Encounter *with the* New Testament ◈

Encounter *with the* New Testament

An Interdisciplinary Approach

Russell Pregeant

Fortress Press *Minneapolis*

ENCOUNTER WITH THE NEW TESTAMENT
An Interdisciplinary Approach

Cover image: Photo © Alinari / Art Resource, NY
Cover design: Christy J. P. Barker
Book design: Zan Ceeley, Trio Bookworks

Additional resources are available on the companion Website, www.fortresspress.com/pregeant.

Library of Congress Cataloging-in-Publication Data

Pregeant, Russell.
    Encounter with the New Testament : an interdisciplinary approach / Russell Pregeant.
        p. cm.
    Rev. ed. of: Engaging the New Testament.
    Includes bibliographical references and index.
    ISBN 978-0-8006-6348-3 (alk. paper)
  1. Bible. N.T.—Introductions. 2. Bible. N.T.—Textbooks. I. Pregeant, Russell. Encounter with New Testament.
II. Title.
    BS2330.3.P74 2009
    225.6'1—dc22

                                                                        2008050423

Manufactured in the U.S.A.

13   12   11   10   09   1   2   3   4   5   6   7   8   9   10

To a special few among the many
from whom I have learned:

William A. Beardslee
John B. Cobb Jr.
Victor Paul Furnish
Walter J. Harrelson
Leander E. Keck
Schubert M. Ogden
W. J. A. Power

Education with inert ideas is not only useless; it is, above all things, harmful. . . .

The solution . . . is to eradicate the fatal disconnection of subjects which kills the vitality of our modern curriculum. There is only one subject-matter for education, and that is life itself in all its manifestations.

—Alfred North Whitehead, *The Aims of Education*

What is written . . . ? How do you read?

—Luke 10:26 RSV

Brief Table of Contents

Additional resources are available on the companion Website,

www.fortresspress.com/pregeant

Contents

INTRODUCTION   Encountering the New Testament   1

1   Some Ways of Reading the Bible   8

PART ONE   BEFORE THE NEW TESTAMENT

PART TWO   THE GOSPELS AND ACTS

PART THREE   THE PAULINE CORPUS

10 1 and 2 Corinthians   231

PART FOUR THE GENERAL LETTERS AND REVELATION

14 The General Letters: Hebrews, James, 1–2 Peter, Jude, 1–3 John   300

Lists of Charts, Maps, and Images

Preface

This book is an abridgment and updating of *Engaging the New Testament: An Interdisciplinary Introduction*, published by Fortress Press in 1995. I have shortened the original text by approximately one-third, largely by reducing many of the analyses of individual writings from detailed accounts to sections entitled "Notes on a Reading of . . ." Otherwise, I have summarized the discussion of some topics and deleted a few sections altogether. But I have also made numerous revisions and introduced a few new topics, such as postcolonial approaches, and have added some features to make the work more student-friendly, such as the sections entitled "Points to Look For in . . ." and summaries following the treatments of each of the Gospels. Also, I have been more systematic in discussing matters of authorship, date, and place of composition.

I am grateful to John Darr of Boston College, along with several other participants in a session of the Society of Biblical Literature at which the original text was the subject of discussion, for suggestions for improvement. I am also indebted to my colleague at Curry College, John Hill, for a painstaking review of the first draft of the abridgment, and to the staff at Fortress Press for their help on this and earlier projects. And I repeat my thanks to John Darr, along with Ron Farmer of Chapman University, who gave the original text trial runs before its publication.

I have retained the dedication of the earlier version with the sad acknowledgment of the death of William A. Beardslee. Here is my original tribute to those from whom I have learned so much:

Victor Furnish and W. J. A. Power, my professors at Perkins School of Theology at Southern Methodist University, provided much of the inspiration and encouragement that led me to graduate school in the field of biblical studies. Schubert Ogden, also at Perkins, fueled my interest in theology, introduced me to life-changing perspectives, and held before me a model of rigorous thinking. At Vanderbilt University, Walter Harrelson not only gave me invaluable insight into the Jewish Scriptures, but also embodied an ideal of teaching I still strive to emulate. And Leander Keck, my dissertation advisor, provided constant challenges, honest criticism, meaningful dialogue, and persistent encouragement.

Years later, William Beardslee and John Cobb extended me a gracious welcome into an emerging circle of persons exploring the interaction between biblical studies and philosophical/theological reflection. To all of these—whom I honor as scholars, teachers, and human beings whose lives are shaped by the biblical vision of peace, justice, community, and love—I express my enduring gratitude.

A final word of heartfelt appreciation goes to my wife, Sammie Maxwell, pastor of Contoocook (New Hampshire) United Methodist Church. Her insight, wisdom, and probing questions are a continued source of nourishment for my own encounter with the biblical text.

Encountering
the New Testament

INTRODUCTION

This book is designed primarily as an introduction to the study of the New Testament in an academic setting. The New Testament itself is a collection of religious writings that, along with the Jewish Scriptures (which Christians have traditionally called the "Old Testament"), are sacred and authoritative for the Christian community. Together, the two collections constitute the Christian Bible.

Aims of This Book

Although many of you who enroll in a New Testament course will likely have some sense of identification with Christianity, some of you may be adherents of other faiths—Judaism, Islam, Buddhism—and others may have no religious faith or background at all. Some of you will attach great importance to religion, while others will treat it more casually or even feel no need of it, and some will not be quite sure where they stand. Motives for taking the course, in any case, will be varied. If some of you seek deeper knowledge of the Christian faith or confirmation of your religious views, others may be searching for perspectives they can accept. And still others may have a purely secular interest in the historical development of Christianity or in the New Testament as literature. Neither instructor nor text should presuppose any particular religious commitment, nor should an academic course in biblical studies become a means of indoctrinating students in one religious view.

As diverse as your religious views may be, each of you will have some sense of values and opinions on the meaning of human life. You will have views on human rights, politics, sexuality, ecology, and economics. And because the New Testament addresses the foundational issues of what life is about and how human beings ought to live, it has clear points of contact with the interests not only of religious but also of nonreligious people.

Unfortunately, these points of contact can easily be overlooked. Western education has too often confused the legitimate demand for objectivity with a kind of value-neutrality that discourages personal involvement. But to study the New Testament writings only as relics from the past is to miss their potential to engage the reader in reflection on life's deepest questions. Ultimately, it is up to you to make connections between the course materials and your life. But I have written this text out of the conviction that it is more exciting and much sounder educationally to have students, instructor, and text involved in an ongoing interchange about the possible importance of what is studied than to consign the text (and perhaps the instructor) to the external role of a provider of "bare" information—as if there were such a thing.

The matter is not fundamentally different in other fields of study. Should a history course approach the past as something "dead" or as a means of reflecting on our present and our alternative futures? Can economics (as is often claimed!) be reduced to sheer quantification, or is every economic decision finally an expression of value judgments? It is arguable that the most subjective, doctrinaire books are actually those that claim to be value free. In fact, the illusion of neutrality may be the subtlest of all the tools of indoctrination.

Although I hope I have maintained an appropriate degree of objectivity, I disavow value-neutrality as an educational ideal. This text, far from addressing readers as disembodied intellects, is written to foster a genuine encounter with the perspectives presented in the various New Testament writings. This means, in part, to inform you about what the New Testament says. But it also means to invite you to ask questions that call for personal involvement: questions as to what the New Testament means by what it says, how one can know what it means, and the possible worth to you, as a human being, of what the New Testament says and means. Chapter 1, which surveys various methods of biblical study, will explain more concretely how the text will proceed and how it will seek to encourage value judgments without relinquishing objectivity.

The New Testament: Origin and Contents

The New Testament writings were produced by many different authors, are of several different literary types, and express varying interests and points of view. It is therefore crucial to study each writing individually and not impose the perspective of one upon another.

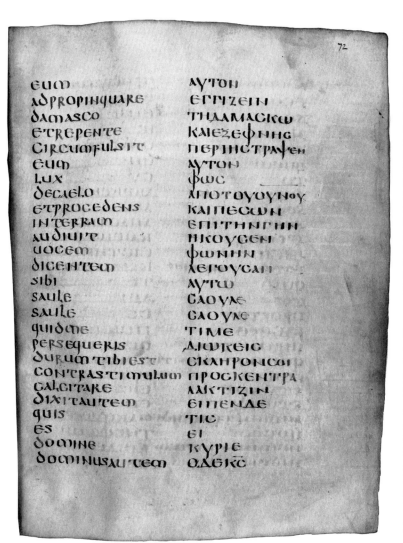

euco	лутон
лдркоріпчилке	еггіzеіп
длопabco	тіллмлсксо
е'ткерепте	клезефннс
сікcumfulsіт	пекінстклуен
еиф	лутон
lux	фос
десльло	хпотоуоупоу
е'ткросеdеns	клі пессон
ін теккли	епітнигнн
лubiui'т	нкоусен
uocem	фоннн
dіcen'тeco	легоусли
sibi	луто
sлule	слоуле
sлule	слоуле
quidoe	тіме
persequeris	дісокеіс
durum tibiest	склнронсоі
cоntrasтіоulum	прoскентрл
cлlcіtлke	лліктізіn
dіхітлuteco	еіпенле
quis	тіс
es	еі
доопіне	куріе
доопіnusлu tem	олекс

FIG. 0.1 (left) We possess no original writings of the New Testament, only copies like this sixth-century manuscript of the book of Acts (here: Acts 9:3-5 in Latin and Greek). The earliest extant manuscripts of Acts are from the third century. Lines 19-21 in the right column are the heavenly Jesus' words comparing Paul to a stubborn mule: "It hurts you to kick against the goads." Those words are missing from all but a few manuscripts, however, and apparently were inserted by a scribe to make this account line up with the similar account in Acts 26 (see 26:14). Acts 9:3-5 in Manuscript E (Number 08, "Laudianus," MS. Laud Gr. 35). Photo courtesy of Bodleian Library, University of Oxford.

FIG. 0.2 (below) The Greek text of Acts 9:3-5 as it appears in a modern critical text, the *Novum Testamentum Graece*, 27th ed. (known by scholars as the Nestle-Aland[27]). The T-shaped mark at the end of v. 4 points the reader to a technical note at the bottom of the page, which indicates that an additional Greek phrase is inserted (following Acts 26:14) in a few manuscripts: E (see Fig. 0.1, above), manuscript 431, and some Syriac manuscripts. Text critics use such information to explore the history of the New Testament text.

3 Ἐν δὲ τῷ πορεύεσθαι ἐγένετο αὐτὸν ἐγγίζειν τῇ Δαμα-
σκῷ, ἐξαίφνης τε αὐτὸν περιήστραψεν φῶς ἐκ τοῦ οὐρα-
νοῦ **4** καὶ πεσὼν ἐπὶ τὴν γῆν ἤκουσεν φωνὴν λέγουσαν
αὐτῷ· Σαοὺλ Σαούλ, τί με διώκεις; ᵀ **5** εἶπεν δέ· τίς εἶ,
κύριε; ὁ δέ· ἐγώ εἰμι Ἰησοῦς ᵀ ὃν σὺ διώκεις·

¶ **9,2** ⸆ *3 1 2* 𝔓⁷⁴ ℵ A 81. 323. 453. 945. 1739 *pc* ¦ *1 2* 33. 1175. 1891 *pc* ¦ *txt* B C E Ψ 𝔐 ● **4** ᵀ(26,14) σκληρον σοι προς κεντρα λακτιζειν E 431 syᵖ·ʰ** mae (*cf* 6 *app*)

But who were these authors, and how did their works come to be included in the New Testament? Although these questions will require detailed discussions at later points, a brief overview of the early Christian movement can provide some preliminary answers.

During the reign of the emperor Tiberius, the Roman occupation government in the province of Judea executed a Jew named Jesus from the town of Nazareth. In the following decade, small groups of his followers gathered regularly for worship, inspired in part by their belief that God had raised him from the dead. The movement was originally a small Jewish sect, composed of people who believed that through this Jesus, God had fulfilled the ancient promises to the people of Israel. Soon, however, non-Jews, or Gentiles, joined their ranks. Christians, as the followers of Jesus came to be called, eventually dropped some of their distinctively Jewish heritage, such as laws of ritual purity, although not without controversy. And before long, Jews were a small minority in a predominantly Gentile faith.

In the Roman Empire, Christianity was one among numerous religious cults. Sometimes viewed as oddities, sometimes seen as a threat and persecuted, Christians were nevertheless successful in winning converts to their faith. Slightly less than three hundred years after Jesus' death, the emperor Constantine gave Christianity a favored position in the empire and thus laid the foundation for its role in Western civilization. In time, a new system of reckoning history made the presumed date of Jesus' birth the dividing point of history.

From the beginning, the figure of Jesus was central to the new faith. But it was no simple matter for Jesus' followers to state who they understood him to be and what his life, death, and resurrection meant. Understanding themselves as heirs to God's promises to Israel, they naturally looked to the Jewish Scriptures as their primary resource. These writings pointed to a hope for God's redemptive action in the future, and Christian interpreters connected that hope to Jesus. But the language of hope in these scriptures took many forms and was subject to varied interpretations. In addition, none of the many religious concepts available in the cultural world of the Roman Empire was fully adequate to the Christian experience of Jesus. Thus, what eventually emerged as the "orthodox" view of Jesus was without exact precedent. It developed through time and was forged only through controversies and splits among groups with various interpretations.

By the middle of the second century, it was apparent that the extreme diversity in doctrine among various Christian groups threatened the continuity of the church's message. One of the ways early Christians sought to define acceptable teaching was through the designation of a body of authoritative Christian writings to set alongside the Jewish Scriptures. The Greek word for a list of authoritative books is *canon*, which means "rule" or "measure." Christianity thus developed its own canon, which became known as the New Testament.

The process of canonization was gradual and informal. Churches in various locales drew up their own lists of authoritative books. These lists differed considerably in the beginning, but by the middle of the fourth century, the present canon had achieved general acceptance.

Not all the Christian works that circulated during the early years became part of the canon. The churches chose those writings that they found meaningful and helpful in their community life, and they justified their choices (probably after the fact) by appealing to various criteria. One of these criteria was "apostolic" origin: they understood the writings included in the canon as in some sense based upon the testimonies of the apostles, the first generation of church leaders, made up primarily but not exclusively of persons believed to have been called into leadership by Jesus himself.

The canon, as it eventually developed, begins with four narrative portrayals of the life of Jesus, designated in English as "Gospels." There follows a work called the Acts of the Apostles, which gives account of the early church in mission. Next come thirteen letters that bear the name of Paul, a devout Jew who joined the Christian movement after Jesus' death and understood himself as the apostle to the Gentiles. Appended to the body of Pauline letters is the book of Hebrews, which bears no author's name but was attributed to Paul by Christians in Egypt. The remaining eight writings, seven of which are traditionally grouped together as the "General Letters," were attributed to various other apostolic figures. (Hebrews is sometimes included in this category, a practice I have followed in this text.)

What the early church believed about the authorship of the writings may not have always been accurate, however. Many scholars are convinced that Paul did not write all the letters that bear his name. And the actual identities of the authors of the Gospels are matters of dispute. It is important, in this connection, to understand that the titles by which these writings are known appear as headings to the ancient manuscripts but do not occur in the bodies of the works themselves. These titles are probably the products of tradition and were not supplied by the authors.

In many cases, we do not know who the authors were or when they wrote. We do know that the authentic letters of Paul, most of which were written during the 50s of the first century, are the earliest of all the canonical writings. The Gospels probably did not begin to appear until shortly before or shortly after the year 70—forty years or so after Jesus' death. We must therefore imagine a long period in which the primary way of transmitting the Christian message was by word of mouth. Jesus' earliest followers told stories of what he had said and done, and they preached about what God had done *through* him. The authors of the Gospels made use of this oral tradition, as well as of some early written material that is now lost.

Which New Testament? Translations, Manuscripts, and Textual Criticism

Because most people who read the Bible today read it in translation, not in the original languages, it matters which translation one uses. Most students of New Testament are aware of the existence of many versions of the New Testament, particularly the newer ones that seek to capture the meaning of the original texts in clear, contemporary English. The move in this direction is all to the good, but readability is not the only issue. Translation is tricky business, and it is important to know whether the translators have made an attempt at objectivity or have presupposed some particular doctrinal point of view. Another question is whether a given version is a genuine translation of the original or simply a paraphrase that tries only to give the "general sense" of the text. Although all translation involves a measure of interpretation, a paraphrase offers far too much opportunity for the injection of some particular theological perspective.

But what is it that translators translate? What do we mean, in other words, when we speak of "the original"? There is, in fact, no such thing as the original New Testament as such, since each of the writings was produced separately. But neither do we have the original (or "autograph") copy of any of the individual books. What we do have is a great number of ancient manuscripts, some containing the entire New Testament and others containing portions of varying lengths.

Not surprisingly, there is often considerable variation in the wording of the manuscripts of a given writing. Copyists made errors and sometimes even changed the text intentionally for various reasons. These variations are for the most part fairly minor, but they are not insignificant. In any case, before setting out to translate a New Testament writing, one must first try to construct the oldest form of the text. And this is the task of a textual criticism. Most textual critics use what is called the eclectic method, which involves comparing the various readings of any given passage and trying to determine which is closest to what the author wrote.

A few scholars speculate that the Gospels were originally written in Aramaic, which was spoken by Palestinian Jews during the time of Jesus. The majority, however, are convinced that Greek was the language of composition of all the books of the Christian canon. What the textual critic must work from, in any case, is nearly five thousand Greek manuscripts, along with many other manuscripts of early versions—translations into such languages as Latin, Syriac, and Coptic. In addition, the writings of early church leaders contain numerous quotations from New Testament writings.

Our answer to the earlier question, then, is rather complex. What New Testament translators translate, and what New Testament interpreters seek ultimately to interpret, are the textual critics' approximations of the oldest Greek texts. This means there will continue to be some disagreement among scholars as to precisely what the New Testament says at various points. But it does not mean that the tasks of textual criticism and translation are hopeless. However significant the variations might be in individual cases, the general sense of each of the writings is clear enough. The task of interpretation is, of course, a somewhat different matter, and we turn to it in chapter 1.

STUDY QUESTIONS

1. How would you describe the educational philosophy presented in the first section of this introduction? State your agreements and/or disagreements with it. Should an academic text be "objective"? Should it be "value-neutral"? Do these two terms mean the same thing?
2. Explain, in a few brief sentences, the steps through which the New Testament came into being. Which writings are the earliest of all the canonical works? When, approximately, did the Gospels begin to appear?
3. After reading this introduction, how would you answer the following question "Who wrote the New Testament?"
4. Define each of the following terms: apostle, canon, Gentile, manuscript.
5. Why is it important to pay attention to which translation of the New Testament one uses?
6. What is the task of textual criticism?
7. In which language were the materials in the New Testament written?

FOR FURTHER READING

Dungan, David L. *Constantine's Bible: Politics and the Making of the New Testament.* Minneapolis: Fortress Press, 2007.

MacDonald, Lee Martin. "Canon of the New Testament." In *The New Interpreter's Dictionary of the Bible,* vol. 1, ed. Katharine Doob Sakenfeld. Nashville: Abingdon, 2006.

Some Ways of Reading the Bible

1

At a corner of Central Park, a man waves a Bible and urges the crowd to be "born again." In Saint Patrick's Cathedral, worshippers receive bread and wine that have been miraculously transformed into the body and blood of Christ. In another city, a woman and a man sit before a television camera and proclaim that the "end of the world" is near. Their reading of the Bible leads them to specific positions on social and political issues: they oppose most government-funded social welfare programs but encourage voluntary giving to alleviate world hunger; they believe that capitalism is biblically based and that the United States is a Christian nation; they honor "womanhood" but oppose the ordination of women as ministers. These media evangelists identify themselves as Protestant. In a study group in a church across town, however, a minister representing a different sort of Protestantism denies that biblical prophecies apply literally to events in the modern world, but she finds biblical support for environmental sensitivity, disarmament, the radical redistribution of wealth, and full equality for women. Her group learns about peasants in Latin America who, together with Roman Catholic priests and nuns, discuss liberation theology—a school of thought that understands the Bible as announcing God's solidarity with the oppressed and calling for fundamental changes in the social and economic order. They notice that the version of Catholic theology held by these peasants, priests, and nuns differs as much from that of some other Catholics as does this Protestant minister's theology from those of the media evangelists and the man in Central Park.

Such diversity of biblical interpretations raises the question of whether it is possible to determine what the biblical texts "really" mean. What would seem to be needed is some way of moving beyond individual prejudices and social conditioning to attain objectivity. Not only is absolute objectivity impossible, however, but one may even question its desirability. To be objective in dealing with a problem is to become detached from the question in the sense of not allowing one's own interests to distort the evidence. But to religious persons, the demand for detachment might seem a denial of their faith.

A book such as this cannot attempt to resolve such questions, but I hope that the following discussion of various ways of studying the Bible will be of some help to students in formulating their own perspectives. Later in this chapter, I will state how the present text seeks to provide an approach to biblical studies that avoids violating the legitimate concerns of both religious and nonreligious students.

Historical Approaches

Scholars today generally acknowledge the value of reading the biblical texts in light of their historical contexts. Although biblical scholarship has sometimes come into conflict with religious groups over the methods and results of historical criticism, this approach is now generally accepted as a valuable step toward objectivity. Interpreters employing this method do not begin with such questions as

"What does this mean to me?" or "What does my religion teach?" They seek first to determine such matters as when and where the work in question was written, who wrote it, for whom it was written, and why it was written. The goal is to understand what the author meant and what the original readers would have understood.

To view a writing this way means learning about the history, culture, and social organization of a time and place far removed from our own; it also means allowing that writing to say something that may strike us as strange or even unintelligible. Because people in ancient cultures held understandings of the nature of the universe that were quite different from our own, we may find that they not only were giving answers that appear strange to us but also were asking different questions. It is natural to seek in the biblical materials some immediate point of contact with our own interests, but the historian's point of view cautions us against forcing either "acceptability" or "relevance" upon the biblical text. This does not mean that one must give up one's prior beliefs as a prerequisite to historical inquiry, but it does mean that we must not allow those beliefs to override the evidence and answer all questions before the investigation begins.

There have been some recent attempts to refine our methods of historical interpretation. Many interpreters are making use of sociological and anthropological methods to determine the social, cultural, and political situations in which the biblical writings were produced. We may therefore speak broadly of social-scientific criticism, which embraces a variety of emphases. When read against the background of class conflict, for example, a text often takes on an unexpected meaning. And recognition of the patriarchal social system that is presupposed in the writings of the New Testament can help identify ways in which the various texts reflect and/or challenge that system.

Another aspect of historical criticism, which overlaps with literary approaches, is rhetorical criticism. This method analyzes ancient writings in light of the rhetorical patterns (the standardized forms of expression) that were current in the environments in which they were written. Asking how a given work would affect its intended audience, the rhetorical critic of the New Testament studies ancient Greek rhetoric and also tries to learn as much as possible about the historical situation of the original readers.

Many recent interpreters find limitations in the historical method, a fact that has led to the explosion of newer methods discussed in this chapter. The present text presupposes the value of viewing the writings of the New Testament historically. But it is naive to think that this approach ensures objectivity. There is no neutral perspective from which to view the past and no given set of questions a historian must ask; all questions reflect the perspectives of individual historians and their cultural settings. So it is important not only to try to allow the Bible to speak on its own terms, but also to recognize that we cannot study the past objectively unless we identify our own biases and ask how they influence our interpretation.

Theological and Ideological Approaches

As classically formulated, the historical method requires that interpreters avoid value judgments as they try to describe the meaning of a text in an objective way. Because of this, some religious interpreters have proposed various types of theological interpretation as supplements to the historical approach.

The term *theological interpretation* sometimes refers to a description of the theological content of a writing. In that case, it is simply one aspect of historical interpretation. But what concerns us here is a second meaning: an interpretation intended to serve the interests of a religious community. Interpreters who practice theological interpretation in this second sense try to show the relevance of a writing for the contemporary readers' faith. They point out that the Bible is, after all, religious literature, so ignoring its possible significance for contemporary believers would be a violation of its very nature.

Alongside theological interpretation are various modes of interpretation that take specific ideologies as their starting points. Although the term *ideology* is sometimes used in a negative way, I use it here simply to mean a set of values to which a person is committed. Thus, ideological interpretation is an approach to the Bible that openly identifies a specific set of interests on the part of the interpreter.

Both theological and ideological interpretation are subject to the criticism that they could allow interpreters to distort the meaning of a text in order to satisfy their preconceived interests. Proponents of these approaches point out, however, that all interpreters bring their own perspectives to the text, whether or not they are conscious of this fact. One may note, for example, that until very recently, biblical interpretation was dominated by relatively affluent white males in the industrialized West, who tended to neglect questions of interest to women, persons of color, and the common people in the developing nations. In any case, the key question to ask in evaluating theological and ideological approaches is whether they actually illuminate the biblical text or simply impose a meaning upon it.

One of the most prominent forms of ideological interpretation is feminist criticism. Much of the work in this area is another refinement of the historical method. By asking formerly neglected questions, feminist scholars have uncovered strong evidence that women played a much greater role in the leadership of early Christian communities than was formerly believed. And they have called attention to alternative strains of Christian tradition that were passed on by women but were eventually suppressed.

Although feminist criticism overlaps with historical criticism, it makes no claim to value-neutrality. Some feminist scholars seek to expose and critique the androcentric (male-centered) nature of both the biblical materials themselves and much modern biblical scholarship. Feminist interpreters often make use of the literary methods discussed later in this chapter. But they add feminist twists by asking such questions as how a writing might appear to a woman rather than a man—and especially to a woman who rejects the male perspective a writing might reflect.

Persons of color and people in the developing nations also have fostered various ideological approaches. For example, African American interpretation, which draws upon the unique experiences of African Americans in U.S. society from the days of slavery to the present, has blossomed in recent decades. And postcolonial criticism draws upon the perspectives of peoples in parts of the world that have experienced the effects of European colonization and the neocolonialism (in which the United States has been a major participant) that followed in its wake. In New Testament studies, postcolonial critics are particularly interested in the attitudes toward the Roman Empire evident in the writings.

Marxian analysis of the class structures of societies and economics sometimes plays a role in some ideological approaches. And we may speak of a broad interest among ideological interpreters in "liberating" interpretation, intended to call into question the various ways in which some groups in the human community oppress others. These forms of ideological interpretation overlap with theological interpretation, since most of their proponents work from within the Christian community.

One theological approach that has influenced modern scholarship is existentialist interpretation. It is grounded in the work of the mid-twentieth-century German biblical scholar and theologian Rudolf Bultmann.

According to Bultmann, the biblical writers viewed the universe as "a three-story structure, with earth in the middle, heaven above it, and hell below it."[1] Bultmann termed this world picture "mythological" and argued that modern people cannot accept it without involving themselves in serious contradictions, for the language of this world picture speaks of what is understood as "otherworldly" in the same terms that we speak of this-worldly realities. The New Testament, for example, routinely understands God's transcendence ("apartness" from the world) as spatial distance. And it views as supernatural interventions events that modern people would attribute to natural causation or human decision.

Bultmann thus proposed a method of interpretation that involves "demythologizing." This term emphasizes the negative task of the interpreter, which is to "strip away" the mythology and look beneath the ancient world picture that determined the authors' language and concepts. The positive term *existentialist interpretation* indicates that the interpreter does so by identifying the "self-understanding"—the notion of what life is all about—that is expressed by the mythological language. In looking for the self-understanding conveyed in a text, one is searching for an "existential" meaning, one that speaks directly to life as all persons ordinarily experience it, without reference to the supernatural. The New Testament, for example, speaks of a final judgment at which a heavenly court decides the eternal fates of human beings. But Bultmann looked beneath the notion of a supernatural end to

history to find an existential meaning and interpreted the final judgment as symbolizing the view that human beings stand before God in every moment of their lives.

Some critics of Bultmann accuse him of imposing a modern point of view upon the Bible. He claimed, however, that the New Testament itself begins the process of existentialist interpretation, since at numerous points, the authors depart from their mythological world picture and reveal the existential "intention" of their mythological language. However one evaluates Bultmann's approach, it clearly stimulates reflection upon the question of what interpreters are looking for when they seek "meaning" in a religious text.

Other forms of theological/ideological interpretation, which sometimes draw upon insights from religions outside the Judeo-Christian tradition, emphasize aspects of biblical texts that exhibit positive views of the natural world and deemphasize God's separateness from the created order. Interpretation from the perspective of process thought, a philosophical/theological school that views the universe as dynamic or ever changing and understands all aspects of reality as interrelated, shares some of these emphases. But a process approach is broader in its interests and has its own specific way of approaching a text. It shares with Bultmann a sense of the cultural distance between the ancient world and our own but envisions more of a dialogue between the two worldviews, in which each is able to question the other in order to achieve a kind of synthesis.

Psychological Approaches

Some recent scholars draw upon the psychological theories of Sigmund Freud and C. G. Jung to interpret biblical texts. Whereas historical interpretation usually identifies the meaning of a work with the author's intentions, psychological interpretation views writing as in part the product of the unconscious mind. Jung claimed that the symbols used in religious lore are closely parallel to the imagery appearing in dreams. Religious writings thus have a special connection to the unconscious. They can express thoughts of which the author was unaware and can also affect the reader on the unconscious level. Psychological interpretation assumes that some psychological patterns are universal, cutting across history and cultures. It can thus to a large extent bypass historical questions. However, since each reader has an individual psychological history, meaning has a very personal dimension.

It is interesting to view stories of Jesus' resurrection from a Jungian perspective. According to Jung, all human beings share, in the depths of their unconscious minds, a set of "archetypes," or fixed patterns of thought, which are the products not of our individual experiences but of our biological inheritance through evolution. Jung believed that the theme of death and resurrection is one of these archetypal patterns. We all have, in the depths of our unconscious minds, "a pattern of being, in which what appears to be irreparable loss is supplanted by unimaginable gain: being hopelessly lost and then found, being hopelessly ill

and healed, being hopelessly locked into a destructive pattern of living and then forgiven and released."[2] A psychological interpretation of the resurrection stories will have no interest in their literal truth but will focus on how they can release the power of the death/resurrection archetype in a reader's experience.

Psychological interpretation can be criticized from the historian's perspective. Are psychological patterns really so universal? Might we not misread an ancient text if we try to correlate it with our own psychological patterns? Clearly, however, psychological approaches have an immediate point of contact in almost every reader's experience and great potential for awakening interest in biblical studies.

Steps toward a Literary Approach: Form Criticism and Redaction Criticism

Interpreters through the centuries have tended to treat the New Testament as a statement of Christian doctrine, focusing largely on its theological content. Modern historical criticism reshaped this theological concern by insisting that we get at the meaning of a writing by placing it in its historical context. It also added a new interest: because a given work might have gone through one or more revisions, and an author might have made use of various earlier materials, scholars sought to reconstruct the history of the work itself.

The biblical writings, however, are more than sources for the reconstruction of history, and although they express theological ideas, very few if any of them can be called theological treatises. Some of the writings are narratives, or stories, and most of the others are letters or at least have some characteristics of a letter. The Bible is, in fact, literature, and recent scholarship has given increased attention to its specifically literary aspects.

The new emphasis came in stages. Two methods of biblical study that were influential in twentieth-century scholarship served as bridges between the historical and the literary approaches.

The first of these is form criticism, which is based on the recognition that the writings of the New Testament often contain small units of preexisting material. The first task of form criticism is the recognition and classification of these small units according to their literary forms or types. Some New Testament authors have apparently quoted early Christian hymns, and the Gospel writers made use of various kinds of earlier material, such as parables, various types of sayings, miracle stories, and pronouncement stories (short accounts ending in a dramatic saying of Jesus).

Insofar as scholars identify specific literary forms, they are involved in a kind of literary criticism. But form critics are also interested in the stages of development the material might have gone through before it found its way into the present writings. For that reason, this method is also called form history.

This interest in development is particularly evident in the study of the Gospels.

When we compare the different Gospels, we sometimes find the same story or saying in several different versions. So the form critic tries to reconstruct the process of development that produced the variations and ultimately to identify the original version. The presupposition is that the stories about what Jesus said and did circulated orally before anyone wrote them down. Presumably, they went through transformations as they moved from one environment to another. Form critics therefore try to determine what specific setting, or life situation, would produce a particular transformation. They are thus concerned not only with literary forms but with history and sociology as well.

Application of form criticism to the Gospels eventually led to the development of redaction criticism. The term *redaction* is the English version of a German word meaning "editing." By identifying how an author has added to, deleted from, or rewritten a source, redaction critics can learn something about that author's interests. For example, by showing that in several cases a writer makes the same kind of change, they identify a consistent emphasis.

Redaction critics are interested in a finished writing as a whole, not simply its component parts. Any student who has written a term paper, however, knows that it is possible to incorporate a quotation one partly disagrees with or perhaps does not fully understand. Approaching a writing as the product of editorial changes of existing material leaves open the possibility that some incorporated material might not reflect the final author's point of view. So redaction critics will sometimes treat a given passage as an "undigested morsel"—something that does not really serve the author's intentions.

Some interpreters have pointed out that redaction critics actually interpret something other than the writing itself: the author's theology. While this might be a valid goal, it is possible to approach a writing differently. We could simply ignore the possible sources that lie behind the text and interpret it as we would any other type of literature. Then we would not be able to write off any passages as undigested material but would be responsible for the entire text as an integrated literary whole.

erary forms, tracing the development of plot and characters, recognizing themes, and appreciating rhetorical devices. Students who have encountered such methods in studying other types of literature may wonder why biblical studies has made so little use of them until recently. The reason is that the Bible's status as scripture conditioned interpreters not only to look primarily for its doctrinal content but also to focus on the question of historical accuracy. It is because biblical scholars were so long preoccupied with doctrine on the one hand and the question of "what really happened" on the other that they gave scant attention to the Bible as literature.

Literary Approaches

Interpreters have traditionally emphasized the rational content of the biblical writings—the theological ideas they contain. Literary approaches introduce another emphasis. Viewing the biblical writings as literature recognizes that they appeal to the readers' imaginative powers, not simply their rational capacities. Telling a story, for example, sets up an imaginative world into which the reader is expected to enter. Understanding the story may involve grasping certain ideas, but more fundamentally, it means entering the world the story creates and participating in what happens.

Literary approaches to the New Testament involve such traditional procedures, familiar to students of other literature, as identifying lit-

Schools of Literary Interpretation

A literary critic can approach a text in three ways: (1) by focusing on the author, thinking primarily in terms of what that author intends for the text to mean; (2) by focusing on the writing itself, asking what the written text means, without reference to the author's intent; or (3) by focusing on the reader, considering how what is written seems designed to elicit specific responses from the reader. These approaches clearly overlap, but it makes a difference which of these three aspects of a text an interpreter emphasizes. Redaction critics, as we have seen, focus on the author's intentions. Two current methods of interpretation, in contrast, tend to play down the role of the author.

One of these, narrative criticism, is text centered—that is, its emphasis is upon what

the written text itself means. It takes account of the reader to the extent that it posits a hypothetical reader, termed the "implied reader," who will understand the text in specific ways. But its emphasis is on the way the text itself prompts the reader's reactions. Thus, as Mark Allan Powell comments, "It is less necessary to know the historical situation of the actual readers for whom the texts was originally intended."[3]

Narrative criticism also tends to treat the implied reader as someone who has perhaps read the text many times, so that in analyzing a text, the critic is free to move backward and forward in the story to gather up the many connections that an attentive reader might make.

The other method, reader-response criticism, tends to identify the reader as a *first-time* reader, so that in analyzing a text, the critic tries to stick to what a reader would know at any given point. It also emphasizes the open-endedness and ambiguity of a text, which give the reader options in terms of how to understand and value it. Reader-response criticism comes in many varieties, however. Extreme versions give the reader almost complete control over the text, so that nearly any reading of it is seen as valid. But more moderate versions are similar to narrative criticism in that they stress the way the text gives directions to the reader. Apart from the question of whether one thinks of the reader as a first-time reader, the moderate versions of reader-response criticism are almost indistinguishable from narrative criticism.

Reader-response criticism seeks to identify the ways in which a given text is designed to elicit responses from the readers, how it seeks to awaken specific emotions or judgments, how it prepares readers for turns in the plot by giving or withholding information, and how it sometimes leaves it to the readers to fill in gaps in the plot and draw their own conclusions. To the extent that it acknowledges that the reader has real decisions to make, it leaves open the possibility of understanding the text in different ways.

There is therefore a sense in which each reader of a given writing reads a different text, since each brings her or his own interests and makes different decisions in reading; even a single reader reads a different story every time she or he reads it. Opponents of this view therefore charge that it leads to a pure subjectivism in which interpreters make the writing say whatever they want it to say, so that there is no way to distinguish valid from invalid readings. Moderate reader-oriented critics avoid the charge by making clear that the reader has a limited range of options in creating meaning and that the role of historical criticism is to help define the limits.

Another current school of interpretation is deconstruction, which denies that texts are capable of presenting straightforward, consistent, and coherent points of view. It therefore tries to show how texts "deconstruct" themselves—how, for example, one set of themes or values in a writing ends up actually making use of its opposite. It shares with the radical reader-response approaches the view that because meaning is open-ended, no interpretation can be final or definitive. But it is distinctive in its denial that a text constitutes a coherent literary whole, that a text in fact offers its reader a "climactic, completed understanding."[4] It is therefore even more vulnerable to the criticism of subjectivity than are the radical reader-response theories.

Deconstruction differs from other modes of interpretation in that, rather than looking for an overall meaning in a writing, it identifies strains of meaning that compete with and subvert the dominant strain. Although disclaiming allegiance to any specific ideology, deconstruction gives voice to points of view that are either neglected or suppressed. Moreover, its emphasis on competing strains of meaning is similar to some interpretation carried out from the perspective of process thought. The latter, however, differs from deconstruction by stressing that one can sometimes bring the competing strains together in a higher synthesis.

The Problem of Multiple Interpretations

Proponents of some of the newer literary methods tend to accept the validity of a variety of approaches to interpretation, including those based on specific ideological commitments. Reader-oriented critics and deconstructionists often grant that all such readings are valid within their own frames of reference but deny universal validity to any one approach. Not surprisingly, then, many biblical scholars are wary of such open-endedness in interpretation. They fear that some of the newer approaches undermine the gains made

by historical criticism. But proponents of these methods believe they are coaxing biblical studies into exciting new territory. So the debate goes on. Meanwhile, the man waving the Bible still preaches at the corner of Central Park, while Latin American peasants continue to read their Bibles as texts of liberation.

This Book's Approach

What is the most important objective for beginning students in biblical studies? Should they gain a basic grasp of the content of the biblical "message"? Should they master a method of interpretation? Should they learn how the Bible came into being? These are all worthy goals, but they raise questions. Which interpretation of the biblical message should students learn? Which method should they be taught? Does knowledge of the way the Bible was produced necessarily lead to an understanding of what it means? Without negating such goals as these, the present book has a prior, more basic objective: to foster a genuine encounter with the New Testament, to enhance the process of questioning and "wrestling" with the biblical texts and with the life-and-death issues those texts raise.

It is precisely with the hope of genuine encounter in mind that I have chosen to write a book that approaches the New Testament writings from several different perspectives. To show that there are many ways in which people have found meaning and value in the New Testament invites students into a conversation; it encourages them to develop their own views as to the meaning and value of the materials they will be reading, even as they explore the opinions of others.

Paradoxically, this approach also contributes to objectivity. Whatever position one takes on the question of multiple interpretations of a text, the fact is that interpreters do offer different readings. Giving students several different perspectives makes it more difficult for them to accept any perspective uncritically—whether this is their prior understanding, the teaching of a religious body, or the views of an instructor or the author of this text.

My hope is to encourage both objectivity and subjectivity in appropriate forms. In asking for objectivity, I affirm the academic environment and reject any attempt at indoctrination; in asking for subjectivity, I acknowledge the nature of the New Testament materials as religious literature, the purpose of which is in fact to encourage readers to embrace certain options regarding faith, belief, thought, and action.

Although I will make some use of many of the approaches to the Bible discussed in this chapter, I will emphasize two methods of study—historical criticism and a moderate version of reader-response analysis—by applying them to each of the New Testament writings. I am convinced that the former, for all its limitations, still provides an important perspective on the text. And the latter has been particularly useful in fostering an initial encounter with the text that can become the basis for further reflection.

Reflection, however, cannot take place in a vacuum; it must be informed by the reader's own life experiences, concerns, and prior understanding. I have therefore not hesitated to allow current interests to influence my agenda. Such matters as economic justice and the status and role of women are pressing concerns in our contemporary world, and the debate over the compatibility of religion with a scientifically informed world picture continues. These and similar concerns define the context within which biblical study in our day actually takes place. My goal has been to let such matters inform my approach to the New Testament without illicitly "modernizing" the ancient texts or ignoring their own frames of reference.

Exegesis, Hermeneutics, and Contemporary Relevance

Another way of describing the intention of the present text is to say that it seeks to involve students in reflection on what biblical interpreters call the "hermeneutical problem." The term *hermeneutics*, which comes from a family of Greek words having to do with explanation or interpretation, has been employed in a variety of ways in modern biblical studies, theology, and philosophy. According to one definition, the heart of hermeneutics is the theoretical question of what actually happens when an interpreter understands a text and/or communicates its meaning. Since theory affects practice, however, one may also speak of particular hermeneutical perspectives that inform given attempts to explain what a text means.

One way of understanding the concept of hermeneutics is to contrast it with *exegesis*, a term that comes from another group of Greek words with the root meaning of "leading out," which also refers to interpretation. Exegesis is systematic explanation of what a biblical text means. Hermeneutics, by contrast, comes into play whenever the process of finding the meaning of a text becomes problematic—that is, when interpreters discover differences between their own world pictures and those represented in the texts, competing strains of meaning within such texts, or different angles of vision from which to approach the task of interpretation. We can clearly identify existentialist and process interpretation, for example, as hermeneutical methods, because they address the problem of differing world-views. And liberating interpretations such as feminist, African American, and postcolonial interpretation also are designed to speak to questions of contemporary relevance.

The hermeneutical question is easiest to identify when the interpreter seeks to render an ancient text meaningful to readers centuries removed from it—that is, to comment on its "contemporary relevance." It might at first seem that, in relation to the New Testament, the question arises only for Christian believers, those for whom this collection of writings is in some way authoritative. But many hermeneutical theorists insist that although there is a difference between understanding a text

and appreciating it—valuing it positively or negatively—the two cannot be separated in an absolute way. Any understanding of a writing involves some kind of interest in it, so that we cannot really understand it without allowing it to engage us in a struggle for meaning and truth, whatever actual judgment we make about it.

When, for example, a reader finds that a writing endorses a patriarchal system in which women are subordinated, does this mean that she or he must *accept* that system in order to find personal value in the text? Or does the reader have a right to reject that aspect of the text while perhaps accepting other aspects? And what if the various writings in the New Testament do not agree on this issue, or what if there are actually competing strains of meaning within a single text? Hermeneutics involves the process of wrestling with questions such as these. It is always "there," whether recognized or not, and every attempt at exegesis really presupposes a hermeneutical stance.

To raise the questions of hermeneutical perspective and contemporary relevance is to risk the charge of introducing a personal agenda into an academic text. Certainly, the choice of which concerns to address involves a degree of subjectivity. But a decision to treat the New Testament from a purely historical perspective would in its own way constitute a hermeneutical move and, as we have seen, would carry no guarantee of objectivity.

The truth is that it is impossible to write a totally unbiased text, and I do not claim to have done so. I had no intention of writing one that is value free. I do hope I have been fair enough on controversial issues to give students some tools for reaching their own conclusions. I hope, in other words, that this text will encourage you to approach the New Testament as a student in the fullest sense— as a whole human being, exercising your critical intellect with enough detachment to see things clearly, yet deeply engaged in your own quest for meaning and value as you attend to voices that claim to speak the truth.

NOTES

1. Rudolf Bultmann, *New Testament and Mythology and Other Basic Writings*, ed. and trans. Schubert M. Ogden (Philadelphia: Fortress Press, 1984), 1.
2. Wayne G. Rollins, *Jung and the Bible* (Atlanta: John Knox, 1983), 83.
3. Powell, *What Is Narrative Criticism?* (Minneapolis: Fortress Press, 1990), 15.
4. Stephen D. Moore, *Literary Criticism and the Gospels: The Theoretical Challenge* (New Haven, Conn.: Yale University Press, 1989), 160.

STUDY QUESTIONS

1. What advantages and/or disadvantages do you see in how this book approaches the New Testament?
2. Evaluate the following statement: "You can make the Bible say anything you want it to say." How would a proponent of historical criticism respond? Deconstructionists? Reader-response critics?
3. Explain why it is or is not important to take into account the historical situations in which the biblical authors wrote.
4. Does the historical approach have any limitations? If so, what are they?
5. Name some types of interpretation based on specific theological or ideological commitments, and give your own preliminary evaluation of such approaches.
6. What advantages and/or disadvantages do you see in interpreting the Bible psychologically?
7. How do literary approaches to the Bible differ from the historical approach?
8. Explain each of these terms: form criticism, redaction criticism, narrative criticism, reader-response criticism, deconstruction, exegesis, hermeneutics.
9. Try to identify the presuppositions, biases, and commitments that you bring to a study of the New Testament. How might each of these help you to become genuinely engaged with the New Testament? In what ways might each make such an engagement difficult? Do you think you can maintain an appropriate balance of objectivity and subjectivity as you approach this study?

FOR FURTHER READING

Bultmann, Rudolf. *New Testament and Mythology and Other Basic Writings.* Selected, edited, and translated by Schubert M. Ogden. Philadelphia: Fortress Press, 1984.

Felder, Cain Hope. *Troubling Biblical Waters: Race, Class, Family.* Maryknoll, N.Y.: Orbis, 1989.

Krentz, Edgar. *The Historical Critical Method.* Philadelphia: Fortress Press, 1975.

McKnight, Edgar V. *What Is Form Criticism?* Philadelphia: Fortress Press, 1969.

Perrin, Norman. *What Is Redaction Criticism?* Philadelphia: Fortress Press, 1969.

Powell, Mark Allan. *What Is Narrative Criticism?* Minneapolis: Fortress Press, 1990.

Rollins, Wayne G. *Jung and the Bible.* Atlanta: John Knox, 1983.

Schottroff, Louise, Silvia Schroer, and Marie-Therese Wacker. *Feminist Interpretation: The Bible in Women's Perspective.* Minneapolis: Fortress Press, 1998.

Schüssler Fiorenza, Elisabeth, ed. *Searching the Scriptures.* 2 vols. New York: Crossroad, 1993–94.

Sugirtharajah, R. S. *The Bible and the Third World: Precolonial, Colonial and Postcolonial Encounters.* Cambridge: Cambridge University Press, 2001.

Tiffany, Frederick C., and Sharon H. Ringe. *Biblical Interpretation: A Roadmap.* Nashville: Abingdon, 1996.

BEFORE
THE NEW TESTAMENT

Prologue to Part One

The primary subject matter of this text is the New Testament itself. Parts 2, 3, and 4 are devoted to treatments of the various writings that make up the canon. These writings, as they currently stand, do not represent the earliest stage of the Christian tradition. Long before the appearance of the Gospels, and even before Paul wrote his letters, Jesus' followers passed on stories and sayings and composed materials for use in their worship. One way of gaining perspective on the New Testament writings, then, is to study the historical process that lies behind them. In chapters 3 and 4 of part 1, I therefore turn our attention to two stages of the traditions that constituted that process.

First, however, it is important to learn something about the historical contexts within which Jesus lived, the early tradition was transmitted, and the writings finally emerged. As Jesus' early followers shaped their understanding of him, the only tools available for them to work with came from their own cultural settings. Of necessity, they used the concepts, modes of expression, and styles of writing available in the Jewish and wider Hellenistic environments. The new faith, although indeed new, was not created "out of nothing."

In chapter 2, then, I will try to describe the features of the New Testament world that are most relevant for understanding the early Christian tradition. This requires a consideration of the history of the Jewish people and that of the Greek-speaking world. It should also be helpful to place both of these histories in the context of the human religious consciousness and of Western history as a way of studying ourselves—our preconceptions and biases—as we approach the world of the past.

Throughout the text, I will designate years as B.C.E. (Before the Common Era) and C.E. (Common Era), rather than B.C. and A.D. In doing so, I follow a practice increasingly employed by biblical scholars "out of deference to those for whom the birth of Jesus marks the beginning of a new era only in a secular sense."[1]

NOTE

1. Robert W. Funk and Mahlon J. Smith, *The Gospel of Mark: Red Letter Edition* (Sonoma, Calif.: Polebridge, 1991), 244.

2

Christian Beginnings in Context

Nature Demystified: A Prologue to Western History

The ancient world picture was a religious world picture. People believed that all components of reality are bound together in a kind of cosmic empathy, or spiritual relatedness. Human beings, animals, plants, and stars all participate in the same life-giving power. When belief in various goddesses and gods eventually developed, these deities were understood as personifications of natural phenomena. The world picture in the modern West, by contrast, makes religious belief optional. Although not excluding a religious interpretation, the Western view no longer *expresses* such an interpretation. People today tend to see the forces of nature as subject to mechanistic laws of cause and effect. We have "demystified" nature, taken the mystery out of it.

This demystification was not complete until modern times, but its seeds were sown in ancient times. Two departures from belief in cosmic empathy contributed to the shaping of Western culture and the modern consciousness: Hebrew monotheism and Greek philosophy.

Hebrew Monotheism

The Hebrew people, who originally organized themselves as a federation of tribes called Israel, possessed a rich heritage of ancestral lore, at the center of which was the tradition of the exodus—the story of how God, through Moses, led a band of slaves out of Egypt and gave them a land of their own. In a partial break with the surrounding cultures, who worshipped a pantheon of deities, the Israelites gave exclusive worship to one god, Yahweh. This change in religious consciousness had several important consequences.

Shift in Focus from Nature to History

Ancient people envisioned their deities as governing the cyclical aspects of life, such as seedtime and harvest, birth and death. But because the Hebrews thought of their God as also acting in history to bring about change, they developed a strong sense of hope for the future.

Heightened Moral Conscience

As transcendent over both nature and society, the Hebrew God occupied a vantage point from which to exercise moral judgment. Understanding Yahweh as particularly concerned for the downtrodden, the Hebrews developed various mechanisms for social justice, such as requiring farmers to leave a portion of their crops for the poor. This concern for the dispossessed became more pronounced when a monarchical form of government had developed and extreme discrepancies in wealth were common. The prophets of the eighth through the sixth centuries b.c.e. not only criticized the worship of foreign deities but also condemned kings and elites of society for exploiting the poor.

Tendency to Identify the Divine with the Male Gender

The pantheons of the surrounding peoples contained both female and male deities, but the imagery for Yahweh in the Jewish Scriptures is primarily (but not exclusively) male.

Steps toward the Demystification of Nature

Yahweh's apartness from the world meant that nature was no longer understood as divine. It was, however, many centuries later that the Western view of nature as an object to be manipulated developed. For the ancient Hebrews, the sovereign over the world was God, not human beings.

Greek Philosophy

The Greeks originally worshipped nature deities but eventually turned their attention to the gods and goddesses of Mount Olympus, who personified such ideals of civilization as law, justice, and intellect. As the political order came to manifest the divine more than did nature, nature became subject to investigation. Thus, people began to ask questions that led to scientific inquiry on the one hand and philosophy on the other.

The philosopher Plato (427–347 b.c.e.) contributed to the demystification of nature by arguing that physical objects such as desks and trees are less real than the ideas, or eternal "forms," by which we identify these objects (desk*ness*, tree*ness*). For him, the universe is more basically mental than physical, since physical reality proceeds from a mental or spiritual ground.

Plato's philosophy is a form of idealism (the view that only the mind is real), but it has characteristics of dualism (the view that there are two types of reality, mind and matter). Because dualism suggests that matter is a deficient form of reality, the later blending of Platonic thought with Christianity led to the image of the universe as a "great chain of being," with the more spiritual kinds of being at the top and the more material at the bottom. Such thinking lent support to the "divine right of kings," the subjugation of women, and other hierarchical social structures. It has been used to justify theories of racial superiority and has governed the way we think about the division of labor, the governing of societies and organizations, and education.

World Pictures in Conflict:
The Context of the Contemporary Interpreter

Hebrew monotheism and Greek philosophy provided Western civilization with a world picture that served for many centuries as a basis for values. A transcendent God reigned over a hierarchically arranged universe. Moral standards, governmental structure, and social organization were understood in terms of the will of God and Plato's eternal forms. By breaking with the notion of cosmic empathy, however, these ways of thinking opened the way for the total demystification of nature that came with the rise of modern science. And this demystification undercut the spiritual basis of values as people began to view nature as composed of mere lifeless matter, without inherent value or purpose. Although many modern people believe in a spiritual reality, such a belief is problematic for some and impossible for others.

One aspect of the modern consciousness is confidence in reason and the human ability to understand the universe and manipulate the environment. This confidence has broken down in recent decades, however, so that many thinkers now speak of a postmodern age that we are now entering. Science itself has undermined our faith in our ability to grasp reality in a comprehensive way. Physicists, for example, have encountered extreme oddities in their studies of light. Observed in one way, it appears to be composed of particles; observed in another way, it consists of waves. And both views seem to be true from within a particular frame of reference. Also, it is increasingly clear that our values and understandings of truth depend on cultural background, social class, and family experience.

Postmodernists in general are doubtful about the human ability to achieve secure knowledge. And one type of postmodernism is skeptical regarding all claims to truth, stressing that knowledge is limited by the perspectives of the knower. Belief in God is as problematic for this school of thought as it is for the modernist. Deconstruction and radical reader-response criticism reflect this view, for in arguing that the reader determines meaning, these approaches deny that there is any definitive interpretation of a text.

Not all postmodernists, however, are so negative regarding knowledge. Process thought, which is sometimes called "constructive postmodernism," agrees that knowledge is limited by perspective but thinks it possible to work out provisional understandings of reality that take this limitation into account. It involves a respiritualizing of nature that recovers a sense of the relatedness of all things without returning to premodern ways of thinking. Constructive postmodernists find it possible to speak of God, but of a God quite different from the all-controlling deity of traditional theology.

Both versions of postmodernism reject hierarchical understandings of reality, and both seek to hear the thoughts of groups traditionally excluded from power. They also agree that literary texts are capable of generating more than one legitimate interpretation.

The primary reason for discussing Hebrew monotheism and Greek dualism is to set the stage for the emerging Christian movement. But before we get to that point, we need to take account of the story of ancient Israel down to the beginning of the Common Era and its encounter with Hellenism, the Greek-like culture that captured the Mediterranean world after the death of Alexander the Great.

Memory and Hope: The Hebrew People and History

Holiness, Pollution, and Sacred History

Despite their partial demystification of nature, the Hebrews shared many aspects of the ancient sense of cosmic empathy. It is against this background that we must understand their practice of sacred rites, taboos, and dietary regulations.

Central to the Hebrew value system was the notion of holiness, which had to do largely with separateness or apartness. God, the truly holy one, was utterly beyond human beings and the things of the world. The Hebrews, as God's people, were obligated to keep themselves in a state of holiness, or apartness from the world at large.

Holiness embraced a moral dimension, but it had other aspects as well, such as the distinction between clean and unclean, which was rooted in a notion of ritual pollution. Cultural anthropology can help us grasp this concept, which must not be confused with a modern interest in sanitation. Ancient people had a deep sense of cosmic order. Since all things are pervaded with power, anything out of its proper place is unclean and therefore dangerous. This explains "why blood, spit, [and] semen are unclean. They belong inside the body. When they come out of their place, such as in a menstrual flow, they are unclean and will defile people."[1] It also explains why a person can become polluted by touching a holy object if that person is not qualified to do so or does so under the wrong circumstances.

Given this concern with purity, everything—space, time, human activity—had to be ordered to meet the requirements of holiness. It was the role of sacred ceremonies and rituals to carry out this ordering. Like other ancient peoples, the Hebrews had a hereditary priesthood that presided over a system of animal and vegetable sacrifices that established relationship with the divine. They also observed numerous festivals throughout the year, as well as the weekly Sabbath, a day of rest.

At the heart of the Hebrew faith was the notion of covenant, a relationship between God and the people of Israel. Yahweh, who had led them out of Egypt, would continue to be their God and grant them abundant life in their land, and they would obey God's commands. Festivals celebrated throughout the year commemorated the events through which God had acted on Israel's behalf, such as the exodus from Egypt. These occasions evoked memory of what God had done in the past and hope for what God would do in the future.

Monarchy and Theology

The establishment of a monarchy altered the concept of the covenant. The second king, David, expanded Israel's borders and captured Jerusalem, which became its capital. His son Solomon built a magnificent temple there to house the cult. Thus Jerusalem and the temple became sacred places, and people came to believe that God had promised that David's kingly line would last through the ages.

This Davidic theology played a key role in later hopes regarding the future. As Israel went through difficult times over the centuries, suffering defeat and occupation by a series of conquerors, people began to expect an ideal king who would usher in the kingdom, or rule, of God. By this, they meant a situation in which God's will was truly done

in the world, so that there would be lasting peace and justice. Because the Hebrew monarchs were consecrated by anointing with oil, they were called God's "anointed." Through the centuries, the notion of an ideal king developed into the expectation of an "Anointed One," or "Messiah," a king in David's line who would establish a new order on earth.

Since this concept has played such a large role in Christianity, it is important to note several points. First, the Messiah was understood as a human being, a king through whom God would establish peace and justice on this earth. Second, a messianic king was only one of several ways of conceiving the reign of peace and justice itself. For example, some people thought God would rule directly, and others spoke of an ideal priest or a "prophet like Moses" who would be God's agent. Third, the hope for a Messiah was not a clear-cut concept passed on from early times. It developed gradually and took many different forms, and there was no consistent "doctrine" of the Messiah when Jesus was born. In fact, Judaism did not give a formal definition of what the Messiah was to be until after the time of Jesus.

The Divided Monarchies and the Babylonian Exile

Eventually, the northern regions broke off to form a separate state. The northern state kept the designation Israel, while the southern monarchy reverted to the tribal name of Judah. Both nations struggled constantly to maintain independence as empires threatened

FIG. 2.1 TIMELINE OF THE NEW TESTAMENT WORLD

Hebrew/Jewish Civilization		Greek/Hellenistic/Roman Civilization
	B.C.E.	
Exodus from Egypt	ca. 1290	
Conquest of Canaan begins	ca. 1250	
Period of tribal confederacy		
David king of all Israel	1000	
Division of Monarchies	922	
Judah (south) **Israel** (north)	700–750	Homer's *Iliad* and *Odyssey*
Assyrian conquest		
of Israel; end of northern	721	
monarchy		
Destruction of first temple;		
Babylonian exile	587	
Beginning of Diaspora Judaism		
Babylonia falls to Persia;	538	
band of exiles returns		
to Judah/Judea		
Persian rule of Judah/Judea		
Building of second temple	347	Death of Plato
	338	Philip II, king of Macedon,
		defeats Greek states and
		forms Hellenic League
	336	Murder of Philip and accession
		of his son, Alexander
	333	Alexander defeats Persians at Issus
ALEXANDER (332) ENTERS JUDEA		
	331	Founding of Alexandria in Egypt
	323	Death of Alexander
THE HELLENISTIC AGE BEGINS		
		Hellenistic Dynasties: Antigonids,
		Seleucids, Ptolemies
	306	Epicurus founds school in Athens
	300	Zeno, founder of Stoicism,
		arrives in Athens
Seleucids take control of Judea	168	

FIG. 2.1 TIMELINE OF THE NEW TESTAMENT WORLD (cont.)

Hebrew/Jewish Civilization		Greek/Hellenistic/Roman Civilization
Maccabean war begins	167	
Rededication of temple	165	
Hasmonean Dynasty founded; formation of Pharisees, Sadducees, Essenes		
POMPEY (63) ENTERS JERUSALEM		
Roman rule of Judea		
	60	First triumvirate rules Rome: Pompey, Crassus, Julius Caesar
	48–44	Julius Caesar, dictator in Rome
	43	Second triumvirate rules Rome: Lepidus, Marc Antony, Octavian
Herod becomes king of Jews	37	
	31	Octavian defeats Marc Antony in the Battle of Actium and secures control of Rome
	27	Octavian proclaimed "Caesar Augustus"
Death of Herod	4	
BIRTH OF JESUS (?)		
	C.E.	
	14	Tiberius becomes Roman emperor
Death of Jesus	ca. 30	
	37	Caligula becomes Roman emperor
	41	Claudius becomes Roman emperor
	54	Nero becomes Roman emperor
Jewish war of independence begins	66	
	68	Galba becomes Roman emperor
	69	After brief reigns of Otho and Vitellius, Vespasian becomes Roman emperor
Romans destroy second temple Jewish academy of Yabneh: beginnings of Rabbinic Judaism	70	
	79	Titus becomes Roman emperor
	81	Domitian becomes Roman emperor
	96	Nerva becomes Roman emperor
	98	Trajan becomes Roman emperor
	117–35	Hadrian becomes Roman emperor
Bar Kochba War	132–35	

their borders. In 721 B.C.E., Assyria conquered Israel, deporting much of the populace and bringing in foreigners to settle. In 587 B.C.E., the Babylonians ravaged Judah, destroyed the temple, and deported the community leaders to Babylon.

The exiles in Babylon found more need than ever to hold on to their traditions. They had already committed some material to writing, but there was no scripture in the formal sense. Thus, the priests began gathering traditional materials into a foundational document. Whether completed during or after the exile, the result was what came to be called "Torah"—the first five books of the Bible, later attributed to Moses himself. *Torah* is often translated "law," but "teaching" is a better rendering. Although containing much law, these books also tell a story beginning with creation, continuing through the Hebrew ancestors and the exodus, and ending as the people prepare to enter the land God had given them. Also important were customs that set the worshippers of Yahweh apart from the surrounding culture. Such observances as circumcision, dietary regulations, and Sabbath rest took on central importance in the period following the exile.

The Reestablishment of Judah/Judea

Empires rise and fall. Babylonia fell to Persia, which allowed its subject peoples a measure of home rule. In 538 B.C.E., the Persian king issued an edict allowing the descendants of the exiles to return to Judah, which now became known as Judea. Many people remained in Babylonia, but others made the long journey home. A new temple was completed by 515 B.C.E., but Jerusalem remained sparsely populated and without fortifications for some time. A part of the old northern monarchy known as Samaria was under separate provincial rule by the Persians, and the Samaritans actively opposed the rebuilding of Jerusalem.

There were also conflicts within Judah itself. Those taken into exile had been the wealthy and powerful, and those who returned were their descendants; those who had remained were largely the poor, many of whom probably took over abandoned homes and farms after the deportations. We can imagine bitter conflicts after the return, and we have clear evidence of the exploitation of the poor by the rich.

The rebuilding of the temple contributed to class conflict. A dispute arose over who had legitimate rights to priestly service, and as a result, some groups were excluded. Those who assumed leadership gained enormous economic power, since the temple was responsible for collecting tithes and taxes. In time, the Persian king took steps to stabilize the situation, sending two emissaries from among the exiles in Babylonia—Ezra and Nehemiah.

Nehemiah instituted reforms to alleviate the exploitative practices of the rich, but his efforts did not change the basic structure of society. The temple aristocracy, tied to the ruling empire, remained in place.

Ezra was instrumental in establishing obedience to the Torah as the definitive mode of religious observance. By obeying God's commands, the people sought to ensure that they would never again bring God's judgment upon them, for many understood the exile as punishment for sin. Obedience to the Torah was a way of being faithful to the covenant, of nurturing memory in order to call forth hope. It is only in this postexilic period, when the traditions that that have lasted into modern times were securely in place, that we can begin to speak of the Israelite people as Jews or of their faith as Judaism.

The Hellenistic Age: Exportation of a Culture

The Persian Empire lasted two centuries and then crumbled before the invading army of Alexander the Great. After defeating the Persian king in Asia Minor in 333 B.C.E., Alexander took Egypt and marched eastward to the edge of India. He conquered, but his reign was cut short. In 323 B.C.E., he died in Babylon, and the new empire disintegrated. He had, however, laid the foundation for a new world.

The Impact of Hellenism

Alexander was a native of Macedonia, a Greek-speaking land to the north of Greece, and his conquests resulted in the exportation of Greek culture, in however superficial a form. Throughout the new empire, he founded Greek-style cities and reorganized many older cities on the Greek model, most notably Alex-andria in Egypt, which became the intellectual center of this new world.

Alexander's generals and their successors fought over the remnants of his empire, and three relatively stable dynasties emerged: the Antigonids in Macedonia, the Seleucids in Syria, and the Ptolemies in Egypt. Although politically divided, the world Alexander left became a network in which the *koine*, or "common," Greek was the language of government and business. Centuries later, the New Testament authors composed their works in this popularized Greek.

The Greeks' name for their homeland was Hellas. The adjective *Hellenic* refers to ancient Greek culture, and *Hellenistic* pertains to the period following Alexander in which Greek culture spread throughout the Mediterranean world. It is unclear to what extent Hellenization reached the masses of people outside the new Greek-style cities, but within these cities, Greek ways prevailed, particularly among the affluent.

The combination of a common language and new trade routes brought heightened awareness of the wider world. Local and national consciousness gave way to a cosmopolitan atmosphere. People began to think of themselves as citizens of the world and also as individuals, no longer bound by ancient traditions but free to choose from among various patterns of life and thought.

The new world was one of intellectual vitality. The library at Alexandria amassed the largest collection of writings the world had ever known. Science and mathematics flourished, significant advances were made in medicine, and seafaring expeditions extended the knowledge of geography. Literature also flourished. Biographies became popular, and a new literary genre reflected the spirit of the times: the romance, or novel, which often combined the motifs of travel, adventure, and eroticism.

Hellenistic Religion

The Hellenistic Age fostered the breakup of traditional faiths, in part because the local deities seemed powerless in the face of Alexander's conquests. The Macedonians brought the Olympian gods and goddesses with them, but interest in these deities had long dwindled among the educated. And the Olympian cult was largely a political affair that evoked little personal devotion.

In this chaotic situation, many came to see life as ruled by either Fate (cosmic necessity, often imaged as a goddess) or Chance (sheer accident). Others turned to astrology as a way of discerning the future and perhaps modifying it in some way, while magic offered a more immediate way of manipulating threatening forces.

Other people found solace in cults that offered initiation into secret "mysteries." Our knowledge of such cults is limited, but the sacred rites typically offered the renewal of the individual's life in this world and the promise of immortality. Originally associated with agricultural themes, they took on the new meaning of personal rebirth and immortality. Particularly popular were the cults of Demeter, "the Mother of Grain," and Dionysus, the god of wine. From Egypt came the cults of Isis and Serapis, a Hellenized version of the older religion of Isis and Osiris.

Syncretism—the combination of motifs of various origins—characterized Hellenistic

FIG. 2.2 **The Parthenon in Athens.** Photo by Marshall Johnson.

FIG. 2.3 **The Odeon (Theater) at the Parthenon.** Photo by Marshall Johnson.

example is Isis, who gradually shed her association with Serapis. A number of hymns to her manifest a clear step toward monotheism.

Not everyone found the religions of the Hellenistic Age acceptable. For some, philosophy provided an alternative, although the distinction between religion and philosophy became somewhat blurred.

Hellenistic Philosophy

For the Greeks, to be human in the fullest sense was to participate in society, and Plato and Aristotle pursued their philosophy on this assumption. Plato sought to know the nature of the universe in order to provide a foundation for just government and social norms. In the Hellenistic Age, however, people felt lost and powerless in a vast civilization. Thus, philosophy underwent a shift of emphases: from concern with social structure to concern with the individual good, and from speculation on the nature of the universe to the development of a personal ethical code. The schools of Plato and Aristotle continued, but three alternative philosophies emerged and flourished: Epicureanism, Stoicism, and Cynicism.

religion in general. Greek ideas penetrated local religions, and vice versa. Eastern deities became identified with Greek gods and goddesses, and various deities combined into one. There was also some tendency toward belief in one universal divine being. The most notable

Epicureanism

Epicurus, who established a school in Athens in 306 B.C.E., returned to a view of the universe that predated Plato. This was a pure materialism in which everything is made of atoms, and there is no spiritual dimension undergirding the physical and no overarching purpose in the universe.

To the Epicureans, it was self-evident that pleasure is the ultimate good; the only question was how to attain it. Rejecting overindulgence partly because of its addictive nature, they pursued the simplest pleasures: to enjoy a bowl of porridge and the association of a few friends. One should live prudently, honorably, and cheerfully and treats others justly, because to do otherwise would bring pain upon oneself.

Although encouraging a type of detachment from the world to avoid pain, they recognized friendship as a basic need and established organizations that took on a religious character. Members honored Epicurus and other leaders in sacred meals and looked to one another for support, believing that one should love one's neighbors as oneself.

Stoicism

Founded by Zeno of Cyprus, who came to Athens in 300 B.C.E., Stoicism gained a large following. The name derives from the word *stoa*, which refers to the porchlike structures in the Greek cities, where people gathered for conversation and activities. It was in such stoas that Zeno generally taught.

For Stoics, fire was the basic element of which everything consists. They identified this fire with God and also called it the universal Logos, or Reason, the principle that holds the universe together. Stoicism is thus a form of pantheism, the view that the universe itself is divine. In Stoic teaching, the world is God's body, in which the Logos dwells as soul. Also, each human being possesses an individual logos—a spark of the divine fire, capable of ordering itself in accordance with universal Reason. Although the god of Stoicism sounds impersonal, some Stoics found room for intense personal devotion to the Logos.

The Stoics made no attempt to avoid pain, since they believed that everything is ruled by Fate or Providence, which they also identified with God. Individuals cannot control external circumstances, but they can control their inner attitudes. Thus, the Stoic ideal was *apatheia*, a state of passionlessness, the refusal to suffer internally. One should also accept one's fate, one's place in the universe, and perform the duties that nature assigns to that station.

Stoic pantheism also implied universal human relatedness. Even though belief in Fate tended to discourage attempts to change society, Stoics often supported social reforms. And Stoic writers produced some striking examples of utopian writings that envisioned thoroughly egalitarian societies.

Cynicism

The third philosophy, Cynicism, was distinguished less by doctrines than by the manner of instruction and lifestyle of the teachers, who rejected both personal wealth and social conventions. The founder, Diogenes, born around 400 B.C.E., lived in a tub and was so flagrant in his violation of cultural norms that Aristotle called him *kuon*—the Greek term for "dog." Out of this designation grew the nickname *kunikos* ("doglike"), Cynic.

Cynicism gave rise to Stoicism and shared its emphasis on detachment from the world, although the Stoics moderated Cynicism's extreme denunciation of civilization. Stressing self-sufficiency and harmony with nature, the Cynics took animal behavior as their model. A typical Cynic sage lived an itinerant life, carrying only a bag, a staff, and a cloak, and slept on the ground or in public buildings; begging was often the Cynic's means of support.

Cynic sages taught in the marketplaces, employing two distinctive ways of making their points. One was the striking example story, which illustrated their version of ethical behavior. The other was the diatribe, a form of argumentation employing such devices as rhetorical questions, vivid images drawn from ordinary life, and the objections of an imaginary opponent.

In New Testament times, we find many popular philosophers wandering from place to place, living a Cynic lifestyle, and teaching in the marketplaces. Their ideas generally reflected a Cynic–Stoic outlook.

The Spirit of the Age

Stoicism was more typical of one aspect of the Hellenistic Age than Epicureanism: its pantheism constituted a partial "remystification" of nature. Epicureanism was virtually alone in moving in the opposite direction. For all the sophistication of the age, there was an overwhelming resurgence of a sense of "the beyond" and of mystery. Some historians have disparaged the change in consciousness as escapism. To what extent, however, is such a judgment the imposition of modern values on the ancient world? Was this change a "failure of nerve"[2] or a creative attempt to see into the depths of human existence?

Crosscurrents: Judaism in the Hellenistic Age

During the Hellenistic Age, Jews existed in a variety of circumstances. Many lived outside Jewish Palestine.[3] There were probably scattered communities of such people even before the Babylonian exile, but that event marked a new chapter in the history of what became known as the Diaspora ("Dispersion"), the great body of Jews living in the Gentile world. In the time of Jesus, Jewish communities flourished throughout the Mediterranean world.

Palestine itself was divided into three regions—Judea, Samaria, and Galilee, where Jesus carried out the greater part of his mission. The Samaritans were a separate religious community, with their own version of the Torah, and at some point, they built their own temple. The Samaritans considered themselves the true worshippers of Yahweh, while Judeans and Galileans believed these people had corrupted the tradition. The animosity was so intense that Jews traveling between Judea and Galilee would bypass Samaria.

Galilee was part of the Jewish community, but Galilean customs probably differed somewhat from those in Judea. The religious leaders in Judea considered Galileans inferior and somewhat impure because of the Gentile influence, while the Galileans probably resented Jerusalem's authority to some degree.

The Challenge of Hellenism

After Alexander's death, Palestine was caught up in the struggles among his successors. After a long rule by the Ptolemies of Egypt, Palestine passed into Seleucid (Syrian) hands in 198 B.C.E. Throughout the Hellenistic Age, Jews in Palestine and the Diaspora struggled to retain their religious heritage in the face of a powerful and appealing culture.

Diaspora Jews were in frequent contact with Gentiles, and the Greek language was a necessity. Nevertheless, they were able to live in closely knit communities and carry on their traditions. One means toward this end was a Greek version of the scriptures. It became known as the Septuagint, from a Latin root meaning "seventy": legend had it that seventy scholars made separate translations and came up with the exact same wording. The scholarly abbreviation for the Septuagint is LXX.

Since Persian times, most of the people in Jewish Palestine had spoken Aramaic, although Hebrew was used in religious study and writing. Hellenism brought Greek to the area, especially the cities, and the upper classes embraced it along with other Greek ways as the passport to social and economic success.

But when young men began to wear Greek clothes and participate in Greek games (and even to have operations to disguise circumcision, since the games required nudity), many pious Jews were scandalized. For some, loyalty to Yahweh meant the complete rejection of Hellenism.

The Maccabean War

The conflict between Judaism and Hellenism in Palestine came to a head during the reign of the Seleucid king Antiochus Epiphanes. He angered Jews by pursuing a policy of active Hellenization, and his selling of the high priesthood to the highest bidder gave rise to an overt protest movement. An important component of that movement was a group known as the Hasidim, "the pious ones." Eventually, Antiochus's raid on the temple treasury following a failed military campaign led to the Maccabean War. A group of Jews seized control of Jerusalem, but the Seleucids recaptured the city and attempted to abolish the Jewish religion in Jerusalem and Judea. In 168 B.C.E. (or 167), they forbade circumcision and Sabbath observance, destroyed copies of the Torah, set up a Syrian-Hellenistic cult in the temple, and ordered Jews to offer sacrifices to foreign deities. Some Jews complied with the order, while others resisted passively and paid with their lives. Still others, under the leadership of the family of one Judas, nicknamed Maccabeus ("The Hammer"), fled to the hills and organized armed resistance.

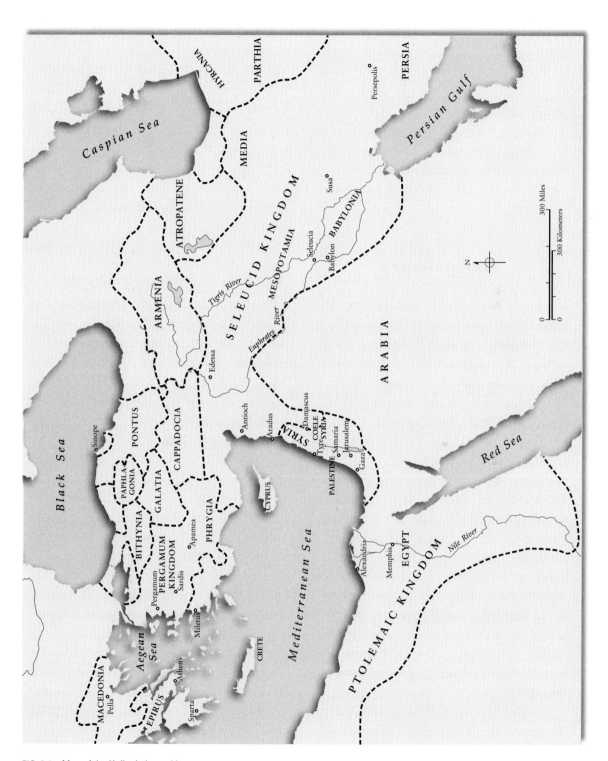

FIG. 2.4   Map of the Hellenistic world.

The Maccabees fought ferociously and by 165 forced a treaty restoring religious rights. Jews commemorate the rededication of the temple, following Judas's triumphant entry into Jerusalem, in the festival of Hanukkah. Judas fought on for full freedom, and after his death, leadership passed to his brother Simon, who negotiated independence and founded the Hasmonean Dynasty, which lasted about a century.

Apocalyptic Literature

During the war, a literary work appeared that had great influence on later Jewish and Christian thought: the book of Daniel. It expressed a way of thinking that had been developing since the early postexilic period. In terms of literary form, it is classified as an "apocalypse," from the Greek word *apokalypsis*, meaning "revelation," and the mode of thinking it expresses is called apocalyptic.

One type of apocalypse is a narrative writing in which an otherworldly being mediates to a human recipient a revelation regarding a supernatural world and a final judgment at which the wicked will be destroyed and the righteous will receive a salvation after death. Apocalyptic teachings regarding such matters as the final judgment and the fate of human beings beyond the grave constitute a particular form of eschatology (from the Greek word *eschatos*, meaning "last"), or doctrine of the "last things."

Apocalypses have often been called the "literature of the oppressed." They express

the hope that God will eventually come to the rescue of the oppressed people of Israel. The prophets had frequently interpreted the Israelites' misfortunes as God's punishment, but they had also promised God's rule in the future. At a time when many Jews were asking how they could deserve so much suffering, apocalyptic writings proclaimed that God would establish the divine rule by bringing history to an end and punishing the unrighteous.

Apocalyptic writers used emotional language and symbolism that often took the form of bizarre imagery. In Daniel, the recipient of the revelation (the character Daniel) describes a vision of four beasts rising from the sea. The fourth beast had ten horns but then grew a little one with eyes and a mouth that was "speaking arrogantly" (Dan 7:7-8). Later, an angel explains the vision: the beasts represent successive empires, and the horns of the last beast are kings. It is clear that the fourth beast represents Alexander's empire, the horns are the Hellenistic kings who succeeded him, and the little horn is Antiochus Epiphanes.

The book of Daniel also gives symbolic accounts of God's eventual defeat and destruction of Antiochus, the vindication of the Jewish people, and the final judgment and resurrection of the righteous. Its ecstatic, imaginative language is not that of reasoned argument but of religious inspiration.

Although written during the Maccabean War, the "story" told in Daniel is set during the Babylonian exile: Daniel's vision thus purports to look *ahead* in history. Readers living through the war therefore receive a word from a hero of the past who assures them that God is in control of history and will eventually set things right.

The theme of the resurrection, which appears in Daniel 12, was unknown in earlier Hebrew thought. As originally conceived, this concept was intimately related to the problem of the suffering of the righteous. Resurrection is God's way of vindicating righteous people who have suffered unjustly in this life.

The book of Daniel found its way into the Hebrew canon, but there were many Jewish apocalypses that did not. Although Judaism eventually turned away from apocalyptic writing, the apocalyptic imagination lived on in early Christianity.

Sociological Makeup of Jewish Society

Ancient agrarian societies were divided into two groups of classes: the upper and the lower, with no middle class in the modern sense.[4] The upper classes probably constituted 5 to 7 percent of the population. The real power rested with a governing class that made up 1 to 2 percent, but other groups were attached to the governing class and enjoyed some of its benefits. Among the latter was a "retainer" class, made up of such persons as bureaucrats, educators, officials, soldiers, priests, and merchants, who served the needs of the governing class. Unlike the modern middle class, the retainers were directly dependent on the governing class.

The lower classes consisted primarily of peasants, or farmers—the largest part of

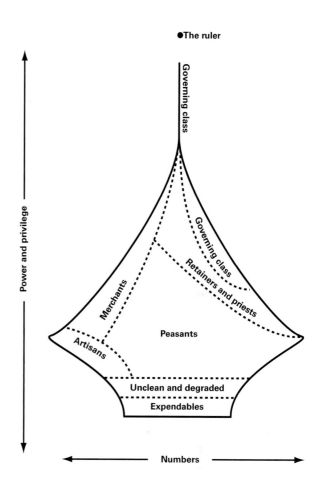

FIG. 2.5 **A graphic representation of the relationship among classes in agrarian societies.** From Gerhard E. Lenski, *Power and Privilege: A Theory of Social Stratification* [New York: McGraw-Hill, 1966], 284.

the population. Left to themselves, peasants would produce only enough food for their families, but the governing classes demanded excess produce to feed the rest of the population and high taxes to fund the government. Although there was wide variation in economic status among peasants, they were usually poorer than those in the upper classes and lacked even the indirect access to power that the retainers had.

A small fraction of the population consisted of artisans, who also belonged to the lower classes. Below them were persons without land or marketable skills, who either performed society's most menial tasks or were left with no means of support at all. In difficult times, when peasants often lost their land, more and more persons fell into the very lowest categories. Many who lost status turned to banditry.

The governing class in Judah during the Hasmonean Dynasty comprised the royal

FIG. 2.6 Caves in which the Dead Sea Scrolls were found. Near the ruins at Qumran, which scholars generally identify as the religious community that produced the scrolls.

Photo by Marshall Johnson.

court and the temple aristocracy. The high priest and the upper echelons of the priesthood belonged to that class, but the majority of priests were among the retainers.

The New Testament frequently mentions persons known as scribes. These also seem to fit primarily into the retainer class. Scholars have often treated the scribes as if they constituted a unified group, but there were many different kinds of scribes with a wide range of functions. In the most general terms, they were persons whose work demanded the ability to read and write. Some were undoubtedly teachers and high officials, but the majority probably performed middle-level bureaucratic functions such as record keeping, collection of taxes imposed by Jewish leaders, and copying of documents. Many scribes were attached to the temple, and well-educated scribes were the ones who preserved much of ancient Jewish tradition in writing.

Pharisees, Sadducees, Essenes, and the Qumran Sect

The first-century C.E. Jewish historian Josephus describes three Jewish factions that were apparently formed during the Hasmonean period: the Pharisees, the Sadducees, and the Essenes. All are mentioned in other ancient sources as well, and the Pharisees and Sadducees appear in the New Testament.

Pharisees

The origin of the Pharisees is uncertain, but many scholars believe they were heirs of the Hasidim, the vigorous opponents of Hellenization at the time of the Maccabean War. The Pharisees advocated meticulous obedience to the Torah and possessed an extensive oral tradition that supplemented the written law. They were known for observance of elaborate religious customs regarding such matters as tithing and Sabbath observance. Ritual purity was a primary concern, particularly with respect to regulations regarding meals. They believed in the resurrection of the dead and eternal reward and punishment.

Sociologically, the Pharisees seem to have belonged to the retainer class. As is often characteristic of groups in this class, they fell in and out of favor with the governing class over the years. It has been argued that by the New Testament period, they had given up the struggle for political power, but the matter is disputed. In any case, their influence on the government was limited during the time of Jesus. Their relationship to the lower classes is somewhat unclear, although they did foster interpretations of the law designed to make it easier for common people to conform to its regulations.

The Pharisaic movement was composed of laypersons rather than priests. In the New Testament, they are frequently associated with "the scribes," which probably indicates that many Pharisees were in fact scribes. In any case, scribes and Pharisees shared a concern for the preservation of tradition.

Sadducees

The Sadducees apparently belonged to the governing class and were probably a much smaller group than the Pharisees. Their mem-bership seems to have come from the Jewish aristocracy, especially the upper levels of the priesthood. Concerned primarily with the temple cult, they had little interest in the application of Torah to daily life after the manner of the Pharisees. They also rejected the resurrection of the dead and eternal reward and punishment, notions that do not appear in the Torah. In this respect, they reflected a conservatism that is typical of the governing class. Although power shifted back and forth between the Pharisees and Sadducees, the Sadducees generally had the greater influence in official affairs.

Essenes

According to Josephus, the Essenes resided in several different locales and practiced a type of communitarian life involving rules of purity more elaborate than those of the Pharisees. Membership entailed an extensive probationary period, strict vows, and severe disciplinary rules. Another ancient source portrays them as a celibate order that perpetuated itself through adoptions, but Josephus's account indicates that not all groups of Essenes avoided marriage. The Roman writer Pliny the Elder refers to a group of Essenes living along the shore of the Dead Sea, although historians are uncertain as to the accuracy of his account.

The Essenes were apparently a fairly small group and considerably less influential in affairs of state during the time of Jesus than were the Pharisees and Sadducees. It would appear, in fact, that they had in large measure retreated from the wider Jewish community in protest against current practices.

The Dead Sea Scrolls and the Qumran Sect

In 1897, an ancient writing that scholars named the Damascus Document was found in a synagogue in Cairo, Egypt. Then in 1947 came discovery of an enormous deposit of manuscripts, largely in fragments, in caves near the ruins of an ancient settlement at Qumran, along the coast of the Dead Sea. The Dead Sea Scrolls, as the materials came to be called, included books of the Jewish Scriptures, along with other writings that are clearly sectarian in nature and bear striking similarities to the Damascus Document. Most scholars believe that the Damascus Document and the sectarian materials among the scrolls reflect the views of the Essenes and that the Qumran settlement was an Essene community. There are other theories, however, and a recent hypothesis is that the group at Qumran was a dissident faction of Sadducees.[5]

Whoever the residents of Qumran were, their writings indicate that they withdrew from the larger Jewish society because they believed the temple leadership was corrupt. The group's theology was highly apocalyptic. They expected a final battle between the forces of good and evil, and they awaited two messianic leaders, one political and one priestly, to lead them into the new age. They forbade marriage because, according to the purity laws in the Jewish Scriptures, sexual contact brought a temporary ritual uncleanness that made warriors unfit for battle. In expectation of the coming age, they sought to maintain a constant state of ritual purity. Thus, they enforced a rigid set of community rules, considering themselves the only true Jews. Prospective members went through a period

of probation, and strict regulations governed all aspects of life.

The sectarian writings among the Dead Sea Scrolls are important to students of early Christianity because of their method of biblical interpretation. The settlers at Qumran read the scriptures in light of their own experience, taking passages in the various books to refer to specific events in the history of their own community. Similar approaches to interpretation were employed by other Jewish interpreters of the time and by the New Testament writers.

Hellenistic Influence on Diaspora Writings

Well before the Babylonian exile, the Israelites appropriated a type of writing prevalent in the surrounding cultures: Wisdom literature, which involved comment on life in general, life as it might appear to anyone in any time. Such literature left little room for such notions as God's covenant with Israel, but some Hebrew versions of it retained a degree of distinctiveness by identifying Torah as the ultimate wisdom.

Hellenistic ideas eventually found their way into Jewish wisdom materials. For example, the Wisdom of Solomon, written in Greek probably around 100 B.C.E., reflects both Platonic and Stoic thought. It advances a notion of personal immortality based not on resurrection but on a dualism of body and soul (2:23; 8:19-20; 9:15)—a Greek, not a Jewish, concept. It also personifies the figure of Wisdom. Because both the Greek and the Hebrew words for "wisdom" are feminine in form, the personified Wisdom appears as female. She is the agent through whom God created the world (7:22; 8:5; 9:9) and, like the Stoic Logos, pervades all creation: "For she is a breath of the power of God and a pure emanation of the glory of the Almighty" (7:24).

The writings of Philo of Alexandria (20 B.C.E.–40 C.E.) go even further in embracing Hellenistic thought. Philo sought to demonstrate the superiority of Judaism, largely by arguing that the Jewish Scriptures contain the same truths put forth by the Greek philosophers. He thus identified the Torah with the "natural law" of the Stoics and interpreted biblical characters as embodiments of Greek virtues. And he employed a method of interpretation often used in relation to the Greek myths: allegorical interpretation, which means finding a symbolic meaning behind the literal details of the text. For example, he interpreted the four rivers in the Garden of Eden as the four cardinal virtues identified by Plato and the Stoics: prudence, temperance, fortitude, and justice.

Logos/Wisdom was an important notion in Philo's thought. It was for him a kind of emanation from God's own being, which gave the world its form, functioned as natural law, and became manifest in virtuous lives. It has been suggested that the figure of Isis influenced the way Philo understood Wisdom.

The Context of Emerging Christianity: The Roman Imperial Period

The Hellenistic monarchies eventually fell, but an eager new master waited in the West

to impose its rule. The Hasmonean rulers thus suffered the fate of the whole western end of the Hellenistic world: while rival leaders contended for power, Rome stepped in. The independence of the Jewish nation came to an end in 63 B.C.E., when the general Pompey marched into Jerusalem.

Roman Occupation of Palestine

Although many Jews were initially relieved to have Rome intervene in a chaotic situation, there was some early resistance against the occupation government, particularly in Galilee, where many Gentiles had converted to Judaism. The early years were also marked with political intrigue, since Rome itself was experiencing a power struggle, and those contending for control of Judea switched sides as the tide turned. By 30 B.C.E., however, Octavian, who became known as Caesar Augustus, had taken control in Rome.

In the midst of this turmoil, Rome appointed a man named Herod as "king of the Jews." He was a native of Idumea, a region south of Judea that was annexed to the Jewish state during Hasmonean times. But the Jewish people saw him as a puppet of Rome and despised him intensely. He maintained foreign mercenaries and a network of informers, and he met any hint of disorder with harsh repression. Although he made some attempts to win the favor of the people and transformed the temple into a magnificent new structure, he was an avid proponent of Hellenism and intensely loyal to Rome; many people were scandalized when he placed a Roman eagle above the temple gate. His maintenance of a lavish royal court and his fetish for building projects led to increased taxes that placed the population under an extreme economic burden.

When Herod died in 4 B.C.E., his territory went to his three sons. Philip ruled an area to the northeast of Galilee. Herod Antipas had Galilee and Perea (a district east of the Jordan River) and governed until shortly after Jesus' death. We will meet him later as the one who executes John the Baptist and who (while temporarily in Jerusalem) questions Jesus prior to his trial. Archelaus, who ruled Judea, was a terrible leader. His brutality provoked such constant unrest that the em-

peror removed him and put his district under a Roman governor.

There was widespread resentment of the occupation government, which was increased by economic hardship, and several revolts took place in Jerusalem and the outlying regions shortly following Herod's death. In Judea, Galilee, and Perea, the insurgents proclaimed their leaders kings and were able to set up brief rules in their respective territories. These uprisings were popular in nature, involving mainly peasants. The leader in Galilee was a bandit chief, and the insurgents in Perea stormed the estates of the rich and confiscated their goods.

FIG. 2.7 **Ancient ruins in Masada.** Photo by Marshall Johnson.

After these revolts were suppressed, relative quiet prevailed until 26 C.E., when Pontius Pilate became governor of Judea. His rule was a complete failure. Consistently offending the people's religious sensibilities, Pilate met their nonviolent protests with brutal repression. The situation deteriorated so much that the Romans removed him from office in 36 C.E., a few years after the crucifixion of Jesus. In 41, they placed the whole of Palestine under a grandson of Herod, who ruled as King Agrippa I and gained a good reputation among the Jews. Following his death in 44, the entire area came under the direct rule of a Roman governor. However, the king's son—Agrippa II—eventually received a small territory in Galilee and Perea. Completely subservient to Rome, he appears in the New Testament in connection with the trial of the apostle Paul.

The eight governors who served in succession from 44 to 66 were of mixed quality, but the insensitivity and incompetence of some led to a full-scale rebellion in 66, in which even a segment of the aristocracy turned against the occupation government. A son of the high priest succeeded in stopping all sacrifices on behalf of Rome and eventually led an insurrection that expelled the governor, Florus, from Jerusalem. When other members of the aristocracy took refuge in the Herodian palace, they lost all vestiges of authority with the people.

The entire country finally united in the rebellion, but the Romans eventually regained control. As they marched through the land, devastating it as they went, many peasants fled and formed bandit brigades. Several such groups eventually sought refuge in Jerusalem, forming a coalition known as the Zealots. They set up a makeshift government but were opposed by the priestly aristocracy and eventually replaced by another revolutionary group. Scholars have often assumed that the Zealots were a long-standing revolutionary party, but the evidence indicates that they were formed only during the Roman siege of Jerusalem.[6]

The final stage of that siege came in 70 C.E., when the Romans recaptured Jerusalem and burned the temple and much of the city. In 73, they took the final group of holdouts at the mountain fortress of Masada, along the Dead Sea. Much later, in 132, a man called Bar Kochba led another ill-fated rebellion, following which the Romans renamed the province Syria Palestina, forbade Jews to enter Jerusalem, and built a temple to Jupiter where Yahweh's once stood. The ancient Jewish state was at an end.

Although there was as yet no formalized concept of the Messiah, the time of Roman occupation was characterized by "messianic" expectations in the broad sense of hopes for a climactic act of God in history. These expectations are evidenced not only by the apocalyptic works produced during the period but also by social movements. The popular kingships set up temporarily after Herod's death, the revolutionary governments that appeared during the siege of Jerusalem, and the Bar Kochba revolt had clear messianic overtones. In addition, various prophetic movements, and even some aspects of the activities of bandits—who generally attacked the holdings of the rich and were often glorified by the poor—in their own ways grew out of a hope for justice that was associated with the expected rule of God.

Continuation of Jewish Tradition

In 68 C.E., when the fate of Jerusalem was already apparent to many, a respected teacher among the Pharisees, Yohanan ben Zakkai, escaped from the city and went to the camp of the Roman general. With Roman approval, he then set up an academy in the town of Yabneh, near the seacoast, with the intention of preserving Jewish tradition. Revered teachers among the Jews were called rabbi, a title that did not at first involve formal ordination. Because of the succession of such teachers during the period that began with the establishment of the academy, the Judaism of the time is called Rabbinic Judaism.

It was during the period of Rabbinic Judaism that the Hebrew canon took final shape. But the closing of the canon did not bring the process of tradition to an end. Drawing upon centuries of lore, rabbinic schools in both Palestine and the Diaspora produced an enormous amount of literature during the early centuries C.E.

One type of such literature is known as midrash, running commentary on scriptures; another type is oral law arranged topically. In time, the Jewish leaders codified the topically arranged material as the Mishnah. Much later, they added to it an enormous body of interpretation to form two works called the Talmud, one produced in Babylon and the other in Palestine, which are second only to the scriptures themselves as authoritative for Jews.

Rabbinic literature is far removed from doctrinal formulation, the presentation of ideas for intellectual assent. Contradictory assertions stand side by side in a free-floating, open-ended discussion. As Christians in the early centuries C.E turned more and more to the formulation of doctrine in the categories of Greek philosophy, Jews continued to wrestle with the application of God's commands to daily life and, simply, to tell stories. In the New Testament, we find Christianity still living in both worlds—on the one hand engaged in open-ended discussion and the telling of stories, and on the other hand moving toward a body of doctrine.

Christians and the Hebrew Canon

Some of the books included in the Septuagint were not subsequently accepted into the Jewish canon. Because the early church quickly became Greek-speaking and naturally used the Septuagint as its Bible, Christians found themselves with a version of the Jewish Scriptures containing books not accepted as fully authoritative by Jews themselves. Christians did not generally hold the "extra" books in as high regard as those in the Hebrew canon, but the inclusion of these books in the later Latin translation (the Vulgate) increased their standing. During the Protestant Reformation, however, Martin Luther placed them at the end of his translation and designated them as "Apocrypha," indicating their secondary status. They have therefore played a less

FIG. 2.8. THE JEWISH CALENDAR AND SEASONAL CYCLE

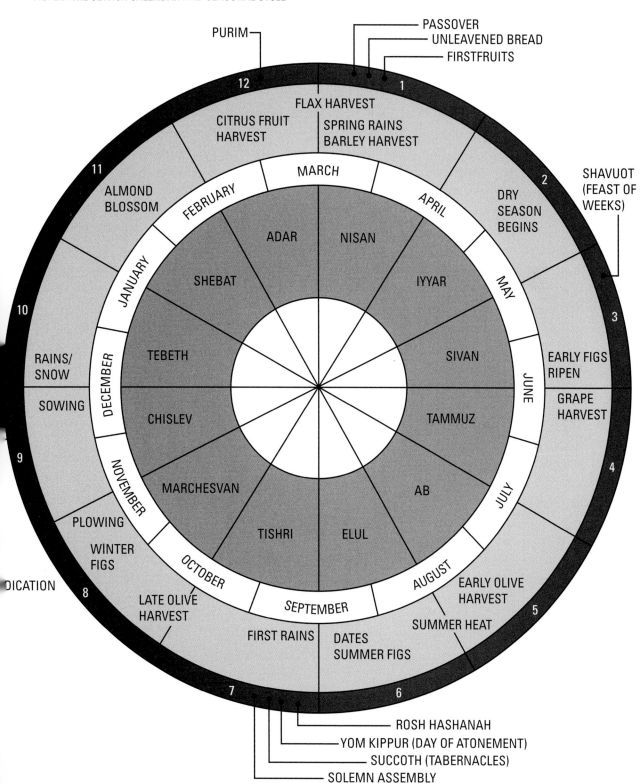

important role in Protestant churches than in Catholicism or Eastern Orthodoxy.

The early Christians supplemented the Jewish Scriptures with a collection of their own writings. Because they believed that God had now (in words taken from the prophet Jeremiah) made a *new* covenant with all humankind through Jesus, they called their own canon the "New Covenant." The Jewish Scriptures became known as the "Old Covenant." The Greek term for "covenant" was translated into Latin as *testamentum*. Unfortunately, current usage of the English equivalent, *testament*, obscures the original force of the term as applied to scripture—that is, its designation of a formally instituted relationship between God and human beings.

Christianity in the Greco-Roman World

The Roman Empire was heir to the Hellenism that had flourished for two centuries, and we may speak of its territory as the Greco-Roman world. The transition from a small Jewish sect in Palestine to a major religion within this wider world involved a conflict in values. In what sense was the Christian message for all humankind without qualification, and in what sense did it remain tied to God's covenant with Israel? The Greco-Roman environment provided social, religious, and philosophical precedents that enabled the new faith to speak meaningfully to the world in which it found itself, but it also posed enormous threats to Christianity's own distinctive claims, as well as to its Jewish heritage.

Jewish Christians and Judaism

The earliest Christians were Jews and continued to think of themselves as such, not as members of a new religion. They understood Jesus as the fulfillment of Jewish hopes and designated him "Messiah," which they translated into Greek as *christos* (Christ). But Jewish messianic hopes included the expectation of a rule of God that would bring peace and justice to the world at large. If Jesus was Messiah, could Gentiles now be included in the community? If so, on what basis? Must the males be circumcised, and were Gentile Christians subject to the ritual requirements of the law? What, in fact, was the status of the Jewish law itself in this new situation?

Most Jews found no reason to accept Jesus as Messiah. The messianic hope was associated with God's rule, but where were the peace and justice expected from that rule? Furthermore, Jesus' life had ended in apparent failure and shameful death. How were Christians to deal with these issues?

Like all Jews, they also had to deal with the problem of Rome. At one point, they probably had to ask whether they should join the resistance. Later, they faced the question of how to view the destruction of Jerusalem and the temple. As the church became more and more Gentile, it lost all connection with Jewish nationalistic hopes. But what, then, were Christians to think of God's promises to Israel?

Christianity and the Sociopolitical Order

Rome was a highly stratified society. It had nurtured democratic ideals in its past, and even the transition from republic to empire under Caesar did not destroy these ideals entirely. The senate retained some power, and there was a strong sense of the rule of law, as opposed to the arbitrary power of a monarch. Also, there were means by which people in the provinces under Rome's rule could obtain citizenship. Senate membership, however, was a matter of social rank, and owners of large estates held a large percentage of the land.

The empire included a vast area composed of agrarian societies that fit the general social pattern discussed earlier in relation to Jewish society. Within this structure, it was taken for granted that persons relatively low on the social scale would look to persons higher up to be their patrons and help them get what they needed in social or financial matters. In turn, those on the receiving end of the relationship were obligated to the patrons and thus became their clients, who would repay the debt in whatever ways the patrons demanded.

Because of society's multiple levels, persons who were clients of patrons above them could also function as patrons of others even further down. Those who played such a dual role functioned as brokers, who negotiated power relationships between persons widely separated on the social scale.[7]

Slavery was widespread. Greco-Roman slavery was generally less brutal than its modern American counterpart: slaves were often well educated, and steps had been taken, largely under Stoic influence, to improve their lot. But slavery is slavery nonetheless, and conditions were extremely severe in some areas. There were several slave revolts, which were harshly repressed.

The empire was male dominated, but the rights of women had been expanded through the years, again under Stoic influence. As over against Jewish society, for example, women in the Roman world had the right to divorce.

How would Christians relate to these social structures? Would they pick up on the Jewish sense of social justice? Would they expand it to include women more fully? Would they embrace the Stoic notion of universal relatedness? Would they advocate social reform? The acceptance of Jesus as Messiah committed Christians to hope for the realization of God's rule, but they had to work out for themselves just what that meant.

One issue Christians could not avoid was the emperor cult. Veneration of the emperor did not always mean that the emperor was literally worshipped as divine. Different emperors interpreted the matter differently, and some discouraged the practice, but the usual view was that divine power was present *in* the emperor. The point in any case was loyalty to the empire itself. Even so, the practice of sacrificing to the emperor was unacceptable to both Jews and Christians, whose monotheism demanded ultimate loyalty to God alone. But the question remained: How were Christians to relate to human governments when such sacrifice was not demanded?

Christianity and Mediterranean Culture

Both Hellenism and the Roman Empire superimposed themselves upon the preexisting world that surrounded the Mediterranean Sea. Although this broad region was composed of numerous societies, many modern anthropologists believe that a general culture cut across all of them. Of particular importance is the identification of honor and shame as the pivotal values within this culture. "Honor," Bruce Malina explains, "is the value of a person in his or her own eyes (that is, one's claim to worth) *plus* that person's value in the eyes of his or her social group."[8] Much energy was directed toward the maintenance of the honor of one's family. To preserve honor was to avoid shame, so that along with a sense of honor, one also needed a sense of shame, "sensitivity for one's own reputation."[9]

To grasp this concept, one must understand that ancient people thought largely in collective terms and were dominated by the opinions of the group. Each group member had specific responsibilities with respect to the maintenance of honor, and these were distributed according to a hierarchical order with clear differentiations according to sex.

There was a clear double standard regarding sexual activity. The woman's virginity prior to marriage was central to the family's honor. For a woman to engage in illicit sexual relations would bring shame, whereas for a male to do so would not. Both honor and shame fell ultimately upon the male, and it was assumed that all women needed the protection and supervision of males. Thus, women who were widowed or divorced or for any reason outside a male-headed household were "viewed as stripped of female honor, hence more like males than females, therefore sexually predatory, aggressive . . . hence dangerous."[10]

The value system of honor and shame was deeply ingrained in the first-century Mediterranean mind, and Christians could not simply abandon it altogether. Their allegiance to Jesus, however, brought them into tension with various aspects of that system. Even on the level of some of society's most tightly held norms, they faced the question as to what constituted honorable and shameful behavior in this new group.

Christianity among the Religions in the Greco-Roman World

The Greco-Roman world was a fertile field for missionary activity, and Christianity was from an early point a missionary religion. But it was not alone in its ability to attract converts.

Judaism itself was well respected in many quarters, and many people were profoundly attracted to Jewish monotheism and high ethical standards. The number of actual converts was limited because of circumcision and dietary regulations, but many Gentiles participated in synagogue worship without becoming Jews. In Acts, such people are called "God-fearers."

The mystery cults were extremely popular, and of particular importance was Mithraism, which was connected with sun worship: initiates became "soldiers" of the god Mithras and eventually achieved unity with Sol, the sun. This cult spread rapidly among the military and at one point was the official religion of the empire.

In many ways, Christianity's most serious rival was not a religion but a philosophy: Stoicism. Like Judaism, it possessed a highly developed moral sense, and its notion of universal human relatedness suited an age of world-consciousness. As with all philosophical movements, however, its appeal was limited mostly to the educated. It did not offer initiation rites, the close communion of a religious fellowship, or the promise of immortality.

A different kind of competition came from a complex of teachings designated by modern scholars as Gnosticism. Not only did gnostic groups compete against Christianity, but the two movements overlapped. There were at one time numerous groups of Christian gnostics, although as official doctrine and organizational structure developed, they were eventually forced to leave the church. The conflict with Gnosticism, which came to a head in the mid second century c.e., was a crucial point in the development of Christian self-definition, for it brought the question of Christianity's relationship to its Jewish heritage together with the broader question of how Christians should balance this-worldly and otherworldly concerns.

According to some gnostic mythology, the present world came into being not as a creation of the supreme God, but through some sort of cosmic accident. From the true God, who is pure Light, there somehow emanated several lesser orders of being. Sometimes the Jewish god is seen as belonging to one of these lesser orders. According to the gnostics, it was this god who, being ignorant of the true God, arrogantly decided to create this world. The present world, therefore, is seen as inherently flawed; it is less than fully real and actually an evil place that never should have come into existence.

Human beings within this world have a dual nature. Their material bodies, as parts of this "lower" world, are corrupt. But trapped within these bodies are spirits, "sparks" from the realm of Light. To remedy this situation, the true God sends a Redeemer from the realm of Light to enter this world. This Redeemer comes in the *appearance* of a human being but is not truly human, since to be material is to be corrupt. The Redeemer then teaches a secret knowledge (Greek: *gnosis*) that enables people to escape from this world at death and return to the realm of Light.

There are some real similarities between Christianity and Gnosticism. But the latter involved a total rejection of the Jewish God and the material world. Where were Christians, who accepted Jesus as the Jewish Messiah, to stand in relation to such a view? In what sense should they reject the world, and in what sense should they accept it?

Life and Mission of the Christian Communities

Jewish heritage, Hellenistic religious and philosophical ideas, and social realities all contributed to the various forms of the emerging Christian consciousness. But the reality of the early Christian movement was more than the sum of all these factors. The new communities were distinct entities within their various environments, held together by what is known in social-scientific terminology as a symbolic universe, a shared way of perceiving reality. Christians embraced the

Jewish belief in one God, modifying it with the conviction that, through Jesus of Nazareth, God had acted decisively not only to fulfill the ancient promises to Israel but also to make salvation available to all people. They also believed that this Jesus, whom God had raised from the dead, would return at the end of the age to bring to completion God's plan for the world. And along with such basic beliefs, they passed on moral teachings and tried to maintain cohesive relationships within the communities.

They also practiced certain rites that served to define their boundaries and create internal cohesion. Their ritual of initiation was baptism, immersion in water, which Jews had long practiced as a way of incorporating Gentile converts into their ranks. They also met together for worship, which was modeled after Jewish worship in the synagogues, involving such practices as prayer, reading of the Jewish Scriptures, and preaching. Originally meeting on the seventh day of the week, the Jewish Sabbath, they eventually adopted the first day as their holy day, associating it with the resurrection of Jesus.

At the heart of their worship life was a sacred meal, the Lord's Supper, which later became known as Holy Communion, or the Eucharist. It was a reenactment of Jesus' final meal with his disciples before his death. At first, the Lord's Supper seems to have been identical to what was known as the love feast, an actual fellowship meal. But eventually the ceremonial reenactment was separated from the full meal and consisted only of the giving and receiving of bread and wine.

As important as their internal life was, Christians also understood themselves as being in mission to the world. So before we come to the New Testament writings as they now stand within the canon, it will be important to look in on the earliest stages of the Christian proclamation. What exactly did the earliest Christians say about Jesus? What were the nature and meaning of their claims? Questions such as these will claim our attention in chapters 3 and 4.

NOTES

1. "Social Criticism: Crossing Boundaries," in *Mark and Method: New Approaches to Biblical Studies*, ed. Janet Capel Anderson and Stephen D. Moore (Minneapolis: Fortress Press, 1992), 151.

2. Gilbert Murray, *Five Stages of Greek Religion*, 3rd ed. (Boston: Beacon, 1951), ch. 4.

3. "Palestine" is the preferred scholarly designation for the land as a whole in ancient times—that is, as inclusive of both northern and southern regions. "Israel" is ambiguous, since it was once used to designate the northern monarchy alone.

4. The discussion in this section draws particularly upon Anthony J. Saldarini, *Pharisees, Scribes, and Sadducees* (Wilmington, Del.: Michael Glazier, 1987); and Richard A. Horsley, *Jesus and the Spiral of Violence: Popular Jewish Resistance in Roman Palestine* (San Francisco: Harper & Row, 1987).

5. See the contrasting views of Lawrence H. Schiffmann, "The Sadducean Origins of the Dead Sea Scroll Sect," and James C. VanderKam, "The People of the Dead Sea Scrolls: Esssenes or Sadducees?" in *Understanding the Dead Sea Scrolls: A Reader from the Biblical Archaeology Review*, ed. Hershel Shanks (New York: Random House, 1992).

6. See Richard A. Horsley with John S. Hanson, *Bandits, Prophets, and Messiahs: Popular Movements at the Time of Jesus* (Minneapolis: Winston, 1985), xiii–xvi.

7. John Dominic Crossan, *The Historical Jesus: The Life of a Mediterranean Jewish Peasant* (San Francisco: HarperSanFrancisco, 1991), 89–90.

8. Bruce J. Malina, *The New Testament World: Insights from Cultural Anthropology* (Atlanta: John Knox, 1981), 27.

9. Ibid., 44.

10. Ibid.

STUDY QUESTIONS

1. How did Hebrew monotheism and Plato's thought alter the ancient consciousness? How does the modern consciousness differ from the ancient, and how does the postmodern differ from both of these?

2. How did the development of a monarchy change the social structure and religious outlook of ancient Israel? What changes came about as the result of the Babylonian exile?

3. Give a brief description of the Hellenistic "world," with particular emphasis on the religious and philosophical options it offered.

4. Explain each of the following terms: cosmic empathy, demystification, materialism, idealism, dualism, exodus, Yahweh, covenant, rule of God, Messiah, messianic age, Torah, Judah, Samaria, *koine*, syncretism, Logos, Septuagint, eschatology.

5. How was Judaism affected by Hellenism?

6. What is apocalyptic literature, and why are historical apocalypses written? Discuss the benefits and dangers of apocalyptic literature from the point of view of a religious community.

7. Give a brief description of the sociological makeup of Jewish society during the Hellenistic Age.

8. Describe the main characteristics of the Essenes, Pharisees, and Sadducees.

9. What specific Hellenistic ideas can be found in writings of the Jewish Diaspora during the Hellenistic Age?

10. What would it have been like to have been a Palestinian Jew during the Roman occupation? How might your social standing have affected your evaluation of the occupation government?

11. Explain the origin of the terms *New Testament* and *Old Testament*. Many recent scholars and theologians have abandoned the use of the latter in favor of such terms as *Jewish Scriptures, Hebrew Bible,*

and *First Testament* (replacing *New Testament* with *Second Testament*). Can you state why these terms might be appropriate in our time?

12. Explain each of the following terms: Apocrypha, zealots, midrash, Mishnah, Talmud.

13. Give a brief description of the patron-client relationship in the world of the Roman Empire. How does the concept of debt figure into this relationship?

14. Give a brief description of how the concepts of honor and shame functioned in the ancient Mediterranean culture. Compare that culture's understanding of the human self with our own view.

15. Discuss the status and role of women in the world into which Christianity was born.

16. What are the specific characteristics of Gnosticism? In what ways did it reflect the "spirit" of the Hellenistic Age? Compare Gnosticism with Christianity as you understand the latter.

17. Give a brief description of the "internal life" of the Christian community.

FOR FURTHER READING

Barrett, C. K. *The New Testament Background: Selected Documents.* 2nd ed. New York: Harper & Row, 1989.

Boring, M. Eugene, Klaus Berger, and Carsten Colpe, eds. *Hellenistic Commentary to the New Testament.* Nashville: Abingdon, 1995.

Collins, John J. *The Apocalyptic Imagination: An Introduction to the Jewish Matrix of Christianity.* New York: Crossroad, 1989.

Horsley, Richard A., with John S. Hanson. *Bandits, Prophets, and Messiahs: Popular Movements at the Time of Jesus.* Minneapolis: Winston, 1985.

Malina, Bruce J. *The New Testament World: Insights from Cultural Anthropology.* London: SCM, 1983.

Pagels, Elaine. *The Gnostic Gospels.* New York: Random House, 1979.

Robinson, James M., ed. *The Nag Hammadi Library in English.* 3rd ed. San Francisco: Harper & Row, 1988.

Roetzel, Calvin J. *The World That Shaped the New Testament.* Atlanta: John Knox, 1985.

Saldarini, Anthony J. *Pharisees, Scribes, and Sadducees: A Sociological Approach.* 2nd ed. Grand Rapids: Eerdmans, 2001.

Vermes, Geza. *The Dead Sea Scrolls in English.* 2nd ed. Hammondsworth, U.K.: Penguin, 1975.

The Gospels, Jesus, and the Earliest Tradition

3

Alongside the early Christians' proclamation that God had raised Jesus from the dead, they transmitted another body of tradition: stories of incidents in Jesus' life and accounts of his teaching. This tradition must have begun during Jesus' lifetime, as those who heard his words and saw his deeds told others what they had seen and heard. A period of oral tradition thus preceded the four Gospels. The primary subject matter of this present chapter is the earliest stage of this Jesus tradition. In chapter 4, I will consider its later stages, along with the resurrection faith.

One cannot, however, consider the Jesus tradition apart from the Gospels themselves, for these writings constitute our primary sources for knowledge of the oral period. So it is important to begin with what contemporary scholarship has to say about what kind of materials the Gospels are and how they came to be. A good starting point is the question of the relationship between the Gospels and the actual, historical person of Jesus, who lived and carried out his ministry in first-century Jewish Palestine.

Jesus and the Gospels

Intentions of the Gospel Writers

Where can we go to find information about Jesus? The easy answer is to the Gospels. However, the Gospel writers were less concerned with historical accuracy than with proclaiming the *meaning* of Jesus' life, death, and resurrection. The author of John, in fact, implies as much in a statement of purpose at 20:30-31: "so that you may come to believe that Jesus is the Messiah, the Son of God, and that through believing you may have life in his name."

In other words, those who wrote the Gospels intended their works to be much more like sermons than newspaper accounts. This does not mean that they are pure invention, containing no historical facts at all. But it does mean that if we want to learn something about the actual person Jesus, we must distinguish between expressions of faith and the historical realities that lie behind those expressions.

"Apostolic Origin" and "Eyewitness Accounts"

Who wrote the Gospels? I noted in the introduction to this book that the early Christians canonized those writings that they believed were of apostolic origin. But in what sense did they understand the Gospels to be apostolic? To whom do the titles "Matthew," "Mark," "Luke," and "John" refer?

The actual texts of the Gospels make no claims regarding authorship. They get their traditional names from the headings of the Greek manuscripts, the oldest of which (with the exception of a fragment of the Gospel of John) come from around 200 C.E. These manuscripts employ the stereotyped titles, such as "According to Matthew," "According to Mark." Since it is unlikely that all four authors chose the same designation, we can

conclude that the titles were added after these books were widely accepted as authoritative. There must therefore have been oral traditions ascribing the books to particular authors.

We cannot be certain to whom the names originally referred. At some stage, early Christians took "Matthew" and "John" to be two of "the Twelve," the group that formed the inner circle of Jesus' disciples during his lifetime. The assumption is that "Mark" referred to John Mark, mentioned in Acts as a companion of Paul. A second-century bishop named Papias claimed that "Mark" made use of information given him by Peter, who was one of the Twelve. Second-century tradition also identified "Luke" with a coworker Paul mentions at Philemon 24, and the assumption has been that he is identical to the Luke of 2 Timothy 4:11 and "Luke, the beloved physician" of Colossians 4:14. The early church thus thought the author was a companion of Paul's, but not someone who actually knew Jesus. "Apostolic origin" thus had a fairly loose meaning; only Matthew and John were supposed to have been eyewitness accounts.

But were they really? It is difficult to believe that *both* are, since they tell different stories; very few incidents occur in both Gospels, while a crucial event, Jesus' action in the temple, comes at different points in the two accounts. They also contain entirely different types of material: Matthew (like Mark and Luke) is composed of short literary units—accounts of Jesus' conversations with various people, miracle stories, sayings—while John is filled with long speeches by Jesus. An early Christian writer described John as a "spiritual" gospel, recognizing it as a highly meditative work with little interest in reporting actual historical details. So if we compare the type of material found in Matthew to that found in John with respect to historical accuracy, the choice will have to be with material of the Matthean type. However much historical information John might contain, it is clearly not an eyewitness account.

The "Synoptic" Problem

But what of Matthew? The question is complicated by the fact that Matthew bears a literary relationship to Mark and Luke. Not only do Matthew, Mark, and Luke tell roughly the same story, but their wording is so similar that some actual copying must have been involved. Because of their close interrelationships, scholars have designated these three works the "Synoptic" (from Greek words meaning "seeing together") Gospels. They have also tried to solve the Synoptic problem, the question of how to account for the literary relationships.

The solution to the Synoptic problem that has dominated critical scholarship since the late nineteenth century is known as the two-document hypothesis. According to this theory, a comparison of materials common to all three Synoptic Gospels shows that Mark appeared first and the authors of Matthew and Luke used it independently in creating their own works. This leaves unexplained, however, the large body of material common to Matthew and Luke but not present in Mark. Thus, proponents of this view posit a second written

source, besides Mark, which both Matthew and Luke used. The designation for this hypothetical document is Q, after the German word *Quelle*, meaning "source." Some scholars expand this solution to a four-source theory, positing two further documents to account for material that is peculiar to Matthew (M) and Luke (L).

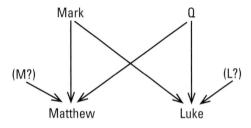

FIG. 3.1   Two (four)-document hypothesis

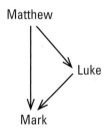

FIG. 3.2   Two-Gospel hypothesis

There are other theories, notably the two-Gospel hypothesis, which holds that Matthew was first, Luke drew upon Matthew, and Mark drew upon both. However, many scholars find it easier to explain why the author of Matthew (and Luke) would in individual instances have changed Mark, rather than vice versa. Sometimes it appears that the author of

Matthew or Luke is cleaning up the Greek in Mark or avoiding a possible misunderstanding; in other instances, it is easier to attribute a theological motive to either of these than to the author of Mark.

But how does all this affect the question of eyewitness accounts? Clearly, the two-document hypothesis calls that notion into question, since no one has ever claimed that Mark is the work of an eyewitness. But even apart from this theory, there are reasons to reject the notion of eyewitness accounts. The Synoptic Gospels are made up of relatively self-contained units of tradition that we call pericopes, which suggests that whichever Gospel came first, it was the work not of an eyewitness but of an author who drew upon oral traditions and ordered them into a coherent narrative. This judgment is strengthened by the observation that each Gospel writer pursues a specific theological agenda.

Christian Faith and the Problem of the "Historical Jesus"

The fact that the Gospel writers' materials were shaped by oral tradition does not mean that they contain no historical reminiscences. While some scholars are extremely skeptical about knowledge regarding the historical Jesus, most think we can reconstruct the main outlines of his teaching and the main thrust of his ministry. But there is general agreement that the Jesus of history is to be found not through an uncritical reading of the Gospel narratives but through a complex process of evaluating the individual units of tradition found within them.

But what does this view of the origin of the Gospels imply regarding Christian faith? Because of a particular understanding of the divine inspiration of the scriptures that some Christians hold, people are sometimes disturbed to learn the Gospels are less than fully accurate in a historical sense.

Although this theological question lies to some extent beyond the scope of this book, it is legitimate to ask whether the religious value of these writings necessarily depends upon their accuracy in historical details. Not all Christians link the doctrine of divine inspiration to such a standard. Many theologians believe that because the Gospel writers themselves focused on the meaning of Jesus' life rather than historical accuracy, believers should do the same.

In any case, most scholars think we can gain some knowledge of the historical Jesus. Some, however, prefer to think in terms of recovering the *earliest level of the Jesus tradition*, rather than finding a way around tradition to pure historical fact. This is a way of recognizing that the material we have is highly selective, since the tradition passes on only what serves its purposes. From this perspective, the only Jesus we can really know is the Jesus who is already part of the church's proclamation.

Whether or not one distinguishes between the earliest tradition and the historical person Jesus, an oral tradition about his words and deeds preceded the written Gospels. And the task at hand is to identify the oldest accounts of what he said and did. For all intents and purposes, the reader of the present text may treat the "historical Jesus" and the "earliest level of the Jesus tradition" as identical.

Jesus as Remembered: Words and Deeds

Identifying "Authentic" Teachings of Jesus

Recognizing that much of the teaching material attributed to Jesus in the Gospels belongs to later stages of the tradition, scholars have proposed criteria for identifying what is "authentic"—that is, what actually comes from the historical Jesus. I will note five such criteria that many scholars accept.

Environmental Appropriateness

Some passages can be ruled out because they reflect an environment different from that of first-century Jewish Palestine. Mark 10:12, for example, presupposes the right of a woman to divorce her husband; since Jewish law granted no such right to women, we must regard this verse as a later Hellenistic expansion of Mark 2:11, in which Jesus speaks on the question of whether a *man* may divorce his *wife*. For most scholars, the criterion of environmental appropriateness functions only negatively, since not all material that could have come from first-century Palestine necessarily goes back to Jesus himself.

Dissimilarity (or Distinctiveness)

On the positive side, many scholars look to the "criterion of dissimilarity" as a way of establishing a core of relatively indisputable material. In their view, we can be certain a teaching comes from Jesus only if it is distinctive over against both first-century Judaism and early Christianity. Material that parallels early Christian theology could easily be the product of the early church. And material that is typical of Judaism could have come from some other Jewish teacher and only later have been attributed to Jesus.

This search for what is dissimilar is probably the only way to achieve relative certainty, but it entails a subtle prejudice. Jesus was, after all, a Jew; to rule out all passages paralleled in Judaism is to stack the cards in favor of a Jesus at odds with his own tradition. So the search for distinctive material should be bracketed by recognition that Jesus must have shared much with his fellow Jews, however much he might have disagreed with some particular school on a given issue.

The matter is somewhat different when we come to parallels with early Christian theology. It is easy to imagine the postresurrection community reading its own faith back into Jesus' teachings. And it does, in fact, seem possible to distinguish between materials that reflect a distinctly postresurrection perspective and materials that do not. Even so, some scholars caution against assuming that Jesus' views were entirely different from those of the early Christian communities.

Embarrassment

Closely related to the criterion of dissimilarity is that of embarrassment. Some scholars argue that there are some Gospel passages that would have been so embarrassing to the early church that it is inconceivable they are the product of invention.

Coherence

Scholars who accept the criterion of dissimilarity sometimes supplement it with that of "coherence." Thus, Norman Perrin argued that once one has established the characteristics of Jesus' teaching, "these characteristics can be used to validate sayings which themselves would not meet . . . the criterion of dissimilarity."[1] One can, in other words, include as authentic other material that is in some significant way similar to that which meets the stiffer requirements.

Multiple Attestation

A final criterion is that of "multiple attestation." Scholars who use this test accept material as authentic if it appears in a cross section of the sources and types of material that lie behind the Synoptic Gospels. It is more applicable to general themes than to specific segments of material. "We may say," Perrin comments, "that a motif which can be detected in a multiplicity of strands of tradition and in various forms (pronouncement stories, parables, sayings, etc.) will have a high claim to authenticity."[2] The presence of a theme in both Mark and Q would also count as multiple attestation, since these are two independent sources.

Parables of Jesus

Although parables were common in Jewish teaching, the earliest layer of parable tradition in the New Testament exhibits a distinctive use of this form. The parables, in other words, tend to meet the criterion of dissimilarity, and many scholars believe that it is in the parables that we come closest to the original tradition regarding what Jesus taught.

Parables are not always easy to understand. Therefore, I begin with two simple examples as a way of getting an initial sense of what a parable is and what, according to the earliest tradition, Jesus taught.

The Treasure (Matt 13:44) and the Pearl (Matt 13:45)

The parables in Matthew 13:44 and 45 make explicit reference to the "kingdom [rule] of heaven," a circumlocution for "kingdom [rule] of God." While not all of Jesus' parables and sayings are so explicit, there is a near consensus that the announcement of God's rule was central to his mission and that the saying in Mark 1:15 expresses a major component of his teaching: "The time is fulfilled, and the kingdom of God has come near."

In each of these parables, God's rule is the subject of a comparison; something that is known, because it is ordinary, reveals the character of the rule, which is unknown in that it cannot simply be observed. We should be careful, however, about identifying the point of comparison. Since Matthew 13:44 says God's rule is "like a treasure," it seems natural to think of the treasure itself as corresponding directly to that rule. But 13:45 says the rule is "like a merchant," when we would logically expect the *pearl* to be the point of comparison. The parable of the Sower in Matthew 13:24-30 similarly presents God's rule as like a person "who sowed good seed," whereas it is not the sower but the whole situation described that corresponds to the rule. In both the Pearl and the Treasure, it is the *action in the story*, not some individual element, that signifies the rule of God.

In the Treasure, a person, presumably by accident, finds a treasure in a field that belongs to someone else, and then, after hiding the treasure, sells everything to buy the field. To understand this story *as parable*, we must get beyond questions based on the story's literal meaning, such as whether it was moral to buy the field without telling the owner about the treasure. To grasp what is being said about God's rule, we must make an imaginative leap from the literal meaning to a metaphorical level. A parable is not an *example* story, and this story is not a lesson in business practice. Before we ask what the parable implies one should do, it is important to ask what happens to the character in the story.

The finder's normal way of planning and carrying out activities is, in the words of John Dominic Crossan, "rudely but happily shattered."[3] Something unexpected and overwhelmingly good happens to this person, who joyfully sells everything and buys the field. What does the parable invite us to say about the rule of God? Perhaps that it interrupts, shatters everyday existence, that it is of such inestimable value and is the source of such

unimaginable joy that those who encounter it will find themselves challenged to give their total selves to live within it.

A similar leap is required by the second story: the Pearl. We should not be misled by the fact that the merchant was looking for pearls. Such a person would hardly have expected to find one so valuable as to demand selling everything to obtain it. Here again, the rule of God occurs as surprise. Like the Treasure, the Pearl is a parable of grace, in which God's rule appears precisely as gift. Yet the gift demands a response, and a radical one at that. Both parables call not only for imaginative interpretation but for imaginative action. To sell everything is risky business.

Defining "Parable"

We should note several things about these stories. First, they deal with common activities, depicting scenes ordinary people would recognize. Second, they command attention, partly through a note of extravagance: selling everything is extreme behavior. Third, these stories leave the reader somewhat puzzled about their exact meaning. That is why they demand an imaginative leap.

But why does anyone tell a story with indefinite meaning rather than simply stating the point? The fact is that we cannot reduce the meaning of a parable to propositional statements, since that meaning depends to some extent upon the circumstances in which the hearers live. Another interpreter might have derived somewhat different characteristics of God's rule from the Pearl and the Treasure than I have. And the hearer/reader's concrete life situation will play a major role in determining the specific action God's rule requires. In short, one tells a parable in order to *engage* those who hear it, to encourage people to make personal decisions and take action.

For this reason, it may be less meaningful to ask "what" a parable means than "how" it means, how it might affect a person's feelings and reasoning processes.[4] To state how a parable works would help define the parameters of its meaning without suggesting that the interpreter has found "the" meaning.

So what is a parable, as exemplified in the earliest level of the Jesus tradition? Consider the classic definition of C. H. Dodd:

> At its simplest the parable is a metaphor or simile drawn from nature or common life, arresting the hearer by its vividness or strangeness, and leaving the mind in sufficient doubt about its precise application as to tease it into active thought.[5]

Not all the stories called parables in the Gospels conform to this definition. Many of them are actually allegories. And although we may think of an allegory as a particular type of parable, it is important to understand how it differs from the type just defined. The individual elements in an allegory (characters, events, places) point outside the story to realities with which the hearers are already familiar. Thus, the way to understand an allegory is to decode it piece by piece—that is, to figure out what person, event, or other reality in the actual world each element in the story signifies.

A good example is Matthew 21:33-41. A householder (God) plants a vineyard (a frequent symbol for Israel in the Jewish Scriptures) and then departs for another country. At harvesttime, the householder sends a first set of servants (the early Hebrew prophets) to get his fruit, but the people reject and kill them; when a second set of servants (the later prophets) arrive, the people reject them also. Finally, the householder's own son (Jesus) appears, but he is killed (crucifixion) outside the vineyard (Golgotha, outside Jerusalem). Then the vineyard owner resolves to put the murderers to death (the destruction of Jerusalem, 70 C.E.) and give their vineyard (Israel's relationship to God's rule) to other tenants (the followers of Jesus).

When we come to the Gospel of Matthew, we will see evidence to confirm this allegorical reading. At this point, it is important to note that scholars do not generally accept allegories as authentic teachings of Jesus. They belong, in their present forms, to some later stage of tradition.

The parables that Jesus told, by contrast, demand acts of the imagination and therefore cannot be decoded. Their individual elements do not point to anything outside the stories; they have no meaning except their contribution to the stories themselves. This kind of parable makes its point as a unified whole: one understands it not by mechanically translating it into other terms but by letting the story make an impact as an integrated totality. Neither the merchant nor the man in the field signifies anything or anyone in the "outside world"; each character is simply "everyone."

The field, similarly, is a piece of furniture in the story, nothing more and nothing less. That is why one should beware the simplistic equation, treasure = rule of God.

Study of the parables is complicated by the fact that many of them have been altered through transmission. Some have been turned into allegories or have been placed in contexts that invite allegorical interpretation. In other cases, the Gospel writers or those who transmitted the stories earlier have added interpretive comments. Thus, sometimes we have to try to reconstruct the original form of a parable before we can interpret it as parable.

The Prodigal Son (Luke 15:11-32)

The disruption brought by the rule of God in the preceding parables is occasion for undiluted joy. In some other parables, however, the matter is more complex, for God's rule brings with it a reversal of conventional expectations and values. Such a reversal is evident in the Prodigal Son.

To get the full impact of this story, we must imagine the response of someone who does not know the outcome. The character of the younger son, whom tradition has named the "prodigal," is a study in self-destruction: he demands what is not yet rightfully his and then wastes it in foolish ways. He reduces himself to a level where, tending ritually unclean beasts, he violates his religious heritage and his family's honor. He does nothing to deserve his father's approval, but in the end, he receives not only acceptance but an extravagant welcome home. Ignoring social standards of dignity, the father actually runs to meet him

and then lavishes gifts upon him. The older brother's negative reaction is understandable.

The author of Luke has placed the parable in a context that encourages allegorization of the father into a God figure. Certainly the story itself asks the reader to imagine that God acts toward human beings as the father does toward the son—in an accepting and forgiving way. But the allusions to God in verses 18 and 21 show that the father does not signify God directly. To get the full shock of the story, we need the reality of this human father's extreme behavior. Hearers need to feel the legitimacy of the older brother's reaction in order to have their own expectations shattered. But what expectations would have been at work in a first-century Jewish audience?

Against the background of a proclamation of God's rule, the story has the potential to convey unexpected acceptance by God. There were people in Jewish society who, sometimes because of the nature of their profession, led lives far beyond the boundaries of the demands of the Torah. Such persons, rejected by the community at large, would naturally identify with the younger son; to them, the reversal of expectations and values would come as a word of grace.

But some people would hear the story differently. In fact, the parable has set the audience up for a negative response by its depiction of the extreme behavior of both the erring son and the father. Some religiously observant folk would feel that, to the extent that the father's acceptance mirrors God's attitude toward the disobedient, the story makes a mockery of both divine justice and the demands of the Torah.

The genius of the parable, however, is that it undermines this latter response by building it into the plot and subjecting it to criticism. Rather than rejoice in the return of his brother, the older son withdraws in resentment; he will not even name the younger as his brother, but refers to him as "this son of yours."

But resentment is not the only attitude the story holds open to the religiously observant. As Dan Via comments, "The father not only goes out to the prodigal son; he also goes out to the elder brother."[6] Reminded that he has always had access to his father's wealth and that the younger son is, in fact, his brother, the older son stands at a crossroads as the story closes. He can continue in resentment, or he can embrace his brother and come to know his father in a new way. Those who react negatively to the first part of the story face a similar choice.

Christian interpreters sometimes identify the attitude of the older brother as a specifically "Jewish" or "Pharisaic" form of "legalism," the view that human beings can merit divine acceptance by their own actions, apart from God's grace. But such interpretation is based on an uncritical acceptance of the New Testament's negative presentation of the Pharisees. Jewish teaching included an emphasis on God's grace and forgiveness: there were clear provisions for the restoration of sinful persons into the community through repentance. And no Jew would have claimed that human beings earn God's favor.

The parable does, however, criticize a tendency common to any society or religious community. And as a story told in a Jewish context, it does so in Jewish terms. The note of extravagance circumvents the procedures associated with repentance in Judaism, such as making restitution for wrongs. The father accepts the erring son before he has a chance to do anything beyond the mere act of returning home in desperation. But the parable does not attack Jewish teaching; it proclaims the rule of God as a gracious gift and, secondarily, undermines the attitude of resentment that prevents some people from understanding it as such.

The Great Supper (Luke 14:16-24)

Another version of the Great Supper appears at Matt 22:1-14. This parable is a good illustration of the process of allegorization, since Matthew's story contains some elements (vv. 7, 11-14), not found in Luke, that make little sense as part of the plot. When the Matthean version is placed beside Matthew 21:33-41, which we previously examined, one can easily see that it is a partial replay of that allegory. Even the Lukan version probably contains some editorial additions. The notation at 14:21 that the new guests are drawn from "the poor, the crippled, the blind, and the lame," absent from Matthew, reflects a specific interest of the author of Luke in social outcasts. Nevertheless, the rich/poor contrast is implicit in the original; for it is only the affluent who are invited to banquets, and people rounded up at the last minute in the streets would almost certainly be poor.

Stripped of its allegorical additions, the story is a tale of the reversal of expectations: invited guests remain outside a banquet hall, while uninvited strangers sit at table! How might a first-century audience hear such a story? The socially acceptable and affluent would identify with those originally invited but would be surprised that these characters make refusals. And, recognizing the banquet as a metaphor for the rule of God, they would be deeply offended. The socially outcast, however, would identify with those brought in from the streets and would hear the parable as a metaphor for God's grace.

Here again, the rule of God appears as a surprising and gracious gift, and here again, we have the criticism of an attitude that prevents the recognition of that gift. In this parable, however, there is a particularly sharp social bite: it is the social standing of those originally invited that is their downfall. Preoccupied with other matters, they ultimately miss the feast enjoyed by the rabble from the streets.

The Good Samaritan (Luke 10:29- 37) and the Leaven (Matt 13:33; Luke 13:20-21)

Interpreters who accept the Good Samaritan as it stands in Luke generally understand it as an example story enjoining the hearer to imitate the action of the Samaritan. There is evidence, however, that both the introduction ("Jesus replied") and the conclusion (v. 37) are attempts to fit the story into its Lukan context. The introductory question asks *whom one should consider neighbor*—that is, who should *receive* neighborly acts—whereas the conclusion holds up the Samaritan as one who *acts* in a neighborly way. Neither introduction nor conclusion, moreover, picks up on the key point, which is the identity of the one who acts charitably: the Samaritan, archenemy of the Jew.

How would this parable affect first-century Jews? The first character to appear is the man who is beaten and robbed. The hearers, who know the treacherousness of the road from Jerusalem to Jericho, will sympathize with him. They will view the priest and the Levite as potential heroes of the story and will feel shock and disappointment when they fail to show mercy. The hearers will also be familiar with a standard triad—priest, Levite, and Israelite (a layperson or ordinary Jew)—that signified the Jewish people as a whole. So perhaps they will now expect "an Israelite" to appear on the scene. But they will undoubtedly have thought of the victim as an Israelite, so that this role is no longer available. What happens instead is unthinkable: a hated Samaritan enters the story as hero.

With whom can the hearers identify in this story? Their only options, as Bernard Scott comments, are "to identify with the half-dead [the victim] and be saved by a mortal enemy or else to dismiss the narrative as not like real life."[7] To accept the Samaritan as hero, however, is to experience the disruption of one's routine ways of thinking. And it is that point, according to Crossan, that the hearer should grasp with respect to the rule of God. Just as acceptance of the Samaritan turns one's world upside down and shatters one's presuppositions, so does God's rule "break abruptly into human consciousness and demand the overthrow of prior values, closed options, set judgments, and established conclusions."[8]

Crossan argues that the parable does not really teach mercy as a value but simply assumes it: the real point of the story is that God's rule shatters conventional wisdom. The parable does not stop with upsetting prior values, however, but points forward to some specific qualities of life within God's rule. As Robert Funk comments, the Samaritan acts in freedom from the constraints society imposes.[9] But this freedom is not utterly formless; it is freedom to risk an act of love, unrestrained by society's prejudices. To accept the Samaritan as good is to acknowledge that God's rule "does not separate insiders and outsiders on the basis of religious categories."[10] The hearer who has identified with the traveler in the ditch is in a position, by accepting the Samaritan as "good," to enter that world of risk and freedom through commitment to human solidarity.

There is a "scandalous" quality about the Good Samaritan that Scott finds also in the Leaven. In the ancient Jewish context, leaven was a metaphor for a corrupting influence (parallel to the proverbial "rotten apple" in our own culture). The parable thus creates the scandal of God's rule appearing in the most unexpected context and subverts the audience's "dependency on the rules of the sacred, the predictability of what is good."[11]

One of the "rules" or boundaries that is shattered, on this reading of the Leaven, is the traditional attitude toward women. In symbolic terms, woman stood for impurity. So in comparing God's rule to a woman's act of leavening dough, the parable attacks the patriarchal structure that was so integral a part of the ancient social structure.

The Parables from a Social-Science Perspective

Some recent scholars have been critical of interpretations of the parables that fail to ask how they would have been heard by persons living under the hardships of social and economic oppression. One example of an attempt to read a parable in this way is William R. Herzog's approach to the parable of the Unjust Judge (Luke 18:1-8). In this story, a woman seeks justice from a judge "who neither feared God nor had respect for people." In keeping with his character, the judge continually puts the woman off. The woman will not give up, however, but doggedly continues making her case until the judge finally gives in—not for the sake of justice, but because she has worn him down by her persistence.

As the parable stands in Luke, it ends with the declaration (vv. 7-8a) that God will give justice to those who persist in prayer. And its meaning hinges upon a particular form of logic known as "from the lesser to the greater." If even an unjust judge finally grants a request for justice, how much more will God come to the aid of those who ask. As interpreters have often noted, however, this is a rather unsatisfying image of God—delaying justice until persuaded by persistent prayer. Herzog argues, however, that if we hear the parable as addressed to a situation of oppression, we can find something very different in it. As a widow, the woman is a marginalized person, outside the realm of patriarchal protection and hence vulnerable to exploitation. But some social theory teaches that oppressive systems work only to the extent that the oppressed are so intimidated that they are in collusion with the system. "Usually that collusion grows out of a fatalism and despair that anything will change." This widow, however, chooses another course, and "her refusal to accept her predestined role breaks social barriers and crosses forbidden social and gender boundaries. The result of her shameless behavior is a just verdict."[12] Read in this way, the parable is a call to resistance against oppressive social structures.

Sayings of Jesus

Many sayings attributed to Jesus are paralleled in other Jewish literature of the time or reflect the interests of the early church. Therefore, we cannot be sure they belong to the earliest tradition. There are, however, enough sayings of distinctive character to give us a broad idea of the content of that earliest level. But because we find them in settings created by the Gospel writers or earlier collectors of tradition, we must take them out of context in order to interpret them.

Paradox and Hyperbole: Sayings That "Jolt"

Some of the most distinctive sayings are closely akin to the parables that jolt the hearer out of ordinary patterns of thought and action. Consider Mark 10:25: "It is easier for a camel to go through the eye of a needle than for someone who is rich to enter the [rule] of God." This saying constituted a direct challenge to a frequent theme in Jewish thought: that material well-being is a reward for righteousness and a sign of God's favor. Equally

radical are the words of Luke 6:20-21, which may be close to the original version of the sayings known as the Beatitudes:

> Blessed are you who are poor, for yours is the [rule] of God.
> Blessed are you who are hungry now, for you will be filled.
> Blessed are you who weep now, for you will laugh.

As F. W. Beare comments, "The Beatitudes put forward a conception of human blessedness which completely reverses all the values of any social order that ever existed."[13] We have seen the theme of reversal in the parables, but the economic and social dimensions of reversal are more prominent in the sayings, which manifest a clear social radicalism that is neatly summarized in Mark 10:31: "Many who are first will be last, and the last will be first." Those in a socially favored position in society tend to think of themselves as religiously and morally superior. But in the teachings of Jesus, that attitude is overturned in the rule of God, which belongs especially to the poor!

As William Beardslee notes,[14] some of Jesus' sayings take the form of paradox, as in the case of Luke 17:33: "Those who lose their life will keep it." This saying jolts hearers out of their projects of "making a continuity" out of their lives—that is, out of the normal attempt to make rational sense of existence and plan for the future. The greater part of human activity goes into survival, but according to this saying, one finds survival only paradoxically: by losing one's life.

The saying about the needle's eye makes its point through hyperbole, or intentional exaggeration. The force of hyperbole becomes particularly clear in the sayings in Matthew 5:39-41:

> But if anyone strikes you on the right cheek, turn the other also; and if anyone wants to sue you and take your coat, give your cloak as well; and if anyone forces you to go one mile, go also the second mile.

The actions recommended here are so extreme as to be almost ridiculous. In the Mediterranean world, with its emphasis upon honor, a blow on the right cheek was the height of insult. The words for "coat" and "cloak" refer to the standard inner and outer garments, so that the second saying actually asks the hearers to give away their last possessions to people unkind enough to bring them to court. And the third saying enjoins loyal Jews not merely to comply with a law compelling them to bear the burdens of the occupying Roman soldiers, but to do twice as much as required!

The extreme nature of the commands prevents one from literalizing them. Life is full of complexities, but these sayings ignore such matters and give absolute, simplistic advice. They force the hearers to exercise their moral imaginations, to question the patterns of revenge and self-concern that often motivate human behavior.[15]

Ethical Content: The Parameters of "Open-Endedness"

The parables and sayings we have seen are open-ended, inviting people to use their own imaginations in making decisions. This is not to say that they give no direction at all, however, for they contain clear moral content. The Good Samaritan, for example, calls the hearer to a freedom specifically to love, and the saying on turning one's cheek is a radical statement of human solidarity. The ethical content of the claim imposed by God's rule, however, becomes clearest in the explicit injunction to love one's enemies:

> But I say to you, Love your enemies and pray for those who persecute you, so that you may be children of your Father in heaven; for he makes his sun rise on the evil and on the good, and sends rain on the righteous and on the unrighteous. For if you love those who love you, what reward do you have? Do not even the tax collectors do the same? (Matt 5:44-46)

In its own way, this material, too, is disruptive of traditional values, but it is not couched in antithetical form and does not resort to hyperbole. It is a straightforward command regarding one's dealings with other human beings.

It is less certain that the specific linking of the first commandment (love for God) with Leviticus 19:18 (love for neighbor) as it is portrayed in the Gospels (Mark 12:28, 34; Matt 22:34-40; Luke 10:25-37) belongs to the earliest tradition. There are "several near-contemporary Jewish summaries of the law which . . . juxtapose commands to love God and one's fellows."[16] Nevertheless, it is only in the Synoptic stories that we find the specific link between Deuteronomy 6:5 and Leviticus 19:18.[17] And the command to love one's enemies is unparalleled in the entire ancient world.

There is thus no doubt that some form of a demand for love of one's human fellows, which permeates the New Testament, was a central component of the earliest Jesus tradition. But if we ask about moral regulations in a broader sense, we run into the problem of distinguishing earlier and later tradition, since the early church would have been inclined to produce such material to settle debates.

The Deeds of Jesus: General Activities

Jesus' first followers told stories about what he did, as well as about what he said, for they understood his deeds as part of his mission. We must proceed somewhat differently in treating Jesus' deeds than in relation to his teachings, for only in a few cases can we give solid evidence that a specific incident goes back to the earliest tradition. But there are some general activities that are deeply embedded in the whole Jesus tradition: his healings and exorcisms, his association with "marginalized" people, and his maintenance of a group of disciples who shared his mission.

Healings and Exorcisms

However one might choose to explain them, it is the healings and exorcisms among the various miracles attributed to Jesus that scholars most often assign to the earliest tradition. The stories involving more elaborate wonders, such as walking on the water and stilling the storm, are generally viewed as belonging to a later phase. Some recent analysts have argued that the stories of healing and exorcisms are also late, but the majority hold that Jesus' earliest followers knew him as one who healed illnesses and cast out demons.

But what specific meaning would such actions have had in first-century Jewish Palestine? It is important, in beginning, to note what meaning they did not have. Modern people often think of a miracle as the suspension of the laws of nature. But ancient people did not have the concept of a rigid natural order that developed in the course of Western history. Stories of miracle workers abounded in the ancient world; people were impressed with miraculous deeds but did not interpret them within the framework of a dualism of "the natural" and "the supernatural."

Jewish people did consider miraculous works as manifestations of God's power, however. They were subject to more than one interpretation, as is clear from the fact that some observers attributed Jesus' exorcisms to an evil power (Mark 3:21-27), but they did constitute evidence that those who performed them were God's agents. So Jesus' followers must have understood his healings and exorcisms as attestations that he was in fact commissioned by God. And they would also have seen them as signs of the rule of God. In apocalyptic thought, demons were agents of Satan, who held sway over the present age. And the view that Jesus was breaking Satan's hold on the world through the exorcisms is explicit in Luke 11:20: "But if it is by the finger of God that I cast out the demons, then the [rule] of God has come to you."

Association with "Marginalized" People

The Gospels abound with stories of Jesus' associations with "marginalized" people, those denied full participation in society. His opponents ridicule his friendship with "sinners and prostitutes" and "sinners and tax collectors." The Beatitudes (Luke 6:20-22) in particular link Jesus with the hungry, the poor, and the miserable, as his healings do with the physically infirm.

Marginalization was in part the result of economic factors: people were often forced into dishonorable professions by adverse circumstances. The story of Zacchaeus (Luke 19) has taught us to view tax collectors as rich, but most of those "who did the actual work were impoverished, or were slaves employed by a 'tax agency,' and quickly dismissed if problems arose."[18] The reality of economic distress is reflected in the fact that when speaking of "the poor," the Synoptic tradition regularly uses the Greek term for the destitute rather than that for the relatively poor. And there is strong evidence of extreme poverty and homelessness throughout the Roman Empire and in Palestine specifically, brought on by a combination of crop failures and insensitive government policy.[19]

In the ancient Middle East, to be a woman was in and of itself to experience marginalization. It is thus a remarkable feature of the Jesus tradition that it continually depicts Jesus in the company of women, without any hint that he shared the traditional restrictions regarding male-female contact and the role of women. We have already seen that in subtle ways his teachings reflect this attitude of openness.

Maintenance of Disciples

The Jesus tradition makes constant reference to a group of disciples surrounding Jesus and to an inner circle of twelve. Although there are slight discrepancies in the lists of this leadership cadre, Paul's citation (1 Cor 15:5) of an early testimony mentioning "the twelve" suggests that the tradition about such an inner circle goes back to the earliest level, whether or not the membership was stable.

The Synoptic accounts of the week before Jesus' death include a story of a final meal with the Twelve, during which Jesus institutes a cultic meal—the Lord's Supper, or Eucharist. Scholars disagree on several points: the extent to which later worship practices have been read back into this event; whether it really was a Passover meal, as the Synoptic texts claim; and whether such an event actually took place at all. Most scholars acknowledge, however, that the story at least reflects the memory that Jesus and his disciples shared fellowship meals during his ministry, a memory also reflected in the stories of the miraculous feedings (Mark 6:30-44; 8:1-10).

In the context of a proclamation of God's

rule, such meals carried a specific meaning. Jewish tradition frequently imaged the "age to come" as a great banquet. Sometimes it is God who presides at the banquet, but in other traditions, notably the Qumran literature, the Messiah assumes this function. Either way, the banquet has "messianic" implications. It symbolizes life free from want, injustice, and suffering.

The tradition regarding these meals also said something very specific about life in God's rule. If we take the parable of the Great Supper as mirroring Jesus' own practice, the gatherings involved a mixture of social classes. According to Crossan, it is this mixture, rather than the presence of the poor in and of itself, that was so distinctive and so offensive, for it was an outright violation of the Mediterranean system of honor and shame, with its distinctions based on class, rank, and sex. What would respectable people say about someone who hosted such inclusive affairs? "He makes . . . no appropriate distinctions and discriminations. He has no honor. He has no shame."[20]

Jesus and the Jewish Law: Deeds and Teachings

The New Testament contains numerous accounts of Jesus' conflicts with the Pharisees over observance of the Jewish law, most notably because of his healings on the Sabbath. In Mark 7:15, moreover, we have a saying that seems to undercut the entire system of dietary regulations: "There is nothing outside a person that by going in can defile, but the things that come out are what defile." We may therefore wonder whether Jesus actually spoke against the law itself.

Not all interpreters are convinced of the authenticity of Mark 7:15, however, and some recent analysts have argued that Jesus' healings did not constitute work and therefore were not violations of the Sabbath law.[21] In any case, scholars have long held that many of the stories of Jesus' conflicts with opponents are products of the later tradition, constructed to give concrete illustration to specific points. The early Christian communities probably came into more serious conflict with the Pharisees than did Jesus himself, and to some extent, they projected these conflicts back into the time of Jesus.

There is, however, one account of Jesus' teaching that suggests a willingness to forgo the demands of the law in some instances. In Matthew 8:21-22/Luke 9:59-60, a person whom Jesus has invited into discipleship asks, "First let me go and bury my father." But Jesus' response is astonishing: "Let the dead bury their own dead." As Perrin comments, "In Judaism the responsibility for burying the dead was one that took precedence over all other duties enjoined in the law."[22] We see here once again a radicalism found in some parables and other sayings. Jesus presents the demands of God's rule as requiring a response that flies in the face of standard expectations.

The saying on burying the dead may indicate that in God's rule, the law would in some way be transformed.[23] Jesus and his earliest followers may have appealed to a "popular tradition," as over against the "official tradition" of the written Torah and the established leadership groups.[24] But it is unlikely that he rejected the law as such.

The ambiguity of the Jesus tradition on the question of observing the ritual requirements of the law does, however, show that his earliest postresurrection followers were divided on the question of where Jesus stood on the issue. According to Crossan, the best explanation for that fact is that Jesus simply ignored these requirements because "he did not care enough about such ritual laws to attack or to acknowledge them."[25]

Specific Incidents:
Baptism, Action in the Temple, Death

There are a few accounts of specific incidents in the Gospels that scholars regard as indisputably historical because the early church would have had no conceivable motive for inventing them.

One of these is Jesus' baptism by John the Baptist. Although such elements in the Gospel accounts as the voice from heaven and the descent of the dove are probably added by tradition, there can be little doubt that Jesus was actually baptized by John, for as Matthew 3:14-15 reveals, the church was embarrassed by the memory of the event and sought to explain it. Many scholars take the baptism story as evidence that Jesus began as a disciple of John and then moved out on his own. The Gospel tradition, however, makes John a self-conscious forerunner of Jesus and understands the baptism as a divine commissioning for Jesus' mission.

Another indisputable event is Jesus' crucifixion. No group who understood the stigma of crucifixion in the Roman world would have invented such a story about their hero. The reason for Jesus' execution, however, is a matter of dispute. It is clear that it was the Romans who actually put him to death, because they and not the Jews used crucifixion as a means of capital punishment. The Gospels also implicate the Jewish leaders, but it is evident that the New Testament writers went to some lengths to shift the blame from the Romans to the Jews.

Some scholars have argued that the Pharisees instigated a plot against Jesus because of his views on the law, but it is improbable that they had the power to manipulate the legal system for their ends. Nor is it likely that conflict over fine points in the law or tradition would have constituted grounds for handing him over to the Romans for execution. It is significant, finally, that the Pharisees are almost entirely absent from the Gospel accounts of the events leading to Jesus' death.

Why, then, did Jesus die? According to E. P. Sanders,[26] another event with a strong claim to authenticity triggered his arrest: his disruption of the activity in the temple court (Mark 11:15-19). To strike at the temple was to strike at the very heart of the established sociopolitical and religious power structure.

If we ask who would have had both the motive and the means to move against Jesus after this event, the answer is the priestly aristocracy. Jesus was a threat to the aristocracy

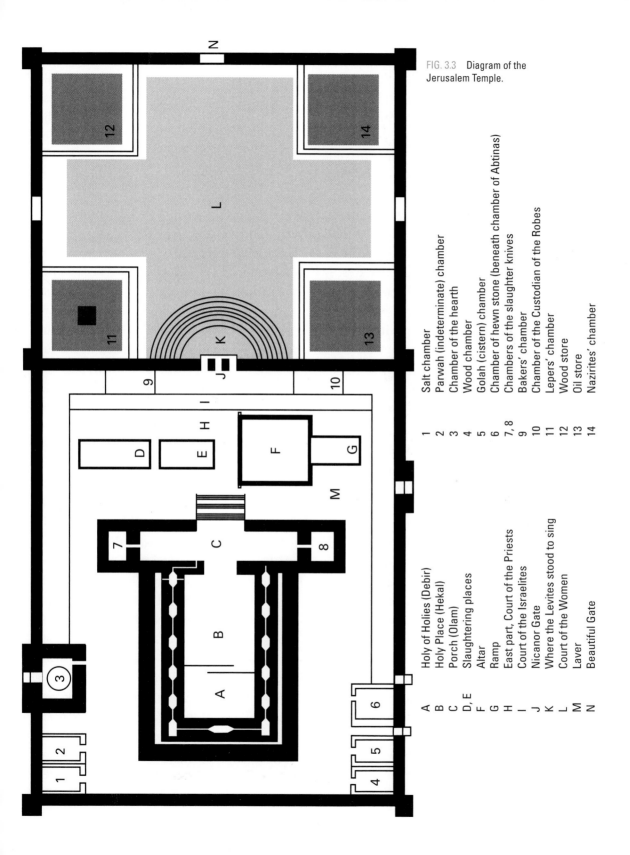

FIG. 3.3 Diagram of the Jerusalem Temple.

1   Salt chamber
2   Parwah (indeterminate) chamber
3   Chamber of the hearth
4   Wood chamber
5   Golah (cistern) chamber
6   Chamber of hewn stone (beneath chamber of Abtinas)
7, 8 Chambers of the slaughter knives
9   Bakers' chamber
10 Chamber of the Custodian of the Robes
11 Lepers' chamber
12 Wood store
13 Oil store
14 Nazirites' chamber

A   Holy of Holies (Debir)
B   Holy Place (Hekal)
C   Porch (Olam)
D, E Slaughtering places
F   Altar
G   Ramp
H   East part, Court of the Priests
I   Court of the Israelites
J   Nicanor Gate
K   Where the Levites stood to sing
L   Court of the Women
M   Laver
N   Beautiful Gate

for the same reason that he was a threat to the Roman occupation government. His proclamation of the rule of God had the potential to create a public disturbance by raising "messianic" expectations, and his demonstration in the temple made the threat concrete. The Romans had no desire to deal with another popular uprising. And any unrest among the populace could damage the positions of those among the Jews whose measure of authority depended upon the Romans' good graces. In the end, the reason for Jesus' death was the Romans' policy of brutal suppression of any hint of popular unrest, together with the aristocracy's policy of collaboration.

Jesus, the Rule of God, and the Future

The proclamation of God's rule was central to Jesus' mission. But what did the rule of God mean? Was it still in the future or already present? Would it change the public, communal world of social and political structures, or was it something internal to the individual? Would it bring the "end of the world"? And what was the relationship between the message about God's rule and the person who brought that message? How, in other words, did the earliest tradition understand Jesus himself?

Present or Future?

Critical scholars are unanimous on one point: the earliest tradition does not speak of the rule of God as something in the *distant* future. Here the agreement ends, however. Some scholars maintain that, in this tradition, God's rule is expected in the immediate future, while others think it is understood as already present. A mediating position is that it was in the process of realization—beginning to break in but not yet fully realized.

The question is complicated by the fact that the notion of God's rule was present not only in apocalyptic but also in Wisdom literature, in which it signified not a future hope but a present reality—God's ongoing rule of the world, into which the individual can enter at any time "by wisdom or goodness, by virtue, justice, or freedom."[27] Some scholars thus argue that the rule of God proclaimed by Jesus was not something to be expected in the future but was available in the present.

An answer to the question of present and future depends to some extent upon which materials one assigns to the earliest tradition, but also upon how one interprets the language employed in those materials. The present book sides with scholars who think the heavily apocalyptic passages attributed to Jesus in the Gospels are products of later tradition. It is also influenced by the view that we should not force the language about God's rule into a rigidly literal mold. Thus, particularly with respect to the parables, I am inclined to view this rule as in some sense already present for those who are open to it.

Nevertheless, there are elements with strong claim to authenticity that seem to involve a future expectation. Consider, for example, the third beatitude, Luke 6:21: "Blessed are you who weep now, for you will laugh." Certainly the blessing is available in the present, but the future tense indicates

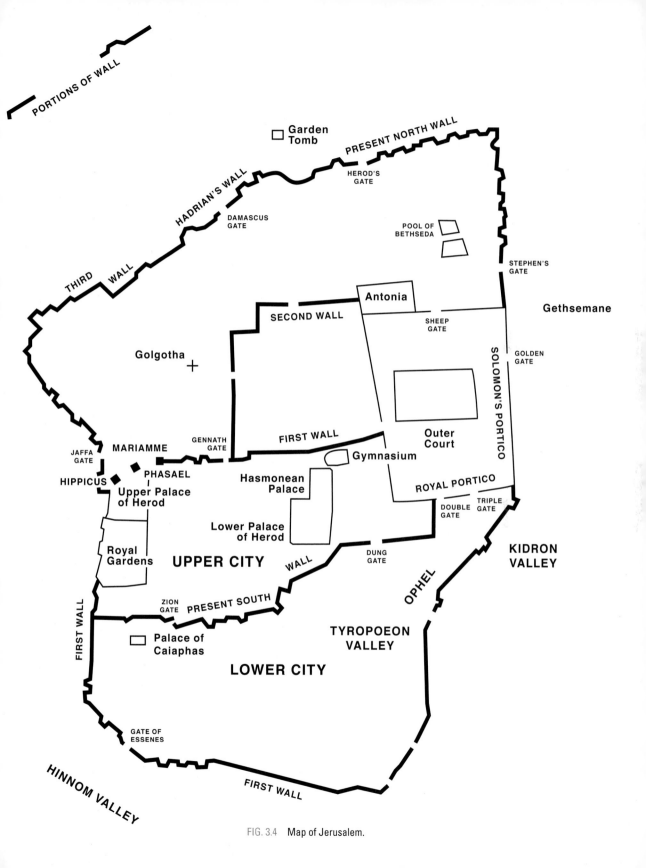

FIG. 3.4 Map of Jerusalem.

that something is yet to come. Similarly, the petition "Your kingdom come" in the Lord's Prayer (Matt 6:10) seems to contain an irreducibly futuristic element.

Individual or Communal?

To the extent that one understands the rule of God as present for Jesus' first followers, one will also tend to see it as a matter of the individual's experience. Conversely, futuristic interpretations tend toward an understanding of that rule as communal, or publicly observable. These issues converge in the consideration of a key saying that clearly denies one aspect of the apocalyptic outlook—the practice of calculating the coming of God's rule by observing historical events: "The kingdom of God is not coming with things that can be observed; nor will they say, 'Look, here it is!' or 'There it is!' For, in fact, the kingdom of God is among you" (Luke 17:20-21). Granted a critical attitude toward apocalyptic *speculation,* the question is whether this saying envisions God's rule as already present in the individual's experience or as a future reality that will one day be "visible" to all. Some interpreters have understood the passage in a highly individualistic way on the basis of a translation of the closing phrase as "*within* you." Most recent scholars, however, understand that phrase to mean "among you" or "in your midst"—that is, in the social-communal setting.

But does this saying mean that God's rule is understood as now present among the people, and therefore experienced by individuals, or does the present tense refer to a future time when it will be present? It is reasonable, in

light of the preceding discussion, to interpret it in this way: individuals are able to experience in the present the power of God's rule, which is not yet manifest in its fullness.

The "End of the World"?

What would the coming order be like? Would it be in heaven or on earth? Would it involve the resurrection of the dead, a final judgment, and eternal life for the righteous? Answers to these questions hinge to some extent on whether one believes that the earliest tradition contained an apocalyptic element, and on how one chooses to interpret that element. Given the rapidity with which the early Christians adopted a fully apocalyptic outlook, it is difficult to deny that some of the apocalyptic material belongs to the earliest level. To say this, however, does not answer the crucial question of how the apocalyptic language was intended.

One indication that the rule of God in the earliest tradition did not refer to a heavenly reality disconnected from the present earthly sphere is to be found in a saying (Matt 19:28) that assigns to the disciples the task of "judging" the twelve tribes of Israel, which should be understood in the sense of "doing justice for" or even "liberating" them.[28] Sanders makes much of this point in arguing that Jesus' mission was a Jewish renewal movement that expected the "restoration" of Israel in the eschatological age.[29] That is to say, the earliest level of tradition apparently understood God's rule as involving the reestablishment of the nation of Israel. We should therefore not imagine that Jesus gathered disciples to assign them work that would be swept away when the new age had come. If his mission had to do with the renewal of Israel, we must assume that the renewed society would continue in the new order.

This is not to deny that Jesus and his followers envisioned the eventual resurrection of the dead and a final judgment or that a "heavenly" reality would somehow be superimposed upon the earthly. But it appears that they did not think of God's rule in abstraction from the ancient hopes of Israel, the human longing for peace and justice, and the hope of the poor for vindication.

Jesus in the Tradition

What role did Jesus himself play in his disciples' understanding? They may not have applied "messianic" titles to him during his lifetime, but they almost certainly understood him as fulfilling "messianic" functions in the broader sense. It is clear that Jesus appears in the earliest tradition as one with special authority, the final messenger before the full establishment of God's rule. And it is likely that his first followers believed he would play a special role within the new order.

It is also clear that these followers believed that Jesus enjoyed a special relationship to God. This is evident in the memory, preserved at a few points in the New Testament (Mark 14:36; Rom 8:15; Gal 4:6), that Jesus called God *abba*—an Aramaic term by which children addressed their fathers and that carried the connotation of "*dear* Father," or even "Daddy." Joachim Jeremias claims that such usage was unique to Jesus, but Geza Vermes argues that it was typical of Galilean charismatics.[30] Either way, it suggests a sense of special closeness between Jesus and God without implying the notion that a human being could be "divine." The term *son of God* was familiar to Jews, but only as a designation for human beings who in some way stood particularly near to God—the king, the *messianic* king, a particularly just man, or a miracle-working charismatic. In a broader sense, the term could apply to any Jew as a member of God's covenant community.

It should also be said that if Jesus' first followers thought of him as having a special relationship to God, their interest was not in that relationship as a matter of speculation but in what it meant for them. They felt themselves drawn into that relationship; they, too, could address God as *abba*.

Jesus and the Empire

Because Jesus directed his social criticisms primarily at the social system and ruling elite of Jewish society, it might appear that he was neutral with respect to the occupying Roman government. More careful analysis, however, reveals a subtle but unmistakable rejection of Roman rule.

To begin with, to proclaim that God's rule is coming is to imply that Caesar's rule is about to end. Jews who believed that Satanic power ruled the present world order would have viewed the Roman presence in their land as a manifestation of that power. In addition, the saying of Jesus that is most frequently used to document Jesus' supposed political neutrality may well mean almost the opposite of what many interpreters have thought. When asked whether it was lawful to pay taxes to the emperor, Jesus asked his questioners to bring him a Roman coin known as a denarius and then posed his own question: "Whose head is this [on the coin], and whose title?" When they replied, "The emperor's," Jesus replied, "Give to the emperor the things that are the emperor's, and to God the things that are God's" (Mark 12:16-17).

Although this saying is often seen as an endorsement of the emperor's authority, Herzog argues that it is really a "coded message" that subtly calls that authority into question. For not only does the image of the emperor violate the prohibition against graven images (Deut 8:5), but the inscription on it makes an idolatrous claim for the emperor's divine status. So when Jesus says the coin can be paid back to Caesar, he is in effect saying, "It must be paid back to him, because it is blasphemous and idolatrous." If Jesus had said this directly, he would have been arrested, but by his "coded" wording, he issued a subtle invitation to a nonviolent form of resistance. The peasants who followed Jesus would have to pay the tax to the emperor, but they would not have to give allegiance to him or to the empire.[31]

Summary and Conclusion: "Radical Grace/Radical Demand"

"The time is fulfilled, and the [rule] of God has come near." Many scholars regard this proclamation, placed on the lips of Jesus at Mark 1:14, as an accurate summary of what he actually taught. For those who first followed Jesus, the rule of God was breaking in; it was experienced in his fellowship meals and manifest in his association with outcasts.

The rule of God was coming, on the one hand, as surprise and gift, reversing human expectations and traditional standards of acceptability. But it also entailed a call to risky and courageous action—action offensive to the social and religious sensibilities of many sincere people, action that challenged accepted forms of authority. Herbert Braun therefore summarizes the teachings of Jesus in the formula of radical grace/radical demand.[32] The announcement of God's rule was a proclamation of grace because it offered acceptance by God as a gift, yet it was, paradoxically, a message of radical demand, since it asked nothing less than total commitment.

For the Jews who first followed Jesus, to accept the announcement of God's rule meant experiencing the disruption of their former lives, but it did not mean denying their Jewish religion, their Jewish God, or their Jewish law. They heard Jesus' words as they would have heard a Hebrew prophet who spoke on behalf of God's covenant with Israel. They found in his presence an energizing, renewing power. And they received the hope that Jesus brought precisely as a renewal of *the hope of Israel*—the hope that God's ancient promises to their ancestors, Abraham and Sarah, were now to be fulfilled.

But was this hope fulfilled? What his followers hoped for on the public and observable level simply did not take place. Jesus suffered a painful and humiliating death. The world did not change in any visible way: Rome continued its brutal rule, and the suffering of the oppressed remained unrelieved. Nevertheless, the movement Jesus founded survived. In chapter 4, we will ask how.

The Son of Man

In its present contexts in the Gospels, the phrase *Son of Man* refers to Jesus, whether in terms of his earthly ministry or in terms of his return in glory at the end of the age. But if we ask how Jesus came to be known as the Son of Man and what the term might have meant in its earliest application to him, problems abound.

The term *son of* . . . in Semitic languages (such as Hebrew and Aramaic) often designates membership in a general category. Thus, "son of a prophet" can refer to a member of a prophetic community, and "son of man" can mean simply "human being." This is clearly the way the term is used in some passages in the Jewish Scriptures, such as Psalm 8:4 and Isaiah 51:12.

In apocalyptic literature, however, the phrase sometimes refers to a heavenly redeemer figure in a way parallel to Jesus' description of his eschatological return. In Daniel 7:13-14, for example, we read, "I saw one like a human being [son of man] coming with the clouds of heaven. And he came to the Ancient One and was presented before him.

To him was given dominion." The reference is apparently to a figure that looks like a human being. In the noncanonical book of *1 Enoch*, the apocalyptic Son of Man is referred to as the Messiah, and a somewhat similar passage appears in another noncanonical work, 2 Esdras. Thus, on the basis of passages such as these, many scholars have argued that prior to the time of Jesus, there was a widespread expectation among Jews of a supernatural redeemer called "the Son of Man." It is often argued that this belief is rooted in ancient Canaanite mythology.

Other scholars dispute this view, however. In Daniel 7:7, the phrase is interpreted as a collective symbol of the people of Israel, and it is uncertain whether in any of the Jewish literature of the period, it is intended as a formal title. In the view of some, there was no concept of a heavenly Son of Man in the sense of a supernatural redeemer figure before the time of Jesus, but the early Christians and the author of *Enoch* both drew upon Daniel 7 in order to create such a concept. Thus, in the case of *Enoch*, an individual or community read Daniel 7 and took the term *son of man* as a literal reference to a heavenly being. In a parallel way, early Christians took the same passage as a reference to Jesus' expected return in glory.

The question of whether there was a pre-Christian concept of an apocalyptic Son of Man remains a matter of debate. The same is true of the question of whether Jesus used the term as a self-reference or his early post-resurrection followers placed it on his lips. Some scholars think Jesus used the term in its apocalyptic sense as a self-reference, but others think the postresurrection community first applied it to him. Some contend that Jesus used it only in the non-apocalyptic sense, as an equivalent of "I" (or "this human being"), and it acquired the apocalyptic sense only later. Yet another view is that Jesus used it in its apocalyptic sense but not of himself and not in a literal way. For example, he could have referred to "the days of the Son of Man" (Luke 17:26) as a way of pointing to the dawn of the rule of God, but after his death, his followers took it as a literal self-designation.

These issues are extremely difficult to decide, but they have little effect on our reading of the Gospels as literary wholes. The term appears in each of them as Jesus' self-designation, but one must determine from each work what nuances it takes on in that context.

NOTES

1. Norman Perrin, *Rediscovering the Teachings of Jesus* (New York: Harper & Row, 1967), 43.
2. Ibid., 47.
3. John Dominic Crossan, *In Parables: The Challenge of the Historical Jesus* (New York: Harper & Row, 1973), 34.
4. James Breech, *The Silence of Jesus: The Authentic Voice of the Historical Man* (Philadelphia: Fortress Press, 1983), 134.
5. C. H. Dodd, *The Parables of the Kingdom*, rev. ed. (New York: Charles Scribner's Sons, 1961), 5.
6. Dan Otto Via Jr., *The Parables: Their Literary and Existential Dimension* (Philadelphia: Fortress Press, 1967), 171.
7. Bernard Brandon Scott, *Hear Then the Parable: A Commentary on the Parables of Jesus* (Minneapolis: Fortress Press, 1989), 201.
8. Crossan, *In Parables*, 65.
9. Robert W. Funk, *Language, Hermeneutic, and Word of God* (New York: Harper & Row, 1966), 219.
10. Scott, *Hear Then the Parable*, 202.
11. Ibid., 328.
12. William R. Herzog II, *Parables as Subversive Speech: Jesus as Pedagogue of the Oppressed* (Louisville, Ky.: Westminster John Knox, 1994), 231–32.
13. F. W. Beare, *The Earliest Records of Jesus: A Companion to the Synopsis of the First Three Gospels by Albert Huck* (New York: Abingdon, 1962), 55.
14. William A. Beardslee, "Uses of the Proverb in the Synoptic Gospels," *Interpretation* 24 (1970): 61–73.
15. Robert C. Tannehill, *The Sword of His Mouth* (Philadelphia: Fortress Press; Missoula, Mont.: Scholars, 1975), 69–70.

16. Victor Paul Furnish, *The Love Command in the New Testament* (Nashville: Abingdon, 1972), 62.

17. Ibid., 62.

18. Elisabeth Schüssler Fiorenza, *In Memory of Her: A Feminist Theological Reconstruction of Christian Origins* (New York: Crossroad, 1983), 127.

19. Luise Schottroff and Wolfgang Stegemann, *Jesus and the Hope of the Poor*, trans. Matthew J. O'Connell (Maryknoll, N.Y.: Orbis, 1986), 16–17.

20. John Dominic Crossan, *The Historical Jesus: The Life of a Mediterranean Jewish Peasant* (San Francisco: Harper, 1991), 262.

21. Geza Vermes, *Jesus the Jew: A Historian's Reading of the Gospels* (New York: Macmillan, 1973), 5.

22. Perrin, *Rediscovering the Teachings of Jesus*, 144.

23. E. P. Sanders, *Jesus and Judaism* (Philadelphia: Fortress Press, 1985), 267, suggests that Jesus did not think of the Mosaic law as final.

24. See Richard A. Horsley, *Sociology and the Jesus Movement* (New York: Crossroad, 1989), 136, who makes this suggestion in relation to the Jesus movement, or early Palestinian Christianity.

25. Crossan, *Historical Jesus*, 263.

26. Sanders, *Jesus and Judaism*, 301–2.

27. Crossan, *Historical Jesus*, 292.

28. Ibid., 203–5.

29. Sanders, *Jesus and Judaism*, 90–119.

30. Joachim Jeremias, *The Prayers of Jesus*, trans. John Bowden and Christoph Burchard (Philadelphia: Fortress Press, 1978), 11–65; Vermes, *Jesus the Jew*, 210–13.

31. William R. Herzog, *Prophet and Teacher: An Introduction to the Historical Jesus* (Louisville, Ky.: Westminster John Knox, 2005), 190.

32. Herbert Braun, "Der Sinn der neutestamentlichen Theologie," *Zeitschrift für Theologie und Kirche* 54 (1957): 341–77.

STUDY QUESTIONS

1. In what sense did the early church understand the four Gospels as of "apostolic" origin?
2. Explain the following terms: Synoptic Gospels, Synoptic problem.
3. Explain the two-document hypothesis.
4. What criteria do scholars use in determining the authentic teachings of Jesus (or the earliest level of the Jesus tradition)?
5. How do the parables Jesus told differ from allegories?

6. What do the parables of the treasure and the pearl teach about the rule of God?

7. Illustrate each of the following themes by references to specific parables: reversal, demand, freedom, grace. In what sense are the parables "scandalous"?

8. What types of deeds seem to belong to the earliest level of the Jesus tradition? How do these deeds complement Jesus' teachings?

9. How would you respond to someone who says, "The Jews crucified Jesus"?

10. Does the earliest tradition present the rule of God as present or as future? As individual or as communal? Does it present that rule as the "end of the world"?

11. Show how the formula "radical grace/radical demand" does or does not adequately summarize the content of Jesus' ministry.

FOR FURTHER READING

Crossan, John Dominic. *The Historical Jesus: The Life of a Mediterranean Peasant*. San Francisco: HarperSanFrancisco, 1991.

———. *In Parables: The Challenge of the Historical Jesus*. New York: Harper & Row, 1973.

Dodd, C. H. *The Parables of the Kingdom*. Rev. ed. New York: Charles Scribner's Sons, 1961.

Herzog, William R. II. *The Parables as Subversive Speech*. Louisville, Ky.: Westminster John Knox, 1994.

Jeremias, Joachim. *The Parables of Jesus*. Rev. ed. Translated by S. H. Hooke. New York: Charles Scribner's Sons, 1963.

Sanders, E. P. *Jesus and Judaism*. Philadelphia: Fortress Press, 1985.

Schweitzer, Albert. *The Quest of the Historical Jesus: A Critical Study of Its Progress from Reimarus to Wrede*. 3rd ed. Translated by W. Montgomery. London: A&C Black, 1954.

Scott, Bernard Brandon. *Hear Then the Parable: A Commentary on the Parables of Jesus*. Minneapolis: Fortress Press, 1989.

Vermes, Geza. *Jesus the Jew: A Historian's Reading of the Gospels*. New York: Macmillan, 1973.

Via, Dan Otto. *The Parables: Their Literary and Existential Dimension*. Philadelphia: Fortress Press, 1967.

The Resurrection Faith and the Expanded Tradition

4

The Movement in Transition

The Christianity that eventually became a major force in the Roman Empire was the result of several stages of development in various geographical settings. Palestinian Judaism was the first environment. The Jesus movement (as scholars have termed this earliest stage of Christianity) took roots in various towns and villages of Palestine and continued there after his death. After the crucifixion, a church formed in Jerusalem that was of great significance in the early postresurrection period.

Influences from the broader Hellenistic environment were at work from the beginning. Greek culture had penetrated various parts of Palestine, and Acts 6 mentions a group within the Jerusalem church called "the Hellenists," who were presumably Greek-speaking Jewish Christians. Hellenistic influence increased as the movement spread into the world of Diaspora Judaism and an important, mission-oriented Jewish Christian congregation developed in Antioch of Syria. When the movement pushed beyond the bounds of the Jewish population to embrace Gentiles, the way was open for a new level of cultural interaction. Thus, it is not surprising that in its earliest stages, the new movement was characterized by considerable diversity.

In the final section of this chapter, we will take a brief look at the expansion of the Jesus tradition as it moved through time and varying environments. But we must first take note of the other stream of tradition that helped shape the emerging movement into the form that eventually became dominant: the resurrection faith, or the conviction that God raised Jesus from the dead.

Accounts of Jesus' Resurrection

Within a few decades of Jesus' death, the Mediterranean world was dotted with congregations of his followers, proclaiming the message of his resurrection. This claim is obviously a matter of faith, not something that historical research can prove or disprove. What we can do from a historian's perspective, however, is examine the materials through which Jesus' earliest followers expressed this conviction and try to determine precisely what this belief meant to them.

Three Types of Accounts

The New Testament never says that anyone witnessed the resurrection itself. The claim is that the already risen Jesus appeared to believers. The resurrection was not therefore something the disciples experienced directly but something they *inferred* from the appearances.[1] Three types of material express this inference: (1) the Gospel stories about the women (or woman) finding Jesus' tomb empty on the third day after his burial; (2) the Gospel stories about the appearance of the risen Jesus to vari-

ous disciples; and (3) creedlike "proclamations" of Jesus' resurrection, which also contain references to the appearances.

The Empty-Tomb Tradition

There are variations in the accounts of the empty tomb, but in all four Gospels (Matt 28:1-10; Mark 16:1-8; Luke 24:1-11; John 20:1, 11-13), one or more women come to Jesus' tomb, discover that his body is missing, and encounter an angel or angels who inform them that he has been raised. In all but Mark, they repeat this to the male disciples, and in two cases the risen Jesus' first appearance is to women (Matt 28:9) or a woman (John 20:14-17). Whether or not one takes these stories at face value, it is remarkable that women are granted such a crucial role in the tradition. Elisabeth Schüssler Fiorenza therefore argues that the women were in fact the first to proclaim the resurrection,[2] and her thesis is strengthened by the fact that the tradition is consistent also in claiming that the women did not abandon Jesus before his death, as the male disciples did. In any case, the function of the stories is clear enough: the empty tomb and the testimony of the angels combine to make the point that God raised Jesus from the dead.

The Developed Appearance Accounts

The Gospels of Matthew, Luke, and John all give accounts of Jesus' appearances to his followers after the empty-tomb story, although they are riddled with ambiguities and inconsistencies. At some points, it seems clear that a physical body is involved (Luke 24:37-43; John 20:27). In other cases, however, the nature of the resurrection body is ambiguous: the disciples do not recognize Jesus (Luke 24:15-16), and he appears and disappears in ghostly fashion (Luke 24:1, 36; John 20:26). Many scholars thus conclucde that these accounts reflect a good deal of embellishment. But they clearly reflect the early belief that Jesus appeared to his followers after his death.

Creedlike Proclamations
and Briefer Appearance Accounts

Our remaining category of materials is that of the creedlike proclamations, which contain briefer accounts of the resurrection appearances. In the following passage from 1 Corinthians, notice three important features: (1) Paul acknowledges that he is passing on a traditional formulation; (2) the entire formulation constitutes a proclamation that Jesus has been raised and an interpretation of the meaning of the resurrection; and (3) the statement includes references to the appearances of the resurrected Jesus.

> For I handed on to you as of first importance what I in turn had received: that Christ died for our sins in accordance with the scriptures, and that he was buried, and that he was raised on the third day in accordance with the scriptures, and that he appeared to Cephas [= Peter], then to the twelve. Then he appeared to more than five hundred brothers and sisters at one time, most of whom are still alive, though some have died. Then he appeared to James, then to all the apostles. (1 Cor 15:3-7)

In Luke 24:34, we find a single sentence that has all the marks of an even earlier version of such a creedlike proclamation: "The Lord has risen indeed, and he has appeared to Simon" (= Peter). Thus, once again, we have clear testimony to the early belief that Jesus appeared to his disciples after his death.

Origin of the Resurrection Faith

Scholars differ in their assessments of the relative historical value of the various accounts. One school of thought is that all of them are late developments, and belief in the resurrection arose out of the communities of Jesus' followers' sense of his spiritual presence with them. Another view is that only some dramatic event or events can explain how that faith came to be. So, wholly apart from the question of whether one believes that God actually raised Jesus from the dead, many scholars think that the disciples must have had experiences that they interpreted as his appearances to them.

It is important to say "interpreted as," because we cannot be certain about their nature. Paul considered his own vision of the risen Jesus, a considerable period after the crucifixion, as belonging to the came category as these earlier experiences: "Last of all, as to one untimely born, he appeared also to me" (1 Cor 15:8). So we may question whether these incidents were such that a neutral observer would have understood them as appearances of the risen Jesus. In any case, as Reginald Fuller remarks, the early tradition

FIG. 4.1 *Christ in the Sepulcher* by Bartolomeo di Tommaso. Perugia, Italy. Photo © Scala/Ministero per i Beni e le Attività culturali /Art Resource, NY.

understood the resurrection "not as the resuscitation of a corpse, but as the transformation of the body" into a "heavenly" or "eschatological" form.[3]

Meaning of the Resurrection Faith

Why did the disciples' experience of Jesus' presence with them suggest the notion of "resurrection"? It was not because Jewish tradition expected that the Messiah would be raised from the dead; we know of no Jewish texts from the period that make that claim. However, most Jews in the first century expected the general resurrection of the dead at the end of the age. While Jesus lived, the disciples hoped for the rule of God; when he appeared to them after his death, they concluded that the age of resurrection had begun. That is why they spoke of Jesus as "the firstborn from the dead" (Col 1:18): they understood his resurrection as the inauguration of the eschatological events envisioned in apocalyptic thought.

The resurrection thus gave early Christianity a strong apocalyptic content. But it also necessitated a revision of the typical apocalyptic scheme. Obviously, the fullness of God's rule still had not come. So the early believers concluded that the new age would arrive in two stages. Jesus had been taken to heaven (exalted) but would eventually return "in his glory" (Matt 25:31); *then* would come the general resurrection, the final judgment, and entrance into eternal life.

At first, Christians expected Jesus' return within their own generation (1 Thess 4:15). When decades passed and he still had not come, they had to wrestle yet again with the disappointment they had experienced. But by this time, they had developed ways of thinking to aid them in that process.

If the resurrection signified the inauguration of the eschatological events, it also implied that God had confirmed the validity of Jesus' mission and the truth of his words. Thus, as they awaited Jesus' return, his followers expressed their faith and hope in ways that gave Jesus himself a central role.

Expression of the Resurrection Faith

Titles of Jesus

The postresurrection followers of Jesus drew upon Jewish tradition for their terminology regarding him. They addressed him in prayer as *Mar*, an Aramaic term of respect meaning "Lord." And in relation to his expected return, they spoke of him as the Son of Man, the heavenly figure in Daniel 7.[4]

Convinced that God had initiated the divine rule through Jesus, believers also drew upon the still rather fluid complex of "messianic" notions and titles such as Messiah, Son of David, and Son of God. This last title, used originally for the reigning king and later for the messianic king, at first carried no "metaphysical" connotations when applied to Jesus but simply indicated his special closeness to God.

As the movement spread from Palestine into the world of Diaspora Judaism and finally into the Gentile world itself, the meanings of the titles applied to Jesus underwent change. When *Messiah* was translated into Greek as *christos,* it tended to lose its specific meaning and become almost a proper name. Son of David and Son of Man, with little appeal to Gentiles, began to drop out of use as titles. In the post–New Testament period, Son of Man became a designation for Jesus' humanity, as opposed to his divinity.

The titles Lord and Son of God blossomed in the Hellenistic world. Since the Septuagint translates *Yahweh* as "Lord," Hellenistic Jewish Christians probably began to transfer "*functions* from God to the exalted Jesus."[5] Then, among Gentile Christians, both "Lord" and "Son of God" came to embrace the notion of Jesus' divine nature. Neither of these titles was in and of itself responsible, however, for the development of the notion that Jesus was Son of God in the "metaphysical" sense of being a divine incarnation.

Christ as God Incarnate

Many scholars believe that Jesus' postresurrection followers came to think of him as divine under the influence of personified Wisdom, which appeared in the literature of pre-Christian Hellenistic Judaism. By some accounts, this happened very early, but others believe that the notion of the incarnation developed only gradually and came to flower in the Gospel of John, where the parallel term *Logos* displaced *Wisdom*: "In the beginning was the Word [Logos], and the Word was with God, and the Word was God" (John 1:1). However it happened, those who believed in Jesus came to think of him in terms of the notions of incarnation and preexistence. They did not mean to deny the unity of God or to identify Jesus Christ with God in simplistic fashion, but they did believe that God was present in Jesus in a unique way.

Worship, Witness, and the "Point" of Christology

The language that Jesus' postresurrection followers applied to him was the product of their worship and witness, not philosophical speculation. Much of it took shape directly through the liturgy, in the form of hymns and prayers, and in their preaching. They reflected on Jesus' status because they had experienced God's rule though him. Their interest was not in Christ-in-himself but in Christ-for-them. New Testament Christology thus has a practical, or functional, dimension that distinguishes it from abstract speculation. What the various writers say about the person of Jesus Christ is always connected to an understanding of what they believe God has done for human beings through him.

The New Testament contains several christological hymns that emphasize the exalted status of the Christ. Not all of them make the explicit point that this exaltation is inherently related to Christ's function, but it is always implicit. And it is crystal clear in Colossians 1:15-20. Beginning with statements on Christ's "nature" ("He is the image of the invisible God, the firstborn of all creation"), it ends in a declaration of what he *accomplished*: "and through him God was pleased to reconcile to himself all things . . . by making peace through the blood of his cross."

The Death of Jesus as a Redemptive Event

Deeply embedded in the ancient Hebrew faith was the hope that God would "save" or "redeem" Israel, that is, establish the nation in security. Apocalyptic thought modified this collective hope by introducing the notion of an individual salvation consisting of eternal life in God's eschatological rule. In neither case, however, was sheer survival the main idea. Jews hoped for survival *as the people of God*, which meant as an obedient society in which justice prevailed. And the eternal life envisioned in apocalypticism was explicitly for "the righteous" among human beings and was characterized by abundance, joy, and the absence of suffering.

Those who responded to Jesus' preaching presumably experienced both hope for the future and the power of God's rule in the present. Similarly, the postresurrection proclamation envisioned a future salvation that could in some measure be experienced in the present. But an important shift had taken place. Jesus' followers now understood him not simply as the one who had announced God's rule, but as the one through whom

God had actually *brought about* the salvation associated with that rule. They began to think of his life, death, and resurrection as a redemptive event that somehow wiped away or atoned for human sin and thereby made salvation available.

Jesus' followers must have come to interpret his death in this way very early, since Paul seems to be drawing upon an existing formulation when he writes, in Romans 3:25, of Christ as the one "whom God put forward as a sacrifice of atonement by his blood." But it is difficult to determine just how such a belief arose.

By some accounts, Jesus' followers simply took over the concept of atonement associated with ritual sacrifices in the Jewish Scriptures. The New Testament makes use of some of the terminology relating to the sacrificial cult, such as *ransom*. But it is significant that Paul does not use the Greek verb for "make atonement" that we find in the Septuagint passages, such as Leviticus 5:6-10, that deal with the slaughter of animals in atonement rituals.[6]

FIG. 4.2   Crucifixion of Christ with the two thieves. Detail from the doors of Saint Sabina Church in Rome. Photo © Alinari /Art Resource, NY.

And it is difficult to imagine that concepts associated with animal sacrifice would, without some intervening factor, have led to the notion that the life of a human being was offered for such a purpose.

Some scholars find such a factor in the figure of the "suffering servant" depicted in Isaiah 52:14—53:12. This servant, whose identity is not explicitly stated, is presented as "despised and rejected by others" (53:3); and it is said of him:

> He was wounded for our transgressions,
>   crushed for our iniquities;
> upon him was the punishment that made
>   us whole;
> and by his bruises we are healed. (53:5)

Christians through the centuries have understood these words as a prophecy of Jesus' death as a sacrifice for human sin, and the New Testament does make such a connection at two points: Hebrews 9:8 and 1 Peter 2:22-25. Both of these writings were probably composed at relatively late dates, however. And although quotations from the "servant song" of Isaiah 52–53 appear six times in the New Testament,[7] in none of these cases is the passage used in relation to atonement. So although Christians came eventually to understand Jesus as the suffering servant, it is not at all clear that this passage is the source of the understanding of Jesus' death as a saving event.

Many scholars look to Hellenistic culture as the catalytic agent in the development of the Christian view of atonement, for Greek literature was filled with such notions as the worthiness of dying for one's friends or one's land and the beneficial effects of a sacrificial death. Also, a noncanonical Jewish writing, known as 4 Maccabees, shows heavy Hellenistic influence and contains an explicit notion of vicarious sacrifice.[8] Reflecting on a family of pious Jews who were killed by the Seleucids for not renouncing their faith, the author speaks of these martyrs as "a ransom for the sin of our nation" and says, "Through the blood of these devout ones and their atoning sacrifice, divine Providence preserved Israel" (17:21-22). The date of composition of 4 Maccabees is uncertain, however; it may not have been written until after 70 C.E.[9] But it remains a strong possibility that Hellenistic models of the benefits of a martyr's death played a role in the development of the notion of Jesus' death as a saving event.

Whatever the specific origin of this notion, the language the New Testament writers employ in this regard is highly metaphorical and cannot be translated into hard-and-fast concepts. Theologians in later centuries tended to take the biblical metaphors literally, however, in their efforts to explain the "mechanics" of Christ's sacrifice by developing formal doctrines of the atonement. Confronted with the term *ransom*, for example, they asked the logical question: If God gave Jesus as a ransom for human sin, to whom was the ransom paid? Some answered "to God's own self," while others said "to Satan." Both answers raise enormous questions on the logical, moral, and theological levels. But most New Testament scholars see the whole argument as based upon a failure to grasp the metaphorical nature of the language. The biblical writers were not interested in explaining the "how" of the atonement but only in proclaiming it.

Whenever and however the concept of Jesus' atoning death appeared, it eventually became an integral part of Christian thought. But it was apparently not universal among Christians in the beginning. As we will presently see, there was at least one other way in which believers understood Jesus' "saving" power.

Expansion of the Jesus Tradition

Process of Expansion

The proclamation of the resurrection could not stand alone. Every religious community needs to nurture its constituents in the faith and develop rules of moral conduct and organizational structure. To what sources could the early Christians look as they faced the task of teaching?

They could, of course, look to the Jewish Scriptures. They could engage in their own *midrash*, the "updating" of scripture through commentary, and this is to some extent what they did. But it was the words and deeds of Jesus himself that had called them into a new consciousness, and it was the proclamation of his resurrection that had renewed their hopes. The real center of their life was thus Jesus, so they primarily turned to his own teachings.

However, Jesus had not taught a comprehensive ethic and had probably said nothing about community organization. Furthermore, his open-ended parables and sayings provided little help in meeting the needs of the community in relation to concrete situations. So his postresurrection followers expanded the tradition of his words and deeds. Faced with issues on which they had no memory of Jesus' teachings, they probably attributed to him sayings of other Jewish teachers and added interpretive comments to sayings of Jesus they did remember. It is likely that they also added the words of Christian prophets, who believed they were speaking on behalf of the risen Jesus, to their stock of Jesus' own sayings.

Outside the "Mainstream"

In what eventually became the mainstream of Christianity, the Jesus tradition and the proclamation of the resurrection complemented one another. But not all of Jesus' postresurrection followers found these two streams of tradition so compatible, and the "mainstream" was not the only line of development followed by the Jesus tradition. A different mode of expansion is attested by the *Gospel of Thomas*, a work discovered in an archaeological find at Nag Hammadi in Egypt in 1945.

Rather than telling a story of Jesus' life, this work takes the form of secret teachings delivered by the risen Jesus. Among the teachings, which are generally esoteric, we find a few parables that are obvious variants of materials found in the Synoptic Gospels. Some scholars think *Thomas* is directly dependent on the Synoptics, but others doubt this and see *Thomas* as representing another way in which the early tradition developed. In a few cases, it preserves materials that appear to be closer to the original in minor details than the Synoptic counterparts.

But what is the "other direction"? The discovery at Nag Hammadi was a library of an ancient Christian monastery containing numerous works that are clearly gnostic in orientation. In the eyes of the gnostics who read such materials, this postresurrection teaching constituted the secret knowledge, or *gnosis*, that set the gnostic (= knowing) believer above other followers of Jesus. From their point of view, what was redemptive was the teaching itself, not Jesus' death and resurrection. This is necessarily so for gnostics, since the Redeemer could not have had a physical body and therefore could not really have died. The death was therefore an illusion, and the "resurrection" could not mean what it did for "mainstream" followers.

Some scholars think the *Gospel of Thomas* also exhibits the tendency to understand Jesus' teachings as having saving power in themselves. But the authors of the New Testament writings curbed this tendency as they brought Jesus' teaching into the canonical writings. The Christianity that prevailed was that which proclaimed the life, death, and resurrection of Jesus of Nazareth as a saving event. It is nevertheless important to remember that it is only in retrospect that we can speak of that form of Christianity as the "mainstream." Each of the variant groups was undoubtedly convinced that it possessed the authentic interpretation of the meaning of Jesus' life.

"Shape" of the Expansion

We saw in chapter 3 one way in which the earliest level of the Jesus tradition was expanded: the allegorization of the parables. But it should be helpful now to give some examples of types of expansion.

Legal Materials

Matthew 5:18, in which Jesus says, "Until heaven and earth pass away, not one letter, not one stroke of a letter, will pass from the law," makes the details of the law binding upon Christians, probably reflecting the position of conservatives in the Palestinian communities who opposed those who were dispensing with ritual requirements.

Prophetic Statements

Luke 10:16 is probably the utterance of a Christian prophet, designed to give encouragement to missionaries by portraying Jesus pronouncing judgment on those who reject their message: "Whoever listens to you listens to me, and whoever rejects you rejects me, and whoever rejects me rejects the one who sent me." Mark 3:29 is best understood in a similar light: "Whoever blasphemes against the Holy Spirit can never have forgiveness, but is guilty of an eternal sin." This probably means that those who reject the words of Christian prophets will not be forgiven—not because they have committed too great a sin, but because the impending eschatological crisis leaves no further opportunity for repentance.[10]

Apocalyptic Materials

Mark 13:24-26 is one of the many apocalyptic sayings that entered the tradition:

> But in those days, after that suffering,
> the sun will be darkened,
>   and the moon will not give its light,
> and the stars will be falling from heaven,
>   and the powers in the heavens will be
>   shaken.
> Then they will see 'the Son of man coming in clouds' with great power and glory.

"Glorification" of the Earthly Jesus

There was a tendency in the expansion of the tradition to attribute characteristics of the risen Christ to the earthly Jesus. In Mark 9:2-8, Jesus' disciples get a preview of the "glorified" Jesus: "He was transfigured before them, and his clothes became dazzling white, such as no one on earth could bleach them." Also, there now appeared nature miracles in which Jesus walks on water (Mark 6:45-52) or stills a storm (Mark 4:37-41). Even the earlier miracle stories are largely the product of the expanded tradition. Whether pre- or post-Easter in origin, they are less reflective of memories of specific incidents than of the general recollection of Jesus as healer and exorcist. As Eugene Boring comments, each story constitutes a kind of "gospel in miniature."[11] As such, it focuses on the Jesus of the past only to convey the power of the risen Jesus as potentially working in the lives of those who hear it.

Controversies and Dialogues

Several other types of stories grew up to illustrate general memories of Jesus' activities or to provide settings for remembered sayings. There are numerous accounts in which Jesus comes into conflict with religious representatives because of his healings or exorcisms (Mark 3:1-6, 22-30), his (or his disciples') disregard of aspects of the law (Mark 2:23-28), or his association with outcasts (Mark 2:15-17). And there are instances in which questions by either disciples or opponents lead to a response by Jesus (Mark 10:17-22).

Historical Stories and Legends

Many stories, ranging from those with a strong historical element to those that are totally legendary, do not fit into any of the previous categories. Critical scholars generally take the accounts of Jesus' birth in Matthew 1:18—2:23 and Luke 1–2 to be late stories showing much Hellenistic influence. And the narratives of Jesus' arrest, trial, and crucifixion were shaped by the theological reflections of postresurrection followers, who combed the Jewish Scriptures to help them interpret these events. Far from the reports of neutral observers, they are theologically weighted accounts that interpret Jesus' death as the fulfillment of prophecy.

Formation of Orthodox Christology: Through the New Testament and Beyond

Jesus' postresurrection followers came to think of him as a divine being, but they also maintained that he was really human. In the second century, however, a tendency began to flourish that many leaders found disturbing. Some Christians, partly under gnostic influence, denied that Jesus was human at all. Their doctrine of Christ is termed *docetic*, from a Greek word meaning "to seem," because for them Jesus only seemed to have a human body.

To combat such notions, the church instituted such tests of "right teaching" as the Apostles' Creed, which emphasizes Jesus' humanity with the statement "[Jesus] suffered under Pontius Pilate, was crucified, died, and was buried." The creed also proclaims Jesus' "divine" status with the affirmation, "[I believe] in Jesus Christ [God's] only Son, our Lord." In later centuries, the church formalized its Christology by employing the Greek philosophical notion of "substance." Jesus Christ, according to what became the "orthodox" formulation is, as Son of God, of one substance with God the Father, and Father, Son, and Holy Spirit together constitute the triune God, or Trinity. The Son, moreover, has two "natures," one human and one divine, which are neither separate (as if he were two persons) nor confused (so that one would negate the other). Those Christians who, in distinction from various groups of dissenters, accepted this view spoke of their faith as both "catholic" (= universal) and "apostolic." This christological formula, adopted at the Council of Chalcedon in 451 C.E., has remained definitive for most Christians through the centuries.

NOTES

1. Philip E. Devenish, "The So-Called Resurrection of Jesus and Explicit Christian Faith: Wittgenstein's Philosophy, Marxsen's Exegesis as Linguistic Therapy," *Journal of the American Academy of Religion* 51 (June 1983): 171–90.
2. Elisabeth Schüssler Fiorenza, *In Memory of Her: A Feminist Reconstruction of Christian Origins* (New York: Crossroad, 1983), 138–40.
3. Reginald Fuller, *The Formation of the Resurrection Narratives* (New York: Macmillan, 1971), 57.
4. See above, pages 81–82.
5. Reginald Fuller, *The Foundations of New Testament Christology* (New York: Charles Scribner's Sons, 1965), 186.
6. Udo Schnelle, *Apostle Paul: His Life and Theology* (Grand Rapids: Baker Academic, 2003), 446.
7. Rom 15:21; 10:16; John 12:38; Matt 8:17; Luke 22:37; Acts 8:32-33.

8. Sam K. Williams, *Jesus' Death as a Saving Event: The Background and Origin of a Concept* (Missoula, Mont.: Scholars, 1975). Although never canonized, 4 Maccabees was read by early Christians and appears in an appendix to the Greek Bible. It is included in the Apocrypha section of the NRSV.

9. Schnelle, *Apostle Paul*, 448.

10. M. Eugene Boring, *The Continuing Voice of Jesus: Christian Prophecy and the Gospel Tradition* (Louisville, Ky.: Westminster John Knox, 1991), 219–20.

11. M. Eugene Boring, *Truly Human/Truly Divine: Christological Language and the Gospel Form* (St. Louis: CBP, 1984), 21.

STUDY QUESTIONS

1. Through what stages of development, defined by geography and culture, did the early Christian tradition go?

2. What are the different kinds of resurrection traditions found in the New Testament? What seems to be the origin of the resurrection faith?

3. What evidence is there that women were among the first, or even perhaps the very first, to proclaim the resurrection?

4. What was the meaning of the proclamation that God had raised Jesus from the dead?

5. How did the early Christians come to think of Jesus as "God incarnate"?

6. What are the various theories as to when and how Christians began to think of Jesus' death as having atoning, redeeming, or saving power?

7. What is the "other direction" of the development of the Jesus tradition that is represented in the *Gospel of Thomas*?

8. In what ways was the Jesus tradition expanded in the postresurrection community?

FOR FURTHER READING

Fuller, Reginald H. *The Formation of the Resurrection Narratives*. New York: Macmillan, 1971.

Marxsen, Willi. *The Resurrection of Jesus of Nazareth*. Translated by Margaret Kohl. Philadelphia: Fortress Press, 1970.

Perkins, Pheme. *Resurrection: New Testament Witness and Contemporary Reflection*. Garden City, N.Y.: Doubleday, 1984.

Perrin, Norman. *The Resurrection according to Matthew, Mark, and Luke*. Philadelphia: Fortress Press, 1977.

Epilogue to Part One

Sociology of the Jesus Movement

Recent scholarship has produced much debate on the sociology of early Christianity. Some analysts view Christianity as a movement of the lower classes, while others think it cut across all social groups. It is important, in dealing with this question, to distinguish between early Jewish Christianity in Palestine—often called the "Jesus movement"—and the forms of Christianity that developed in the wider reaches of the empire. It is with the Jesus movement that we are concerned at this point.

We know from Paul's letters that the Jerusalem church was impoverished, and we have seen that the earliest Jesus tradition, which was preserved in the Palestinian communities, reveals a deep sense of identification with the poor. Gerd Theissen has argued, however, that most of the adherents of the Jesus movement were not among the very poor but were in danger of falling into that category.[1] From his perspective, the Jesus movement was liberal in orientation, comprising persons from various strata of society who opposed the policies of the aristocracy and stood in solidarity with the poor. But it depended on the generosity of affluent persons to subsidize those who formed its core and were its true leaders, wandering charismatic prophets, who voluntarily abandoned home and possessions and accepted poverty.

Theissen's view has been influential, but critics have challenged him on numerous points. It is not at all clear, for example, that the poverty indicated in the early Jesus tradition is voluntary. Wolfgang Stegemann notes that texts such as Matthew 6:25 ("Do not worry about your life, what you will eat or what you will drink, or about your body, what you will wear") are best understood as words spoken to people who are worried about the basic necessities of life.[2] And Richard Horsley argues that the core of the movement was not the wandering charismatics but the people in the local communities.[3] Rather than a liberal group in solidarity with the poor, then, the Jesus movement was, in the eyes of some analysts, a more radical movement comprising the very poor themselves.

Another aspect of the sociology of the Jesus movement that has attracted attention is the status and role of women in its ranks. It is striking that Jesus appears in the early Palestinian tradition in close association with the female Wisdom. Luke 7:35, for example, defends both John the Baptist and Jesus with a saying that casts them in the role of Wisdom's envoys: "Wisdom is vindicated by all her children." But was this openness to female imagery matched by social egalitarianism? There is some indication that it was.

Matthew 23:9 ("And call no one your father on earth, for you have one Father—the one in heaven") is a recognition of God's sovereignty. But as Elisabeth Schüssler Fiorenza has shown, it is also an implicit critique of male-dominated society. This is clear, at least, if one reads it in relation to Mark 10:29-30: "There is no one who has left house or brothers or sisters or mother or father or children or fields . . . who will not receive a hundredfold now in this age—houses, brothers and sisters, mothers and children, and fields." Although fathers are among the items left behind, they do not appear among the items one regains in the new community: "Insofar as the new 'family' of Jesus has no room for 'fathers,' it implicitly rejects their power and status and thus claims that in the messianic community all patriarchal structures are abolished."[4]

We have in fact a striking example of the new community's abolition of an important patriarchal privilege. Since divorce was an exclusively male prerogative in Jewish society of the time, the early Christian prohibition of it functions in and of itself as an endorsement of women's rights. And Mark 10:8, which follows a quotation from Genesis on marriage, further emphasizes the point by proclaiming male-female solidarity: "So they are no longer two, but one."

In a similar vein, Schüssler Fiorenza sees an expression of broad social radicalism in Mark 10:15: "Whoever does not receive the kingdom of God as a little child will never enter it." This statement, she says, "is not an invitation to childlike innocence and naiveté but a challenge to relinquish all claims of power and domination over others."[5]

It should now be evident that the early followers of Jesus challenged certain social norms and stood in opposition to the ruling aristocracy. And it might seem natural to ask whether they were content to pursue an "alternative" lifestyle among themselves or made active attempts to change society as a whole. To pose the question this way, however, may rest upon a misunderstanding. If Jesus led a Jewish renewal movement, his followers would not have been completely cut off from the communities in which they lived. Certainly, they did not withdraw from society as did the settlers at Qumran, and they had no sense of constituting a new "religion." They probably thought of themselves as the nucleus of God's coming rule. Although hardly social reformers in the modern sense, they would nevertheless have expected that the kind of community life they nurtured among themselves was precisely what would characterize Israel as a whole when the rule of God arrived in its fullness.

A Continuing Question: Christianity and the Social Order

The preceding questions should be of interest to anyone considering the relationship between religious faith and the social order. They are particularly important for Christian theology. Most liberation theology attempts to move directly from the words and deeds of Jesus that challenge the power structures of his time to a contemporary rejection of analogous systems. From this perspective, it is important to document the specifics of Jesus' social views. Another approach is to begin not with Jesus' solidarity with the poor specifically but with his general love ethic and then apply it to a wide range of situations.

Both of these approaches take the Jesus tradition as normative for Christianity. While they do not deny the importance of the resurrection faith, they understand it as deriving its meaning from the stories of a Jesus who associated with the outcast and was opposed by the powerful. Because of this emphasis upon the human Jesus (or the earliest Jesus tradition), these views might be of significant personal interest to persons beyond the bounds of the Christian faith.

A fundamentally different option is to understand the resurrection faith and incarnation theology as normative for interpreting the life and teachings of Jesus, rather than vice versa. This approach would tend to support a somewhat more doctrinally oriented and otherworldly version of Christianity.

One should not, of course, assume a one-to-one correlation between a given approach and a specific position on religion and society. The latter view has often been enlisted in liberation causes, and the "historical Jesus" approach has sometimes produced an individualistic piety that deemphasizes the social dimension of faith. Nevertheless, it makes some difference where one comes down on this issue when considering the question "What is Christianity?" Theologians who start with the historical Jesus or the Jesus tradition are critical of theology that begins with the incarnation rather than their more "concrete" Jesus, while those who take incarnation theology as normative are suspicious of attempts to find a Jesus behind the canonical materials.

NOTES

1. Gerd Theissen, *Sociology of Early Palestinian Christianity*, trans. John Bowden (Philadelphia: Fortress Press, 1978).
2. Wolfgang Stegemann, "Vagabond Radicalism in Early Christianity," in *God of the Lowly: Socio-Historical Interpretations of the Bible*, ed. Willy Schottroff and Wolfgang Stegemann, trans. Matthew J. O'Connell (Maryknoll, N.Y.: Orbis, 1984), 161–62.
3. Richard A. Horsley, *Sociology and the Jesus Movement* (New York: Crossroad, 1989), 112–16.
4. Elisabeth Schüssler Fiorenza, *In Memory of Her: A Feminist Theological Reconstruction of Christian Origins* (New York: Crossroad, 1983), 147–50.
5. Ibid., 148.

STUDY QUESTIONS

1. In what ways did the Jesus movement depart from existing social norms?
2. What issues are at stake between Theissen and his critics?

FOR FURTHER READING

Horsley, Richard A. *Sociology and the Jesus Movement*. New York: Crossroad, 1989.

Schottroff, Luise, and Wolfgang Stegemann. *Jesus and the Hope of the Poor*. Maryknoll, N.Y.: Orbis, 1986.

Schüssler Fiorenza, Elisabeth. *In Memory of Her: A Feminist Theological Reconstruction of Christian Origins*. New York: Crossroad, 1983.

Theissen, Gerd. *Sociology of Early Palestinian Christianity*. Translated by John Bowden. Philadelphia: Fortress Press, 1978.

THE GOSPELS
AND ACTS

Prologue to Part Two

Getting Started

The New Testament begins with four stories of Jesus' life: the Gospels. In the canonical arrangement, the Acts of the Apostles comes after the Fourth Gospel, John. It is apparent, however, that the author of Luke also wrote Acts and that the two volumes constitute a genuine narrative unity. For that reason, I will treat Luke-Acts as a single, two-volume work. I will also begin with Mark rather than Matthew, simply because I find a study of Mark helpful in dispelling preconceptions.

Each chapter begins with a brief consideration of questions concerning authorship and the date and place of composition, followed by a list of "points to look for" when reading the writing in question. Then follows a reader-response treatment of that work. To illustrate the reader-response method, I will give a detailed reading of Mark and John, but I will confine myself to abbreviated treatments of Matthew and Luke-Acts.

Entering the Story Worlds

In dealing with the precanonical levels of tradition, we intentionally took passages out of their present contexts in order to understand what they meant to the earliest followers of Jesus. Now we are going to read the canonical books as they stand—as whole, integrated literary works. Passages that meant one thing when read in light of the pre-Easter or the early church situation may mean something quite different within the context of a Gospel narrative.

To read the Gospels and Acts in this way, we must let each writing establish its own "story world." We will have no interest in whether the events described in any of these stories "really happened." Our only concern will be for the story each narrative tells—how it attempts to engage the reader in reflection upon the meaning of Jesus' life.

It may at some points be difficult to maintain this perspective. Perhaps the hardest task is to remember to treat the characters in the story *as characters* and not make an unconscious leap to actual human beings who once lived. If Jesus does something puzzling in the story (as he will often do in Mark), we must not ask why the historical person Jesus would have done that. The appropriate question is why, in the context of the story world, the *character* Jesus did that.

The other half of the matter is that the Gospel writers present their stories as interpretations of a person who actually lived and died. In this regard, what they did in constructing their story worlds is not fundamentally different from what Jesus' earliest followers did in passing on the original stories of what he said and did. For the pre-Gospel Jesus tradition was itself *interpretation* of Jesus.

It is also important to grant each Gospel its unique perspective and not read into it the perspective of another. We have no right, for example, to import into Luke the particular form of incarnation theology, based largely upon the Gospel of John, that made its way into the orthodox creeds. Only when we allow each writing its own way of depicting Jesus will we be able to understand what each has to say about the meaning of his life.

The "Narrator," the "Reader," and the Reading Process

The various schools of literary criticism necessarily employ particular technical vocabularies. I have sought to reduce such terminology to a bare minimum by limiting myself to two technical terms, *the narrator* and *the reader*. In explaining my use of these two terms, I will also define more precisely the reader-response approach I will employ.[1]

The Narrator

By "the narrator," literary critics do not mean the author, the actual person who wrote the story. They mean the "voice" that tells the story. In some literary works, the narrator is one of the characters in the story. More frequently, the narrator is anonymous. All four Gospels employ an anonymous narrator, although in a few passages in Acts, which are told in the first person plural, the narrator appears to be an unidentified character in the story.

Narrators, as Mark Allan Powell puts the matter, "vary as to how much they know and how much they choose to tell." When narrators are characters, their knowledge will probably be limited to what such characters would reasonably know. The narrators in the Gospels, however, fall near the other end of the spectrum. Powell describes them as "highly knowledgeable," noting that they know "the inner thoughts and motivations of the characters they describe." But, at least in the case of the Synoptic Gospels, they show some limitations. They neither offer "descriptions of heaven and hell" nor "presume to speak directly for God," as Jesus does.[2]

The Reader

The reader might seem to be a self-explanatory term, but it is easily misunderstood. When reader-oriented critics refer to the reader, they are not speaking of some actual person but to a construct of their own devising, designed as an aid to interpretation. The critic, in other words, tries to imagine how a reader who follows the narrator's leads would read the story. By intentionally taking up the stance of this hypothetical reader, the critic sharpens her or his perceptions and approaches the narrative in a focused and systematic way.

The various schools of literary interpretation vary somewhat in their definitions of the reader. Narrative criticism tends to think of the reader as someone who knows the entire story very well, who has read it before and is therefore able to perceive all sorts of relationships between the various parts of the story.[3] The advantage of defining the reader this way is that it allows the critic great freedom in noting such relationships.

Reader-response criticism, by contrast, tends to posit a first-time reader, who does not know the ultimate outcome of the story. Such a reader may make guesses about what is to happen next, but may in fact be surprised as the story unfolds. The advantage of this approach is that it helps to preserve the sequential nature of the narrative. In taking up the perspective of the reader who is naive regarding what is to come, the critic is able to imagine that reader's questions, remembrances, and feelings, such as disappointment, confusion, or amazement.

Neither of these schools of criticism is primarily interested in who the actual first readers of the work were. But many representatives of both camps recognize that the critic's historical knowledge is often essential, precisely because the text itself sometimes implies a reader who has such knowledge. The Gospels, for example, presuppose readers who are familiar with the Jewish Scriptures. To the extent that critics stress the importance of identifying presupposed knowledge, they are attempting to endow their hypothetical readers with some of the qualities of actual readers.

The Reading Process

A reader-response approach requires some definition of what happens in the reading process. When actual readers read a story, they remember a good bit of what has happened before, and they anticipate what is to come. They form opinions about the characters, becoming attached to some and repelled by others, and they hope for certain turns of events and build up dreads about others. In doing all this, they are active participants in the story.

But their participation goes even further. A story cannot tell everything. It always leaves something to its readers' imaginative powers. So readers must make concrete what the narrator leaves in general terms, and they must even fill in gaps in the plot and in the development of characters. In the end, they try to understand the story as a coherent whole and often assign some specific meaning to what they have read. And they sometimes come away with insights regarding life in general or their own lives. Readers do not write their own stories, but they do participate in making narrators' stories complete and in bringing them to life.

Readers also move "in" and "out" of the story, sometimes utterly caught up in it but at other times disengaging themselves in order to reflect on ideas and even to assess their own reactions. Sometimes readers finish a story with a keen sense of satisfaction. But they must often revise their judgments and expectations along the way, and sometimes they must acknowledge that their hopes were dashed by the development of the story.

Because actual readers perform all these actions, reader-response critics try to bring to expression some of the key thoughts and feelings that a reader focused intently on the narrator's clues might reasonably have. There is, of course, subjectivity in this method of criticism, since it involves the critic's own imagination. And the possibilities for a reader's actions are far broader than any critic could begin to "record"! But the value of this approach is that, by focusing on the reading process, it can help actual readers with their own task of truly encountering the text.

The Approach of the Present Text

In the initial approach to each of our four narratives, I will assume the role of the reader-response critic, which means trying to take up the perspective of "the reader." In doing so, I will posit a first-time reader who does not know the ultimate outcome of the story but who is able to remember in perfect detail everything that has gone before. In terms of more specific knowledge, my reader also knows the Jewish Scriptures in Greek (the Septuagint) and shares the broad outlines of the common knowledge of the Hellenistic culture.

I will, of necessity, be selective in actions I assign to this reader. But I will always seek to focus on lines of thinking and feeling that are in fact invited by the narrator's voice.

My attempt at "objectivity" cannot, however, assure the reader of *this* text that the reader I posit is approaching these stories in a valid way. The point of the critic's observations is to assist others in doing their own reading and evaluation. I should also say that I do not assume that my reader's responses are the only possible, or only valid, ones. I present them as specific "performances" of the texts, which are not intended to rule out other, perhaps quite different, ways in which one might find meaning in them.

One final note on terminology: When I want to indicate the actual author of a New Testament writing, I will say so explicitly. For example, I will refer to "the author" or "the author of Mark." I have reserved the names Matthew, Mark, Luke, and John to refer to the writings themselves.

What Is a Gospel?

The English word *gospel*, derived from the Anglo-Saxon *godspel*, translates the Greek *euangelion*: the meaning, in each case, is "good news." The Gospel of Mark begins with an indication that the story of Jesus is to be understood as precisely that: "The beginning of the good news of Jesus Christ." In designating the four stories of Jesus' life as "Gospels" and placing them together at the head of the canon, church tradition does more than recognize the literary similarities among these works. It indicates the centrality of the Jesus story in Christian faith, and it characterizes that story precisely as did the author of Mark: "good news" for humankind.

This fact in itself should tell us something about the nature of these writings. Scholars have long debated whether and in what sense they are to be understood as "biographies" of Jesus. Some have argued that the Gospels constitute a unique literary genre in the ancient world, while others have found significant ways in which they parallel ancient biographies. This debate need not concern us here. The important point is that the Gospel writers—sometimes called "the evangelists" (those who announced the good news)—wrote with the explicit intention of engendering or nurturing Christian faith. Their purpose, we should remember, was not to report factual material in a neutral way but to convince those for whom they wrote of the truth of their witness to the meaning of Jesus' life, death, and resurrection.

NOTES

1. For a fuller statement of the approach that has most influenced my own, see John A. Darr, *On Character Building: The Reader and the Rhetoric of Characterization in Luke-Acts* (Louisville, Ky.: Westminster John Knox, 1992), ch. 1. Darr's views are presented in more detail in his doctoral dissertation (Vanderbilt, 1987), "'Glorified in the Presence of Kings': A Literary-Critical Study of Herod the Tetrarch in Luke-Acts."
2. Mark Allan Powell, *What Is Narrative Criticism?* (Minneapolis: Fortress Press, 1990), 25–26.
3. Ibid., 19–21.

STUDY QUESTIONS

1. Explain the terms *narrator* and *reader* as used in reader-response criticism.
2. Explain the difference between reader-response criticism and narrative criticism.
3. Are the Gospels written from an "objective" point of view? Should they be?

FOR FURTHER READING

Burridge, Richard A. *What Are the Gospels? A Comparison with the Graeco-Roman Biography*. Cambridge: Cambridge University Press, 1992.

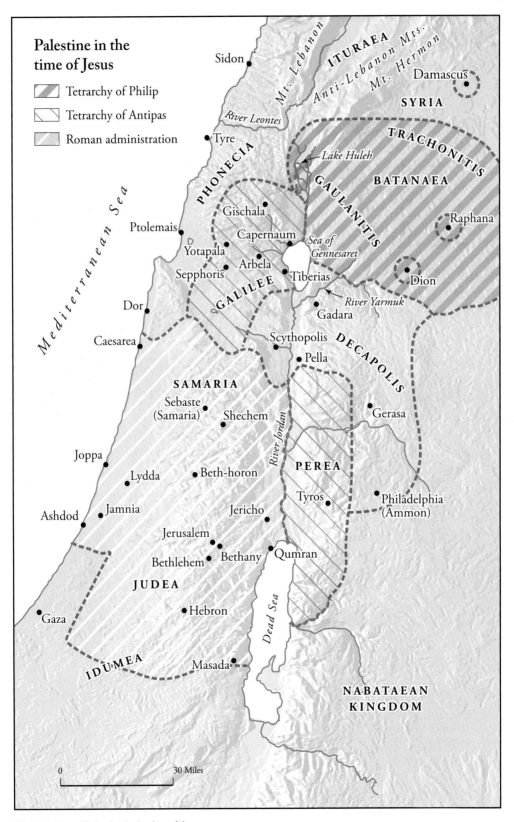

Tetrarchy of Philip

Tetrarchy of Antipas

Roman administration

Mediterranean Sea

Sidon

Mt. Lebanon

ITURAEA

Anti-Lebanon Mts.

Mt. Hermon

Damascus

SYRIA

River Leontes

Tyre

PHONECIA

TRACHONITIS

Lake Huleh

BATANAEA

GAULANITIS

Raphana

Ptolemais

Gischala

Capernaum

Yotapala

Arbela

*Sea of
Gennesaret*

Dion

Sepphoris

Tiberias

GALILEE

River Yarmuk

Dor

Gadara

Caesarea

Scythopolis

DECAPOLIS

Pella

SAMARIA

Sebaste
(Samaria)

Shechem

Gerasa

River Jordan

Joppa

PEREA

Lydda

Beth-horon

Ashdod

Jamnia

Jericho

Tyros

Philadelphia
(Ammon)

Jerusalem

Bethlehem

Bethany

Qumran

JUDEA

Dead Sea

Gaza

Hebron

NABATAEAN
KINGDOM

IDUMEA

Masada

0   30 Miles

FIG. 5.1   Map of Palestine in the time of Jesus.

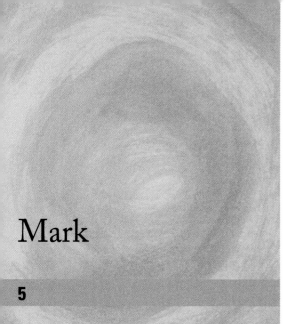

Mark

5

Authorship, Date, and Place of Composition

Second-century tradition attributes the Gospel of Mark to someone named Mark, who supposedly received his information from Peter. It is often assumed that this is the John Mark who appears as a companion of Paul in Acts and the Mark to whom Paul refers in his letters. Mark was a common name, however, so that even if a Mark was the author, we cannot be certain about these connections. In any case, the evidence of a long period of oral tradition preceding the written Gospels makes the claim regarding Peter suspect.

Chapter 13, with its description of a tumultuous situation and its prediction of the destruction of the temple, leads most scholars to think Mark was written around 70 C.E., either in the midst of the Jewish war against Rome or soon after it. Early traditions place the writing in Rome, and some scholars accept this as fact. Others, however, favor Galilee or Syria, partly because these regions are prominent places in the narrative. Wherever the Gospel was composed, most interpreters believe that the author wrote for a community of believers who faced grave danger because of their allegiance to Jesus.

Points to Look For in Mark

- The theme of secrecy (Jesus keeping his identity hidden)

- The role of the two giving-of-sight stories, which bracket the three predictions of Jesus' death and resurrection, in interpreting this secrecy

- The role played by the parable of the Soils in the narrative as a whole

- The failure of the disciples

- The emphasis on the suffering of Jesus and its implications for the disciples

- The meaning of the strange ending

- The author's use of paradox and irony

Mark's Story of Jesus: A Reading

1:1-13

In the first sentence, the narrator indicates that what is to follow is "good news" and concerns Jesus, the Messiah (Christ) and Son of God. The reader is therefore prepared to hear a story about God's fulfillment of the ancient promises to Israel and will identify either Jesus or John the Baptizer, who appears in verse 4, as the figure mentioned in the quotation from the Jewish Scriptures: the "voice of one crying out in the wilderness," sent to "prepare the way of the Lord."[1]

When John appears, he preaches baptism, forgiveness, and repentance. His message suggests both renewal and fulfillment, as does the place of his activity: the river Jordan, scene of the Hebrews' entrance into the promised land. The announcement that someone else is to come, who will baptize with the Holy Spirit, is another sign of fulfillment, since many Jews believed that the Spirit had departed Israel and would return only in the new age. It will also be clear that the reference is to Jesus, who comes on the scene and is baptized (1:9).

By treating the reader to Jesus' vision of the Holy Spirit and audition of the voice of God, the narrator establishes credibility regarding the earlier proclamation of who Jesus is and reinforces the term used earlier: *Son of God*. When the Spirit drives Jesus into the wilderness, we begin to sense a "cosmic" conflict. Satan tempts Jesus, seeking to subvert his mission, and the wild beasts suggest danger. But the ministering angels signify God's presence with Jesus and approval of his mission.

1:14—3:6

A turn in the plot comes in 1:14-15, with John's arrest and the beginning of Jesus' proclamation, in Galilee, of the rule of God. The immediate response of the Galilean fishermen to Jesus' invitation to discipleship creates a sense of rapid movement: the mission is under way.

When Jesus begins to teach in a synagogue (1:21), the narrator signals a rift between Jesus and the religious authorities by observing that the people contrast his authoritative words to the teachings of the scribes (1:22). And Jesus' exorcism of a demon not only demonstrates his power but also introduces a theme of secrecy. In 1:25, he silences the demon, and in 1:34, after a report of many healings and exorcisms, we read that "he would not permit the demons to speak, *because they knew him.*" After healing a man with leprosy, Jesus warns him to "say nothing to anyone."

In the stories in 2:1—3:6, the theme of conflict with the religious authorities becomes explicit. Scribes and Pharisees criticize Jesus for pronouncing a man's sins forgiven, for eating with "tax collectors and sinners," and for violating the Sabbath. In each story, Jesus in some way bests his opponents, quoting scriptural precedent or uttering a saying that presumably silences them. He also makes oblique references to his own status, speaking of the "Son of Man" and of the "bridegroom" who will soon be "taken away."

The saying on new wine and old wineskins in 2:22 indicates that Jesus in some way signals a new beginning. But the expected rule of God is dawning in the midst of conflict, a point underscored by the conclusion to the series of stories: the Pharisees begin to hatch a plot "to destroy him" (3:6).

3:7—5:43

In 3:7-12, the narrator shifts the scene and again summarizes Jesus' activity. Demons continue to recognize Jesus, who explicitly forbids them to make his identity known.

Then at 3:13, Jesus withdraws to a mountain, where he appoints twelve disciples as an inner circle, gives them authority to preach and cast out demons, and gives the nickname "Peter" to Simon. The reader will assume that these chosen ones will have a significant and positive role to play in the drama.

An unexpected twist to the conflict develops at 3:21: Jesus' own family members try to stop his activity, as the scribes contend that he is demonically possessed. Jesus' reply to the scribes in the debate in 3:22-27 shows that he is in mortal combat with Satan (the "strong man" of 3:27). And by casting out demons, he is binding Satan in order to plunder his house, that is, to break the demonic hold upon the world. A few verses later, Jesus declares that those who do God's will are his true family (3:33-35), which indicates that all who hear him must make a decision that may wrench them away from prior commitments—even those to their own families. The implication is that to reject Jesus' mission is to side with the demonic.

In chapter 4, where Jesus begins to teach beside the sea (of Galilee), we learn something of the specific content of his teaching. But here things get more complex and confusing. When the disciples ask for an explanation of the parable of the Soils, Jesus comments that the parables are intended to keep those "outside" from getting the point, while the disciples have been given the "secret" of God's rule. Then, disheartened at the disciples' dullness, he chastises them for not understanding but gives an allegorical explanation of the parable (4:13-20).

The reader will try to identify the various types of soil in the parable and explanation with varying responses to Jesus' own preaching (sowing), and it is already apparent that the Jewish authorities constitute the first type, in which the word takes no root at all. But Jesus' question and statement at 4:21-22 speak directly to the reader's own life: those who desire to be good soil must bear fruit by preaching the word themselves. After some additional parables and sayings, the narrator makes the summary statement that Jesus taught in parables "as they were able to hear it" (4:33).

The narrator also notes that Jesus explains things privately to his disciples (4:34), which gives the impression that they are beginning to understand. The story in 4:35-41, however, dispels this notion. Caught in a storm in their little boat, the disciples are terror stricken. When Jesus miraculously calms the storm but rebukes the disciples for their lack of faith, two themes reach a higher pitch. Jesus' awesome power extends now even to nature itself, but the disciples cannot grasp what is happening. *Who is this?* they ask. The irony is apparent. Although given the secret of God's rule, those closest to Jesus seem to resemble the good soil

FIG. 5.2   **The Great Temple of Artemis in Gerasa, Jordan.** Photo © Erich Lessing / Art Resource, NY.

less than they do the rocky soil—which starts well but ends in failure!

The heightening of Jesus' powers continues. Across the lake, in Gentile territory, which is unclean in Jewish eyes, he heals a demoniac possessed by a "legion" of demons and sends them away in a dramatic fashion (5:1-13). But in sharp contrast to his practice in Galilee, Jesus commands the man to tell what has been done for him. And the man does so, exemplifying the good soil of the parable far better than do the disciples.

Back in Jewish territory, Jesus performs two feats that are even more astonishing. A woman is healed merely by touching his garment, and he raises a twelve-year-old girl from the dead. Then the note of secrecy reemerges: Jesus insists that no one should know of this deed (5:43). Thus, a certain paradox cannot escape the reader. In his conflict with Satan, Jesus is exercising enormous power, dem-

onstrating his status as Son of God. Yet his identity and mission are cloaked in an air of secrecy and mystery. Why?

6:1—8:26

Following these dramatic events, Jesus returns to his home area, only to be met with rejection. His saying on a prophet's lack of honor among his own people (6:4) recalls the earlier conflict with his family, just as his surprise at the unbelief he now encounters is reminiscent of his reaction to the disciples' dullness. Jesus thus appears as powerful but not omniscient or all-powerful. His ability to perform miracles depends on the faith of those to whom he ministers.

Jesus now sends his disciples on a mission, giving them "authority over the unclean spirits" (6:7), which creates the impression that

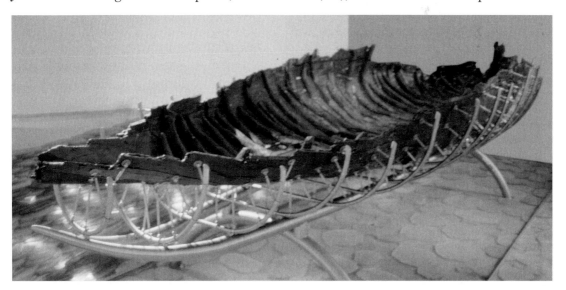

FIG. 5.3 The so-called "Galilee-Boat" was discovered in 1986 in the Sea of Galilee and is located now in Ginosaur, Israel.
Photo © Erich Lessing / Art Resource, NY.

they are at last realizing their potential. They are successful both in healings and in exorcisms, the very works Jesus himself has performed. But will this impression hold?

The speculation about Jesus at 6:14-16 raises the issue of his true identity. And the flashback revealing Herod's murder of John the Baptizer at 6:17-29 keeps the motif of conflict alive as a series of accounts dramatizes Jesus' power. Highlighted by a miraculous feeding (6:30-44) and an eerie scene on the sea, the series ends with a description of the masses flocking to Jesus for healing (6:56). We thus get the impression that Jesus is having success in his mission. But along the way, the positive view of the disciples has been undermined by descriptions of their obtuseness in the feeding story (6:37) and their display of fear on the sea (6:49), but most of all by the narrator's comment at 6:52 that "their hearts were hardened."

The note of success at 6:56 creates a contrast between the people's reaction and that of the Pharisees in the ensuing material, as the conflict with them reemerges. A dispute over "the tradition of the elders" regarding ritual law (7:1-16) gives Jesus the opportunity to brand the Pharisees hypocrites who neglect human need and place human tradition above God's commandments. Intruding at 7:19 to point out that Jesus' words abolish the dietary regulations, the narrator invites the conclusion that Jesus is breaking sharply with established tradition—but precisely in order to honor God's command.

At 7:24, Jesus once again travels into Gentile territory, where he is bested by a Syro-phoenician woman in a verbal encounter regarding the "rights" of Gentiles to his ministry. The story encourages reflection on the place of Gentiles in Jesus' mission, and the Gentile woman's faith once again creates a contrast with the response of the Pharisees. When, after another miraculous feeding, the Pharisees approach Jesus (8:11-13), their hypocrisy is evident. They converse with him only to test him, asking for a sign on the heels of awesome deeds of power!

Jesus' warning to the disciples at 8:15 reinforces the negative view of the Pharisees, but the conversation that follows reemphasizes the disciples' own inadequacies. They take Jesus' symbolic statement about yeast in a crudely literal fashion. And his displeasure is evident in the question he poses regarding the significance of the twelve and seven baskets of bread left over from the feedings: "Do you not yet understand?" The implication is that they do not. The seven and the twelve seem to have significance, but it remains unexplained.

The note of mystery and secrecy thus reasserts itself, and it continues in 8:12-26. Jesus heals a blind man—halfway! Has Jesus failed? He tries again, and the man sees clearly. What does this strange story mean?

8:27—10:45

At 8:27, Jesus, again in Gentile territory, confronts the disciples, for the first time, with the question of his identity. Given all the evidence for Jesus' status that the story has brought forth, Peter's answer will seem correct: "You are the Messiah." But Jesus' reply is puzzling. Employing the same Greek verb (*epitimao*) with which he earlier silenced demons, he rebukes (NRSV: "sternly ordered") the disciples "not to tell anyone about him." Has he accepted Peter's confession that he is the Messiah? Has he rejected it?

We do not get a direct answer to these questions. Jesus immediately begins to teach the disciples privately, telling them "quite openly" about the coming death and resurrection of the Son of Man, whom the reader will identify with Jesus himself. But Peter now rebukes (*epitimao*) Jesus, indicating his unwillingness for Jesus to die. In the harshest terms, Jesus again rebukes Peter, calling him "Satan"! Then he speaks to the crowd and the disciples, linking the role of discipleship to his own coming fate.

The contrast between Jesus' present openness and his earlier secrecy is unmistakable. At least part of what has been hidden, and must remain hidden to outsiders, is that Jesus, to fulfill his mission, must die. And to follow Jesus means to bear one's own cross. Hiddenness and mystery thus give rise to paradox and irony. One must lose one's life to find it (8:35). Was this what Peter could not—would not—understand? We can sympathize with Peter's reaction. Impressed with the awesome power of the Son of God, the reader will find Jesus' talk of death and denial abrasive and must wrestle with the paradox.

When in 9:2 Jesus takes the disciples to a mountaintop and is transfigured before them, there is additional, dramatic testimony to his status: the appearances of Moses and Elijah and once again the voice from heaven proclaiming him Son of God. But the disciples are bewildered. Peter does not know what to say, and all the disciples are afraid and cannot understand Jesus' reference to his coming resurrection. Then, at the foot of the mountain, Jesus finds that those left behind have failed in an attempt to cast out a demon. He performs the exorcism, but not before he has accused the disciples: "You faithless generation."

Noting at 9:30-32 that Jesus is traveling *secretly* through Galilee and speaking for a second time about his coming death, the narrator calls attention yet again to the disciples' fear and lack of comprehension. Then at 9:34, it becomes clear that the disciples have been haggling over who among them is the greatest. Could any conversation be less appropriate to the situation? The pattern following the first prediction is repeated: again Jesus teaches about discipleship. But the disciples do not really understand him and are not prepared for the kind of discipleship he demands.

At 10:1, the scene shifts, and Jesus is in a public setting, where he continues his teaching by addressing specific areas of ethical concern. When Jesus reprimands the man who calls him "good" (10:17-18), noting that God alone deserves such praise, he makes a distinction between God and himself as the one who proclaims God's rule. And in directing the inquirer to God's commandments (10:19), Jesus begins a characterization of that rule that continues into the material that follows (10:23-31). The radical character of this teaching—evident, for example, in the demand he makes on the inquirer at 10:21—

invites reflection on life in the new age. And Jesus' promise of goods and families "now in this age" (10:30) suggests that the community he is gathering is called to manifest God's rule in the here and now. We thus get a glimpse of life, as it should be, in the postresurrection community. Like the call to discipleship, it is riddled with paradox: one leaves everything but gains more—"with persecutions" (10:30)!

At 10:32-34, Jesus informs his followers that they are headed to Jerusalem, where he will die. This account of Jesus' third prediction of his death and resurrection reemphasizes the aura of terror and mystery and also repeats the familiar pattern linking Jesus' suffering and death with discipleship. The paradoxes of 10:43—great among you/your servant; first among you/slave of all—are powerful reminders of the irony of losing one's life to find it. But the narrator now provides a new element, Jesus' statement on the meaning of his death: "For the Son of Man came not to be served but to serve, *and to give his life a ransom for many*." Somehow, in a way that is not elaborated but only suggested through the metaphor of "ransom," Jesus' death and resurrection will *set human beings free*.

The reader has thus gained some insight into the secrecy that has shrouded the narrator's tale from the beginning. Jesus is not a triumphant Messiah, but one who must suffer, and those who follow him must be prepared to suffer also. This insight is couched in paradoxical form, however, and central characters in the drama do not grasp it. The air of mystery prevails. Nevertheless, the theme of prediction, linked to the narrator's use of

the Jewish Scriptures, keeps alive the impression that God is active in all that is happening. Jesus knows what is to come.

10:46—12:44

When Jesus and his followers come to Jericho, which lies at the base of the mountain atop which Jerusalem is set, it becomes clear that this is the last leg of the fateful journey. And the incident that occurs here directs attention forward to Jerusalem. A man who is blind addresses Jesus as "Son of David," that is to say, as Messiah-King, and Jesus heals him without a word of rebuke. Jewish monarchs reign from Jerusalem; will Jesus claim his crown when he arrives? No, because at 10:32, Jesus said that he will die in Jerusalem. But what, then, of the messianic title?

The incident at Jericho also points backward to the earlier story of a blind man, the odd two-stage healing that preceded the three instances in which Jesus predicted his death and linked it to discipleship. Together the two stories bracket these predictions and invite the reader to reconsider them in light of the metaphors of blindness and sight and of the distinction between partial "seeing" and full "seeing." It is already apparent that Jesus' mission involves his death and that discipleship means bearing one's cross. What the metaphor of stages of sight adds is a confirmation that acceptance of Jesus' suffering, and of one's own as a disciple, represents a deeper level of understanding than is possessed by those who expect a more visible, less paradoxical victory of their Messiah. But how does one reconcile the notion of a suffering Messiah and suffering disciples with the expectation of a messianic king who would establish peace and justice?

There is no immediate answer to this question. And it is surprising that we now witness a scene in which Jesus appears as a quite public and apparently triumphant Messiah: his entrance into Jerusalem (11:1-11). Not only do the crowd's accolades imply his status as Davidic king, but the colt on which he rides conjures up the image of the "messianic" procession in Zechariah 9:9.

It is thus clear that Jesus is wielding messianic authority when, on a second incursion into the city, he carries out a brief "occupation" of the temple and condemns both the commerce in the court and the exclusiveness of the temple worship. His citation of a scriptural passage that designates the temple "a house of prayer *for all the nations*" (11:17) calls to mind that he earlier extended his ministry into Gentile territory and abolished the system of clean and unclean foods. Apparently, Jesus is in some way opening God's rule to the Gentiles.

The connection between the temple incident and the story that frames it (the strange account of the cursing of the fig tree in 11:12-14, 20-25) will be difficult to grasp at this point. But the contrast between the unfruitful tree and the promise Jesus gives in verses 22-25 suggests that while faithlessness bears no fruit, faith can move mountains!

The statement in 11:18 that the chief priests and scribes set out to kill Jesus suggests that his interchanges with the Jewish leaders in 11:27—12:44 signify an irreparable breach between the two opposing camps. In addition, the narrator's comment at 12:12 ensures that the reader will interpret the preceding parable as a condemnation of Jesus' opponents. And the story of the poor widow, who gave "everything she had," creates a sharp distinction between those of sincere faith, who stand for love of God and neighbor (12:28-34), and those who pretend faith but "devour widows' houses" (12:40). The Jesus now on his way to his death is also the compassionate friend of the poor and the one who truly understands the nature of God's coming rule.

Less clear at this point are the implications of Jesus' rejection of the scribes' identification of the Messiah as Son of David (12:35-37), arguing that the Messiah is in fact David's Lord! Jesus has already passed up two opportunities to disclaim the title Son of David, if that were his intention. The movement of the plot, however, is clear. Jesus is on his way to his death, which is very near.

13:1—15:47

13:1-37

Jesus' prediction of the destruction of the temple in 13:1-2 directs attention to the future. Then the disciples' question, put to him as Jesus sits "on the Mount of Olives opposite the temple" (13:3), raises the expectation of information about the end of the age. The first part of Jesus' answer—predictions of tumultuous events and the persecution of his followers, qualified by the disclaimer "but the end is still to come" (13:7)—disconnects the events surrounding the temple's destruction from the actual end of the age. And the narrator's "aside" in 13:14 ("let the reader understand") suggests that the "desolating sacrilege" (an event predicted in Dan 9:2) will be fulfilled in the reader's own time. The point is that Jesus' followers after his death should not be led astray by false prophets and false christs who interpret contemporary events as the actual end of the age.

Jesus' words give not only information, but also encouragement. For he promises that those who endure the trials to come will "be saved" (13:13) and reinforces the point with the reminder, "I have already told you everything" (13:23). Knowledge thus has the function of supporting courage and faithfulness in a time of crisis.

Having made clear that the destruction of the temple is only the prelude to the end of the age, Jesus can now (13:24-28) speak of the actual end: the whole cosmos will be disrupted, but then the Son of Man will return. In light of Jesus' predictions of his death and resurrection, it is clear that he will return in glory at the end of the age. His followers can therefore endure the sufferings ahead in confidence of the final deliverance of those who remain faithful.

The saying about the fig tree (13:28-31) continues the hopeful mood, making clear that the signs just elaborated will indicate the nearness of Jesus' return. The positive image of the tree nevertheless calls back the negative image of the tree Jesus cursed at 11:14, and the

connection between that tree and the temple becomes clear. Like the fig tree, the temple, which was not bearing fruit, had to die!

Jesus has asked his disciples to read the signs of the time and take heart. But immediately there comes a disclaimer. No one, not even the Son, knows the time of the end (13:32). The note of hope thus leads into a solemn injunction to "watchfulness" (13:33-36).

The discourse in chapter 13 combines with Jesus' earlier predictions to "explain" the paradox by referring to his eventual return as the triumphant Son of Man. Yet the disciples' inability to grasp the matter and Jesus' ominous words about the persecution of his followers keep the themes of mystery, paradox, and irony alive. The reader has only a promise, qualified by warnings of grave difficulties that lie ahead. In the present, one must still follow a suffering Messiah by taking up one's cross. No intellectual clarification can unravel the inherent irony of such a proclamation of "good news." But there is that promise by Jesus, whom the narrator has encouraged the reader to accept as Son of God.

14:1—15:47

A reference to the plot of the chief priests and scribes (14:1-2) and the story of the woman who anoints Jesus (14:3-9) bring the focus back to his death. As events unfold and Jesus' death draws near, the theme of the disciples' failure comes to a head. Judas, one of the Twelve, gives the chief priests the opportunity to carry out their intentions (14:20-11), and during the Passover meal, Jesus predicts that they will "all become deserters" (14:27).

Quickly, events bear him out: the disciples sleep while he prays (14:32-42) and then flee when he is arrested (14:50), and Peter denies him three times (14:66-72).

The crowds of people also fail Jesus in the end, in effect pronouncing his death sentence (15:1-15). But there are minor characters who appear momentarily to minister to Jesus and share his suffering: Simon the leper, who has him to dinner (14:3); the woman who anoints him; Simon of Cyrene, who carries his cross (15:21); a group of women among his followers, some of whom had "provided for him" in Galilee, who watch his crucifixion "from a distance" (15:40-41); and Joseph of Arimathea, who provides a tomb (15:46). Their actions appear as examples of "faith, being least, being a servant"[2]—that is, as models of discipleship. And they contrast sharply with the conduct of the Twelve and the crowds, who neither took up their crosses nor followed Jesus. The actions of those around Jesus during his final days thus serve as positive and negative paradigms for action in the postresurrection situation.

The harshest judgment must fall upon the various "authorities." They are cowardly types who fear the reaction of the masses and must arrest Jesus secretly and convict him by false witnesses. Utterly unable to comprehend Jesus' message, they are outright opponents of all that he stands for. Pilate, it is true, makes an attempt to release Jesus. But in the end, he acquiesces to the crowds out of fear (15:14-15). The authorities involved in the arrest, trial, and crucifixion are thus of a piece with the earlier Jewish leaders whose intention in questioning him was always to entrap him, never really to hear him.

The Jesus depicted in these final scenes is in many ways a figure who contrasts with the powerful wonder-worker of the early chapters. He admits to intense agony and prays for deliverance from his fate (14:34-36); he utters a cry of despair from the cross and dies with a cry of pain (15:34, 37). Yet he is resolute and obedient to God's will. He has the strength of silence in the face of false accusations, and he at last makes the open claim to messiahship that leads directly to his condemnation (14:62). In everything, he carries out the intention of God. As he has predicted many things before, now he predicts his disciples' failure but also a reunion with them in Galilee after his resurrection (14:27-28). As he had spoken of his death as a "ransom," at the Passover meal he interprets it in terms of the renewal of the covenant and points ahead to the new community and the rule of God (14:24-25). Even his cry of despair from the cross (15:34) is a quotation from the Jewish Scriptures (Ps 22:1).

Here again, we encounter the irony that has pervaded the story. Jesus, the powerful wonder-worker, suffers a humiliating death, yet he wins a moral victory in facing it courageously, fulfilling his mandate from God. The Roman centurion's words at the cross, in fact, provide a confirmation of the victory: "Truly this man was God's Son!" (15:39).

We should not, however, miss the paradox and irony in the centurion's declaration. Just when Jesus' weakness and helplessness become most apparent, someone is finally able

to understand fully who he is. He has suffered humiliation and death, and we quickly
learn that he is buried (15:46), so the note
of tragedy is real. Yet Jesus has predicted his
resurrection and triumphant return, and the
reader has learned to trust his predictions. At
his death, moreover, there are signs of God's
reading of this tragic event: the darkness cov-
ering the land and the rending of the temple
veil (15:33, 38), which suggests the renewal of
the covenant to include Gentiles. Despite the
solemnity of the moment, one can read on in
the hope that Jesus' victory is more than the
merely moral victory of the one who dies nobly
in an ultimately lost cause. The paradox must
be unraveled, the ambiguity dispelled.

16:1-8

The reader's hopes are immediately raised.
The women come early Sunday morning to
anoint the body that was buried Friday after-
noon. But the tomb is empty! And a mysterious young man in white proclaims Jesus'
resurrection, reminding the women of Jesus'
promise that he will "go ahead of" his followers to Galilee. However, the women flee in
astonishment and, ignoring the command of
the mysterious figure, tell no one about what
has happened, "for they were afraid." On this
ambiguous note, the Gospel ends abruptly.[3]
Where *now* does the reader stand?

The implication is that Jesus has in fact

FIG. 5.4   Crucifixion scene from the bronze doors of St. Mary's Cathedral in Hildesheim, Germany. Photo © Foto Marburg / Art Resource, NY.

been raised. But there are no resurrection appearances, and we hear nothing about the establishment of the postresurrection community. The Twelve have vanished from the story, and the last accounts we had of them involved their desertion or betrayal of him. Only the women among his followers stood by him, and it is appropriate that they witness the empty tomb. But in the end, they were too fearful to carry out their task.

Ultimately, the reader stands in ambiguity, caught between hope and fear—precisely where human beings often find themselves as they struggle in the midst of life's difficulties. This ambiguity, however, is not a void. Jesus has made promises, and the reader has "heard" them. He has performed wonders, and the reader has "seen" them.

True, the story has involved dashed hopes and stark tragedy. But it has also given encouragement, through the story of how Jesus met his own fate, for choosing hope rather than fear in the face of difficult circumstances. In the ambiguity that prevails at the end, one can now think back to the theme of secrecy at the beginning of the story. In the context of his powerful deeds, Jesus commands secrecy about his messiahship. Facing death, however, he openly asserts his identity, and at his death, the centurion recognizes him as Son of God. We are thus invited to apprehend Jesus' identity in a paradoxical way—to see in his "weakness" the power of God, to see in his "failure" God's way of ransoming the world, and to see in the ambiguous witness of the empty tomb a sign of ultimate victory. Jesus kept his identity secret in the beginning because it was only in

light of his death that the meaning of his messiahship could be rightly understood.

A question remains, however. If even the women who witness the empty tomb do not pick up the task of witnessing, then is there anyone else equipped to do so? "Of course there is," Mary Ann Tolbert comments: "the audience itself."[4] The narrator's abrupt ending thus contains an implicit demand upon those who read it, a call to tell again the story that has just been read—that is, to be themselves the "good soil" in which the gospel message takes root.

Summary

In the early chapters of Mark, Jesus appears as the powerful, miracle-working Son of God who heals illnesses, casts out demons, manifests sovereignty over nature, and even raises the dead. Strangely, however, he seeks to keep his identity secret. He silences demons who identify him and tells obscure parables so that outsiders will not understand. However, he also gathers disciples, trying to teach them "the secret of the kingdom of God" (4:11), their and reveals to them the meaning of both his messiahship and the discipleship: both entail suffering, rather than the triumph that might be suggested by his powerful deeds. But in the end, they desert him in his hour of need, and the Gospel ends with the ambiguous story of the empty tomb and the failure of the women to tell the story of his resurrection. Still, the reader has witnessed Jesus' deeds and heard his words of promise. And in contrast to the failed disciples, positive models of courageous witness have appeared along the way—Jesus himself, the earlier actions of the women, and the "little people" who served Jesus in his hour of need. So the challenge is this: Will those who read the story be willing to follow a Messiah who walks the way of the cross?

Mark and Liberation

In a feminist evaluation of Mark, Joanna Dewey begins by noting that Mark is, "like other Christian writings," a male-centered text. The male disciples are the center of focus throughout the story, and it is only toward the end that we learn "that there were women who had traveled with Jesus in Galilee, who had followed and ministered, and who had come to Jerusalem with him; that is, that there were women disciples." And this belated introduction of the women, she argues, is "too little and too late to modify our imaginative reconstructions."[5]

Nevertheless, Dewey describes Mark as "perhaps the most liberating gospel in the Christian Testament for any oppressed or marginalized group":

> [It] presents a nonhierarchical, non-authoritarian, egalitarian view of community. Women are understood as people in their own right. Children, the weakest in society, are at the center of God's realm. Those with more power in the world are called to serve

rather than rule over those with less power and status. Wealth is viewed as a hindrance to entering God's realm.

In addition, Jesus' habit of ignoring purity regulations "wipes out the discrimination against women that was based on purity codes."[6]

Several scholars find the Gospel of Mark particularly amenable to interpretation through sociopolitical categories. Ched Myers argues that the story of Jesus in Mark presents a call to discipleship that explicitly embraces the social, economic, and political aspects of life.[7] He describes Mark as a "subversive" document that presents an alternative to the existing societal structures. And he finds a challenge to Roman power in the designation of the story in 1:1 as *euangelion*—"gospel," or "good news." Because this term was used in relation to military victories, its application to the story of Jesus challenges the sovereignty of the empire. And the story of the exorcism at 5:1-13 symbolizes the downfall of Roman power. To call the demons "Legion" is to associate them with the legions of Roman soldiers that imprisoned the land, and to have them drowned in the sea is to suggest their destruction in a new exodus. Even the Markan metaphor for discipleship—to take up one's cross—has, in light of the corpses of rebels that hung from Roman crosses along the Palestinian roadsides, a political thrust.

According to Myers, Mark's subversiveness extends to the Jewish establishment. Jesus' activities in Galilee challenge the system of ritual purity and the authority of the leadership, and the parable in 12:1-11 condemns the ruling class in the guise of the evil tenants of the landowner's vineyard. Economic concerns also are evident. Jesus criticizes the scribes at 12:40 because they "devour widows' houses" and condemns the temple in 11:17 because it has become "a den of robbers." Also, over against the exploitative economics of the existing system, Mark presents an alternative economic order based on sharing. This, according to Myers, is the meaning of the promise of the reception of houses, lands, and families at 10:29-31. This new order will not come through military endeavor, however, nor will it simply appear out of nowhere. It will grow slowly, like the seeds at 4:26-32, from a small beginning. It is a revolution from below—nonviolent but thoroughly subversive of the present order.

Free Will, Determinism, and the Power of God

Mark presents Jesus' death as in accordance with God's will, and the notations that the events in the story are fulfillment of scripture lend a predestinarian air to the whole drama. The secrecy theme reinforces this aspect of the story; the fact that Jesus teaches in parables to prevent outsiders from understanding suggests that the course of events is foreordained. Nevertheless, the story has elements that make no sense apart from the assumption of contingency. When Jesus is surprised by his disciples' misunderstanding, the implication

is that he is genuinely trying to communicate with them and that their response is not predetermined. Similarly, the condemnation of Judas for his betrayal implies his freedom to have acted otherwise (14:21)—although it is said in the same breath that Jesus' death is predicted in scripture!

In addition, the story loses its dramatic punch if the actions of the characters have been totally programmed in the mind of God ahead of time. Jesus' struggles with the authorities, the faith of the people who ask for healing, the wavering attitude of the crowds—none of these crucial elements in the action carries any real weight apart from the assumption of contingency. Nor indeed does the pivotal scene in Gethsemane, which implies that Jesus could have acted other than as he did and even suggests that *God* might have acted otherwise, by coming up with an alternative plan.

From a strictly literary point of view, it may be satisfactory to say that Mark is finally paradoxical, combining contingency and predestination in a way that defies logic. The Bible is in fact full of paradoxes such as this, and they probably presented no problem to ancient readers. Twenty-first-century Western readers bring a different world picture to their reading, however, and some interpreters influenced by process thought have suggested we need to bring the ancient world picture into conversation with it if we want to render Mark intelligible and meaningful in our own reflections on reality. Because a sense of free will is an important aspect of our contemporary self-understanding, it might be helpful to ask which is finally more important in Mark: the predestination or the contingency. If we opt for the latter, they argue, we can read Mark as saying not that Jesus' death was predestined but that it became necessary under the circumstances of his rejection.[8]

The theme of predestination overlaps with the problem of God's power. Predestination assumes that God wields power unilaterally, while contingency implies that God's power is "relational"—that it is not utterly coercive, does not utterly control other beings. Certainly, Mark presents God as being in some sense in control of the drama that is Jesus' life. Yet for the most part, God acts only through Jesus and, at the crucial point, not through Jesus' power but through his weakness. In the end, God raises Jesus from the dead, but strictly speaking, this is not a unilateral act, since it was contingent upon Jesus' obedience. Thus, Mark can lead to critical reflection upon the question of God's power as presented in scripture.

NOTES

1. See Mary Ann Tolbert, *Sowing the Gospel: Mark's World in Literary Perspective* (Minneapolis: Fortress Press, 1989), 239–48. In both Matthew and Luke, this scripture is applied to John the Baptist. But in Mark the passage occurs before John's appearance, so it may refer to Jesus.
2. David Rhoads and Donald Michie, *Mark as Story: An Introduction to the Narrative of a Gospel* (Philadelphia: Fortress Press, 1982), 29–30.
3. Some ancient manuscripts contain additional verses that bring Mark's ending into closer conformity with those of Matthew and Luke by depicting Jesus' appearances to various followers. The scholarly consensus, however, is that none of the longer endings belongs to the original versions; they represent the attempts of later copyists to provide a more "suitable" conclusion.
4. Tolbert, *Sowing the Gospel*, 297.
5. Joanna Dewey, "The Gospel of Mark," in *Searching the Scriptures: A Feminist Commentary*, ed. Elisabeth Schüssler Fiorenza (New York: Crossroad, 1994), 470.
6. Ibid., 470–71.
7. Ched Myers, *Binding the Strong Man: A Political Reading of Mark's Story of Jesus* (Maryknoll, N.Y.: Orbis, 1990).
8. William A. Beardslee, John B. Cobb Jr., David J. Lull, Russell Pregeant, Theodore J. Weeden Sr., and Barry Woodbridge, *Biblical Preaching on the Death of Jesus* (Nashville: Abingdon, 1989), chs. 4–5.

STUDY QUESTIONS

1. How does the narrator try to convince the reader of Jesus' identity in Mark 1–5? Describe Jesus' ministry in these chapters. What is the "strange tension" that develops as he carries out this ministry?
2. What is the meaning of the "strong man" story in 3:21-30?
3. Why, according to Mark, does Jesus tell parables?
4. Does Jesus accept Peter's profession of faith in Mark 8? Explain your answer.
5. What distinctive themes hold the section 8:27—10:45 together? What is the specific role and meaning of the two stories of healing the blind?
6. What questions does Mark 13 answer, and what effects might it have on the reader?
7. Where does the ending of Mark leave the reader? Explain why you do or do not think this ending is effective.
8. Evaluate the approaches to Mark discussed in the sections "Mark and Liberation" and "Free Will, Determinism, and the Power of God."

FOR FURTHER READING

Kelber, Werner H. *Mark's Story of Jesus*. Philadelphia: Fortress Press, 1979.

Kingsbury, Jack Dean. *Conflict in Mark: Jesus, Authorities, Disciples*. Minneapolis: Fortress Press, 1989.

Myers, Ched. *Binding the Strong Man: A Political Reading of Mark's Story of Jesus*. Maryknoll, N.Y.: Orbis, 1990.

Rhoads, David, and Donald Michie. *Mark as Story: An Introduction to the Narrative of a Gospel*. Philadelphia: Fortress Press, 1982.

Robbins, Vernon K. *Jesus the Teacher: A Socio-Rhetorical Interpretation of Mark*. Philadelphia: Fortress Press, 1984.

Tolbert, Mary Ann. *Sowing the Gospel: Mark's World in Literary-Historical Perspective*. Minneapolis: Fortress Press, 1989.

Matthew

6

Authorship, Date, and Place of Composition

Second-century tradition attributes the Gospel of Matthew to the former tax collector Matthew (Matt 10:3), one of Jesus' twelve disciples. However, its probable dependence on Mark and its apparent knowledge of the destruction of the temple in 70 C.E. make this highly unlikely. Most scholars think it was written sometime between 80 and 90 C.E. Like its author, its place of composition is unknown, but the most widely accepted theory is that it comes from Antioch in Syria, where it was quoted by a bishop named Ignatius early in the second century.

Points to Look For in Matthew

- Five long discourses of Jesus, each with a distinctive theme

- Emphasis on fulfillment of scripture

- The view that the Jewish law remains in effect, with Jesus as its definitive interpreter

- Radical demands in the Sermon on the Mount (chapters 5–7)

- Centrality of the love commandment and its role as the interpretive key to the law

- Portrayal of Jesus as humble and compassionate

- The church as a central theme

- Severe criticism of the Pharisees

Notes on a Reading
of Matthew

1:1—4:16

The introductory section establishes Jesus' status and sets the stage for his ministry:

— The genealogy (1:1-17) attests his Jewish heritage through Abraham and his messianic credentials through David.

— The stories of his miraculous birth (1:18-25) and baptism (3:13-17) present him as God's Son, and the baptism and temptation (4:1-11) scenes show him to be obedient to God.

— The visit of the wise men (2:1-12) and the reference to Gentiles (4:15) hint at his significance for Gentiles. The portrayal of Herod shows that those in power are not receptive to a new "king of the Jews."

— The quotations from the Jewish Scriptures show that prophecy is being fulfilled and that God is at work in these events. The inclusion of women in the patrilineal genealogy suggests that God works in unexpected ways.

— John the Baptist's call for repentance in the face of the coming rule of heaven (a circumlocution for "rule of God") anticipates Jesus' own message; his condemnation of the Pharisees (3:7-11) casts them as enemies of that rule.

4:17—9:34

The phrase "from that time" at 4:17 indicates a turn in the plot: Jesus begins his ministry, which initially parallels John's, since he preaches repentance in the face of God's coming rule. The account at 4:23-25 combines with the call of the disciples (4:18-22) to create the impression of initial success.

FIRST DISCOURSE
The Ethics of the Rule of Heaven (5:1—7:28)
Jesus delivers his first discourse (known traditionally as the Sermon on the Mount), which concerns the ethics of God's rule.

Significant Aspects of Jesus' Teaching

— The Beatitudes (5:1-11) pronounce blessings associated with God's rule, partly contrasting with John's emphasis on repentance, but the final beatitude envisions persecutions for Jesus' followers.

— Jesus (5:17-19) has come to fulfill the law and the prophets, not abolish them (so the Jewish law remains in effect); verse 20 shows that his followers must demonstrate a higher righteousness than that of the scribes and Pharisees.

FIG. 6.1 Saint Matthew the Evangelist from the Gospel of Ebbo. Photo © Erich Lessing / Art Resource, NY.

— The "you have heard . . . but I say to you" sayings in 5:21-48 demonstrate Jesus' authority to interpret the law, showing that the "higher" righteousness is measured in qualitative rather than quantitative terms. His interpretations intensify and radicalize the commandments, demanding obedience from within.

— Jesus' radical demands include love of enemies and prohibitions of anger, lust, divorce, retaliation, serving of two masters, and judgment of others. Other instructions concern almsgiving, prayer, fasting, and worrying over material goods.

— In 7:12, Jesus summarizes his ethical teaching with the "Golden Rule," stating that "this is the law and the prophets"— that is, that the demand to treat others as you would have them treat you is the heart of the law's commands.

— The discourse concludes with a series of eschatological warnings. The phrase "when Jesus had finished saying things" at 7:28 signals that the discourse is finished.

The discourse represents Jesus' messianic teaching, and chapters 8–9 recount his messianic deeds—primarily healings and exorcisms. But the scribes' reaction to Jesus' exercise of authority in 9:3 and the Pharisees' objection to his eating with sinners and tax collectors in 9:22 add to the negative impression of the Jewish leadership. The reader may now look back and discern two contrasting responses to Jesus. Matthew, like the Galilean fishermen, followed Jesus without a word, but the Pharisees cannot see Jesus' deeds for what they obviously are. To justify his eating with sinners, Jesus quotes Hosea 6:6: "I desire mercy, not sacrifice." Just as the Golden Rule summarizes the law, mercy takes precedence over ritual requirements.

The disciples do not get off without criticism in this section. Jesus refers to them as "you of little faith" when they show fear in the story of the stilling of the storm (8:23-27).

9:35—11:1

In 9:35-38, the narrator summarizes Jesus' activities and also stresses his compassionate nature. The saying on the need for laborers in the "harvest" sets the stage for the second discourse.

SECOND DISCOURSE
The Mission to Israel (10:1—11:1)

Jesus appoints twelve disciples, names them apostles, gives them authority to perform deeds similar to his own, and sends them in mission (10:1-4). The mission is limited to Israel, but the prediction of persecution from Gentiles as well as Jews (10:18) hints at an eventual Gentile mission. At 11:1, the narrator signals the end with the same grammatical construction that closed Jesus' teaching in chapters 5–7: "Now when Jesus had finished."

11:2—12:50

The opposition to Jesus is brought to center stage in two ways. First, his answer to John the Baptist's question from prison leads into his positive evaluation of John, in which he identifies him as his forerunner (11:10). This leads to a criticism of "this generation" for rejecting both John and himself; Jesus pronounces woes on the Galilean cities for failure to repent (11:20-24). Second, Jesus engages in controversies with the Pharisees over healing on the Sabbath (12:1-14), exorcisms (12:22-32), and signs.

In 11:25-28, Jesus praises God for hiding "these things" from the wise and revealing them to infants, implying a contrast between the scribes and Pharisees on the one hand and his followers on the other; in verses 29-30, his invitation to bear his "easy yoke" is an implicit criticism of the burdensome yoke of Pharisaic interpretation. Jesus appears as humble and compassionate, in contrast to the hardhearted Pharisees. By the time Jesus speaks in 12:46-50 of his "true family" as those who do his Father's will, it is clear that the Pharisees do not belong to it.

13:1—16:20

THIRD DISCOURSE
Parables on the Rule of Heaven
versus Satan's Rule (13:1-53)

Jesus delivers his third discourse, built around a series of parables, beside the sea. Between the parable of the Soils (13:2-9) and its explanation, he reveals the reason for parables. Although disciples have the "secrets of the kingdom," he speaks in parables to those outside because they do not understand (not so that they will not understand, as Mark 4:12 has it). But 13:51 shows that the disciples should, and in fact do, understand: "Have you understood all this?" Jesus asks. "They answered, 'Yes.'"

The parables depict a conflict between the rule of heaven and that of Satan. In his explanations of the Soils and the Weeds among the Wheat, Jesus reveals that it is the devil who "snatches away" the seed sown in human hearts (13:18) and who corrupts the wheat field with weeds (13:39). The shorter parables illustrate characteristics of God's rule.

At the end of the discourse, Jesus refers to "scribes trained for the kingdom of heaven" (in contrast to the scribes who oppose Jesus) as "like the master of a household who brings out of his treasure what is new and what is old." The reader will hear this statement in light of Jesus' affirmation of the continuing validity of the law (5:17-20), balanced by his messianic interpretations of it, as well as his words and deeds that herald the dawn of the rule of heaven.

The familiar conclusion formula at 13:53, marking the end of the discourse, leads into a dispute over Jesus' authority (13:54-58): the people in his home area question the source of his wisdom and mighty works. The theme of opposition continues in the story of the death of John the Baptist (14:1-13), which explains why Herod (Antipas) takes Jesus to be John raised from the dead.

Familiar Themes in 14:13—16:19

— Jesus continues to perform mighty deeds: miraculous feedings (14:13-21; 15:32-

39), walking on water (14:22-33), and healings (14:34-36; 15:29-31).

— Jesus argues with the scribes and Pharisees over their traditions, giving his own understanding of the rules of purity (15:1-20).

— Several stories illustrate varying responses to Jesus and degrees of faith. Peter's failed attempt to walk on water results in another accusation of "little faith" (14:31), which contrasts with that of the people in 14:34-36 who are healed by touching his garment and the "great faith" of the Canaanite woman (15:21-28). But the story of walking on water ends with the disciples declaring that Jesus is the Son of God and worshipping him. The reader will understand that this response is appropriate. And all degrees of faith contrast with the attitude of the Pharisees, whom Jesus labels hypocrites in 15:7.

— Although the disciples showed understanding in 13:51, the conversation on the "yeast of the Pharisees" (16:5-12), where Jesus once again uses the term "little faith," shows that it is limited. But when Jesus explains that "leaven" means the teaching of the Pharisees and Sadducees, they do understand. The reader should conclude that faith is a process of learning and growth.

In the climactic scene at Caesarea Philippi (16:13-20), Jesus confronts the disciples with the question of his identity (16:15). Peter's response echoes the disciples' preliminary declaration on the lake but adds to it the term *Messiah*. Jesus' response is positive (in contrast to that in Mark 8:30), and he gives him the symbolic name of Peter, "the rock" (*petros*), and then founds the church on "this rock" (*petra*). He also gives Peter the authority to "bind and loose"—technical terms in the rabbinic vocabulary indicating pronouncement on what is and what is not required by law.

The scene concludes with Jesus' injunction to the disciples "not to tell anyone that he was the Messiah," which recalls subtler notes of secrecy earlier in the story (9:30; 11:25; 12:16).

16:21—20:34

The phrase "from that time on" at 16:21 indicates a shift in Jesus' emphasis and a turn in the plot. He now concentrates on the disciples, teaching them in 16:21-23 and 17:22-23 about his coming death and resurrection. But the disciples' actions are ambiguous. Peter objects to Jesus' suffering (16:21-23), and all three who are present manifest fear when Jesus is transfigured before them (17:6); but they understand when Jesus identifies John the Baptist as Elijah (17:11-23).

FOURTH DISCOURSE
Life in the Church (18:1-35)
Having founded the church and predicted his death, Jesus delivers a discourse on church life (18:1-35), preparing his disciples

for the postresurrection situation. His teachings include humility, illustrated by children; a warning against causing another to sin; encouragement to restore lost members; and forgiveness. In a segment on settlement of disputes, he grants to the church collectively the power to "bind and loose" (18:18), earlier conveyed upon Peter, and promises his continuing spiritual presence with the gathered community (18:20).

The conclusion formula at 19:1 marks off the preceding material as a fourth discourse. Much of Jesus' teaching that follows parallels material in the first discourse, but now it is focused more explicitly on the community of believers. Overturning a "concession" in the law, he forbids divorce but (in contrast to Mark 10:11) makes an exception in the case of unchastity (19:1-12). He counsels a rich young man to sell everything and give the proceeds to the poor and then teaches on poverty and riches (19:23-30). The parable in 20:1-15, when read in connection with the mother of James and John in 20:20-27, speaks to the issue of struggles for status in God's rule. Jesus' third prediction of his death in 20:17-19 sets the stage for his entry into Jerusalem, and the healing of two blind men in 20:29-34 both illustrates Jesus' compassion and provides an opportunity for the use of a messianic title: Son of David. The Messiah is about to enter the Holy City—not to triumph, but to die.

21:1—25:46

Dramatic Events and Controversies
in 21:1—22:46

— Jesus enters the city in a triumphant procession, with messianic overtones, and makes a demonstration in the temple (21:1-17). Both the people in the processional and the children in the temple hail him as Son of David.

— He engages in controversy with the chief priests over his authority and tells a series of parables depicting God's judgment on the Jewish leaders (21:8-14).

— He disputes with the Pharisees (22:15-22, 34-46) and the Sadducees (22:23-33).

— When asked about the greatest commandment, he responds with two: love God and love the neighbor. Stating, "On these two commandments hang all the law and the prophets," he makes explicit the hermeneutical principle that has been at work in all his interpretations of the law (22:34-39).

FIFTH DISCOURSE
The Judgment of God and the End of the Age
(23:1—25:46)
In a transitional speech in chapter 23, Jesus denounces the scribes and Pharisees, accusing them of hypocrisy and neglecting "the weightier matters of the law: justice and

mercy and faith" (23:23). He predicts that they will persecute or kill "prophets, sages, and scribes" whom he will send. And in keeping with the parables in the previous chapter, he pronounces that God's judgment against all the injustices of past generations will fall upon the present one. The stage is set for the apocalyptic section of the discourse.

Elements in the Apocalyptic Section

— *24:3-8.* Wars, famines, and earthquakes will be signs of the end of the age, but they must be distinguished from the end itself.

— *24:9-14.* Jesus' followers will be persecuted; the "good news of the kingdom" must spread throughout the world before the end.

— *24:15-28.* Jesus gives instructions for when the final events begin and warnings against false messiahs.

— *24:29-31.* Jesus' return as Son of Man is predicted.

— *24:32-36.* Jesus concludes the apocalyptic section with an injunction to look for signs, followed by a call to watchfulness that qualifies the injunction: "But about that day and hour no one knows, neither the angels of heaven, nor the Son, but only the Father" (23:36).

— *24:45—25:30,* Jesus tells parables that serve as warnings to be watchful as his

followers await the end of the age. The discourse concludes with a depiction of the final judgment, in which the Son of Man will judge persons on the basis of their deeds of mercy (25:31-46).

26:1—28:20

After the conclusion formula at 26:1, marking off the fifth discourse, Jesus refers to the imminence of his crucifixion, and the chief priests and elders plan his arrest (26:3-5). Jesus' words regarding the woman who anoints him not only connect this act to his death but also point beyond it to the mission of the church: "wherever this good news is proclaimed in the whole world" (26:13). With the report of Judas's deal with the high priest (26:14-16), the stage is fully set.

The Final Events

— Jesus observes a Passover meal with his disciples, and his comment at 26:18 underlines what the reader already knows: the meal is a prelude to his death. His predictions of Judas's betrayal (26:20-25), the defection of all the disciples, and Peter's denial (26:31-35) suggest that what is happening is under God's direction. Designation of the bread and wine as his body and blood (26:26-29) points to the later cultic meal of the church as a mode of his presence with his followers after his death. The phrase "forgiveness of sins" reminds the reader that Jesus has spoken of his death as a ransom (20:28), and the reference to the eschatological banquet at 26:29 gives assurance that the ultimate outcome of the tragic events to come will be victory.

As Jesus prays in Gethsemane (26:36-46), the disciples fall asleep. Jesus' predictions are borne out by Judas's betrayal, which leads to his arrest, and Peter's denials of Jesus (26:69-74).

— Jesus answers the high priest's question about his messiahship obliquely, but he predicts the coming of the Son of Man (26:64).

— In a story unique to Matthew, Judas hangs himself (27:3-10).

FIG. 6.2 *The Last Supper* by Sadao Watanabe.

— Brought before Pilate (27:1-2, 11-26), Jesus refuses to answer any questions. Pilate, giving the crowd a choice to release either Jesus of Nazareth or the "notorious prisoner" Barabbas, honors his wife's dream that warned against condemning the innocent Jesus. He tries to persuade the crowd to choose Jesus, but the chief priests and elders stir them up to demand his death. Pilate washes his hands to signify his innocence, and the people respond, "His blood be on us and on our children!" (27:25).

— The soldiers mock Jesus (27:27-31), then he is taken to Golgotha and crucified. An earthquake occurs at the moment of his death; the soldiers are terrified and say, "Truly this man was God's Son!" (27:54). The narrator notes that a group of women who followed Jesus from Galilee are present (27:55-56).

— Jesus is buried (27:57-61), and Pilate, at the suggestion of the chief priests and Pharisees, orders soldiers to guard the tomb for fear that his disciples will steal the body and claim that he was raised from the dead.

— On the morning after the Sabbath, Mary Magdalene and another Mary find the tomb empty. An angel appears, rolls back the stone that sealed the tomb, and shows them that it is empty. Instructed to tell the disciples, they set out to do so and are met by Jesus. They take hold of his feet and worship him, and he instructs them to tell the disciples to meet him in Galilee.

— The guards, who were present at the tomb when the angel appeared, report the event to the chief priests, who bribe them to circulate the story that the body has been stolen.

— The disciples meet Jesus on a mountain in Galilee, where they worship him. He reasserts the authority God has given him and now sends them out on a new mission—no longer restricted to Israel, but to all the world. They are to make disciples; baptize them in the name of the Father, the Son, and the Holy Spirit; and teach them to obey everything Jesus has commanded. Jesus' role as teacher is thus reaffirmed at the very end, as is his promise—made in the church discourse (18:20)—of his abiding presence: "And remember, I am with you always, to the end of the age."

Summary

Matthew's story breaks down into three major parts, separated by the two instances of the phrase "from that time" (4:17; 16:21). Following the introductory section on Jesus' genealogy, birth, and preparation, he begins (4:17) his ministry of teaching, preaching, and performing mighty deeds in Galilee. At 16:21, he begins to teach his disciples about his death and resurrection, and the narrative takes the reader through his ministry in Jerusalem, death, and resurrection. Distributed throughout the narrative are five great teaching discourses on (1) the ethics of the rule of heaven; (2) the mission to Israel; (3) the rule of heaven versus Satan's rule; (4) life in the church; and (5) the judgment of God and the end of the age.

In Matthew, the Jewish law remains in effect, but Jesus is its definitive interpreter, using the love command as the hermeneutical key. In the final scene, his own words are what he urges the missionaries to teach new disciples to obey. Throughout the story, Jesus appears as humble and compassionate, in contrast to the scribes and Pharisees, who are characterized as rigid and hard-hearted. There is a strong sense of fulfillment of prophecy, Jesus' role as the Davidic Messiah is stressed, and the discourse in chapter 10 limits the disciples' initial mission to Israel. Even so, indications of the eventual inclusion of the Gentiles occur throughout, and the final scene envisions a mission to all the world.

Only Matthew among the Gospels uses the word *church*, and a climactic moment in the narrative is Jesus' founding of the new community after Peter's declaration of Jesus' status as Messiah, Son of God. The disciples in Matthew are complex characters, showing understanding at some points but inadequacies at others. They desert Jesus before his death, but they are reunited with him after the resurrection and are entrusted with the task of preaching the gospel to the world.

Issues in the Study of Matthew

Matthew's Community and the Synagogue

Scholars have usually viewed Matthew as the "most Jewish" of the four Gospels. Its positive view of the Jewish law (5:17-20) and the frequent use of rabbinic modes of argument are among the factors that create this impression. Some, however, have found Matthew quite "un-Jewish." Matthew 28:16-20 is a ringing affirmation of the Gentile mission, and the theme of Gentile inclusion is subtly woven into the narrative. Kenneth Clark speaks of a "Gentile bias" in Matthew,[1] and John Meier claims that the author betrays an ignorance of Jewish traditions.[2] Meier argues, for example, that a failure to grasp the Hebrew poetic device of parallelism used in Zechariah 9:9 has Jesus seated upon two animals at the same time at Matthew 21:7.

Such contrasting views are a sign of Matthew's complexity. Clearly, there are tensions within the text. Redaction critics have often claimed that these competing points of view are products of layers of tradition, assigning the heavily Jewish material to an earlier stage. Literary critics, however, insist that we read the text as a coherent whole, and it is difficult to claim that the Jewish Christian material has no real function on the level of the text as it stands. And while some scholars endorse the "Gentile bias" thesis, the majority continue

to think of the author of Matthew as Jewish and the community as predominantly Jewish. As Donald Senior comments, "The gospel's occasional bitter critique of the Jewish leaders can be explained by the rupture between the church and synagogue. And [the author's] alleged 'errors' are extremely subtle" and are more understandable if Matthew was written in the Diaspora.[3]

But has there, in fact, been a rupture between Matthew's church and the synagogue? Recent scholars argue that the sharp distinction between a community "in" or "out" of Judaism is too simplistic. Anthony J. Saldarini has drawn upon the sociological category of deviance to characterize Matthew's group as a marginalized sect within the larger community, on the verge of separation.[4] Others think it is a deviant group that has only recently left or been pushed out of the larger community.

A key question in this debate is whether Matthew's community still practices circumcision. Does the absence of references to it mean that it is simply assumed or that it is no longer practiced? Scholars remain divided on the issue.

The Role of Peter

There is general agreement that Peter plays a special role in Matthew, but not on how this role affects the Gospel's understanding of the church. Traditionally, Roman Catholic interpretation has understood 16:16-19 as representing the founding of the papacy— a reading that Protestants, not surprisingly, have resisted. But few contemporary Catholic scholars would defend this traditional position, and few Protestants still "survey the biblical evidence on Peter with the object of discrediting the papacy."[5] At issue in the current debate is whether Peter symbolizes church leadership or, more generally, discipleship per se. Certainly at 16:16-19, Peter receives certain powers and responsibilities. But are these prerogatives of church officers, or are they the responsibility of the church as a whole?

There is a strong egalitarian strain in Matthew: the power to "bind and loose" conferred on Peter at 16:19 is given to the whole community at 18:18, and 23:9-12 warns against exalting some members above others. Thus, Jack Kingsbury claims that Peter's "primacy" in Matthew is purely temporal—that is, he is the first to confess Jesus and thus becomes the spokesperson for the disciples.[6] Other scholars point out, however, that only Peter is given the "keys" to God's rule, called "blessed," and named as the "rock" on which Jesus founds the church. Thus, they argue, the Matthean emphasis upon Peter is of a piece with other portions of the New Testament (for example, John 21; Luke 5:1-11; 22:31-32; and 1 and 2 Peter) that understand Peter as a symbol of "pastoral leadership."[7]

FIG. 6.3   **Christ handing the law and keys to Saint Peter. Gospel cover from Norvara, Italy.** Photo by Gérard Blot © Réunion des Musées Nationaux /Art Resource, NY.

The Role of Personified Wisdom in Matthew's Christology

In 11:19, Jesus defends both John the Baptist and himself against their critics with the saying "Yet wisdom is vindicated by her deeds." What does he mean by this? Some scholars argue that Matthew has a Wisdom Christology—which is to say, it identifies Jesus with the figure of personified Wisdom, familiar in earlier Jewish thought. Jack Suggs, for example, has argued that a comparison of Matthew and Luke shows that the author revised certain Q passages in order to have Jesus assume the role of Wisdom, so that he speaks *as* Wisdom in such passages as 11:28 ("Come to me, all you that are weary") and 23:34 ("Therefore I send you prophets, sages, and scribes").[8] On this view, Matthew constitutes a major step toward the explicitly incarnational Christology (that is, the notion that Jesus was the embodiment of a preexisting aspect of God) found in the Gospel of John.

Other interpreters, however, think the author has Jesus assume Wisdom's role precisely as a way of avoiding reference to Wisdom herself. Some, notably Frances Taylor Gench, believe that Jesus speaks as God's Son, rather than as Wisdom.[9] And I have argued that there is reason to doubt that a purely literary reading of the Gospel, without regard to the author's redaction of Q, can attest the incarnation motif. But it does seem that the motif of Wisdom's rejection by the world, also found in earlier speculation, has influenced the way Jesus' story is constructed in Matthew.[10]

In an interesting move, Celia Deutsch has refined this debate by stressing the metaphorical character of the Wisdom terminology. On her view, the author leaves aside such traditional aspects of the figure of Wisdom as her role in creation but uses the figure metaphorically to tell us "something about who Jesus is," just as the figure of Jesus also "tells us something about the nature of Wisdom."[11] It is clear, in any case, that personified Wisdom in some way plays into the Christology of the Gospel of Matthew.

Matthew's Theology and Jewish-Christian Relations

Anyone sensitive to the problem of Christian anti-Semitism will read certain aspects of the Gospel of Matthew with some degree of horror: the sweeping denunciation of the Pharisees, the notion of the destruction of the temple as God's punishment, and especially the verse in which the Jewish crowds assume responsibility for Jesus' death: "His blood be on us and on our children!" (27:25). Such thinking has fed the Christian hatred of Jews that contributed so much to the tragedy of the Holocaust. What is found in lesser degrees in other New Testament materials reaches its height in Matthew and John. Thus, Lloyd Gaston argues that Matthew "can no longer be part of the personal canon of many" and that much Christian theology "needs to be rethought after Auschwitz, and one good place to begin is Matthew."[12]

Both Jewish and Christian scholars have addressed this problem in recent years, and a helpful distinction has emerged. It is important to distinguish between a racially based anti-Semitism, which is a clear form of bigotry, and an anti-Judaism that is a religious polemic grounded in theological disagreement. Although a few interpreters find actual anti-Semitism in the New Testament, the majority do not. But Matthew and other New Testament writings do contain severe statements that could be seen as anti-Judaic—that is, condemnatory of the Jewish religion.

New Testament passages have in fact fed both anti-Judaism and anti-Semitism through the centuries. But it is important to place the harsh statements of the New Testament in the context of their ancient environment and its rhetorical conventions. As Scot McKnight notes:

Rhetorically potent language is used throughout the ancient world to erect, fortify, and maintain the boundaries that distinguish one religious community from another or to separate, within the same religious community, the obedient from the disobedient. This form of religious rhetoric is especially prevalent in the Hebrew prophetic tradition that, through this kind of communication, seeks repentance on the part of the sinful.[13]

The last sentence is crucial. The strong language of the New Testament stands clearly in the tradition of the Hebrew prophets who hurled bitter condemnations against their own kings, religious leaders, and people.

This observation is strengthened if we identify with more precision the environment that produced the harsh statements in Matthew. Bruce Malina and Jerome Neyrey trace this level of Matthean tradition to an early period in which the followers of Jesus were clearly a deviant group within Jewish society, a group that had a strong sense of internal identity but was unable to exercise much influence on society at large. In that situation, the Jesus people did what was typical of such groups: they attacked the "enemy," their fellow

FIG. 6.4   **Entrance to the ancient synagogue of Qazrin in the Golan Heights, Israel.** Photo © Erich Lessing /Art Resource, NY.

Jews who remained outside their movement, with charges that fit the anthropological model of "witchcraft" accusations. And, as is evident from Matthew 12:24, their rivals the Pharisees, who for their part were unable to completely counter the Christians' influence, did the same.[14] The whole matter appears in a different light if one accepts the view that the quarrel in Matthew is not between two separate religious communities but between a deviant minority and the majority.

The tragedy is that Christians have often read the polemical statements in Matthew as objective descriptions of the Jewish people as a whole. To do so, of course, is no more valid than to take the Pharisees' charges against Jesus in Mathew 12:24 as a just description of his intentions. And it should also be said that when we read Matthew from a literary perspective, to some extent the Pharisees represent a type of distorted religious consciousness that can exist in any religious community.

Some other aspects of the treatment of the Jews in Matthew may be more troublesome than the invectives against the Pharisees. To hold the Jewish people as a whole responsible for Jesus' death and to speak of God's rejection of Israel can scarcely appear to Jews themselves as anything other than anti-Judaism. But traditional interpretations of Matthew may be in error on both these points. What does it mean that the crowds accept responsibility for Jesus' death on behalf of themselves and their children at 27:25? This verse is traditionally understood as signifying the guilt of the Jewish people as such. Some commentators, however, argue that it means specifically that two gen-

erations are held responsible—the generation contemporary with Jesus and the next one, which suffered the destruction of the temple in 70 C.E. As problematic as this notion might be for modern readers, it is a far cry from condemning all future generations of Jews.

In any case, Matthew's way of dealing with the relationship between Judaism and those who follow Jesus is not the only option the New Testament offers. Paul, for example, presents a very different view, and this alone should encourage one to ask whether a literal acceptance of Matthew's view, however we might interpret it, is a necessary part of a Christian's affirmation.

A Feminist Reading of Matthew

Many scholars have noted that, although for the most part Matthew remains within a patriarchal framework, the presence of women in the patrilineal genealogy represents a partial break with that framework. Elaine Wainwright has, in a number of works, pursued a feminist reading of the Gospel as a whole. With respect to the genealogy, she points out that each of the women who appear in it is "dangerous to the patriarchal system . . . because she is not properly related to a man either in marriage or as a daughter." (For example, Mary the mother of Jesus was not married when she was found to be pregnant, Rahab was a prostitute, and Tamar conceived a child with her father-in-law.) Wainwright goes on to argue that this phenomenon plays up the power of women and functions "as a critique of patriarchy."[15]

Wainwright also finds that at some points, women appear in a more positive light than men. The woman who anoints Jesus at Bethany (26:6-13) shows more understanding of Jesus' destiny than do the disciples, and the faith of the Canaanite woman (15:21-28) overshadows the disciples' "little faith" (8:26; 14:31; 16:8; 17:20). In addition, the Canaanite woman's challenge of Jesus is a dramatic violation of social standards, since it is an intrusion into the male world of public debate.[16] Although all these aspects of Matthew are overshadowed by the Gospel's dominant patriarchal outlook, they set up a tension in the mind of the reader. Women and men in Matthew's community who were resistant to the patriarchal system could have felt empowered by them. Readers today might also make use of them in their hermeneutical reflections as they ask about the relevance of an ancient text to the times in which we live.

Postcolonial Questions

A question of interest from a postcolonial perspective is how the Gospel of Matthew relates to the Roman Empire. For some interpreters, Matthew has shifted the blame for Jesus' death from the Romans to the Jewish people to the extent of creating a pro-Roman perspective. Warren Carter, however, finds significant indications of an anti-Roman stance in Matthew. He views Pilate's washing of his hands, for example, as futile: "A quick hand washing and a few words cannot remove the legal responsibility with which Pilate is charged as governor and agent of Roman power. Nor can they absolve him of his guilt in the murder of an innocent man."[17]

Carter also views the presentation of Jesus in Matthew as a direct challenge to Roman claims. Roman "imperial theology claims that the emperor and empire are the gods' agents chosen to manifest the divine will, presence, and blessing among humans."[18] Against this background, Jesus' titles in Matthew (Christ, King, Son) and his role as the one who brings societal well-being stand as blatant counterclaims to Rome's pretensions. Moreover, in the presentation of Herod in the story of Jesus' birth, "Two systems clash, the imperial and God's," and the imperial system is exposed "as ruthless and murderous. . . . It is not ultimate."[19] Carter also reads Jesus' claim in 28:18 to have received "all authority" from God as yet another challenge to imperial rule: "The verse evokes Dan. 7:13-14, where God gives dominion and reign/empire to one 'like a son of man.' This transfer occurs after a struggle with imperial powers."[20]

Other postcolonial readers disagree, however. Musa W. Dube comments that 28:18 comes "only after the image of a politically harmless Jesus has been established." And she cites as evidence such passages as Jesus' healing of the centurion's slave (8:5-13) at a point in the story when the mission was supposed to be exclusively to Israel; 22:15-22, where

Jesus encourages the payment of the temple tax to Rome; and Pilate's attempt to set Jesus free (27:15-27).[21] As one might expect, Carter reads these passages differently, which shows how it is possible for different readers to find different meanings in a given text.

If we shift our perspective from ancient Rome to colonialism and neocolonialism in more recent times, Matthew 28:16-20 takes on great importance. This passage, where Jesus commissions his disciples to "make disciples of all nations," has been celebrated as the Great Commission, an imperative to win the world for the Christ. In recent years, however, a number of scholars have criticized this passage for what they see as an imperialist attitude: the notion that God wishes all persons in the world to become followers of Jesus. As Dube comments, the passage "advocates imposing sameness on a world of differences, for surely discipling nations to 'obey' all that Christ commanded makes little allowance for diverse teachings of other cultures."[22] The problem is compounded by the fact that Western nations have tended to fuse the Christian faith with Western values, economics, and politics to the extent that, in some cases, Christian missions have been indistinguishable from Western imperialism.

These are serious questions, but another consideration might put them in a different light: Does Matthew as a whole in fact assume that all persons in the world should become Christians? The answer, on one level, is probably yes, insofar as we consider the dominant strains of meaning in this Gospel. However, there are some signs of an undercurrent of meaning that suggest otherwise. For example, a number of commentators have observed that in the depiction of the last judgment in 25:31-46, the criterion for distinguishing between those who gain eternal life and those who do not is not whether they accept Jesus as the Christ but whether they have ministered to needy human beings, with whom Jesus has identified. This is not the only way to interpret the passage, but some who read it this way see it as the basis for hermeneutical reflection on the issue of christological exclusivism.[23]

NOTES

1. Kenneth Clark, "The Gentile Bias in Matthew," *Journal of Biblical Literature* 66 (1947): 165–72.

2. John Meier, *The Vision of Matthew: Christ, Church, and Morality in the First Gospel* (New York: Paulist, 1978).

3. Donald Senior, *What Are They Saying about Matthew?* (New York: Paulist, 1978), 12.

4. "The Gospel of Matthew and Jewish-Christian Conflict," in *Social History of the Matthean Community: Cross-Disciplinary Approaches*, ed. David L. Balch (Minneapolis: Fortress Press, 1991), 60.

5. Senior, *What Are They Saying?* 74.

6. Jack Dean Kingsbury, "The Figure of Peter in Matthew's Gospel as a Theological Problem," *Journal of Biblical Literature* 98 (1979): 67–83.

7. Senior, *What Are They Saying?* 76.

8. M. Jack Suggs, *Wisdom, Christology, and Law in Matthew's Gospel* (Cambridge: Harvard University Press, 1970).

9. Frances Taylor Gench, *Wisdom Christology in Matthew* (Lanham, Md.: University Press of America, 1997).

10. Russell Pregeant, "The Wisdom Passages in Matthew's Story," in *Treasures New and Old: Contributions to Matthean Studies*, ed. David R. Bauer and Mark Allan Powell (Atlanta: Scholars, 1996), 197–232.

11. Celia M. Deutsch, *Lady Wisdom, Jesus, and the Sages: Metaphor and Social Context in Matthew's Gospel* (Valley Forge, Pa.: Trinity Press International, 1996).

12. Lloyd Gaston, "The Messiah of Israel as Teacher of the Gentiles," *Interpretation* 29 (1975): 34.

13. Scot McKnight, "A Loyal Critic: Matthew's Polemic with Judaism in Theological Perspective," in *Anti-Semitism in Early Christianity*, ed. Craig A. Evans and Donald A. Hagner (Minneapolis: Fortress Press, 1993), 55.

14. Bruce J. Malina and Jerome H. Neyrey, *Calling Jesus Names: The Social Value of Labels in Matthew* (Sonoma, Calif.: Polebridge, 1988), ch. 1.

15. Elaine Wainwright, "Matthew," in *Searching the Scriptures: A Feminist Commentary*, ed. Elisabeth Schüssler Fiorenza (New York: Crossroad, 1994), 642–43.

16. Elaine Wainwright, *Shall We Look for Another? A Feminist Rereading of the Matthean Jesus* (Maryknoll, N.Y.: Orbis, 1998, 88.

17. Warren Carter, *Matthew and the Margins: A Sociopolitical and Religious Reading* (Maryknoll, N.Y.: Orbis, 2000, 527.

18. Ibid., 551.

19. Warren Carter, *Matthew and Empire: Initial Explorations* (Harrisburg, Pa.: Trinity Press International, 2001), 57–74 (quotation from 67).

20. Carter, Ibid., 551.

21. Musa W. Dube, *Postcolonial Feminist Interpretation of the Bible* (St. Louis: Chalice, 2000), 130–41 (quotation from 140).

22. Ibid., 138.

23. See Russell Pregeant, *Christology beyond Dogma: Matthew's Christ in Process Hermeneutic* (Philadelphia: Fortress Press; Missoula, Mont.: Scholars, 1978), 115–20.

STUDY QUESTIONS

1. What specific contributions does each of the following passages make to the reader's understanding of Jesus before the beginning of his ministry? (a) the genealogy (1:2-17); (b) the birth (1:18-25); (c) the baptism (3:13-17)

2. Identify as many elements as you can in 1:1—4:16 that stress the Jewish nature of the story being told. Now identify the passages that stress Gentiles. How would you explain the meaning of this dual emphasis?

3. How would you summarize Jesus' teaching in chapters 5–7 (the Sermon on the Mount)? Why do you think scholars refer to Jesus' demands as constituting a "higher righteousness"?

4. What does the discourse in chapter 10 reveal about the role of the disciples? Which aspects of the discourse apply most directly to the postresurrection church?

5. What contrasting views of Jesus are found in 13:52—16:20? What is the significance of 16:13-20?

6. What is the purpose of Jesus' teaching of the disciples in 16:1—18:35?

7. How does the parable (allegory) beginning at 20:1 draw together all the material from 19:1?

8. Give allegorical interpretations of the parables in chapters 21–22. How are they related to the conflicts in which Jesus has been involved?

9. What is the function of chapters 24–25?

10. What is the significance, for the reader, of the behavior of the disciples as Jesus is arrested, tried, and executed?

11. In what ways does 28:16-20 draw together themes from the Gospel as a whole?

12. Compare the treatment of the resurrection in Matthew with that in Mark.

13. Looking back over the entire Gospel, compare Matthew's overall treatment of the disciples with Mark's.

14. Imagine that two of your friends, one of whom is Christian and one of whom is Jewish, are discussing the question of whether the New Testament is anti-Judaic or possibly anti-Semitic. What would you contribute to the discussion?

FOR FURTHER READING

Bauer, David R., and Mark Allan Powell. *Treasures New and Old: Recent Contributions to Matthean Studies.* Atlanta: Society of Biblical Literature, 1996.

Harrington, Daniel J. *The Gospel of Matthew.* Collegeville, Minn.: Liturgical Press, 1991.

Kingsbury, Jack Dean. *Matthew as Story.* Philadelphia: Fortress Press, 1986.

Powell, Mark Allan. *God with Us: A Pastoral Theology of Matthew's Gospel.* Minneapolis: Fortress Press, 1995.

Pregeant, Russell. *Matthew.* St. Louis: Chalice, 2004.

Saldarini, Anthony J. *Matthew's Christian-Jewish Community.* Chicago: University of Chicago Press, 1994.

Senior, Donald. *What Are They Saying about Matthew?* New York: Paulist, 1983.

Stanton, Graham, ed. *The Interpretation of Matthew.* Philadelphia: Fortress Press; London: SPCK, 1983.

Luke-Acts

7

Authorship, Date, and Place of Composition

It is evident that a single author composed the Gospel of Luke and the Acts of the Apostles. Both are addressed to "Theophilus," and Acts 1:1 refers back to a "first" writing, which tells the story of Jesus. The two books, moreover, share a distinctive literary style employing sophisticated Greek; they also exhibit narrative and theological unity. Acts supplements the story of Jesus with an account of the early days of the church, as his postresurrection followers carry the gospel message from Jerusalem into the heart of the Greco-Roman world. Scholars today therefore speak of the combined volumes as Luke-Acts, since they constitute a single, two-volume work. Despite their separation in the New Testament, it makes sense to treat them together.

Second-century tradition identifies the author as Luke, a companion of Paul mentioned in his letter to Philemon (v. 4) and two letters attributed to Paul (Col 4:14 and 2 Tim 4:11). Some scholars accept this tradition, often citing the occasional passages in Acts that shift from the third person to the first person plural (generally referred to as the "we" passages). And because the Luke mentioned in Colossians is called "the beloved physician," a few have tried to document a medical vocabulary in Luke-Acts.

There are good reasons to doubt this tradition, however. A comparison of the portrait of Paul in Acts with what we can learn of him through his own letters shows that the author probably did not have firsthand knowledge of him. As to the "we" passages, they are best explained as a common literary device for drawing the reader into a scene. And as to the supposed medical language, there was in fact no technical medical vocabulary at the time. The author was obviously well educated, had a fine command of Greek, and was familiar with Jewish traditions. He has most often been thought of as a Gentile, but he could have been a Hellenized Jew. Scholars have suggested a number of cities in the Mediterranean world as the place of composition, but there is no compelling evidence for any of them. Luke seems clearly dependent on Mark and reflects a time in the late first or even early second century; the usual estimate is 85 to 95 C.E.

The identity of Theophilus has been the subject of much speculation. Some scholars think he was a Roman official. Others point out that the name means "God-lover" and suggest that the author used it symbolically, as a way of addressing readers who are new or potential Christians. The dedication of historical works to particular individuals, however, was common in the Greco-Roman world. Whether Christian or not, Theophilus was most likely an actual person.

Points to Look For in Luke

- Luke's continuation of the story of God's dealings with Israel

- Themes of God's action on behalf of the poor; repentance for the forgiveness of sins/Jesus' acceptance of sinners; the action of the Holy Spirit; inclusiveness, particularly of the poor, women, and Gentiles; hope for the redemption of Israel; prophets and prophecy; Jesus' innocence; the role of the disciples as witnesses to what they have seen and heard

- The prominence of Jerusalem and the journey motif

- Emphasis on the question of when the end of the age will come

Notes on a Reading of Luke

1:1—2:52

The preface (1:1-4), directed to Theophilus, states the purpose of the writing: to provide an "orderly" account of "the events that have been fulfilled among us" with a view toward establishing "the truth" about the events about to be related. The narrator cites eyewitnesses as the ultimate source of the traditions, but the phrase "handed on to *us*" (rather than to *me*) sounds less like a claim to have known those eyewitnesses personally than a reference to a chain of tradition going back to those witnesses.

Links between the Story of Jesus and the Larger Story of God's Dealings with Israel

— The style of writing imitates that of the Septuagint.

— Three scenes occur in the temple (1:5-24): the prediction of John the Baptist's birth; Jesus' presentation as an infant (2:22-38); and the twelve-year-old Jesus' discussion with the teachers (2:41-52).

— Mary's song (1:46-56) evokes memories of Hannah's song in 1 Samuel 2:1-10 at the birth of Samuel, as well as other scriptural hymns, and of God's mighty acts on behalf of Israel.

— Zechariah's prophecy (1:67-80) is also in a scriptural style and recounts God's blessings, making specific mention of the house of David.

— The theme of prophecy is prominent: not only is Zechariah's speech itself prophecy, but it also predicts that John will be a prophet (1:76); a woman prophet named Anna hails the birth of Jesus in 1:36-38.

— The theme of the gift of pregnancy to an elderly, infertile woman was common in the Jewish Scriptures.

These chapters also establish themes that will be important as the story develops, in addition to prophecy and the mighty acts of God: the action of the Holy Spirit (1:15,

35, 41; 2:25, 26, 27); the forgiveness of sins (1:27); God's action on behalf of the poor and judgment of the rich (1:51-53); the division within the house of Israel that Jesus will bring (2:34-35); fulfillment of the ancient promises to Israel and hope for its redemption (1:54-55, 67-68, 72-75; 2:38). We also see a pattern in which prominent roles are given to women (Elizabeth, Mary, Anna) and stories of men are paired with stories of women: Mary and

FIG. 7.1 *The Annunciation (Ecce Ancilla Domini!)* by Dante Gabriel Rossetti.

Zechariah have long speeches; Simeon and Anna both hail the infant Jesus.

The reader should finish the introductory section with a sense of Jesus' special role in a course of events through which the Holy Spirit is fulfilling the ancient promises to Israel. The time of salvation has come, since Jesus has been born as the Davidic Messiah and Son of God who will establish God's rule. The stories also echo a typical pattern in Hellenistic biographies in which childhood incidents foreshadow greatness, creating the expectation that Jesus will convey great benefits in the manner of emperors and heroes.

3:1—9:50

The narrator signals a new phase of the story in 3:1 by providing a historical context for the ensuing events. The reference to the emperor Tiberius encourages the reader to think not only of Jewish history, but of world history—a point that recalls the earlier indication of the inclusion of Gentiles.

In 3:1-18, John the Baptist appears. Jesus comes for baptism in 3:21-22, and the narrator gives his genealogy, tracing him back through David and Abraham to Adam, signifying both his messianic credentials and his universal significance. Jesus goes into the wilderness to be tested by Satan (4:1-13), after which he comes to his hometown of Nazareth and is rejected in the synagogue (4:16-30).

In the chapters that follow, Jesus performs healings and exorcisms (4:31-41; 5:12-26; 6:6-19; 7:1-17; 8:26-56; 9:37-43), calls his disciples (5:1-11; 5:27-32; 6:12-16), sends them out with the authority to preach and heal (9:1-6), and preaches the Sermon on the Plain (parallel in part to Matthew's Sermon on the Mount). He also performs miracles: the stilling of a storm (8:22-24), the feeding of five thousand (9:12-17), and the raising of a girl from the dead (8:40-56). He tells parables (8:4-15), predicts his death and resurrection twice (9:21-27; 9:43b-45), and is transfigured before his disciples (9:28-36). Just before his second prediction of his death, Peter responds to his question with the declaration that he is "the Messiah of God" (9:18-20).

Reiteration of Themes and Emphases from Chapters 1–2

— John the Baptist fulfills Zechariah's prophecy, preaching repentance for the forgiveness of sins (3:3, 8).

— John's words on sharing (3:11) echo the concern for the poor, and in the synagogue at Nazareth, Jesus reads a scripture passage that proclaims "good news for the poor" (4:18). Jesus expounds on the theme explicitly in 6:20-26, where he begins the Beatitudes with a blessing on the poor and follows with a series of woes upon the rich (vv. 24-25).

— John's words to tax collectors (3:12-13) continue the theme of inclusiveness, and in 5:27-32, Jesus calls Levi the tax collector (parallel to the call of Matthew in Matthew 9:9) as a disciple and defends

FIG. 7.2   The baptism of Christ and the temptation of Christ, from the Psalter of Ingeburg of Denmark.

Photo by René-Gabriel Ojéda © Réunion des Musées Nationaux / Art Resource, NY.

this practice before the Pharisees. Jesus' stories about Gentiles receiving blessings from God in 4:22-28 also extend this theme.

— The Holy Spirit descends upon Jesus at his baptism (3:21-22) and drives him into the wilderness for the testing (4:1-12); the Spirit empowers him as he returns to Galilee, and the scriptural passage he reads begins with "The Spirit of the Lord is upon me."

— Jesus identifies himself as a prophet, and his stories in the Nazareth synagogue about Gentiles involve two Hebrew prophets.

— Jesus' rejection at Nazareth illustrates the division he causes within the house of Israel. This theme continues as Jesus enters into controversies with the scribes and Pharisees (5:33—6:11).

— Jesus' healings and exorcisms signify the dawn of God's rule and its blessings, showing him to be a mighty benefactor and the promised Messiah-Savior.

9:51—19:27

In 9:51, Jesus sets out for Jerusalem. The narrator notes that the time "for him to be taken up" has drawn near, and the interchanges in 9:57-62 point to the metaphorical meaning of Jesus' journey. They are reminders of the cost of discipleship, of "following" Jesus on his way. The disciples' arrogant response to the Samaritans' rejection of Jesus at 9:52-56, however, shows that they still have much to learn. As the narrative unfolds, it becomes clear that the narrator will use the journey (which turns out to take much more time than 9:51 might have suggested) to expand upon Jesus' teachings.

10:1—13:35

The journey motif recedes into the background but comes to the fore in 13:31-35, when Jesus responds to the Pharisees' warning about Herod with the declaration that he must be on his way, because "it is impossible for a prophet to be killed outside of Jerusalem." The saying is also a reminder of the importance of Jerusalem and Jesus' role as prophet.

Contributions to the Reader's Understanding

— The account of the mission journey and return of seventy emissaries (10:1-23), into which Jesus' condemnation of unrepentant cities is inserted, illustrates contrasting responses to Jesus. Jesus and the seventy rejoice at the signs of ultimate victory, but not all who hear the message respond positively. The Beelzebul incident and Jesus' sayings on the return of the unclean spirit and the sign of Jonah (11:14-23) make a related point: Jesus casts demons out, but unless one allows God to fill the empty "space," they will return.

— The parable of the Good Samaritan (following an endorsement of the two great commandments) teaches inclusiveness (10:25-37), and the story of Mary and Martha (10:38-42) redefines women's work and promotes devotion to Jesus' teaching.

— The Lord's Prayer and the discourse that follows it give instructions on how to pray, counsel perseverance in prayer, and give assurance of God's care.

— The saying on the eye as the lamp of the body and the denunciation of the Pharisees (11:33—12:12) promote wholeness in one's devotion, in contrast to external obedience. The story of the healing of a crippled woman (13:10-17) illustrates both Jesus' compassion and the Pharisees' hard-heartedness.

— Jesus' warning against the Pharisees (12:1-12) shows that one's response to him has eschatological consequences. But there is a qualification in 12:10: denial of Jesus is a forgivable offense, but blasphemy against the Holy Spirit is not. In light of the reference to the persecution of the future church in verses 11-12, it appears that those who rejected Jesus during his life will have a second (but final) chance when confronted with Christian preaching.

— The parable of the Rich Fool (12:13-21) reiterates the need for decision and emphasizes the danger of riches, and in 12:22-34, Jesus counsels trust in God rather than worldly goods.

— The theme of preparation for the coming judgment dominates 12:35—13:30, and in 12:49-53, Jesus expounds on his role as one who brings division by demanding a decision for or against him. In all of this, the reader is garnering teaching pertinent to life in the postresurrection situation but also observing Jesus in conflict and on his way to his death. The parables of the Mustard Seed and the Yeast (13:18-20), however, illustrate how God's majestic rule will emerge from seemingly insignificant beginnings.

14:1—19:27

Once again, the journey motif recedes, and this time, it does not reemerge until shortly before Jesus' entry into Jerusalem. In 18:31-34, Jesus predicts his death for the third time, reminding the reader of his destiny in Jerusalem. When he heals a blind beggar in Jericho, the man follows him—symbolizing the journey of discipleship.

Themes in 14:1—18:30

— Jesus' healings (14:1-6; 17:11-19) once again illustrate his merciful and beneficent character.

— Jesus' discourse in 14:7-12 and parable of the Great Dinner in 14:15-24 counsel humility and an inclusive hospitality that shows concern for "the poor, the crippled, the lame, and the blind" (14:13).

The parable of the Pharisee and the Tax Collector also teaches humility. And the theme of poverty and riches appears in the parable of the Rich Man and Lazarus (16:18-31) and in Jesus' encounters with the rich ruler (18:13-3) and Zacchaeus (19:1-9). In 14:33, Jesus demands that those who follow him give up all their possessions.

— The Zacchaeus story also illustrates repentance and forgiveness of sins, and this motif is played out in the parables of 15:1-32: the Lost Sheep, the Lost Coin, the Prodigal Son, and the Pharisee and the Tax Collector.

FIG. 7.3   *The Prodigal Son among Swine* by Albrecht Dürer.

— Negative images of the Pharisees appear in 14:1-6 (the healing of the man with dropsy) and 16:14-18 (Jesus' sayings on the law, God's rule, and divorce), where they are characterized as "lovers of money."

— The healing of the ten lepers teaches thankfulness and praise toward God, and the notation that the one grateful leper was a Samaritan (17:16) picks up on the theme of inclusiveness.

— Jesus' discourse in 14:25-33 plays up the cost of discipleship and loyalty to Jesus as a possible source of family division.

— In 17:20-36, Jesus responds to the Pharisees' question about the time of the coming of God's rule with a dual answer: it is already "among you," but Jesus delivers an apocalyptic discourse that includes a warning not to be misled by false claims.

The travel narrative ends with the parable of the Ten Pounds. At 19:11, the narrator notes Jesus' proximity to Jerusalem and has him tell a parable to dispel the impression that God's rule is "to appear immediately." The image of the nobleman who went away to receive sovereignty over the people stands allegorically for Jesus himself. The story points beyond Jesus' imminent death to his glorious return and indicates that the fulfillment of God's promise will come not when Jesus is in Jerusalem but at the end of history. It also encourages reflection on the actions of the servants as models of good and bad discipleship, and it reaches its climax in a note of judgment. The nobleman's punishment of the citizens who tried to sabotage his reign is the narrator's pronouncement of judgment against those who rejected Jesus.

19:28—24:53

Jesus' entry into Jerusalem at 19:28-44 reminds the reader that Jesus has been presented as the messianic king destined to bring fulfillment of God's promises. But the Pharisees' criticism at 19:39 contrasts with the recitation of the kingship psalm by "the whole multitude of the disciples" in verse 37. The "triumphal entry" will thus appear as ambiguous, fraught with conflict.

Jesus' lament over Jerusalem also clashes with the proclamation of peace in 19:38, which echoes the words of the shepherds at 2:14. Jerusalem does not recognize "the things that make for peace," and Jesus predicts its destruction because it fails to recognize its time of "visitation from God." In 1:68, Zechariah's oracle proclaimed that in Jesus, God had "visited" (NRSV: "looked favorably on") the people for the purpose of redemption. But now the visitation of Jerusalem brings judgment, because the rejection of Jesus is the rejection of God. Jesus brought the real possibility of the restoration of Israel under God's rule, but in failing to recognize him as the messianic king, the people turned down that possibility. Therefore, the peaceful Jesus brings not peace but a sword (12:51-53). But the reader will hope that the peace of God's rule will eventually prevail.

After Jesus' action in the temple in 19:45-48, a series of conflicts arises. The chief priests, scribes, and elders question Jesus' authority (20:1-8), and his allegorical parable, the Tenants, symbolizes God's judgment against them (20:9-18). They try to trap him with a question about paying taxes to Caesar, and when the Sadducees try their own trick question regarding the resurrection of the dead (which they reject), Jesus' answer wins the approval of the scribes. This suggests that even among the Jewish leaders, the rejection of Jesus is not absolute. But after demonstrating from scripture that the Messiah is not subordinate to David, Jesus warns his disciples against the scribes, whose love of status and injustice toward the poor will merit condemnation. Then he contrasts the scribes to the poor widow who gives proportionately more than they do to the treasury (21:1-4). Following Jesus' eschatological discourse in 21:5-36, in which he predicts the destruction of the temple, the chief priests and scribes plot to kill Jesus, and Judas makes a deal with them (22:1-6).

The Final Events in Jesus' Life

— *22:7-30.* At the Passover meal, Jesus institutes the Lord's Supper, criticizes the disciples for their dispute over who is the greatest, predicts his betrayal and death and Peter's denial, and gives instructions on discipleship.

— *22:31-53.* Jesus and the disciples go to the Mount of Olives, where he prays and the disciples fall asleep. Then a crowd comes, led by Judas, and Jesus is arrested.

— **22:54-62.** When Jesus is led to the high priest's house, Peter denies him.

— **22:63-71.** Jesus is mocked, beaten, and brought before the council and questioned, but he gives no direct answers.

— **23:1-25.** Jesus is brought before Pilate, who finds no fault in him, and in 23:6-12 (in a scene found only in Luke), he is brought to Herod (Antipas), who is in Jerusalem at the time. Herod and his soldiers ridicule him and send him back to Pilate, who tries to have him released, but the crowd demands his death.

— **23:26-49.** Jesus is crucified between two criminals. One of them mocks Jesus but is rebuked by the other one, who asks Jesus to remember him when he comes into his rule. Jesus, in a statement that gathers up the theme of forgiveness of sins and acceptance of sinners, replies, "Truly I tell you, today you will be with me in Paradise." As Jesus dies on the cross, his last words are "Father, into your hands I commend my spirit."

— **23:50-56.** Joseph of Arimathea, a righteous member of the council, asks for Jesus' body and buries him, as the women from Galilee look on.

In the account of Jesus' trial and crucifix-ion, the theme of Jesus' innocence emerges. Pilate himself had reached that verdict, and at the death scene, it is reiterated first by one of the criminals with whom Jesus is executed and then by a centurion: "Certainly this man was innocent" (23:47).

The account of the postresurrection events in Luke 24 is extensive. The women from Galilee (now named as "Mary Magdalene, Joanna, Mary the mother of James, and the other women with them") come to the tomb on the first day of the week (24:1-12) and receive the resurrection proclamation from "two men in dazzling clothes." But when the apostles are informed of this incident, they consider the report "an idle tale," although Peter comes to the tomb and finds it empty.

The scene shifts (24:13-35): Two of Jesus' followers, walking to the village of Emmaus, unknowingly encounter the risen Jesus and ironically try to fill him in on the recent events in Jerusalem. After he has documented from scripture that it was necessary for the Messiah to suffer and then enter into glory, and has broken bread with them, they recognize him. Then he vanishes. Back in Jerusalem, they find that Jesus also appeared to Simon Peter. Then he appears in the midst of the disciples and gives proof that he is not a "spirit." They are joyous but only half-believe. So Jesus once again documents the scriptural necessity of his death in terms that more clearly recall his earlier predictions.

Jesus tells the disciples (24:44-49) that they are to preach the message of "repentance and forgiveness of sins," but now specifically in his name, "to all nations, beginning from

Jerusalem," where he commands them to stay until they "have been clothed with power." The disciples are qualified for this mission because they are witnesses of "these things": his deeds, his death, and his miraculous presence with them after his death.

After Jesus is taken into heaven (24:50-53), the disciples return to Jerusalem, where they joyously bless God in the temple. The story thus remains a Jewish story: pious Jews, disciples of Israel's Messiah, await the fulfillment of his promise. Their mission, which will be a mission to all the world, must begin here in the heart of Judaism.

Points to Look For in Acts

— Continuation of themes from Luke, with new variations: God's action on behalf of the poor; repentance for the forgiveness of sins/the acceptance of sinners; the action of the Holy Spirit; inclusiveness, particularly of the poor, women, and Gentiles; hope for the redemption of Israel; prophets and prophecy; innocence (now of the apostles, as they are arrested); the role of the disciples as witnesses to what they have seen and heard

— The prominence of Jerusalem and the journey motif; the role of the city of Rome

— The question of when the end of the age will come

— Speeches in which Peter, Stephen, and Paul express the theology of Luke-Acts

Notes on a Reading of Acts

1:1-26

Referring to the "first book," Acts 1:1-4 points back to Luke 24: Jesus' resurrection appearances, his ascension, and his command to wait in Jerusalem. The passage also expands on Luke 24: Acts 1:6 makes clear that the awaited "power from on high" (Luke 24:49) is the baptism of the Holy Spirit of which John the Baptist spoke (Luke 3:16). Verse 3 discloses (in contradiction to Luke 24) that Jesus remained on earth for forty days after the resurrection, teaching the apostles.

The narrator also uses the term *apostles* here, although other disciples figured in the stories in Luke 24. The reason becomes clear in 1:6-11, the expanded ascension scene: the emphasis is on the apostolic mission. The apostles ask whether he is about to bring the restoration of Israel, but Jesus answers that it is not for them "to know the times or periods" God has determined. And he commissions them to be his witnesses "in Jerusalem, in all Judea and Samaria, and to the ends of the earth." The scene closes with the words of two heavenly figures, pointing to Jesus' eventual return as the completion of God's redemptive activity.

On that note of hope, the narrator proceeds to the story of the reconstitution of the Twelve, symbolic of the twelve tribes of Israel, through the replacement of Judas. The worldwide mission is about to begin.

2:1—8:40

The theme of the Holy Spirit's actions reaches an apex in 2:1-13, as tongues of fire descend on Jesus' followers during the Jewish feast of Pentecost, with Jews from every nation present. The miracle of tongues reverses the confusion of languages that divided the world in the story of the Tower of Babel in Genesis 11. The symbolism is that the mission, empowered by the Sprit, will reunite humankind. Peter then addresses the crowd:

Peter's Speech

— He recounts the story of Jesus, testifying that he and the other apostles were witnesses to all that happened.

— All this was fulfillment of prophecy, according to God's "definite plan and foreknowledge" (2:23).

— He tells his Jewish audience that they killed Jesus through "those outside the law" (the Romans), but God raised him from the dead.

When the crowd is moved by the speech, they ask Peter what to do; he answers by calling for repentance and baptism for the forgiveness of sins. Many respond, and the mission is under way.

Life and Activities of the Jerusalem Community

— The group is adding members rapidly (1:47; 6:7), and the apostles perform many "wonders and signs" (2:43; 3:1-10; 5:12-16).

— The believers share their goods in a communal economy (3:43-47; 4:32—5:11).

— Peter makes another speech (3:11-26), similar to the first. Added emphases are that the people acted "in ignorance" when they put Jesus to death (3:17) and references to Jesus as the "prophet like Moses" (3:23) and his return at the end of the age, which Peter terms "the time of universal restoration" (3:21).

— Peter and John are arrested (4:8-12), and Peter speaks again, now adding that salvation is available in Jesus' name alone (4:12). They are released with a warning not to preach in Jesus' name, but they protest that they "cannot keep from speaking about" what they saw and heard. The entire community prays for boldness (4:23-31), and a reference to God's "plan" (4:28) reinforces the thematic status of this notion: the unfolding events represent the fulfillment of God's promises to Israel.

FIG. 7.4   Pentecost from the Gospel by the painter Simeon of Arces, Yerevan, Armenia. Photo © Scala /Art Resource, NY.

— The high priest and the Sadducees have the apostles arrested, but they are miraculously released and continue preaching. They are brought before the council, but a Pharisee named Gamaliel persuades the council to release them, suggesting that time will tell whether what they are doing is of God (5:17-42).

— A dispute arises between the Greek-speaking Jewish Christians ("the Hellenists") and the Aramaic-speaking Jewish Christians ("the Hebrews") over distributions for the widows. Seven deacons are appointed to attend to the Hellenists' widows, and among them are men named Stephen and Philip (6:1-7).

— Stephen is arrested and charged with blasphemy; false witnesses claim that he taught that Jesus would destroy the temple. He makes a speech (7:1-53) that tells the whole story of Israel, stressing the Israelites' disobedience. Referring to the temple, he proclaims that God "does not dwell in houses made with human hands" (7:48); he ends by accusing the people of continual disobedience to the Holy Spirit and murder (of Jesus).

— Stephen, who is "filled with the Holy Spirit" and has a vision, is stoned to death, forgiving those who kill him. The narrator introduces a man named Saul, who consents to Stephen's death, and then describes Saul's persecution of the church (7:54—8:3).

The preceding events fulfilled Jesus' command to preach in Jerusalem. Now (8:4-8), because of persecution, all members of the community except the apostles flee from Jerusalem. So the second part of the command, to bring the message to "all Judea and Samaria," is fulfilled as those who have fled preach in the surrounding towns and the deacon Philip goes to Samaria, where two events occur. First, hearing that God's word has taken hold there, Peter and John come to continue the work, and they encounter a man named Simon, who tries to purchase the power of the Holy Spirit (8:9-25). In the second event, Stephen meets an Ethiopian eunuch and baptizes him.

9:1—20:38

In 9:1, the focus shifts to Saul (whom we later learn is also called Paul), who has a dramatic conversion experience on the road to Damascus, is accepted by Christians there (by divine direction), and begins to preach in that city. Jews in the city try to kill him, but he escapes and goes to Jerusalem, where (with some difficulty) he is again accepted by the Christians and begins to preach.

The focus shifts again in 9:32, this time to Peter. After a long series of events, Peter preaches to the household of a Roman centurion named Cornelius and some Gentiles accept the message and receive the Holy Spirit (10:34-47). The narrative includes a vision in which Cornelius is told to send for Peter (10:1-9), as well as a vision in which Peter receives divine permission to disregard Jewish

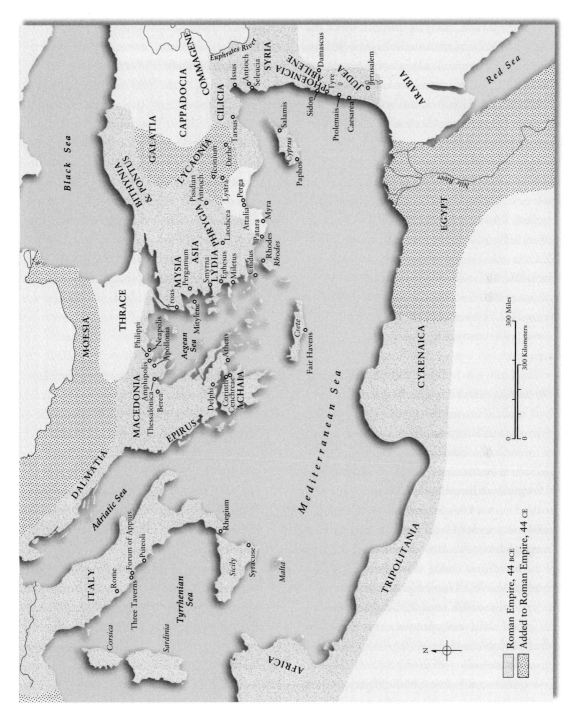

FIG. 7.5   Map of the Roman Mediterranean world, first century C.E.

dietary regulations, thus opening the way for an unhindered Gentile mission (10:9-16). In chapter 11, Peter reports this to the church in Jerusalem, and after some initial objections to his eating with Gentiles, the community decides that "God has given even to the Gentiles the repentance that leads to life" (11:18).

In 11:19-28, the mission of those who had fled Jerusalem continues to the north in Phoenicia, Cyprus, and Antioch, where both Jews and Gentiles accept the word. Back in Jerusalem, James the brother of John is killed, and Peter is imprisoned but is miraculously released. After a notation on the death of Herod Antipas (12:20-25), the focus shifts to Saul.

Paul's Missionary Career

— The Holy Spirit directs the church in Antioch of Syria to commission Saul and Barnabas as missionaries. They preach in Cyprus, Pisidian Antioch, Lystra, and Derbe, and then return to Syrian Antioch. Now referring to Saul as Paul, the narrator recounts his speech in 13:16b-43, which illustrates his approach: rehearsing the history of Israel, Paul proclaims that repentance for the forgiveness of sins is available through Jesus. In 13:36, he mentions God's plan (NRSV: "purpose"). Typically, some Jews and many Gentiles respond, but other Jews reject the mission and try to stop it.

— From Antioch, Paul and Barnabas go to Jerusalem, where the subject of the inclusion of Gentiles apart from circumcision is debated by the apostles and elders (15:1-21). Some Christian Pharisees argue that circumcision is necessary, but Peter and James defend the practice of Paul and Barnabas, and the group decides in their favor. They send a letter to Antioch to this effect, requiring only that converts obey the rules that rabbinic tradition believed applied to all humanity (15:22-35).

— Paul and Barnabas disagree over whether to include Mark, who had earlier deserted their mission, and Paul now travels with Silas and Timothy. Three references to divine intervention (16:6-10) assure the reader that God is directing the course of events.

— In Philippi, they convert a woman named Lydia, and she and her household are baptized (16:11-15). When they cast a "sprit of divination" from a young girl, they are imprisoned because of the complaints of her owners who profited from her fortune-telling. After the missionaries pass up a miraculous opportunity for escape, the jailer is converted (16:16-34).

— They preach in Thessalonica and Beroea, with results similar to those on the first journey, and then come to Athens, where Paul gives a speech. He proclaims that all persons stem from the same ancestor and further defines the scope of God's plan of salvation by alluding to its beginning (in creation, 17:24) and end (Jesus' return and final judgment, 17:30). He speaks of the times before Christ as "the times of human ignorance" and issues a call to repentance (17:16-34). And he reiterates a point from Stephen's speech: "God does not live in shrines made by human hands" (17:24).

— In Corinth, Paul lives with a couple, Priscilla and Aquila, and we learn of his tent-making trade. He gains both Jewish and Greek converts, but opposition from other Jews provokes his declaration, "From now on I will go to the Gentiles" (18:6).

— Having returned to Antioch of Syria, Paul strikes out for Galatia. In 18:24, the narrator introduces Apollos, a missionary from Alexandria who knew only the baptism of John but taught about Jesus. Priscilla and Aquila complete Apollos's instruction in Ephesus, where they had journeyed with Paul. This story leads into an account of Paul's dealings with converts in Ephesus (19:1-7) who had received only John's baptism and knew nothing of the Holy Spirit.

— The account of Paul's healings and exorcisms in 19:11-20 shows the parallel between Paul and Jesus and distinguishes Christian exorcism from a magical approach in which Jesus' name itself carries power.

— The Spirit convinces Paul to go back to Jerusalem and then to Rome. Before his departure from Ephesus, however, a controversy arises: the "Way" has turned so many residents away from "idolatry" that the local artisans who make images of the deities are losing business (19:21-41)!

— In Troas, Paul raises a young boy from the dead, and in Ephesus, he delivers a farewell speech to the elders of the Christian congregation (20:18-35), telling his friends he must go to Jerusalem, never to see them again. He stresses that because he has declared God's whole plan (NRSV: "purpose"), he is innocent of the blood of all who heard him. This will remind the reader of the themes of a "second chance" for Jews and of God's intention to bring salvation to the Gentiles.

Paul journeys by sea to Caesarea, where he stays for several days and encounters a prophet who predicts that Jews in Jerusalem will bind him and hand him over to the Gentiles (21:1-16). Then he goes on to Jerusalem (21:17-40), where he undergoes a rite of purification to combat criticism that he is turning people away from the law. But he is accused of bringing Gentiles into the temple and is arrested. He makes a speech (22:1-29), in which he cites his Jewish origin and relates his conversion experience. The people listen until he mentions his commission to go to the Gentiles; at this, they cry out against him.

Paul's Long Imprisonment

— *22:30—23:11.* Paul is brought before the council, where he states that he has been a zealous Jew, who once persecuted the church, and then relates his conversion experience. He pits Pharisees and Sadducees against each other by claiming that he is on trial "concerning the hope of the resurrection of the dead"; no decision is reached.

— **23:12—24:27.** Because of a plot to kill him, he is sent to Caesarea, where he defends himself before the Roman governor, Felix. Hoping for a bribe, the governor makes no decision but keeps Paul in prison for two years.

— **25:1-12.** When a new governor, Festus, replaces Felix, Paul claims that he has committed no offense "against the law of the Jews, or against the temple, or against the emperor" and then (as a Roman citizen) appeals directly to the emperor. Festus grants the request.

— **25:13—26:32.** King Agrippa (son of Herod Antipas) asks that Paul be brought before him. Paul states that he has belonged to "the strictest sect" of Jews, the Pharisees, and is on trial because of his "hope in the promise made by God" to the ancestors of the Jews (26:4-8), and he again mentions the doctrine of the resurrection. Once again, he tells the story of his conversion (26:12-18). In the final interchange (26:24-29), Paul appears as a model of faithful witness, and Agrippa's words in 26:32 attest Paul's innocence: "This man could have been set free if he had not appealed to the emperor."

— **27:1—28:10.** Paul sets sail for Rome as a prisoner, and along the way, the ship is beset by a storm. He encourages the crew by telling them that an angel appeared to him and said that he must stand before the emperor and all on board would be safe. Later, a shipwreck results in a landing on the island of Malta, where Paul is bitten by a viper but survives, prompting speculation that he is a god.

— **28:11-30.** Paul arrives in Rome, where he lives under house arrest. He calls together the Jewish leaders and in two sessions tries to persuade them to accept his message, making his case from the law and the prophets. He ends with this declaration: "Let it be known to you then that this salvation of God has been sent to the Gentiles; they will listen." In the last two verses, the narrator reports that Paul lived in Rome (still under house arrest), proclaiming God's rule "and teaching about the Lord Jesus Christ" quite openly and unhindered.

Luke-Acts thus ends on a positive note, and the reader may now make a final assessment. Paul is in prison, there are hints that he will die there, and the church faces opposition. But God, who raised Jesus from the dead, stands by those who preach forgiveness of sins in his name. Although many Jews have rejected this message, other Jews have accepted it, as have many Gentiles. And the church, personified in Paul, continues to make that word known, confident of ultimate victory. The mission is on its way "to the ends of the earth," because now it has reached Rome, the center of the empire.

Summary

The Gospel of Luke begins and ends in the temple, and in various ways, it links the story of Jesus to the broader story of God's dealings with Israel. The hope for the redemption/restoration of Israel is a central theme. But the story also makes clear that God's plan includes the salvation of the Gentiles. The Holy Spirit is active throughout the narrative. Both Jesus and John the Baptist appear as prophets, and the theme of prophecy is prominent. John preaches a message of repentance. Jesus does the same, also teaching and carrying out a ministry of compassion, appearing as a great benefactor. His ministry is also one of inclusion, embracing the poor and outcast, women, sinners, and Gentiles. The themes of "good news to the poor" and judgment on the rich are evident throughout the story. Women have prominent roles, and stories of women are often paired with stories of men. The role of the disciples is to witness to all that they heard and saw. Their performance is imperfect, but in the end, they are reunited with Jesus. The account of Jesus' trial stresses his innocence. The resurrected Jesus commands the disciples to stay in Jerusalem and await the power God will send upon them. In the final verses, he ascends into heaven, and the disciples return to the temple.

Acts begins with a reiteration of the ascension story and an account of the days of the early church in Jerusalem, with a focus on the empowerment of the church by the Spirit at Pentecost. The disciples appear as powerful witnesses whose mighty deeds resemble those of Jesus, and the community grows. The story picks up on the theme of poverty and riches by describing a communal economy in the Jerusalem church. The speeches of Peter and Stephen begin to convey an understanding of God's plan of salvation for the world, beginning with Israel, and this understanding is developed further in the later speeches of Paul. The witness of the church spreads from Jerusalem into Judea and Samaria, and then begins to penetrate the Gentile world. Peter's interaction with Cornelius opens the way for a full mission to the Gentiles, and this theme becomes programmatic as Paul is converted and becomes God's primary agent of that mission. His preaching typically results in some Jewish converts, opposition from other Jews, and major progress among Gentiles. Paul returns to Jerusalem and is arrested, despite his efforts to refute charges that he is subverting the Jewish law. After a long imprisonment, during which Paul defends himself by claiming that he is preaching on behalf of the hope of Israel and belief in the resurrection of the dead, he is sent to Rome to await a trial before the emperor. The story ends with Paul under house arrest, still preaching the gospel. The mission, which began in Jerusalem, is now set to extend to "the ends of the earth."

Questions about the Author's Purpose

Should we think of the author of Luke-Acts as a historian? Scholars generally agree that literary sources lie behind Acts, just as (according to the two-document hypothesis) Mark, Q, and perhaps other written sources lie behind Luke. It is equally clear that the author has revised those sources to make theological points. So if we speak of Luke-Acts as a "history," it is not a neutral but very much a "theological" history. The author wrote not in order to communicate factual data but to present the stories of Jesus and the early church as the avenues through which God has worked in the world. Although there is much to learn about the early church from Acts, we may not simply assume the historical factuality of any particular account but must view all material critically.

Many interpreters have noted the emphasis on the innocence of both Jesus and Paul regarding the charges against them and have understood Luke-Acts as a piece of political apologetic. On this interpretation, the author is trying to show Roman officials that the empire has nothing to fear from Christianity. However, not only is it difficult to accommodate the author's theological interests to this narrowly political reading, but some interpreters have questioned whether the author's view of Rome is as conciliatory as this view supposes. Pilate, for example, is hardly a heroic character, even if he did consider Jesus innocent, nor is Felix, who kept Paul in prison in the hope of a bribe.

Other readings of Luke-Acts emphasize the way the author has presented Peter and Paul. Paul appears in Acts as completely at one with the Jerusalem leadership. And it is Peter who makes the initial breakthrough in converting Gentiles and who, along with James, is most vocal in defending the Gentile mission. Judging from Paul's own letters, however, not only did Paul understand himself as commissioned to preach to the Gentiles, but he came into conflict with Peter and the Jerusalem leadership on certain aspects of this matter. Some scholars thus argue that Luke-Acts was an attempt to reconcile the Pauline and Petrine wings of the church or to defend Paul against the attacks of Jewish Christians. A variant of the latter view is that the author was not in fact a Gentile, as has generally been thought, but a Hellenistic Jew who wrote in order to show the validity of the Gentile mission precisely from the perspective of the Jewish Scriptures.

Yet another theory is that the author wrote to combat some form of Gnosticism. Luke 24 emphasizes the physical nature of Jesus' resurrected body, and Acts frequently refers to Jesus as a "man." One can understand all this as refutation of docetic Christology, typical of Gnosticism, just as one can see the emphasis on the apostolic witness as a way of setting the "mainline" church tradition over against "heretical" teachings.

All these readings of Luke-Acts assume that the author was trying to deal with some specific problem, whether in the church or between the church and the empire. But another way of understanding Luke-Acts is to see it as an evangelistic document—that is, as written to convert people in the Greco-Roman world to Christianity, or as instruction for new converts.

Theological Questions

History and Eschatology

Hans Conzelmann's *The Theology of St. Luke*, originally published in German in 1953, was a major force in developing the methodology of redaction criticism. It also put forth an understanding of the purpose and theological perspective of Luke-Acts that has influenced much subsequent scholarship.

According to Conzelmann, Luke-Acts was a response to a crisis of faith within the church. Near the end of the first century, Christians were becoming disillusioned because Jesus' expected return in glory had not taken place, and the author's solution was to offer a revised eschatology. According to this scheme, the end of history should not be expected in the near future. Rather, the present age was but part of a three-period history of God's actions in behalf of human salvation.

The first period was the time of the "law and the prophets," which lasted through the ministry of John the Baptist. The second was the "middle of time"—the time of Jesus, in which Satan was absent and salvation was fully present. The third was the time of the church and its mission to the world. This was the period in which the original readers of

Luke-Acts lived; the author's message to these people was that, rather than expecting deliverance in the near future, they should order their daily lives in accordance with Christian teaching. That is why Jesus tells his disciples to take up their cross "daily" (Luke 9:23): the author presents a call to discipleship for the "long haul"—a message for a church that must learn to settle down and live in the world.

Despite the enormous influence of Conzelmann's views, many recent interpreters

FIG. 7.6 **The Stoa of Attalos II, ca. 150 B.C.E., in the Agora in Athens, Greece.** Photo © Vanni /Art Resource, NY.

have doubted that the writer of Luke-Acts really intended the complex historical periodization (which even breaks Jesus' life down into three phases) that Conzelmann imagined. For them, it is more accurate simply to speak of the author's interest in the theme of promise and fulfillment. Along with doubt about Conzelmann's periodization goes doubt that the delay of Jesus' return was the author's main concern. Scholars disagree as to whether this question was as important for first-century Christians as others have thought. In any case, it seems clear that Luke-Acts contains both an element of "realized" eschatology and a strong emphasis upon a final consummation; what is less clear is whether the author specifically envisions that consummation as lying in the *distant* future.

Jews and Judaism

Many scholars, including Conzelmann, have found a harsh anti-Jewish strain in Luke-Acts. In seeking to make Jesus and his later followers look innocent before the Romans, it is argued, the author put all the blame for the deaths of these martyrs on the Jews. Along similar lines, a typical understanding of the Gentile mission is that it arises specifically out of the Jews' refusal of the message. That is to say, the church preaches to the Gentiles *because* the Jews refuse to hear it.

Luke-Acts certainly attributes guilt to the Jews, but it also stresses that many Jews embraced the Christian proclamation. And although the refusal of the message by some Jews in Acts becomes the occasion for the Gentile mission, it is clear from the beginning of Luke that this mission is part of God's plan.

Many scholars see the church as a kind of "new Israel"—a replacement for "old" Israel. Jacob Jervell, however, has made a good case for a different understanding.[1] Given the emphasis on the loyalty of Jesus and his followers to Jewish institutions, and given the early emphasis on the Gentile mission, it makes sense to see the church more as a "purified" Israel, into which Gentiles are included, than as a new institution.

The Significance of Jesus' Death and Resurrection

A striking feature of Luke-Acts is the apparent absence of any notion of the saving significance of Jesus' death. There is, for example, no Lukan parallel to the description of the meaning of Jesus' death in terms of "ransom" in Mark (10:45) and Matthew (20:28). Jesus' death and resurrection are central to Christian preaching in Acts, as is an emphasis on forgiveness of sins, yet there is no causal connection between the two. The missionaries preach repentance for the forgiveness of sins in Jesus' name, but they never state that it is won by his death. One must therefore ask what precise role Jesus' death and resurrection play in the theology of Luke-Acts.

The answer may lie partly with the presentation of Jesus as a prophet. Robert Tannehill argues that in Luke-Acts, Jesus' death is necessary because persecution and death belong to the prophetic model on which Jesus' role is fashioned.[2] Acts 17:31 may also help answer this question: following a reference to the final judgment, Paul concludes, "And of this [God] has given assurance . . . by raising [Jesus] from the dead." Jesus had offered God's benefits and had preached the coming of God's rule, repentance, forgiveness of sins, and his own glorious return at the judgment. To say that the resurrection constitutes God's "assurance" regarding the judgment is therefore to present it as a confirmation of Jesus' words and deeds.

"The Way"

The central section of Luke describes Jesus' journey to Jerusalem, and the latter part of Acts traces Paul's journey to Rome via Jerusalem. In Acts, the narrator speaks of Christianity itself as "the Way." And in a broad sense, the whole story of God's dealings with Israel is the recitation of God's movement through history. But the definitive element in all this is Jesus' own "way," symbolized in his journey to his death in Jerusalem. Just as the lives of Peter and Paul parallel the life of Jesus, so Luke-Acts calls the Christian to follow in the footsteps of all these who have followed God's way. This means participating in the mission of proclaiming forgiveness of sins in Jesus' name, and it means "following" Jesus through the daily acceptance of one's own cross.

The Rule of God and the Hope of Israel

Some questions remain about the precise nature of God's rule in Luke-Acts. We noted a strong sociopolitical element in the poems in Luke 1—not only an emphasis on vindication of the poor, but also a recognition of the hope for the restoration of Israel. The "material" aspect of salvation appears prominently also in Jesus' teachings and deeds and in the life of the church in Acts. But what becomes of Israel's hope of restoration?

One way to answer this question is to interpret the political component as a false understanding. On this view, the disciples' misunderstanding of Jesus flows from their "nationalistic" view of God's promise to Abraham. Luke 24:21 and Acts 1:6-7 thus appear as reflections of this false view, which Jesus corrects: salvation means life in God's *heavenly* rule.

The problem with this interpretation, as Tannehill shows, is that not only do the poems in Luke 1 endorse the political hope, but Peter in Acts 3:21 "still hopes, and encourages the people of Jerusalem to hope, that they will share in the 'times of restoration of all that God spoke' through the prophets."[3] Thus, when Jesus mourns that Jerusalem does not know "the things that make for peace" in Luke 19:42, he is mourning the loss of a real possibility. That is to say, Jesus' coming to Jerusalem gives to the Jewish nation the genuine option of accepting him, which would in fact lead to peace and justice in the political sense.

One may of course ask how the notion of a real possibility of Israel's repentance can be combined with the notion that Jesus predicted his death as part of God's plan. But this kind of paradox is common in biblical thought.

We may also ask how this earthly political hope fits in with the author's view of salvation as entailing resurrection and eternal life. We should beware, however, of imposing modern distinctions upon the biblical writers' framework. The author could have imagined a hypothetical role for a restored Israel within world history that reaches its end in a general resurrection of the dead followed by an eternity of peace and justice. To ask whether God's rule at that point is "in heaven" or "on earth" may not have been within the writer's purview. The truth is that the apocalyptic tradition in general becomes extremely vague precisely at this point. It is clear enough that for the author of Luke-Acts, God's rule was not some *merely* heavenly/spiritual reality that could be divorced from peace, justice, and material well-being in human society.

Deconstructing Luke-Acts on Poverty and Riches

William A. Beardslee has applied a deconstructionist approach to the theme of poverty and riches in Luke-Acts. When we read this work as a whole, Beardslee notes, we find a rather moderate stance on the question. Although the earliest Christian community is depicted as eliminating poverty altogether through the communal ownership of all goods, it is clear that the narrator does not expect the later churches to imitate this practice in a literal way. The ideal of this earliest community serves rather as an inspiration to a generalized concern for the poor that is to be expressed largely through almsgiving.

When a passage such as Luke 6:20 ("Blessed are you who are poor") is read in light of the whole narrative of Luke-Acts, its radical implications are moderated. A deconstructionist approach, however, refuses to gloss over the tensions between individual strands of meaning and the overall thrust of the work. Thus, Beardslee asks, "Can the hearer's identification with the poor, which the beatitude calls for, be so readily expressed in the limited moves for the poor that Acts describes?" The saying, he notes, resists integration into the whole. And it is the negative function of a deconstructionist approach to note that resistance and upset the attempt to find in the narrative an integrated, consistent point of view.

The positive function, in the present instance, is to enable the reader to hear the radical challenge of the saying itself. When we do that, Beardslee explains, what happens is

> exactly the opposite of finding a place for the poor in a structured society. The structure is broken; the line between the hearer and the poor is erased; we find ourselves open to, at times perhaps even identified with, the subjects of the saying. A vivid, shattering awareness of the possibility that there, among the poor, is the place of happiness or blessedness,

does not produce a plan of action. . . . It does break the established lines of relatedness, by opening up a new and hitherto unrecognized relatedness to the poor. It challenges the structure of power which established a place for the poor.[4]

A Matter of Race in Acts

In a study of Acts 8:26-40, the conversion of the Ethiopian eunuch, Clarice J. Martin shows that Ethiopians were known in the Roman Empire as black and goes on to argue that the eunuch's blackness has thematic value in the Acts narrative as illustrative of the universality of the Christian mission.[5] She also gives reason to believe that Ethiopia was viewed as "the end of the earth," thus supporting the view that the Ethiopian's conversion anticipates the extension of the Christian mission to the world at large (Acts 1:8). A striking aspect of Martin's argument is her documentation of the way in which commentators have routinely dismissed the question of ethnicity: while some have contended that the eunuch's race is indeterminate, others have denied its importance in the narrative. Her study thus illustrates how the historical method is limited by the perspectives of those who practice it.

Suppression of the racial motif began long before the historical method was born, however. As Cain Hope Felder shows, this motif is largely overshadowed in Acts itself by a concentration on the Roman centurion Cornelius as representative of the mission to Gentiles—a role the Ethiopian could conceivably have played. The reason, Felder argues, is the author's acceptance of the notion of "a Roman-centered world."[6] We may thus observe a tension between competing elements in the narrative itself. The author uses a story of a black person to signify inclusiveness but partially disempowers it by giving a related story programmatic status.

NOTES

1. Jacob Jervell, *Luke and the People of God: A New Look at Luke-Acts* (Minneapolis: Augsburg, 1972).
2. Robert C. Tannehill, *The Narrative Unity of Luke-Acts: A Literary Interpretation*, vol. 1, *The Gospel according to Luke* (Philadelphia: Fortress Press, 1986), 286–89.
3. Tannehill, *Narrative Unity of Luke-Acts*, vol. 2, *The Acts of the Apostles* (Philadelphia: Fortress Press, 1990), 55.
4. William A. Beardslee, "Post-Structuralist Criticism," in *To Each Its Own Meaning: An Introduction to Biblical Criticisms and Their Application*, ed. Steven L. McKenzie and Stephen R. Haynes (Louisville, Ky.: Westminster John Knox, 1993), 229–30.

5. Clarice J. Martin, "A Chamberlain's Journey and the Challenge of Interpretation for Liberation," *Semeia* 47 (1989): 105–35.

6. Cain Hope Felder, *Troubling Biblical Waters: Race, Class, and Family* (Maryknoll, N.Y.: Orbis, 1989), 48.

STUDY QUESTIONS

1. In what ways does Luke 1–2 prepare the reader to understand the role of Jesus? In what ways does this material encourage the reader to connect Jesus to the history of Israel? In what ways does it point beyond historical Israel?

2. How does Jesus define his mission in the story at 4:16-30? What links can you find between his definition and the themes in Luke 1–2?

3. How does the narrator play up the theme of decision regarding Jesus in 9:51—13:30?

4. Pick materials in 13:31—19:27 that seem particularly relevant for life in the postresurrection community. At what points does the narrator focus on economic concerns? At what earlier points were such concerns emphasized?

5. In what ways does Jesus, as his death grows imminent, point beyond the disciples' coming failure to their positive role in the postresurrection community?

6. How do Jesus' words on the cross pick up on themes already familiar to the reader?

7. How does the ending of Luke parallel its beginning? Describe the role of the disciples as Jesus defines it in Luke 24.

8. What links can you find between Acts 1 and Luke 24?

9. What is the significance of the dramatic event described in Acts 2?

10. What does the reader learn from the speeches of Peter and Stephen in the early chapters of Acts?

11. What is the significance of the account of Peter's encounter with Cornelius?

12. What is the issue at the "conference" described in Acts 15, and how is it resolved?

13. What does the reader learn from Paul's speech in Athens at Acts 17?

14. How do Jews respond to Paul's preaching? How do Gentiles respond? How does the narrator want the reader to evaluate the progress of the mission?

15. Give a brief description of how Paul eventually comes to Rome.

16. What is the significance of Paul's final speech to the Jewish elders in Rome?

17. Identify the themes that you think are most prominent in Luke-Acts.

18. Was the author a historian? Explain your answer.

19. Assess the various attempts to describe the author's purposes in writing.

20. What seems to be the significance of Jesus' death and resurrection in Luke-Acts?

21. Describe the roles played by women in Luke-Acts.

FOR FURTHER READING

Conzelmann, Hans. *The Theology of St. Luke.* Translated by Geoffrey Buswell. New York: Harper & Row, 1961.

Danker, Frederick W. *Luke.* 2nd ed. Philadelphia: Fortress Press, 1987.

Darr, John A. *On Character Building: The Reader and the Rhetoric of Characterization in Luke-Acts.* Louisville, Ky.: Westminster John Knox, 1992.

Edwards, O. C., Jr. *Luke's Story of Jesus.* Philadelphia: Fortress Press, 1981.

Jervell, Jacob. *Luke and the People of God: A New Look at Luke-Acts.* Minneapolis: Augsburg, 1972.

Juel, Donald. *Luke-Acts: The Promise of History.* Atlanta: John Knox, 1983.

Kingsbury, Jack Dean. *Conflict in Luke: Jesus, Authorities, Disciples.* Minneapolis: Fortress Press, 1991.

Krodel, Gerhard. *Acts.* Philadelphia: Fortress Press, 1981.

Powell, Mark Allan. *What Are They Saying about Acts?* New York: Paulist, 1990.

———. *What Are They Saying about Luke?* New York: Paulist, 1989.

Tannehill, Robert C. *The Narrative Unity of Luke-Acts: A Literary Interpretation.* 2 vols. Philadelphia: Fortress Press, 1986, 1990.

John

8

Authorship, Date, and Place of Composition

Second-century tradition assigned this Gospel to John, son of Zebedee, one of "the Twelve" among Jesus' disciples. And it has often been assumed that the unnamed "disciple whom Jesus loved," who appears late in the story, was the same person. None of this is likely, however, since references to Christians being expelled from the synagogue suggests a late date of composition. Estimates differ, but many scholars place it between 90 and 100 C.E. An alternative suggestion for the author is a "Presbyter John" from Ephesus, although there is no solid evidence that there was such a person.

John was long considered the most Hellenistic of all the Gospels, owing to the author's use of dualistic categories and the Greek concept of Logos. However, the discovery of the Dead Sea Scrolls has documented the presence of dualistic thought in Palestinian Judaism, and the references to expulsion from the synagogue have convinced many scholars that this Gospel comes from a Jewish Christian community. Early tradition associates the Gospel with Ephesus, but various scholars suggest other settings, including Palestine or Syria.

These questions are complicated by evidence that we might not have John in its original form. Chapter 21 appears to be a later addition, and there are at least seeming discrepancies in theological outlook within the main body of the work. For example, a radical emphasis on "realized," or present, eschatology sometimes gives way to statements of the more traditional, futuristic view. And there is some reason to believe that the sequence of materials found in the present text is not that of the original. Thus, many scholars are convinced that the Gospel as we have it has gone through one or more revisions.

Most scholars believe that the Gospel of John came from a highly distinctive, sectarian form of Christianity and that the final author edited it to bring it into greater conformity with a developing "mainstream" theological position. Interestingly, however, one of the most distinctive aspects of this Gospel—its notion of Jesus as the incarnation of the pre-existent Logos—became a central aspect of that "mainstream" or "orthodox" view.

Points to Look For in John

- Emphasis on Jesus' divine nature and preexistence

- Use of irony and double meanings

- Dualisms of light/darkness, above/below, flesh/Spirit

- Emphasis on realized eschatology

- Theme of eternal life

- Jesus' role as revealer

- Jesus' use of "I am"

- Sense of alienation from the world

John's Story of Jesus: A Reading

1:1-18

"In the beginning was the Word"—the Logos. Thus begins the Gospel of John, inviting the reader into a "world" beyond the world of human events and a "time" before historical time. There is an implicit narrative element here, since the initial phrase echoes the beginning of the creation story in Genesis 1. But the focus is on "Logos," which reminds the reader that God creates through the divine Word. The role of Logos in creation also evokes overtones of personified Wisdom, who assumes this role in wisdom literature,[1] as well as fainter echoes of related motifs in Philo and the Stoic philosophers. Told alternatively that the Logos "was with God" and "was God," and is "light" and "life," the reader will associate this Logos with God in a paradox of identity/not-quite-identity. The contrast of light with darkness also introduces a stark dualism of opposing forces.

Verse 6 intrudes abruptly, injecting a narrative element from the world of human events. John (the Baptist) appears, but the interlude is long enough only to establish John as witness to the light, in distinction from the light itself.

The Logos/light reappears in 1:10-11. The light was in the world but rejected by his own people. The reader might think already of Jesus, but perhaps of God's word spoken through the prophets, or even of a divine communication to the world at large. Then the declaration in verses 12-13, that those who believe in the light become children of God, encourages a distinction between "natural" and "divine" birth and a negative view of the world as it is. But then, pointedly—even abrasively, on both Jewish and Hellenistic presuppositions—verse 14 asserts that the Logos became *flesh*! God's eternal Word thus enters human history in the most radical way. Here, in the flesh, the narrator declares, "we have seen his glory." And in the narrator's "we," the reader hears the voice of the Christian community.

An additional reference to John the Baptist and of his subordinate status (1:15) brings us to the end of the introduction. The Son, now named as Jesus Christ, is the source of fullness, grace, and truth. Contrasted with Moses, who brought only the law, he is the one "close to the Father's heart, who has made [God] known." It is now clear that Jesus is the true revealer of God who, as the light of the

world, stands in opposition to the forces of darkness.

1:19-51

Verse 19 brings us into historical time unambiguously, finding John the Baptist under questioning by religious authorities. Four brief scenes reinforce the contrast between Jesus and John, who denies that he is the Messiah or even Elijah or "the prophet"[2] and witnesses to Jesus. John's grounding of his witness outside his own perceptions reaches beyond human testimony to that of God, who has prepared John to recognize the "sign" of the Spirit/dove. The reader must fill in a gap here with prior knowledge of Jesus' baptism, but the significant point is that John identifies Jesus as "Son of God" and "the Lamb of God who takes away the sin of the world" (1:29).

In the third scene (1:35-42), two of John's disciples follow Jesus to the place where he is staying, and we begin to sense the connection between "following" Jesus and witnessing to him. One of the disciples, Andrew, witnesses to his own brother, Simon Peter, concerning Jesus, and this pattern of following/witnessing recurs in the fourth scene as Jesus calls Philip, who in turn brings Nathanael to him.

2:1—4:54

A series of miracles or "signs," notably the changing of water into wine in 2:1-11 and the healing of the official's son in 4:46-54, keep the focus on Jesus' identity. The status of the signs as "evidence," however, is ambiguous. For although the sign manifests Jesus' "glory" and evokes faith from the disciples (2:11), Jesus does not entrust himself to those in Jerusalem who believe in him because of his signs (2:23-25). And then at 4:48, Jesus explicitly criticizes the desire for a sign.

In a subtler fashion, the narrator also encourages the reader to understand the signs in a particular way. On the literal level, the changing of water into wine seems a rather picayune miracle. But Jesus' words at 2:10-11 suggest a deeper meaning: the "good wine," through which Jesus reveals his "glory," symbolizes the qualitative difference he brings to the world. What human beings have formerly settled for is no longer good enough. Such a reading is reinforced in two ways by the story of Jesus' demonstration in the temple. First, the narrator's intrusion (2:21), which explains Jesus' comment on destroying the temple as a reference to his body, sanctions symbolic interpretation. Second, Jesus' action is an act of renewal, parallel to the changing of water into wine.

The reader is also learning to identify *mis*understanding. Not only do the Jews miss the symbolic nature of Jesus' words about the "temple," but Nicodemus, a Jewish official, takes his statement on the new birth—the spiritual birth "from above"[3]—in a crassly literal way (3:4). In 4:11, the Samaritan woman similarly misunderstands Jesus' reference to "living water," giving him an opportunity to speak about "eternal life," and in 4:33 the disciples miss the spiritual meaning of "food."

We can also see that Jesus' words carry double meanings. His explanation of the new birth to Nicodemus employs an analogy between "wind" and "spirit," both signified by the single Greek word *pneuma*. Likewise, the Samaritan woman's misunderstanding results from the fact that the Greek term for "living water" would normally indicate *spring* water.

Jesus' identity is never in doubt. Not only does the prologue identify him as the Logos incarnate, but characters in the story immediately invest him with christological titles, and he openly declares his messianic role at 4:26. This emphasis is reinforced by the treatment of the theme of Jesus' death at this early stage

FIG. 8.2 Jacob's well at Sychar (John 4:5), near Shechem, which is present-day Nablus in Palestine. Photo by Marshall Johnson.

in the Gospel. John the Baptist's designation of Jesus as "Lamb of God" alludes to his coming death and resurrection, as do the reference to his "hour" at 2:4 and the term "lifted up" at 3:14. This theme becomes explicit in 2:21-22, which also provides a glimpse of the postresurrection community.

In the encounter with Nicodemus, the question of Jesus' identity merges with that of what he accomplishes: Jesus not only refers to himself as the Son but also explains that God's gift of the Son brings eternal life. And he goes on to speak of the consequences of how one responds to the Son: those who choose the Son, or the light, receive eternal life, but those who refuse him side with darkness and bring judgment upon themselves.

The characters in the stories represent varying responses. John the Baptist and the disciples are the initial believers, even if their faith needs development. Nicodemus shows great interest, and the Samaritan woman raises the question of his messiahship and even tells others about his miraculous powers. Yet neither makes an explicit declaration of faith. Others believe simply because of the signs, and Jesus remains untrusting of their faith. The Samaritans to whom the woman witnesses, however, go a step further. They believe first because of the woman's testimony but then because of what they hear him say, and then they proclaim him "Savior of the world" (4:42). The implicit point is that one must look through the signs and come to complete faith in Jesus through hearing his own words.

Jesus' condemnation of those who reject him (3:18) underscores the urgency of deci-sion and locates the judgment on unbelief in the present. Similarly, in 4:23, Jesus speaks of the eschatological age in which the Jewish-Samaritan distinction is abolished as "now here." Since Jesus is the light of the world/Logos incarnate, the eschatological realities of judgment/eternal life are already present in him.

The healing of the official's son (4:46-54) reinforces the view that life is present in Jesus. And the faith of the official and his household adds to the impression of Jesus' success in revealing his identity.

5:1—10:42

The picture becomes more complicated in chapter 5.[4] Because of a Sabbath healing, "the Jews" seek to kill Jesus because he "called God his own Father, thereby making himself equal to God" (5:16-18). As Jesus travels back and forth between Galilee and Jerusalem, where he attends Jewish festivals, he faces increasing opposition over the issue of his identity.

The questions put to Jesus give him the opportunity for lengthy discourses elaborating his identity and exposing the misunderstanding of his questioners. And typically their misunderstandings flow from the attempt to understand heavenly things from an earthly perspective. The interchanges are thus packed with ironies that the reader has been trained to detect. "The Jews" search the scriptures to find eternal life, but fail to understand that these scriptures point to Jesus as the bearer of life; they are ironically accused by Moses himself (5:39-47)! They reject Jesus as Messiah because they know his earthly origin, thereby missing his heavenly origin (7:27-29). And when Jesus tells the Pharisees he will return to the one who sent him, we can decode a reference to the resurrection, but the Pharisees ask whether he intends to go into the Dispersion to teach the Greeks. The irony is that Jesus' mission will indeed lead into that larger world—through his death and resurrection.

When "the Jews" accuse Jesus of claiming "equality with God," the implicit charge is attempted displacement of God, or idolatry. Jesus' reply, however, reveals a misunderstanding: "The Son can do nothing on his own" (5:19). In claiming God as his Father, Jesus does not displace but simply *reveals* God. His work is God's work, which is to give life (5:21), and God's work is also to bring about belief in Jesus as revealer (6:29).

When the disciples encounter Jesus walking on the sea in 6:16-21, he replies with the Greek phrase *ego eimi*—"It is I," or "I am," a formula for God's self-revelation in the Septuagint and of Hellenistic deities as well. The allusion becomes even clearer at 8:58, where Jesus says, "Before Abraham was, I am."

This provocative declaration contains a central aspect of the Gospel's claim about Jesus' identity. The "I am" in 8:58 occurs in a conversation with "the Jews who had believed in him" (8:31), and it is to these believers that Jesus says, "You are from your father the devil" (8:44). The implication is that belief in Jesus is inadequate apart from acceptance of his status as incarnation of the preexistent Logos. From one angle and then another, Jesus proclaims

his identity as the one from above. "I am [*ego eimi*] the bread of life" (6:35), he says, and "I am the light of the world" (9:5); and, finally, in a term that evokes scriptural associations with God, "I am the good shepherd" (10:11; see, for example, Ezek 34:11, 15).

All these terms mean in essence the same thing: Jesus is the true giver of life. It is already clear that the life he gives is a present reality, and that theme is reinforced in 5:24. But now Jesus adds a futuristic element: there will be a final resurrection and judgment (5:28-29; 6:39-40). And both aspects of true life, the present and the future, come into play as Jesus uses language alluding to the Eucharistic meal of the church: "Those who eat my flesh and drink my blood have eternal life, and I will raise them up on the last day" (6:54).

This language, together with the contrast between Jesus as the bread of life and Moses' manna, is offensive even to many of Jesus' disciples (6:61). Thus, when some disciples turn away from him at 6:66, we can associate them (and "the Jews who had believed in him" at 8:31) with later Christians who do not share the "high" Christology of the Gospel of John. That would seem to be the implication of 6:70-71: if one of the Twelve could turn out to be a "devil," then others among the believers could also have a false understanding.

The postresurrection situation is also in view in 9:22. The parents of the man born blind "were afraid of the Jews; for the Jews had already agreed that anyone who confessed Jesus to be the Messiah would be put out of the synagogue." It is thus apparent that in John the exclusion of Jesus' followers from the synagogue (which is in the reader's time an accomplished fact) was rooted in the failure of the Jews to grasp who Jesus was.

The false understanding of Jesus is not a matter of simple misperception. Those who fail to grasp who Jesus is do so because they think in earthly terms, and they think in earthly terms because they are "from below" (8:23). But those who accept Jesus are those whom God "draws" (6:44). It might thus appear that salvation is purely deterministic: some have the power of perception, and some do not. In 9:40-41, however, Jesus clears this matter up. When the Pharisees ask if they are blind, Jesus replies, "If you were blind, you would not have sin. But now that you say, 'We see,' your sin remains." So although one's decision about Jesus flows from one's origins (from above or below), Jesus' coming as the light now enables people to *choose their origins*. In the presence of the light, one becomes free to decide whether to see or to step back into the darkness.

In chapter 10, Jesus' conflict with his opponents comes to a head. In 9:38, the blind man's worship of Jesus exemplifies the proper response. Against that background, Jesus launches his discourse on the good shepherd (10:1-18), which leads to an attempt to stone him (10:31) and a renewal of the charge that he claims to be God. Following an argument from scripture, Jesus points back to his "works" as evidence of who he is, but this leads to an attempted arrest.

Following Jesus' escape, the narrator adds that many came to believe in him (10:40-42). We are thus confronted with paradox and irony: many believe, but "the Jews" are now clearly against him. And the reason is clear: he claims equality with God!

11:1—12:50

We now meet a family in Bethany, the sisters Mary and Martha and their brother, Lazarus, who has fallen ill. Jesus' indication that both God and the Son will be glorified by this illness raises expectations (11:4), although it is puzzling that Jesus tarries before proceeding to Bethany. But the explanation comes quickly: correcting the disciples' misunderstanding of his words about awakening Lazarus from his "sleep," Jesus says that Lazarus is dead (11:14). So it is clear that it will be through Lazarus' "awakening" that the glorification will come.

Anticipation blends with foreboding, however; the disciples are reluctant to go to Judea because "the Jews" are seeking Jesus' life. Yet in the end, Thomas articulates their decision: "Let us also go, that we may die with him" (11:16). The statement points ahead to Jesus' coming death but also raises the question of the completeness of Thomas's faith: He is willing to die, but is there a note of despair in his statement?

Jesus' encounter with Martha (11:21-27) is a lesson in faith development. Following her initial expressions of faith in Jesus' power and confidence in the final resurrection, Jesus insists that *he is* the resurrection and the life. And when she makes a strong confession of faith, it is clear that Jesus is correcting a purely futuristic eschatology by presenting "resurrection" and "life" as a present possibility.

The characters in the story, however, do not grasp the point so quickly. Mary and "the Jews" who are with her can only weep. In keeping with the theme of misunderstanding, it is this weeping, not Lazarus's death, that distresses Jesus. Death means nothing in the presence of the one who *is* resurrection and life! Yet "the Jews" show misunderstanding again in their interpretation of Jesus' tears. Even Martha cannot apply her new understanding to the immediate situation but can only voice concern about the odor of the body.

Jesus' comment and prayer (11:40-42) combine to emphasize that the miracle takes place through God's power and that Jesus is sent by God. Then Jesus calls Lazarus, who emerges from the tomb—demonstrating that Jesus brings life, here and now, to those who have faith.

In a monumental ironical twist, the raising of Lazarus—the most dramatic of Jesus' signs—leads directly to the decision of the Jewish leaders to put him to death (11:45-53). They are afraid that Jesus' popularity will lead to a Roman reaction and the destruction of the temple. The high priest argues that it would be expedient for one person to "die for the people," but the narrator intrudes with the ironic truth: the high priest unwittingly prophesies that Jesus' death "saves" the nation in a paradoxical sense that extends to the whole world. This point reappears in 12:19 in the declaration (voiced, ironically, by the Pharisees) that "the world has gone after him."

Jesus' death now looms large. So thick is the air with the plot against him that the people in Jerusalem wonder whether he will show up for Passover. Judas, the betrayer, stands out in the story of Martha's anointing of Jesus (12:1-8), which Jesus interprets in relation to his death. At 12:16, however, we get a glimpse beyond the resurrection to a time in which the disciples look back and interpret everything that has happened in light of scripture.

In 12:20-26, some Greeks tell the disciple Philip that they want to see Jesus. When the message is conveyed to Jesus, he speaks mysteriously of his coming glorification, of losing one's life to find it, and of serving him. The point is that after the resurrection, the "Greeks" will be able to know Jesus by "serving" him!

At 12:27-50, the words of Jesus, the narrator, and a heavenly voice combine to encourage several conclusions regarding Jesus' ministry and coming death. His death is, paradoxically, a victory through which he will draw all humanity to himself; it is simultaneously the judgment of the world, which defeats Satan. Not only will God's name be glorified through Jesus' death, but it has already been glorified, presumably through his total ministry (12:28). The miraculous signs will naturally come to mind, but Jesus emphasizes the saving power of his *sayings* (12:47-48). The point is apparently that Jesus' words, deeds, and death bring salvation by revealing God and confronting the world with the choice between light and darkness, judgment and eternal life. The decision one makes regarding Jesus is a decision about God.

13:1—17:26

In 13:1, Jesus begins to prepare the disciples for his absence. The narrator states that Jesus has *loved* his followers to the end. And now his act of radical humility and his commands to wash one another's feet (13:14) and love one another (13:34; 15:10-12) define the life of the future community. The questions and answers regarding "where" Jesus goes have great importance. That he goes to God (14:2, 28), that he will come again and take the believers with him (14:3), and that in the meantime he will send the Spirit of truth (14:16-17, 26; 15:26; 17:13) are promises of enormous comfort. The predictions of Judas's betrayal and Peter's denial, together with Jesus' own warnings about the hostile world (15:18-20; 16:2), point up the difficulties of discipleship. But the Spirit will serve as Advocate, or Comforter (14:26), and will teach whatever is needed in the later situation. And the one who has loved his followers while he was with them now leaves his "peace" with them.

The hostility of the world defines the need for such empowerment, but 17:20-24 suggests the missional nature of the community. As believers in the reader's time have come to faith through the witness of the original disciples (17:20), so the eventual unity of that community will be a witness to the entire world (17:23). And the subject of that witness is a point that has been stressed from the beginning: Jesus is the one sent from God. This point is emphasized in 14:8-11 in Jesus' exchange with Philip, and at the conclusion of Jesus' prayer, it blends with the love theme: just as to know Jesus is to know God, to know that Jesus is sent by God is to know God's love for the Son and to share love within the community (17:25-26).

The movement toward Jesus' death includes the naming of his betrayer, which leads to the introduction of the disciple "whom Jesus loved" (13:23). This unnamed figure remains mysterious at this point, but the fact that Peter asks him to interpret Jesus' words suggests his importance.

FIG. 8.3 **The Last Supper, ca. 1355–56, from the Four Gospels in Slavonic.** Photo © HIP /Art Resource, NY.

The theme of Jesus' death is entwined with that of the world's hostility. Disciples can expect rejection by the world because Jesus himself was rejected. Jesus, however, promises peace to the followers, who must remain in the world: like him, they "do not belong to the world" (17:16). And the "unworldliness" of the community explains the sense in which Jesus' love commandment is "new," even though it is found in the Jewish Scriptures. The love envisioned is a possibility that comes not from this world but from beyond. To live in its power is to have "eternal life," which the narrator draws into the present by having Jesus define it as a *quality* of life: "And this is eternal life, that they may know you, the only true God, and Jesus Christ whom you have sent" (17:3).

18:1—21:25

The reader comes to the arrest, trial, and crucifixion scenes with a clear image of Jesus as totally in command of the unfolding events, fully knowledgeable of the future, and concerned with the future welfare of the community of believers. The image holds: the narrator stresses Jesus' knowledge of "all that was to happen to him" (18:4), and Jesus' only concern is for his followers (18:8). Before the high priest, he declares that he has always spoken openly (18:20), and he informs Pilate not only of his own divine origin and purpose (18:36) but also of the power "from above" upon which Pilate himself depends. The references to fulfillment of scripture (18:9; 19:24, 36-37)

increase the impression of divine activity in all these events.

Irony now abounds. While the high priest questions the innocent Jesus, Peter—undergoing a less formal interrogation inside the high priest's court—saves his own neck by denying his leader. Confronted with their true king, the Jews demand his death and the release of a robber. As concerned as they are with their law (19:7, 31), they condemn an innocent person, charging the Son of God with blasphemy. And then there are Pilate's words and deeds. His claim to power (19:10) is itself ironic, in

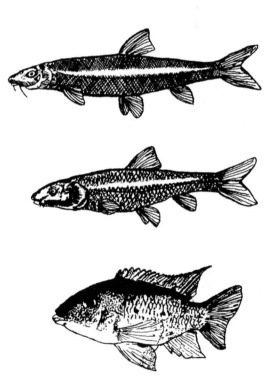

FIG. 8.4 Common fish in the Sea of Galilee. The two upper ones are bottom fish (Kersin and Kishri), feeding on mollusks and caught with lines and hooks. The third fish (tilapia) is a surface fish caught with nets. It is erroneously sold under the name of "Saint Peter Fish."

light of Jesus' reply, as is his mocking designation of Jesus as king, through which he hopes to shame the Jews into relenting (19:14-16). Even more glaring are his cynical attitude toward truth, even as he stands in the presence of it (18:38), and his inscription on the cross (19:19-22). Jesus will indeed be recognized as king by speakers of Hebrew, Latin, and Greek—which is to say, throughout the world.

Both negative and positive models appear in these scenes. If "the Jews" embody a false religious attitude and Pilate illustrates the misuse of secular power, Peter's denial stands for a failure in discipleship. Joseph of Arimathea and Nicodemus, however, appear as ambiguous figures, mixtures of devotion and fear (19:38-42), while the four women who stand near the cross are models of faithfulness. Another positive model at the cross is the "disciple whom [Jesus] loved."

Although Jesus appears fully in command and knowledgeable of the future, his death is real. This point is underscored by the notation that it was unnecessary to break his legs and by the reference to an unnamed eyewitness (19:35).

The process of coming to mature faith is illustrated in the stories of the resurrection appearances. Mary Magdalene, the first to see the empty tomb, thinks the body has been stolen. Later recognizing the risen Jesus, she tries to "hold on to" him (20:17), unable to grasp that in the postresurrection situation, one has a different relationship to him. In the end, however, she becomes a witness. The larger group of disciples is hiding in fear when Jesus encounters them, but Jesus grants them peace and breathes the Holy Spirit upon them (20:22). Thomas proceeds from doubt to the fullest declaration of faith in Jesus in the entire Gospel (20:28), a declaration that recognizes his unity with God as stated in the prologue.

These transformations define the faith of the later community. Jesus' response to Thomas's declaration shows that the faith of the postresurrection believers is in no way inferior to that of the eyewitnesses. And it is to such faith that the narrator now explicitly invites the reader at 20:30.

Despite the climactic sound of 20:30, the story is not finished. The scene at the empty tomb (20:1-10) left the state of Peter's faith unresolved. That story, moreover, suggested a comparison of Peter with the disciple whom Jesus loved. This still mysterious figure not only beat Peter to the tomb but came to faith immediately upon seeing that the body was gone. Thus, at 20:29, the reader could look back and understand him as the truest model of faith for the later community: he alone believed without seeing! But at 20:30, one may still wonder who he is and still have questions about Peter.

Chapter 21 addresses these concerns. The fact that the disciples are once again fishing in Galilee suggests that they still lack full understanding. Thus, Peter's interchange with the risen Jesus serves as another example of the maturation of faith: he learns that love of Jesus means service to the faith community. In addition, Jesus' command to Peter, "Feed my sheep," is a recognition of his position of leadership within the community—a point that

FIG. 8.5 *The Incredulity of St. Thomas*, 1250, by Guido da Como. Pistoia, Italy. Photo © Alinari / SEAT / Art Resource, NY.

draws the Johannine community closer to the larger body of Christians. The parenthetical comment in 21:19, which makes clear that Jesus predicts Peter's martyrdom, also enhances Peter's stature.

Peter also serves as a foil to give information about the disciple whom Jesus loved. His question regarding this disciple sets up the solution of a problem in the community. The story assumes the reader's knowledge of a tradition that Jesus had said that the disciple whom he loved would not die. The narrator, however, not only has Jesus phrase the matter differently but also intrudes with an explanatory comment: Jesus said only that this disciple would "remain until I come" (21:22). This suggests that this disciple has in fact died, and verse 24 may explain the sense in which he remains: he is the one who "is testifying to these things" (21:24)—that is, the source of the traditions on which the story just told is based.

We must therefore recognize a second narrator, who provides a second conclusion to the story. That narrator, looking back over the whole story of Jesus' words and deeds, then adds the final note in the second conclusion: Jesus in fact did so many things the entire world could not contain a record of them!

Summary

Jesus appears in the world as the incarnation of the preexistent Logos, whose mission is to make God known, and the plot revolves around the issue of accepting him in this role. He gathers followers and performs numerous signs, through which his glory as God's preexistent Son is made manifest. He teaches about his own identity, using metaphors such as "light of the world" and "the bread of life that came down from heaven," and he is opposed by Jewish leaders who accuse him of blasphemy. He offers eternal life, which is defined in qualitative terms and is available in the present, to all who believe in him. His teachings are filled with double meanings, and he is continually misunderstood because people think in earthly rather than heavenly terms. The decision with which he confronts his hearers is couched in dualistic terms, such as light versus darkness and flesh versus spirit. The narrative is dotted with accounts of people on faith journeys and illustrations of degrees of faith in Jesus.

The turning point in the plot is Jesus' raising of Lazarus from the dead, which leads to a plot to put him to death. The second half of the story is devoted to Jesus' farewell speeches to his disciples and the account of his arrest, trial, death, and resurrection. Late in the story, the figure of "the disciple whom Jesus loved" appears and is presented as the model of faithfulness and subtly elevated above Peter. In the final chapter, Peter's central importance is affirmed, and the death of the beloved disciple is hinted at in a notation that identifies him as the source of the traditions behind the Gospel.

Historical and Theological Questions concerning John

There has been much debate over whether the author of John used one or more of the Synoptic Gospels, but there is no consensus on this question. John is on the whole a very different story from those told in Matthew, Mark, and Luke, yet at some points, it seems to presuppose elements in them. The question is whether the author drew directly on the written Gospels or simply on a fund of oral tradition.

To the extent that we imagine an independent strain of tradition, we also open up the question of relative historical reliability. Most scholars grant far greater historical credibility to the Synoptics. Few indeed would follow John in placing Jesus' demonstration in the temple at the beginning of his ministry, since such an act would probably have led to his arrest. Some suggest, however, that John might be based on more historically accurate tradition in some instances. A case in point is the date and nature of Jesus' final meal with his disciples. In the Synoptics, it is a Passover meal, but in John, it takes place on the day before Passover. The question is whether the author of John altered tradition to make Jesus' death coincide with the slaughter of the Passover lamb in the temple or the Synoptic tradition modified an earlier version to make the final meal into a Passover celebration.

A particularly intriguing question is the identity of "the disciple whom Jesus loved." If we reject the traditional view of authorship, what are we to make of this character? Some scholars see him as a purely "ideal" figure—that is to say, as a "type" of the perfect follower of Jesus. Raymond E. Brown, however, argues that this "beloved disciple" was in fact a historical figure, although not the son of Zebedee and not the author of the Gospel.[5] An eyewitness to Jesus' ministry, he was a key figure in passing on a variant form of early tradition within the Johannine community.

There is widespread agreement on the existence of such a "Johannine" community, a form of Christianity whose theology is represented in the Gospel and letters of John. Brown has gone so far as to offer a reconstruction of the history of this group. On his hypothesis, the man later called the "beloved disciple" was a member of a community of Jews in or near Palestine who deviated from the mainstream of Jewish teaching only in accepting Jesus as the Davidic Messiah. They eventually included in their fellowship, however, other Jewish Christians who believed that Jesus had been with and seen God and had made God's words known. The acceptance of this latter group brought the Johannine Christians into conflict with other Jews, who accused them of abandoning monotheism and finally expelled them from the synagogue.

The "beloved disciple," according to Brown, exercised important leadership as the community struggled toward a new self-definition. Alienated from the larger Jewish community, the Johannine Christians forged a tightly cohesive group that branded other Jews as children of the devil and came to believe that the eschatological promises were already fulfilled within their own community.

Assuming that it was at this stage that the author wrote, Brown identifies several groups regarding whom the author expresses varying attitudes. The term *the Jews* designates Jewish people who do not accept Jesus as Messiah; for them, the Gospel of John apparently holds out no hope. Use of the broader term *the world* in an equally negative fashion indicates that the community experienced a sense of alienation within the wider Hellenistic environment. And some negative statements regarding John the Baptist suggest that a community of his followers might still have existed outside the church at this time. But the author, more inclined to correct their views than to condemn them, seems to leave open the possibility of their conversion.

The author also seems to take a negative, but not absolutely condemnatory, attitude toward Jews who secretly believe in Jesus but will not say so publicly—perhaps because they blame the Johannine Christians and their high Christology for the tragic split that had occurred. More moderate still is the author's position on non-Johannine Christians, represented by Peter and the other members of the Twelve. While the author clearly asserts the superiority of the "beloved disciple" over Peter—and hence Johannine over "apostolic" (or what eventually became "mainstream") Christianity—the inclusion of the Twelve at the Last Supper places these disciples and their later followers among Jesus' "own," for whom he prays in his final prayers.

On this reading, the story of Thomas's postresurrection doubts may point to an inadequacy Johannine Christians found in the teaching of the early "apostolic" church. "We may make an informed guess," Brown writes, "that the precise aspect missing in the faith of the Apostolic Christians is the perception of the pre-existence of Jesus and of his origins from above."[6] In time, however, the "mainstream" church adopted the Johannine view of Jesus as the incarnation of the preexisting Logos.

Applying Bultmann's Existentialist Interpretation to the Gospel of John

According to Rudolf Bultmann, a modern person cannot, without serious contradiction, believe the New Testament message in a literal way. All talk of the incarnation of a divine pre-existent being, or of Christ's atoning sacrifice, resurrection, and eventual return, is inherently mythological, for it rests upon presuppositions radically at variance with those that undergird the modern turn of mind. Not only that, but the New Testament's eschatological expectations run headlong into the brute fact that Christ's second coming never took place.

The discrepancy between ancient and modern presuppositions was not, however, Bultmann's only justification for his attempt to demythologize the New Testament. He claimed that "there is nothing specifically Christian in the mythical world picture," that it "is simply the world picture of a time now past that was not yet formed by scientific thinking."[7] As evidence that the real message of the New Testament was not bound to this ancient worldview, Bultmann pointed to early

forms of existential interpretation within the New Testament itself. He found steps in this direction in the letters of Paul and the Gospel of John. Most notably, the Gospel of John entailed a demythologizing of the primitive Christian eschatology:

> For John the coming and departing of Jesus is the eschatological event. "And this is the judgment, that the light has come into the world, and men loved the darkness rather than light, because their deeds were evil" (John 3:19). "Now is the judgment of this world, now shall the ruler of this world be cast out" (12:31). For John the resurrection of Jesus, Pentecost and the [second coming] of Jesus are one and the same event, and those who believe have already eternal life.[8]

On Bultmann's view, the Gospel of John makes all talk of Christ's return at the end of history into a symbolic representation of what happens, through faith, in the experience of believers in the here and now. It is clear, for example, that John 14:23 "is not talking about a realistic [second coming] of Jesus":[9] "Those who love me will keep my word, and my Father will love them, and we will come to them and make our home with them."

Eschatology is not the only element of early tradition that Bultmann finds challenged in John. John 16:26-27 explicitly rejects the mythological view of Jesus as a heavenly intercessor between God and humanity: "I do not say to you that I will ask the Father on your behalf; for the Father himself loves you, because you have loved me."[10] And in making Jesus' crucifixion itself already a "triumph over the world and its ruler,"[11] John deprives the resurrection of its significance.

Needless to say, Bultmann's treatment of John opens up many questions and necessitates consideration of one's own presuppositions and hermeneutical perspective.

Applying Jungian Psychology to the Gospel of John

John is a fertile field for psychological interpretation, and Jung's understanding of the Christ-symbol owes much to this Gospel. Five basic concepts in Jungian psychology—collective unconscious, archetype, individuation, ego, and self—will be helpful in understanding the psychological significance Jung saw in this symbol.

In addition to Freud's notion of the unconscious dimension of the individual mind, Jung spoke of a collective unconscious, a fund of psychological patterns shared by the entire human species by virtue of its evolutionary history. Within this collective unconscious are innumerable archetypes, or "tendencies to structure images of our experience in a particular fashion."[12] We cannot know the archetypes directly, but we can identify the specific images through which they express themselves.

Jung's positive view of religion was rooted in his perception that religious symbolism parallels material that is expressed in dreams. Far from the neurotic phenomenon that Freud proclaimed it, religion appeared to Jung as something constitutively human: its symbols tell us something of fundamental importance about who we are in our psychological depths.

Individuation is Jung's term for healthy psychological development, or self-realization. This process takes place in two stages. During roughly the first half of life, a person is faced with the task of developing a strong ego, of distinguishing oneself from parents and environment. In the second half, however, a person will ideally develop a new center of the psyche, which Jung called the Self. "In Jung's model, the Self is the regulating center of the entire psyche, while the ego is only the center of personal consciousness."[13] Persons who have developed the Self have transcended a narrow understanding of who they are and experience themselves as connected to the wider community, human history, and the universe itself. Guiding the process of achieving an "ego-Self axis," a grounding of the ego in this broader psychic center, is the archetype of Self.

The concept of the Self takes psychology to its limits. We cannot truly say what the Self is, for we know ourselves as egos, while the Self remains indescribable. Mysterious source of our own self-realization, it is "indistinguishable from a God-image." Thus, human self-realization "amounts to God's incarnation."[14] To become a fully functioning person, in other words, is to integrate the God-image into one's own being. The psychological value of the Christian myth of the incarnation therefore lies in its expression of the human potential for self-realization.

In Jung's terms, there is a psychological equivalence between incarnation and individuation. To be incarnate is to take on the conditions of human existence, and individuation is the process that defines our humanity. This realization also puts us in touch with the significance of another aspect of the Christ-symbol: "Because individuation is an heroic and often tragic task, the most difficult of all, it involves suffering, a passion of the ego."[15] The lure of self-realization, in other words, is a frightening lure; it is not easy to abandon our narrow and neatly defined patterns of behavior in quest of that elusive, larger Self. We are afraid of losing ourselves altogether. "Through the Christ-symbol," however, we can "get to know the real meaning" of our suffering: it is the gateway toward the realization of our wholeness.

For Jung, Christ constituted an archetype of the Self, which explains the enormous appeal of the Christian message as it expanded into the ancient world. The psychological significance of the Christ-drama is that it symbolizes the transformation of the individual human life by a "higher destiny."[16]

The Johannine Logos and Ecological Theology

The reader who comes to the New Testament looking for direct support for environmentalism is likely to be disappointed. It can hardly be said that the early Christian writings exhibit a developed ecological consciousness.

And later Christian theology in the Western world has put such great emphasis on the theme of God's action in human history that it has tended to neglect the question of God's relation to nature.

The Eastern Orthodox churches, however, have nurtured a mystical theology, based largely upon the notion of the Logos in John 1, that refuses to make such a sharp distinction between nature and history. It is not surprising, then, to find a contemporary Orthodox thinker, Paulos Mar Gregorios, making use of the Johannine notion of the Logos as the basis of an ecological theology:

> Neither art nor literature, neither mountain nor river, neither flower nor field came into existence without Christ and the Holy Spirit. They exist now because they are sustained by God. The creative energy of God is the true being of all that is; matter is that spirit or energy in physical form. Therefore, we should regard our human environment as the energy of God in a form that is accessible to our senses.[17]

Gregorios's proposal, made from a very traditional point of view, entails nothing less than the respiritualization of nature. Process theology obtains a similar result from a nonsupernaturalist perspective. Stressing the interrelatedness of all parts of reality and understanding the universe itself as the "body" of God, it too has a strong ecological emphasis that can be related to John 1.

NOTES

1. See, for example, Proverbs 3:19; 8:22-23; and Wisdom of Solomon 9:1-2 (which also uses the term *logos*); personified Wisdom speaks of herself as having gone out from God's mouth in Ecclesiasticus 24:3.

2. Presumably, the eschatological "prophet like Moses" expected in some Jewish circles on the basis of Deuteronomy 18:15-18; see Raymond E. Brown, *The Gospel according to John I–XI* (Garden City, N.Y.: Doubleday, 1966), 49.

3. NRSV: the Greek word *anothen* can mean either "from above" or "from the beginning," hence the frequent translation "again."

4. The treatment of this section omits 7:53—8:10, the story of the woman caught in the act of adultery, because it does not appear in some of the best ancient manuscripts and was probably not found in the original text of John.

5. Raymond E. Brown, *The Community of the Beloved Disciple: The Life, Loves, and Hates of an Individual Church in New Testament Times* (New York: Paulist, 1979). This view is a departure from Brown's earlier work, *The Gospel according to John I–XI*, in which he argued that John the son of Zebedee was indeed the beloved disciple.

6. Brown, *Community of the Beloved Disciple*, 79.

7. Rudolf Bultmann, *New Testament and Mythology and Other Basic Writings*, ed. and trans. Schubert M. Ogden (Philadelphia: Fortress Press, 1985), 3.

8. Rudolf Bultmann, *Jesus Christ and Mythology* (New York: Charles Scribner's Sons, 1958), 33.

9. Rudolf Bultmann, *Theology of the New Testament*, trans. Kendrick Grobel (New York: Charles Scribner's Sons, 1955), 2:84.

10. Ibid., 87.

11. Ibid., 56.

12. James A. Hall, *Jungian Dream Interpretation: A Handbook of Theory and Practice* (Toronto: Inner City, 1983), 10.

13. Ibid., 11.

14. C. G. Jung, *Collected Works*, 2nd ed., trans. R. F. C. Hull (Princeton, N.J.: Princeton University Press, 1969), 11:157.

15. Ibid.

16. Ibid.

17. Paulos Mar Gregorios, "New Testament Foundations for Understanding the Creation," in *Liberating Life: Contemporary Approaches to Ecological Theology*, ed. Charles Birch, William Eakin, and Jay B. McDaniel (Maryknoll, N.Y.: Orbis, 1990), 40.

STUDY QUESTIONS

1. What does the narrator tell the reader about Jesus' identity in chapters 1–3?
2. How do Jesus' "signs" contribute to the reader's understanding?
3. List ways in which the narrator "educates" the reader in how to read this Gospel.
4. What are the most prominent examples of symbolic language in chapters 5–12?
5. Describe Jesus' interactions with the Jewish people in chapters 5–12. How is Jesus' relationship to God understood in these chapters?
6. What theological points does the raising of Lazarus make, and how does this story contribute to the plot?
7. Give examples of the use of irony in chapters 1–12.
8. What is the significance of Jesus' symbolic action in 13:1-30?
9. What is the primary content of Jesus' farewell discourses and prayer for the church?
10. What can you tell from this Gospel about the identity of the "beloved disciple"? What does his significance seem to be?
11. What is the significance of Mary Magdalene's postresurrection encounter with Jesus? What is the significance of Thomas's encounter with Jesus?
12. What themes are developed in chapter 21?
13. Explain why some scholars doubt that we have the Gospel of John in its original form.
14. Explain how Bultmann employs this Gospel in his demythologizing project, and give your own evaluation of his use of specific passages.
15. How does the Gospel of John contribute to Jung's interpretation of the Self?
16. Explain how some theologians find John 1 useful in reflecting on ecological themes.

FOR FURTHER READING

Brown, Raymond E. *The Community of the Beloved Disciple: The Life, Loves, and Hates of an Individual Church in New Testament Times.* New York: Paulist, 1979.

———. *The Gospel according to John.* 2 vols. Garden City, N.Y.: Doubleday, 1966, 1970.

Bultmann, Rudolf. *The Gospel of John: A Commentary.* Translated by G. R. Beasley-Murray et al. Philadelphia: Westminster, 1971.

Culpepper, R. Alan. *Anatomy of the Fourth Gospel: A Study in Literary Design.* Philadelphia: Fortress Press, 1983.

Dodd, C. H. *The Interpretation of the Fourth Gospel.* Cambridge: Cambridge University Press, 1953.

Kysar, Robert. *John's Story of Jesus.* Philadelphia: Fortress Press, 1984.

Smith, D. Moody. *Johannine Christianity: Essays on Its Setting, Sources, and Theology.* Columbia: University of South Carolina Press, 1984.

Epilogue to Part Two

Diversity within the Canon:
Four Stories of Jesus

The differences in content and theological perspective among the four canonical Gospels make difficult a one-to-one correlation between New Testament passages and definitive Christian belief. The relationship between the New Testament and Christian doctrine would therefore seem to be a more open-ended and imaginative process than many believers have envisioned. The desire for unity and simplicity is strong, however, and many Christians through the centuries have had difficulty with the diversity of the Gospels. A man named Tatian in the late second century produced a conflation of all four Gospels into a single narrative, entitled *The Diatessaron*. It is in some ways remarkable that the church chose to canonize the diverse documents rather than attempt a harmonization such as Tatian's.

Beyond the Canon: Limits of Diversity

The toleration of diversity was not limitless. We know of numerous early Christian writings, which have been termed the "New Testament Apocrypha," that the church rejected. Many of these are usually designated gospels, although not all are narrative accounts of Jesus' life. Some have been completely lost but are mentioned by early Christian writers; others have been preserved only in fragments and/or brief quotations in other works.

Some of these writings are clearly dependent on either the canonical Gospels or the same strands of tradition found in them. They often take the form of lengthy expansions of specific episodes in the canonical accounts. There are, for example, several infancy narratives with extended accounts of Jesus' birth and childhood. And some of the apocryphal gospels are gnostic in orientation. These often take the form of sayings of the risen Jesus, as does the Coptic *Gospel of Thomas*, discussed in chapter 3.

The rejection of the gnostic gospels by the early church has made them a gold mine for flights of fancy throughout the centuries. They have been used to convince gullible readers that a secret tradition, historically accurate and theologically sound, has been maliciously suppressed by a conniving church hierarchy.

It is true that the church suppressed these materials, but that does not mean one can pronounce them to be the authentic Jesus tradition. My purpose is not to defend the canonical tradition but to argue that we can answer the question of historical accuracy only through historical research. And no one familiar with the work done in the past century on the development of the Jesus traditions should be susceptible to the extravagant claims of some of the popular writers on the apocryphal materials. Although some of the works claim an apostle as author, no serious scholar takes such claims at face value.

Although most scholars are convinced that these materials have very little to contribute to our knowledge of the historical Jesus, some do find them useful at a few points. Many scholars think that on occasion the gnostic *Gospel of Thomas* may have preserved a saying of Jesus in an earlier form than did the Synoptic tradition. And John Dominic Crossan has made some limited use of the *Gospel of Peter* in his treatment of the resurrection tradition.[1] These scholars, however, make their cases on the basis of historical criteria, and their claims are debated in an atmosphere of scholarly reflection.

Apart from the question of the historical Jesus, these writings contribute much to our understanding of the diversity of Christianity in the early centuries. The church suppressed them because they were read and had influence.

Some Motifs in the Apocryphal Gospels

Some of the apocryphal gospels exhibit a delight in storytelling, which sometimes takes rather bizarre (if perhaps entertaining) forms. One example is an infancy gospel written under the name of Thomas (but different from the gnostic *Gospel of Thomas*). Expanding on the brief references to Jesus' childhood in Luke, it depicts a divine child with more miraculous power than human concern. Along with stories such as his bringing clay sparrows to life with a clap of his hands and stretching a beam of wood to help Joseph in the carpenter's shop, we also find some that take a less innocent turn. For example, here is what happens when another child bumps shoulders with Jesus: "Jesus was exasperated and said to him: 'You shall not go further on your way,' and the child immediately fell down and died" (4.1).[2]

At other points, the storytelling reflects more pious and theological interests. A book written in the name of James, often called the *Protevangelium of James*, contains several motifs that became a part of accepted tradition. The notation that Mary was a descendant of David reinforces the Davidic lineage of Jesus in the face of the objection that Joseph was not his biological father. And the tradition that Joseph had children by an earlier marriage reconciles the canonical references to Jesus' siblings with the tradition (not mentioned in the canon) of the perpetual virginity of Mary.

This book exalted Mary and by implication held up celibacy as an ideal, thus contributing to movements that became popular within the church. Such was not the case, however, with the emphases found in some other apocryphal gospels, which are clearly Jewish Christian in orientation.

Although Jesus and his first followers were Jews, within a generation the church had become largely Gentile, dispensing with much of its Jewish heritage. But other groups preserved various aspects of that heritage, although doing so cut them off from what eventually became the mainstream movement. Some Jewish Christian communities apparently continued to require circumcision, and some rejected the virgin birth of Jesus. At the same time, there is evidence of the influence of gnostic thought along the way.

One of the Jewish Christian works, which scholars have called the *Gospel of the Ebionites*, seems to have been closely related to the canonical Matthew. But it dispensed with the genealogy and birth stories, perhaps in order to avoid the virgin birth motif. Another such work, known as the *Gospel of the Hebrews*, embraces a motif that was probably characteristic of Jewish Christianity in general: the exaltation of James, the brother of Jesus, who led the church in Jerusalem for many years.

The Jewish Christian groups remained outside the majority church by choice. The matter was different, however, with gnostic Christians, whose writings provide interesting glimpses into the diversity of the early Christian movement.

Scholars have generally argued that the eventual concentration of power in the office of the bishop was largely a response to rampant diversity in doctrine among various Christian groups. Elaine Pagels, however, suggests that the reverse process might have been at work in the case of Christian gnostics. The leaders of what became the majority church might have rejected gnostic writings because they constituted a challenge to the official authority structure.[3]

The issue of authority is clear in the *Gospel of Mary*, in which a woman, presumably Mary Magdalene, has more accurate teachings than Peter and the other apostles. After Mary reports her conversation with the risen Jesus, Andrew disputes her testimony, and Peter adds these questions: "Did he really speak privately with a woman [and] not openly to us? Are we to . . . listen to her? Did he prefer her to us?"[4] Levi's defense of Mary, however, serves to legitimate secret gnostic teachings:

> "Peter, you have always been hot-tempered. Now I see you contending against the woman like the adversaries. . . . Surely the Savior knows her very well. That is why he loved her more than us. Rather let us be ashamed and put on the perfect man, and separate as he commanded us and preach the gospel, not laying down any other rule or other law beyond what the Savior said."[5]

Whether official authority in the church developed to combat gnostic teachings or the gnostics were rejected because they denied official authority, the result was the same. The increasingly hierarchical majority church rejected the gnostic groups, whose teachings differed significantly from what became the "orthodox" view. The conversation between Mary and Jesus in the *Gospel of Mary* provides a case in point:

"I," she said, "saw the Lord in a vision and I said to him, 'Lord, I saw you today in a vision.' He answered and said to me, 'Blessed are you, that you did not waver at the sight of me. For where the mind is, there is the treasure.' I said, to him, 'Lord, now does he who sees the vision see it <through> the soul <or> through the spirit?' The Savior answered and said, 'He does not see through the soul nor through the spirit, but the mind which [is] between the two—that is [what] sees the vision.'"[6]

This teaching contrasts with the view that Jesus' resurrection involved a physical body, for it interprets his appearance to Mary as a matter of "the mind." Pagels, however, comments that the New Testament does not consistently stress the physical nature of the resurrection. And the gnostics' point regarding the resurrection was that it "was not a unique event in the past: instead, it symbolized how Christ's presence could be experienced in the present."[7]

Around 180 C.E., a bishop named Irenaeus mentioned a *Gospel of Judas* in a book dedicated to the refutation of heretical teachings. This writing was lost, however, until its discovery in Egypt in the 1970s, and its first modern publication was not until 2006. It is gnostic in orientation and is distinctive in its presentation of Judas as a heroic figure. It takes the form of a secret revelation that Jesus gives to Judas three days before his last celebration of the Passover prior to his death. In this story, Judas' betrayal of Jesus actually serves Jesus' purpose, because it relieves the spiritual Jesus of his fleshly body. Thus, Jesus places Judas above the other disciples: "But you will exceed all of them. For you will sacrifice the man that clothes me."[8] It is Judas who knows that Jesus has come from "the immortal realm"[9] and who is therefore the ideal disciple.

The Canon as Theological Problem

Behind the popular fascination with the apocryphal materials lurks a question of real substance. To the pure historian, all sources are fair game. There is no reason to deny the legitimacy of looking to the apocryphal materials, along with any other documents we can get our hands on, for reconstructing the history of early Christianity. For the theologian and the Christian believer, however, the phenomenon of rejected tradition invites reflection on the limits of acceptable belief and raises the issue of how rigidly one should understand the boundary between the canonical and the noncanonical.

According to one school of thought, the canon defines absolutely and for all times what is acceptable and unacceptable Christian doctrine. According to another, the boundaries of the canon are only relative, for they were drawn by human beings who were subject to all the limitations of historical existence. From this latter perspective, not all material within the canon is of equal value, and not all outside it is to be rejected absolutely. As the church finds itself in new circumstances, it discovers new needs, new interests, and new perspectives. Thus, the church should continually mine the marginalized and rejected traditions for new insights, and it should take the boundaries of the canon as an important indicator of authentic Christian belief but not as an absolute limit.

This debate is a theological and hermeneutical one that cannot be settled by historical research. But it is important to understand that what the authors of some of these materials did was not in principle different from what the authors of the canonical Gospels did. They reflected on the meaning of Jesus' life and/or teachings from some particular perspective, re-shaping traditional materials on the basis of their own interests and intentions. However one might evaluate them theologically, for the historian they remain a part of the broad stream of Christian tradition.

Ethics and Hermeneutics

Christians often read the canonical Gospels not only to mine them for their theological content, but also as sources of ethical norms. In doing so, they encounter the hermeneutical problem in some very concrete ways.

One difficult issue is that of divorce and remarriage. The problem on one level is that the various Gospel sayings on the issue (Matt 5:31-33; 19:9; Mark 10:11-12; Luke 16:18) are not entirely consistent with one another. Mark and Luke seem to prohibit divorce altogether, whereas Matthew seems to allow it in cases involving a wife's unfaithfulness.

The problem on another level is how the Christian community should apply the New Testament teachings in contexts far removed from the ancient world. From one perspective, the biblical passages are normative in a direct and literal way, and no further considerations are relevant. From another perspective, however, a number of questions arise. Which, if any, of the various forms of the teaching actually come from Jesus himself? And what are the possible motives behind these particular sayings? Some scholars, for example, think that Jesus issued a strict prohibition against divorce, but did so as a way of extending women's rights.

Consideration of issues such as these leads to deeper questions. Are Christians necessarily bound to the literal commands of Jesus and/or the Gospels, or should they seek to formulate ethical teachings in the "spirit" of the New Testament and/or the early Christian witness? And how much weight should be given to one's own culture and circumstances in formulating such teachings?

Another often-debated issue is the use of violence. The strong condemnation of violence in the Sermon on the Mount (Matt 5–7) has led many Christians to adopt various forms of pacifism. Others, however, have endorsed the right to self-defense and the defense of others and have maintained the appropriateness of participation in wars and revolutions fought for just causes. Here again, the question of the nature of biblical authority comes into play.

As complex as the process of deriving ethical norms from the New Testament is, Christians through the centuries have generally agreed on the centrality of the command to love God and one's neighbor. There have been widely varying ways of applying this standard concretely, but most who engage in ethical reflection based on the New Testament give a prominent place to the love command.

NOTES

1. John Dominic Crossan, *The Historical Jesus: The Life of a Jewish Mediterranean Peasant* (San Francisco: HarperSanFrancisco, 1991), 385–91; and *The Cross That Spoke: The Origins of the Passion Narrative* (San Francisco: Harper & Row, 1988).

2. Wilhelm Schneemelcher, ed., *New Testament Apocrypha*, vol. 1, *Gospels and Related Writings*, rev. ed., trans. R. McLachlan Wilson (Cambridge: James Clark; Louisville, Ky.: Westminster John Knox, 1991), 444.

3. Elaine Pagels, *The Gnostic Gospels: The Early Church and the Crisis of Gnosticism* (New York: Random House, 1979), chs. 1–2.

4. James M. Robinson, gen. ed., *The Nag Hammadi Library in English*, 3rd ed. (San Francisco: Harper & Row, 1988), 473.

5. Ibid.

6. Ibid., 472.

7. Pagels, *Gnostic Gospels*, 5–6, 11.

8. Rudolphe Kasser, Marvin Meyer, and Gregor Wurst, eds., *The Gospel of Judas from Codex Tchacos* (Washington, D.C.: National Geographic, 2006), 43.

9. Ibid., 22.

THE PAULINE CORPUS

Prologue to Part Three

The figure of Paul looms large in the New Testament. Thirteen of its writings are letters in which the author is self-identified as Paul. Another work, the book of Hebrews, made its way into the canon because some early Christians attributed it to Paul. And the book of Acts is devoted largely to an account of his work as missionary and apostle.

As one New Testament writer (2 Peter 3:15-16) acknowledges, Paul's letters are not always easy to understand. It is thus important, in approaching these works, to know something about who Paul was and about the background against which he wrote.

The Letters, the Book of Acts, and the "Historical" Paul

Since Acts is our only source for Paul's life outside his own writings, it might seem that it would be the best introduction to his letters. However, a comparison of Acts with the letters reveals that Acts presses Paul's life into a mold designed to make specific theological points. Paul appears in Acts as acting in full accord with Peter and the leaders of the Jerusalem church, but in Galatians he reveals a deep-seated conflict between himself and these other leaders. Not only does he differ from them on an important matter of policy, but he clearly understands his own commission as apostle as completely independent of the authority of Peter or Jerusalem. Galatians 2:7, more-over, discloses that Peter brought the gospel to Jews and Paul brought it to Gentiles, whereas in Acts, it is Peter who initiates the Gentile mission.

Scholars generally agree that when Paul's letters conflict with Acts, the letters are to be preferred. There is less consensus on the extent to which we can rely upon Acts in relation to matters that Paul does not mention at all. I will begin by noting some details we can learn from the letters alone.

Paul says he was born into a family of practicing Jews and was himself a Pharisee totally committed to the Jewish law (Phil 3:5-6; 2 Cor 11:22; Rom 11:1). His use of the Jewish Scriptures, moreover, attests his thorough familiarity with them. That he seems to use the Septuagint and demonstrates familiarity with Greek literary conventions shows that he was, more specifically, a Hellenized Jew.

Paul also mentions that he once persecuted the church (Gal 2:13-14). Although he does not disclose his motivation, we may speculate that he "saw the developing freedom with regard to the law, especially among Hellenistic Jewish Christians, as a threat to Judaism and as an affront to God."[1]

In response to a dramatic experience, Paul became a follower of Jesus. He never describes the details of this experience, but he interprets it as an appearance of Jesus to him (1 Cor 9:1; 15:8) and a commission to become an apostle to the Gentiles (Gal 1:1, 10).

Following his "call," he went to "Arabia" (by which he meant the region just south of Damascus, Syria) and then, three years later, visited Peter in Jerusalem (Gal 1–2). After that, he spent more than a decade preaching in Syria and in Cilicia of Asia Minor before journeying again to Jerusalem for a meeting with the other leaders to hammer out some questions raised by his inclusion of Gentiles into the Christian fellowship. He reports an agreement at this meeting, but it apparently did not settle all questions, for he later had a confrontation with Peter and others (Gal 2:11-14) over whether Jewish Christians should eat with Gentile Christians who had not undergone circumcision and did not observe the law.

We also know from Paul's letters that he carried his missionary activity beyond Asia Minor to Macedonia and Greece, founded churches in the Gentile world, and played an ongoing role in their supervision. And it is clear that he generally supported himself through the practice of a trade, which he never explicitly names.

Paul claimed apostolic status on the basis of his revelatory experience and exercised authority over the churches he founded, although this authority was sometimes disputed (Gal 2:11-14). When he could not visit a congregation, he communicated by letter. In some cases, the letters are responses to crisis situations, and he exercised his authority through them. He was not, by the way, the only person other than the Twelve who functioned as an apostle, for he mentions others outside this circle as apostles also.[2]

As a sign of his solidarity with the Jerusalem leadership, Paul agreed to take up a collection, among his Gentile churches, for "the poor" in the Jerusalem church (Gal 1:10). Successful in this endeavor, he wrote the church at Rome about his intention to deliver the collection to Jerusalem and then visit Rome on his way to Spain to continue his missionary work (Rom 15:22-29).

The letters give us no information beyond this point. Early church tradition has it, however, that Paul made his way to Rome but not to Spain: imprisoned during a time of persecution, he was put to death by the Roman government. It is a tradition that most scholars have accepted.

We can be virtually certain of these details about Paul's life; the question is whether we should accept some other details recounted only in Acts. Was he really born in the city of Tarsus in Asia Minor, and was he really a Roman citizen? Did he actually study with the Jewish teacher Gamaliel in Jerusalem, and was his trade in fact tent making? A good rule of thumb is that the points that most obviously serve the theological interests of Acts must remain the most suspect.

Most scholars grant some credibility to the Acts accounts of Paul's missionary travels, but there is little consensus on how much weight to give them. The reconstruction of Pauline chronology remains a complex matter, as the section below, "Chronologies of Paul," will show.

Studying Paul's Letters

If interpreters have tended to treat the New Testament writings as sources of doctrine, they have done so particularly in the case of Paul's letters. But just as contemporary scholarship has rediscovered the Gospels as stories, it has also rediscovered Paul's writings as letters. It has thus become commonplace to say that they should be studied not as theological treatises but as communications between two parties on specific occasions. Paul wrote not in order to work out the details of Christian teaching in an abstract way but to deal with concrete questions and problems. So it is important to try to reconstruct the specific situations that occasioned Paul's letters.

This does not mean the letters were private communications. Paul wrote as an apostle, and he addressed his readers in the second person plural. It is clear also that he expected the letters to be read to the entire congregations (1 Thess 5:27; Phlm 2). We must therefore imagine that he composed them carefully. While not formal doctrinal statements, they are the products of considerable reflection.

It is nevertheless important to remember that they are letters and to note that letter writing in the Greco-Roman world followed conventions regarding both formal structure and phraseology. A comparison of Paul's letters to others written in that environment shows that he followed the conventional format but modified it to suit his purposes.

William G. Doty gives the following outline of the typical Greek letter:

Introduction (prescript or salutation)
    including: sender, addressee, greetings, and often additional greetings
    or wish for good health
Text or Body, introduced with characteristic introductory formulae
Conclusion
    including: greetings, wishes, especially for persons other than the addressee;
    final greeting or prayer sentence; and sometimes dating[3]

Paul modifies the Hellenistic introduction with his phrase "Grace to you and peace," and he makes the conclusion into a benediction. He also generally replaces a typical sentence of thanks to the gods for the writer's rescue from danger with a sometimes elaborate thanksgiving for the faith of the congregation to which he writes.[4] And following the main body of the letter, he

PLATE A *Saint Matthew and the Angel* by Girolamo Forabosco. Pinacoteca Nazionale, Ferrara, Italy. Photo © Finsiel/Alinari / Art Resource, NY.

INCIPE VANGL LVCA

PLATE C   Saint Luke the Evangelist. Miniature from the Samuhel Gospel, Bayerische Staatsbibliothek, Munich, Germany. Bildarchiv Preussischer Kulturbesitz / Art Resource, NY.

PLATE B   Saint Mark the Evangelist. Polychrome wooden statue. Tarragona, Spain. Photo by C. Sappa © DeA Picture Library / Art Resource, NY.

PLATE D *Saint John the Evangelist* by Pacino da Bonaguida. Accademia, Florence, Italy. Photo © Finsiel/Alinari / Art Resource, NY.

PLATE E   *Saints Peter and Paul* by El Greco. Hermitage, St. Petersburg, Russia. Photo © Scala / Art Resource, NY.

PLATE F   Statue of Augustus (Octavian), first Roman emperor, 27 B.C.E.–14 C.E., from the Serapion at Thessalonica. Photo from *The Cities of Paul*, Fortress Press, 2004 © The President and Fellows of Harvard College.

PLATE G   The Roman aqueduct at Caesarea Maritima. Photo by Marshall Johnson.

PLATE H   Herod's palace at Masada. Photo by Marshall Johnson.

PLATE 1   Herodian floor mosaic from Masada (*in situ*). Photo by Marshall Johnson.

PLATE J   *Saint John the Baptist Preaching* by Pieter Brueghel the Elder. Oil on wood. Budapest, Hungary. Photo © Erich Lessing / Art Resource, NY.

PLATE K   Stone carving of the Ark of the Covenant at Capernaum. Photo by Marshall Johnson.

PLATE L   Byzantine ruins at Capernaum. Photo by Marshall Johnson.

PLATE M   Mountain of the Beatitudes near Tabgha and Bethsaida, with a view of the north end of the Lake of Galilee, Israel. This is the traditional place of the Sermon of the Mount. Photo © Erich Lessing / Art Resource, NY.

PLATE N Feeding of the multitudes, baskets with fish. Mosaic in Hora Church, Istanbul, Turkey. Photo © Erich Lessing / Art Resource, NY.

PLATE 0   Valley leading eastward from Jerusalem to Jericho. Photo by Marshall Johnson.

PLATE P   *The Transfiguration* by William Blake. Photo © Victoria and Albert Museum, London / Art Resource, NY.

PLATE Q   The Garden of Gethsemane, with view across the Kidron Valley to the eastern wall of Herod's Temple. Photo by Marshall Johnson.

PLATE R   Inscription dedicated to and honoring Emperor Tiberius, with the name of Pontius Pilate, prefect of Judea. Caesarea, Israel.

PLATE S   Drawing for *Southwest Pieta* (1983) by Luis Jimenez. © 2009 Estate of Luis A. Jimenez Jr. / Artists Rights Society (ARS), New York.

typically adds specific exhortations regarding behavior, the scholarly term for which is *parenesis*.

Paul also makes use of modes of argumentation drawn from both Greek and Jewish learning. Rhetoric, the art of persuasion through speaking and/or writing, was a major component of Greek and Hellenistic education and the subject of much reflection and analysis. And Jewish teachers, who in this period sometimes studied Greek rhetoric, had their own distinctive modes of argumentation.

Critical Questions about the Letters

Thirteen letters bear Paul's name, but many scholars are convinced that some of these were written by other people. We are apt to think of writing in someone else's name as dishonest, but it was not considered so in the ancient world. Those who used Paul's name did so to lend authority to their attempt to say what they genuinely believed Paul would have said in a particular situation.

In chapters 9–11, I will treat the seven letters that are almost universally accepted as authentically Pauline: Philemon, 1 Thessalonians, Philippians, Galatians, 1 and 2 Corinthians, and Romans. The remaining six will come under discussion in chapter 13.

The question of authenticity is not the only critical question the student of Paul faces. Some of the letters read very unevenly, leading scholars to suspect that we do not have them in their original forms. There is general agreement that 2 Corinthians is a composite of more than one letter, and many scholars have made a similar judgment regarding Philippians. At some points, however, the presence of material that seems out of place is best attributed to an editor's interpolation. And in still other cases, scholars suspect that readers made comments in the margins of manuscripts, and later scribes copied them into the text. It will be important to take note of such possibilities as we seek to read and interpret the letters of Paul.

Paul in Context

Paul's letters are the earliest of all New Testament writings. Although we will approach these letters primarily in order to understand Paul, and only secondarily as sources for the history of the early church, they provide us with some important insights into early Christianity. In chapter 3, we drew upon Paul in reconstructing the resurrection tradition. At this point, we may note that his letters are also an important source for the early tradition regarding Jesus' words at the Last Supper (1 Cor 11:23-26). There are also numerous points at which scholars identify traditional materials of other types, such as the Christ hymn at Philippians 2:6-11, which Paul has quoted.

The recognition of these traditional formulations also shows us that, despite his insistence on his independence from the authority of the Jerusalem leadership, Paul worked, spoke, and wrote from within an ongoing tradition.

This tradition had made inroads into both the Jewish Diaspora and the Gentile world itself prior to Paul's own missionary activity. The story of Stephen and the "Hellenists" in Acts 6 reflects the presence of Hellenized Jews within the early Christian community in Jerusalem, and later passages in Acts (8:1; 11:19-26) report that the departure of Christians from Jerusalem following Stephen's martyrdom led to a mission to Diaspora Jews and to Gentiles. The historical likelihood is that it was only *Hellenized* Jewish Christians who were forced to flee Jerusalem and that it was they who extended the Christian mission into the synagogues of the Diaspora.[5] They apparently had some success in this endeavor, and not only among Jews. It was commonplace that Gentiles who were attracted to Jewish monotheism and ethics, but perhaps unwilling to undergo circumcision or observe dietary regulations, attached themselves to synagogues without formally converting. From their point of view, Christianity would have appeared as a "universalized" form of Judaism, which in a real sense it was. It was undoubtedly among such people, known in Acts as "God-fearers," that Christianity first moved outside the Jewish community.

It should thus be clear that the picture of Paul as the "second founder" of Christianity, who single-handedly transformed the simple message of Jesus into a complex Hellenistic cult, is a distortion. The Gentile mission was in progress before Paul became a part of it. It is nevertheless apparent that he was a major figure in that mission.

A Note on Method

The primary method with which I will approach the Pauline letters will be reader-response criticism. Because this method is normally used in relation to narratives rather than letters, however, it will be necessary to make certain modifications to the version employed in studying the Gospels in part 2.

The prologue to part 2 calls attention to two technical terms used by reader-response critics: *the narrator* and *the reader*. The concept of narrator serves us well in reading a story, but a letter is not a story. Since Paul identifies himself as the writer of the letters we will be studying, I will refer not to a narrator but to Paul himself when dealing with the letters of undisputed authenticity.

I will preserve the term *the reader*, but you should be aware of a subtle shift in meaning. Historical knowledge plays some role in the construction of the readers in the analyses of the Gospels in part 2. It is necessary, for example, to posit readers who are familiar with the Septuagint. But my emphasis there is not upon what we can learn about the *original* readers of these works but upon how the writings themselves implicitly define their own readers. When we approach the authentic letters of Paul, however, the situation is a little different. Each letter is addressed to a specific audience. So although we will look primarily to the letters themselves for help in constructing "the readers," the readers we construct will represent actual, historical situations.

The disputed letters present a special case, since Paul may not be the actual author, and we cannot be certain of the original audience. I will discuss the modifications necessary in their case at the beginning of chapter 13.

Having stressed the differences between letters and stories, I must now point out that a letter nevertheless presupposes a story of sorts—the story of how the person who wrote the letter came to do so. People write letters for specific reasons, which sometimes involve earlier interactions with their intended audiences. Before analyzing each of the undisputed letters, then, I will try to reconstruct the story behind it. It is important to do this, since reading a letter is—as Leander Keck has remarked—"somewhat like overhearing a telephone conversation: one must always infer what is being said on the other end of the line, as well as the context of the conversation."[6]

I will provide full readings of two of the undisputed letters, Philemon and Romans, and will confine myself to notes in the cases of the others. In chapter 13, I will offer a full reading of Ephesians and treat the other disputed letters in notes.

Chronologies of Paul

by John A. Darr

Our resources for calculating the sequence, time, and date of events in Paul's ministry are essentially restricted to the Pauline letters and to the Acts of the Apostles. Neither of these sources is directly concerned with Pauline chronology, although Acts may provide a rough schema of Paul's later ministry. Since Paul's letters dealt primarily with religious issues and were geared to current circumstances in his churches, there was little opportunity for him to recount his personal history in his writings (with one important exception). The modern historian is therefore forced to reconstruct the chronology of Paul's life from meager and diverse sources that must be constantly evaluated and interpreted. This results in a wide range of scholarly opinions as to the dating of Paul's various activities. Nevertheless, two basic approaches to Pauline chronology may be delineated:

1. *Chronologies based on the sequential outline found in Acts.* In this category, the general procedure has been to fit the various phenomena mentioned by the Pauline letters into the narrative framework provided by Acts (the three missionary journeys, Paul's trip to Rome, etc.). This procedure implies a highly positive evaluation of the basic historical trustworthiness of Acts. Dates are supplied by those references that can (to the scholar's satisfaction) be supported by

extrabiblical historical evidence, such as ancient inscriptions mentioning Roman officers with whom Paul dealt.

2. Chronologies based on the Pauline letters. A number of scholars have been skeptical of the historical narrative found in Acts and have preferred to base their chronologies almost exclusively on evidence gleaned from the Pauline letters, scanty though it may be. The reasoning behind this approach is that Paul's own letters constitute primary evidence, while the Acts account can be considered only secondary evidence at best. Acts is not to be trusted, except at those points where it is supported by a specific statement in Paul's letters. Thus, use of the Acts material must be restricted and is advisable only after the essential structure of Pauline chronology has already been developed on the basis of the letters alone. Dating is achieved by reference to certain extrabiblical evidence.

The primary question in a study of Pauline chronology is the placement of the so-called Jerusalem conference in which Paul took part. This incident is crucial in that Paul himself, in one of his few backward glances, recounts all of his previous visits to Jerusalem up to and including the conference visit (Gal 1–2). Acts also knows of Paul's important visit to Jerusalem but mentions at least one "extra" visit not accounted for by Paul in Galatians. How are we to place the various visits of Paul to Jerusalem? The answer to this question is the basic distinguishing characteristic of all modern reconstructions of Pauline chronology. Historians highly dependent on Acts have identified the conference visit with the event in either Acts 15 or Acts 11:30. The chronologies based on Paul's writings reject both these options and point instead to Acts 18:22 as an oblique reference to the real conference visit of Paul. For apologetic reasons, the author of Acts inserted two fabricated Jerusalem visits early in Paul's career. The real conference visit took place late in Paul's career and was marked by the instigation of Paul's "collection for the poor in Jerusalem." The progress of this collection process can be traced through almost all of Paul's letters and thus provides a point of reference for Pauline chronology.

The two most significant extrabiblical pieces of evidence used in Pauline chronologies are the following. First is the so-called Gallio inscription, uncovered at Delphi, from which it has been deduced that Gallio held office at Corinth from the year 51 to 52. Gallio is mentioned in Acts 18:12 in connection with Paul's activities in Corinth. The second piece of evidence is Claudius's edict expelling the Jews from Rome, which is generally assumed to have been issued in the year 49 (based on Orosius) and to have been the reason for Aquila and Priscilla arriving in Corinth from Rome (Acts 18:2). The near coincidence of these dates is taken by many to be a sure sign that Acts' picture of Paul's *first* ministry at Corinth is essentially accurate. Other incidents in Paul's European ministry are then ordered around this time period. Those who are less accepting of Acts' historical accuracy point out that the Claudius edict may well be dated at 41 rather than 49, and thus a chronology based on Acts 18:2, 12 will begin to unravel. These latter scholars see two widely separated Pauline missions to Corinth, one near the beginning or middle of Paul's career (thus the reference to Aquila and Priscilla) and one at the end (thus the Gallio reference in Acts). The author of Acts simply mixed these two traditions in one narrative about Paul at Corinth.

The evolution of Paul's thinking within his letters has often been used as an *internal* source of evidence for Pauline chronology. Determining the sequence and spacing of Paul's letters through careful comparison of their content could provide a valuable criterion for the chronologist. Toward this end, at least three areas of Pauline thought have been examined:

1. *Ecclesiology* (the doctrine of the church). Can we perceive in Paul's letters a growing awareness of the ongoing institutionalization of the early church (the establishment of specific church offices, a centralization of authority, developed sacramentalism, and so on)? Scholars who feel that Paul wrote the Pastoral Letters find this criterion especially significant and helpful; others do not.

2. *Christology* (the doctrine of Christ). How is it that in some letters (1 Thessalonians, Philippians) Paul does not speak of Christ's death as an atonement, while in other letters (Romans, 1 Corinthians) Christ's atoning death is a prominent theme? Could this disparity be another indication of long-term development in Paul's thinking?

3. *Eschatology* (the doctrine of the end). In 1 Thessalonians, Paul apparently feels that Christ's second coming is imminent and that virtually all Christians will still be alive when Christ returns (cf. 4:13ff). In 1 Corinthians, however, Paul takes for granted that many Christians will die (indeed, *have* died) before the second coming (cf. 6:14; 11:30; 15:6, 18, 51). In the latter case he speaks of a bodily transformation of Christians that will take place at the eschaton (end); yet bodily transformation is not even alluded to in 1 Thessalonians, where one would expect it to be a major motif. Does this indicate a progression in Paul's thought, and if so, how much time would have passed between the writing of 1 Thessalonians and 1 Corinthians? Since answers to these and other such questions are subjective, few concrete results have been obtained, and no consensus of opinion has been established concerning the sequence or spacing of the letters. There is, however, widespread agreement among scholars that 1 Thessalonians is our earliest authentic letter written by Paul, and that Romans is our latest. Conjectures concerning the sequence of the letters are often used as warranting or supporting arguments for chronological schemas, but rarely form the foundation of such reconstructions.

Some of the basic types of Pauline chronology are schematized below. It should be emphasized that these charts are not comprehensive summaries of the full-scale chronological reconstructions by the scholars in the footnotes. Rather, they are intended to provide elementary conceptualizations of these varying chronologies. The sequence and spacing of events in the charts are much more important than the absolute dates (which for the most part are highly conjectured). Note once again the different placement of the "Jerusalem conference" and the varying degrees of reliability accorded the account in Acts.

FIG. 9.1 **CHRONOLOGIES DEPENDENT ON THE OUTLINE OF ACTS**

The Jerusalem Conference Visit of Paul (Galatians 2) = Acts 11:30[7]

	C.E.	
Paul's conversion	33	
Paul's first Jerusalem visit	35	Acts 9:26
Paul in Syria and Cilicia	35–46	
Paul's conference visit to Jerusalem (Galatians 2)	46	Acts 11:27-30; described as a famine visit
Paul and Barnabas in Cyprus and Galatia (first missionary journey)	47–48	
Letter to the Galatians	?48	
Council at Jerusalem; Paul's third Jerusalem visit	49	Acts 15 Claudius's edict (49) = Acts 18:2
Paul and Silas travel from Syrian Antioch through Asia Minor to Macedonia and back (second missionary journey)	49–50	
Letters to the Thessalonians	50	
Paul in Corinth	50–52	Gallio inscription (51–52) = Acts 18:12
Paul's fourth Jerusalem visit	52	Acts 18:22
Paul in Ephesus	52–55	
Letters to the Corinthians	55–56	
Paul in Macedonia, Illyricum, Achaia	55–57	
Letter to the Romans	57	
last visit to Jerusalem	57	Acts 21:17
imprisonment at Caesarea	57–59	
Paul's arrival at Rome	60	
Paul under arrest in Rome	60–62	
?Writes the *Captivity Letters*		
Paul visits Spain	?65	
Paul dies	?65	

The Jerusalem Conference Visit of Paul (Galatians 2) = Acts 15[8]

	C.E.	
Paul's conversion	35	Acts 9
Paul's first Jerusalem visit	38	Acts 9:26
Paul in Syria and Cilicia	38–47	
Famine relief visit to Jerusalem	46	Acts 11:30; ?12:25
First missionary journey	47–48	Acts 13, 14
(Cyprus and Galatia)		
Council at Jerusalem (conference visit)	48	Gal 2:1-10 = Acts 15
Second missionary journey (Asia	49–52	Acts 15:36—18:22
Minor, Macedonia, Caesarea)		
Jews expelled from Rome	49	Claudius's edict (49) = Acts 18:2
Paul reaches Corinth	50	
Letters to the Thessalonians	50	
Gallio becomes proconsul of Corinth	51	Gallio inscription (51–52)
Letter to the Galatians	52	
Third missionary journey	52–56	Acts 18:23—21:15
(Macedonia and Achaia)		
Three years spent at Ephesus	52–55	
Letters to the Corinthians	55	
Letter to the Romans	56	
Paul's arrival at Jerusalem	56	
Paul's imprisonment at Caesarea	56–58	Acts 24:27
Paul's arrival at Rome	59	Acts 28:16
Paul at Rome	59–61	
Philippians, Philemon,		
Colossians, Ephesians		
Paul's martyrdom	61 (64)	Neronian persecution (64)

The Jerusalem Conference Visit of Paul (Gal 2:1-10) = Acts 15 = Acts 11:30[9]

	C.E.	
Paul's conversion	30–32	
Paul's first Jerusalem visit	32–34	
Paul's conference visit to Jerusalem	44/45	Gal 2:1-10 / Acts 15 / 11:30
Mission to Cyprus and Asia Minor	46	
Quarrel with Barnabas (equated with the disagreement in Gal 2:13)	46/47	
Mission to Macedonia and Achaia; *1 Thessalonians*	47–51	
Mission in Galatia, Phrygia, and Asia; collection journey; *Galatians, 1 and 2 Corinthians, Romans*	52–58	
Arrest in Jerusalem and Caesarean imprisonment; *Philemon*	58	
Journey to Rome	60	
Roman imprisonment; *Philippians* (?)	60–	

FIG. 9.2 **CHRONOLOGIES DERIVED FROM PAUL'S LETTERS**

The Jerusalem Conference Visit of Paul (Galatians 2) = Acts 18:22
(J. Knox and G. Lüdemann)[10]

	C.E.	
Paul's conversion	33/34	Gal 1:15, 16:2; 2 Cor 12:2
Paul's first Jerusalem visit	36/37	Gal 1:18
Mission activity in Syria, Cilicia, and Galatia	36/37–38/39	Gal 1:21
Independent Pauline mission activity in Macedonia, Achaia, and perhaps elsewhere	38/39–50/51	
Paul in Corinth; *1 Thessalonians* Aquila and Priscilla come to Corinth from Rome	41	Claudius's edict (41) = Acts 18:2
Paul's conference visit to Jerusalem (a dramatic and skewed rendering of this is [mis]placed at Acts 15)	50/51	Gal 2:1 = Acts 18:22
Collection for the Jerusalem church and other mission activity in Asia Minor and Greece	50/51–54/55	
Paul in Galatia	51	
Paul based in Ephesus	51–53	
1 Corinthians	52	
Quick trip to Corinth and back to Ephesus	52	Gallio inscription (51–52); Acts 18:12
Paul travels to Troas and Macedonia; *2 Corinthians and Galatians*	53	
Paul arrives in Corinth; *Romans*	54	
Final journey to Jerusalem to deliver the collection. (We have no hard evidence on Paul after this.)	54/55	

The Jerusalem Conference Visit of Paul (Galatians 2:1-10) = Acts 18:22 (R. Jewett)[11]

	C.E.	
Paul's conversion	34	
Activities in Arabia; return to Damascus	35–37	
Escape from Aretas IV; first	37	2 Cor 11:32-33
Jerusalem visit		Acts 9:23-26
Activities in Syria and Cilicia	37–46	
First missionary journey:	43–45	
Antioch, Cyprus, Pamphylia,		
and South Galatia		
Second missionary journey:	46–51	
North Galatia, Troas, Philippi,		
Thessalonica, Berea Athens,		Claudius's edict (49)
Corinth; *1 and 2 Thessalonians*		
Hearing before Gallio at Corinth	51	Gallio inscription
Second Jerusalem visit;	51	Acts18:22/Gal 2:1-10
apostolic conference		
Conflict with Peter	52	Gal 2:14-17
Third missionary journey	52–57	
North Galatia		
Ephesus; *Galatians*	52–54	
Ephesian imprisonment; *Philippians*	54/55	
Visit to Corinth; return to Macedonia	55	
and Asia; *1 and 2 Corinthians*		
Back to Corinth; *Romans*	56/57	
Philippi to Jerusalem; arrest	57	
Imprisonment in Caesarea	57–59	
Imprisonment in Rome	61	
Execution in Rome	62	

NOTES

1. Leander E. Keck, *Paul and His Letters*, 2nd ed. (Philadelphia: Fortress Press, 1989), 27.

2. James the brother of Jesus (Gal 1:19; 1 Cor 15:7), Barnabas (1 Cor 9:6), and Andronicus and Junia (Rom 16:7).

3. William G. Doty, *Letters in Primitive Christianity* (Philadelphia: Fortress Press, 1973), 14.

4. Ibid., 22, citing John L. White, "The Structural Analysis of Philemon: A Point of Departure in the Formal Analysis of the Pauline Letter" (photocopy for the Society of Biblical Literature on the Form and Function of the Pauline Letters, 1971).

5. See Marcel Simon, *St. Stephen and the Hellenists in the Primitive Church* (London: Longmans, Green, 1958).

6. Ibid., 1.

7. Based on F. F. Bruce, *Paul: Apostle of the Heart Set Free* (Grand Rapids: Eerdmans, 1978), 475.

8. Based on B. W. Robinson, *The Life of Paul*, 2nd ed. (Chicago: University of Chicago Press, 1928), 240–41.

9. A. J. M. Wedderburn, "Keeping Up with Recent Studies, VIII, Some Recent Pauline Chronologies," *Expository Times* (January 1981): 107. Notice that the second and third missionary journeys of Acts are inverted and also that the first journey is placed after the conference rather than before it. While maintaining that Acts is basically trustworthy, adherents of this approach feel that the account of the famine visit (Acts 11:30) resulted from a simple historical misinterpretation by the author of Acts and not from any conscious attempt to distort the facts. A famine did take place, and the Antioch church did send aid to Jerusalem. However, it may be that Paul himself never did accompany Barnabas on a trip solely for the purpose of bringing relief to Jerusalem and/or that Paul took a donation to Jerusalem at the same time he went for the conference visit (Acts 15/Gal 2:1-10). In either case, the author of Acts (or his sources of information) was not clear in making these historical distinctions. Thus, we have two accounts rather than one. Conjectures of this sort are intended to solve (somewhat at the expense of Acts' trustworthiness) the problem of an "extra" Jerusalem visit by Paul in Acts while at the same time preserving the basic integrity of the greater part of Acts.

10. This table is constructed from two slightly varying chronologies that employ the same basic presuppositions and methodology; the spacing and sequence of events are similar despite the difference in absolute dates (indicated by the diagonals). This display does not represent the entire range of dates proposed by these scholars, but it does accurately represent the sequential aspects of their chronologies of Paul: J. Knox, *Chapters in a Life of Paul* (Nashville: Abingdon, 1950), 83–88; G. Lüdemann, *Paulus, der Heidenapostel*, vol. 1, *Studien zur Chronologie* (Göttingen: Vandenhoeck & Ruprecht, 1980), 272–73.

11. R. Jewett, *A Chronology of Paul's Life* (Philadelphia: Fortress Press, 1979), foldout. This simplified chart can present only a fraction of the information Jewett includes in his complex chronology. Note that although Jewett places the conference visit at Acts 18:22 and opts for only three Jerusalem visits (as per the letters), he is much more dependent on Acts for his chronological framework than Knox (see previous table).

STUDY QUESTIONS

1. Assess the historical value of the various sources for the life and work of Paul.
2. Why is it not appropriate to speak of Paul as the "second founder" of Christianity?

Philemon,
1 Thessalonians,
Philippians,
and Galatians

9

Philemon

The Story behind the Letter

Paul indicates in the letter to Philemon that he is writing from prison, and there is a postscript in some manuscripts indicating that he was in Rome. If this tradition is accepted, the date would be somewhere between 59 and 62 C.E. However, we know that the destination of the letter was Colossae, since Colossians 4:9 places Onesimus (the bearer and subject of the letter) in that city. This makes Rome problematic for two reasons. First, Philemon 22 expresses Paul's desire to visit Philemon, but Colossae is to the east of Rome, whereas Paul's intention was to go to Spain if he was released from prison. Second, the distance between Rome and Colossae is so great that it seems odd for Paul to ask Philemon to prepare a room for him in the near future. Some scholars therefore think the letter dates from another imprisonment. However, since Paul was imprisoned often (2 Cor 11:23), if we rule out Rome, we are left with guesses as to the place and date.

Alone among the extant letters of Paul, the Letter to Philemon is addressed to an individual. Philemon was a Christian, apparently converted by Paul's preaching. He was also in some sense the leader of a local Christian congregation, since it met in his house. In writing the letter, Paul presupposed some earlier events linking himself and Philemon.

Philemon had a slave named Onesimus, who was now with Paul, serving him during his imprisonment. Most interpreters have assumed that he had escaped from Philemon,

215

but it is just as likely that Philemon sent him to Paul. Paul mentions the possibility that Onesimus might owe something to Philemon, and many interpreters have speculated that he stole something. If there was a debt, however, we could as easily think of a loan. In any case, he apparently became a Christian through Paul's influence. Paul, for his part, had become deeply attached to Onesimus. But now he sends him back to Philemon with a letter, addressed primarily to Philemon but also to the church that meets in his house and other specific members.

Points to Look For in Philemon

- The role of familial language in Paul's method of persuasion

- Paul's sense of apostolic authority

- The presuppositions behind Paul's request to accept Onesimus as a brother

The Letter to Philemon: A Reading

The opening salutation (vv. 1-3) places the communication in the context of Christian faith and reinforces this point with the secondary address: although in one sense for Philemon, the letter is for the whole house church. That Paul writes also on behalf of Timothy, an associate in his work, adds to the "semi-official" nature of the communication. In addition, the salutation underscores Paul's imprisonment, which he interprets as "for Jesus Christ."[1] Philemon must therefore read the letter as a fel-

low Christian, as a fellow worker of someone imprisoned because of his faith, and as a member of a Christian community.

Paul's prayer of thanksgiving for Philemon's faith, love, and work in the church (vv. 4-7) reinforces the point in another way. Having read this much, Philemon must now read on as someone who has up to this point proved a faithful Christian servant.

Addressed initially as a "coworker," Philemon is confronted in verse 8 with Paul's apostolic authority: Paul asserts that he could simply command what he is about to ask. The emphasis upon authority, however, gives way to a different approach. Without yet stating what he is getting at, Paul indicates that he prefers, out of love, to issue an appeal, rather than an order, for Philemon to do his "duty" in relation to Onesimus. His appeal nevertheless uses some strong persuasion. While not confrontational in tone, it buries Philemon in the ethos of the Christian fellowship: Paul is "father," Onesimus his "child"—indeed, Paul says, his "own heart." Making a pun on the slave's name, which means "useful," Paul says that Onesimus will now be useful both to Philemon and to himself and then notes that he would like to have Onesimus stay with him during his imprisonment.

Only in verses 15-16 does Paul finally make his request: that Philemon should receive Onesimus back, "no longer as a slave but more than a slave, a beloved brother." Only at that point does he refer to the matter of Onesimus's possible debt, which he quickly defuses with an offer to make restitution himself.

Having thus made his appeal to Philemon's love and free will, Paul picks up the pen at verse 19 (apparently having dictated to a scribe up to this point) and finishes the letter in his own hand. But his tactics shift again. He reminds Philemon of his own debt to Paul, presumably his conversion, and issues what comes close to a command. Then he asserts his confidence that Philemon will render *obedience* and "will do even more than" he asks. To top off all this, Paul mentions his coming visit before adding the final greetings.

Where does the letter leave Philemon? At the very least, he will perceive it as his Christian duty to receive Onesimus back without reproach and treat him as a brother in Christ. He will also know that, should he not do so, other church members who read the letter will be available to call him to account and that Paul himself hopes to visit after his release from prison. The implication is that to fail to do what Paul asks is to deny the bonds that Christians know in Christ.

This is the very least that Philemon can hear in the letter, but there are additional undertones. What is the "even more" that Paul suggests? Should Philemon send Onesimus back to continue to aid Paul? More fundamentally, what are the implications of receiving Onesimus back as a brother? Does a person hold a brother or a sister as slave? Does not the master-slave relationship violate the meaning of Christian fellowship?

A Socio-literary Analysis

Norman Petersen has analyzed the Letter to Philemon with a method combining sociological and literary approaches.[2] What interests Petersen is not Paul's theology, but the sociology implicit in what he calls Paul's "narrative world."

To understand the term *narrative world*, it is helpful to reflect on the fact that the "story behind the letter" just recounted was reconstructed from the letter itself; we have no independent knowledge of the events. While one can legitimately approach this reconstruction as "what actually happened," it is just as possible that Paul completely distorts the actual events. But this makes no difference in terms of Petersen's interest. The point is that Paul implies a story that contains characters who relate in particular ways within a particular story world. And because the story implies a world, it also embodies a system of social relations among the characters.

According to Petersen, in Paul's story, the Christian fellowship constitutes a kind of anti-structure over against the sociological structure of the world at large. In the "outside" world, masters own slaves and relate to them in terms of a superior-inferior hierarchy. In the church, however, there can be no master-slave relationship. In Christ, all have equal status as siblings in one family; Onesimus and Philemon are therefore brothers!

The matter is complicated by the fact that Paul asserts his hierarchically based authority to enforce the anti-hierarchical nature of the church. But this contradiction is partially mitigated by the fact that Paul refers to Philemon as "coworker" and "brother" (v. 7). In the world outside, by contrast, there is nothing to bridge the chasm between master and slave. Although not utterly devoid of hierarchical relations, the church stands for anti-structures that "*invade* the world's social structures in the story of Philemon."[3]

In Petersen's scheme, the relationships among human beings constitute only one level of Paul's narrative world. Those relationships are supported by a "symbolic universe"—a set of symbols expressing one's most basic assumptions about reality—in which God and Christ appear as characters. Thus, Philemon's decision regarding Onesimus involves a choice of symbolic universes. To refuse to accept the slave as brother would be to opt for the symbolic universe of the world at large; it would be a denial of Christ.

The Onesimus incident has thus precipitated a crisis in Philemon's life. He has apparently lived rather comfortably in two worlds—the world at large, in which he was master over a slave, and the world of brothers and sisters in the church. "Now," however, "he finds that 'being in Christ' makes a totalistic claim upon him from which there are no exceptions. *If he is to remain in the service of Christ the Lord, he cannot be 'in Christ' only when he is 'in church.'*"[4]

Concluding Comments

Can the Letter to Philemon teach us anything about the early Christians' stance regarding slavery? The fact that Philemon continued to hold slaves after his conversion suggests that Christians did not automatically abandon the practice of slavery within the fellowship. It seems clear, however, that Paul was able to call upon a set of assumptions shared in the church that contained the seeds of a challenge to that practice.

So what have we learned about Paul from this letter? For one thing, we have seen how he made use of a letter to carry out his apostolic function. We have also had a glimpse of his understanding of his apostolic authority. And most important, we have learned something about what was important to Paul and about the basis from which his thinking proceeded. One's being in Christ is not, in Paul's view, one aspect of life parallel to other aspects. It is the very center and substance of one's existence. It is the norm by which one orders

FIG. 9.3 **The apostle Paul baptized by Saint Ananias. Twelfth-century mosaics in the Capella Palatina in Palermo, Italy.** Photo © Erich Lessing /Art Resource, NY.

one's whole life and makes all decisions. It is everything.

1 Thessalonians

The Story behind the Letter

Acts 17:1-15 gives an account of Paul's sojourn in Thessalonica, and most scholars make use of this account in fitting his work there into a chronological scheme. The prevailing opinion is that 1 Thessalonians is the oldest writing in the New Testament and that Paul composed it in Corinth around 50 C.E. Some scholars place it earlier or later, however.

The "story" we can derive from the letter itself is this. Paul and his companions come to Thessalonica, the capital of the Roman province of Macedonia, and are successful in gaining converts and founding a community. When Paul moves on, he becomes concerned about the converts and sends Timothy to inquire about them. Timothy returns to Paul with a generally positive report, but with some questions also. In response, Paul writes the letter known as 1 Thessalonians.

FIG. 9.4 **Walls of Thessalonica.** Photo from *The Cities of Paul,* Fortress Press, 2004 © The President and Fellows of Harvard University.

Points to Look For in 1 Thessalonians

- Paul's use of the notion of imitation
- Paul's characterization of his ministry in Thessalonica
- Paul's views on eschatology

Notes on a Reading of 1 Thessalonians

1:1—3:13

Following the greeting, Paul launches a lengthy thanksgiving to God for the faith, love, and hope of the Thessalonians (1:2-10). As Paul had served as an example to them, they become an example to others. He also encourages the readers to remember the joy they experienced in accepting the gospel under adverse circumstances (1:6) and reminds them of the content of their faith: they have turned from idols to await the return of Jesus, whom God raised from the dead (1:10).

Paul's Ministry in Thessalonica

— *2:1-12.* The ministry of Paul and his companions was gentle and nurturing, not self-seeking (an implicit comparison to the charlatans among the wandering philosophers). They supported themselves and burdened no one.

— *2:13-16.* Paul gives thanks that the Thessalonians received God's word. He acknowledges that they became imitators of the other churches, suffering the same things from their own people that the others did from the Jews.

— *2:17—3:5.* He expresses distress that he could not visit them earlier and explains that he sent Timothy in his place to comfort them in their distress and inquire about the state of their faith.

— *3:6-13.* Paul is encouraged by Timothy's positive report. He reminds the readers of the sufferings of himself and his associates and concludes with a prayer combining his desire for a visit with a pronouncement of God's blessings.

4:1—5:28

With a transitional phrase ("finally" in English), Paul turns from thanksgiving to exhortation, referring to prior "instructions." He addresses sexual ethics in 4:3-8 and in 4:9-12 enjoins mutual love, a quiet lifestyle, manual labor, and noninterference in the lives of others.

In 4:13, Paul addresses a question the Thessalonians have asked. Apparently, some members of the community have died since Paul left, and their fellow Christians wonder whether they will share in the salvation at Christ's return. Paul says (4:13-18) that when the end comes, the "dead in Christ" will be raised, and then dead and living together will be caught up "in the clouds . . . to meet the Lord in the air." This end (5:1-11) will come "like a thief in the night" (which makes speculation as to the time useless). It should not surprise the readers, who are "children of the light," but they should be watchful and encourage one another.

In 5:12, Paul turns again to the life of the fellowship, encouraging the readers to be at peace among themselves and counseling respect for the leaders, admonition of idlers, and encouragement of the fainthearted. He closes (5:23-28) with words of benediction, encouragement, and exhortation. The readers should feel comforted in the midst of their difficulties and strengthened by Paul's acknowledgment of their faith and reminders of his ministry among them.

Critical Problems

First Thessalonians is a simple pastoral letter, devoted largely to the task of encouraging new Christians to continue in the faith. And Paul's theology seems straightforward and uncomplicated: as far as we can tell from this letter, Christian faith consists mainly in accepting Jesus, whom God raised from the dead, as the agent of salvation (5:9) and in faithfully awaiting his return.

Some questions, however, are not so easily answered. Does the fact that Paul goes to such lengths to defend the behavior of his group when they were in Thessalonica mean that someone there has been critical of him? What are the "afflictions" (3:3 RSV) the Thessalonians have suffered? And was there some misunderstanding at work in their questions about the end?

On one reading (reflected in the NRSV translation of 3:3), the Thessalonians have undergone persecution, which has caused their eschatological anxiety. And if one accepts the Acts account, this persecution was at the hands of the Jews. Abraham Malherbe, however, thinks Paul refers to the new Christians' psychological distress, brought on by the alienation from friends, associates, and family that accompanied the abandonment of their former lives. He argues that, at 2:14, Paul refers to rejection not by Jews but by fellow Gentiles.[5]

Malherbe also claims that Paul's self-defense at 2:1-8 follows a pattern common among Hellenistic philosophers distinguishing themselves from those among their number of bad reputation.[6] While many scholars try to identify specific opponents of Paul at Thessalonica, Malherbe finds their attempts unnecessary. On his reading, 1 Thessalonians is a letter born solely of pastoral concern.

Some scholars, however, think a conflict lies in the background. Robert Jewett argues that when Paul stresses that his mission was not "in vain" (2:1), we must imagine that some group in Thessalonica has claimed that it was.[7] Jewett thinks the community was made up largely of people on the lower end of the social scale, who would at one time have been attracted to the cult of Cabirus, which once flourished in Thessalonica. This religion was ecstatic in nature and offered the "divinization" of the initiates. By the time of Paul, however, it had been absorbed into the imperial cult that flourished at Thessalonica. The followers of Cabirus among the common people would likely have become alienated from the cult, feeling it had been co-opted by the rich and powerful.

Perhaps, then, the new converts brought expectations that led to disappointment with Paul. They might have expected dramatic demonstrations of charismatic power. And they might have interpreted Paul's message as an extreme form of "millenarianism" that placed so much emphasis upon the nearness of the new age that it seemed appropriate to shirk all worldly responsibilities. That would explain why Paul addressed the issue of "idlers" in 5:14. It might also explain the Thessalonians' distress at the death of community members.

Paul's instructions, however, can be interpreted as part of the stock advice of those who nurtured Hellenistic philosophical and religious groups. And Malherbe notes that some philosophical schools were criticized for their lack of social responsibility.[8] It is possible that Paul's concern was simply to distinguish the Christians from groups that tended to opt out of society altogether.

Philippians

The Story behind the Letter

Like the Letter to Philemon, Philippians was written from prison. And because Paul refers to "the whole imperial guard" (1:13) and "the emperor's household" (4:22), the usual assumption has been that he wrote from Rome. There were seats of Roman government in other major cities, however. And the great distance between Rome and Philippi raises questions about the feasibility of the communications between Philippi and the place of Paul's imprisonment. Also, as in Philemon, Paul expresses his desire to visit the recipients, whereas his intention was to go from Rome to Spain. If Paul wrote from Rome, the date would have been 59–62 C.E.

We know from 1 Thessalonians that Paul experienced extreme opposition in the mission in Philippi before coming to Thessalonica. According to Acts 16, the Roman authorities imprisoned him and his companion Silas for creating a disturbance. The letter to the Philippians shows, however, that Paul was successful in founding a Christian community there, one with which he developed a special relationship. The letter also reveals that at some point he had received financial assistance from the Philippian Christians, delivered by Epaphroditus. Having fallen ill and subsequently recovered, Epaphroditus is now returning to Philippi with the letter.

Further reconstruction of the story behind the letter is complicated by a critical problem. At 3:1, Paul seems to be bringing the letter to a close, but at 3:2 he suddenly launches a biting attack upon some unnamed proponents of circumcision and then goes on to criticize those whose "god is the belly" (3:19). Again at 4:2-9, the letter seems to be moving toward a conclusion. Now, however, Paul proceeds (4:10-20) to thank the Philippians for their gift.

Many scholars take these breaks in thought sequence as evidence of the composite nature of the present letter. One among several reconstructions is that 3:2—4:1 and 4:10-20 are fragments of other letters that an editor has woven into the "main" letter. Others remain unconvinced by this evidence, however, and interpret the material following 3:1 as a series of postscripts. In the treatment that follows, I will proceed through the letter as it stands.

Points to Look For in Philippians

- Paul's attitude toward his imprisonment and suffering

- Paul's feelings toward the Philippian congregation

- Paul's biographical statements

- The view of Christ in 2:6-11

Notes on a Reading of Philippians

1:1—3:1

Following the salutation, Paul offers a thanksgiving (1:3-11) that encourages the Philippians to persevere in their faith, assured of God's work among them in preparation for the "day of Christ," and expresses his affection for them. The thanksgiving also comforts the readers in the face of Paul's imprisonment by including them as "partakers" in this experience and in the grace that somehow issues from it.

Paul's Points in 1:12—3:1

— *1:12-18a.* Paul discusses his imprisonment; it has advanced the gospel by emboldening others in their proclamation. While some of these preach in order to increase Paul's suffering in prison, it does not matter as long as the gospel is preached.

— *1:18b-26.* He rejoices despite his sufferings, believing he will be released. He ponders whether he prefers to live or to die and be with Christ, but assures the readers he will preserve his life for their sake.

— *1:27-30.* His readers should stand fast; their suffering for Christ is a privilege.

— *2:1-18.* He counsels humility, quoting a hymn (2:6-11) in order to present Christ, who took on human form and was obedient to death, as an example. He exhorts his readers to live blamelessly in a crooked world and to rejoice with him.

— *2:19—3:1.* He will send Timothy to Philippi. Epaphroditus has recovered and will come there also, so that the Philippians may rejoice with him. Paul closes this section with another injunction to "rejoice in the Lord."

The readers will feel included in a community grounded in Christ and dedicated to selfless concern for others, and they will be motivated to give attention to the quality of their life together. They will sense a warm bond with Paul himself, be inspired by his courage in the face of adversity, and reflect on the joy mediated by their faith.

3:2—4:1

Warning the readers against the "evil workers" who propose circumcision, Paul adds a biographical point. Having found righteousness before through Christ, he counts his former blamelessness under the law of no worth. He follows with statements on the hope for resurrection (3:10) and the goal of the Christian life (3:12-16). Presenting himself as a model for imitation, Paul warns against those whose "god is the belly" (3:19) and counsels steadfastness (4:1).

4:2-9

Addressing a dispute by two women leaders in the community, he asks his readers to help them reconcile. Returning to the theme of rejoicing, he counsels his readers to engage in prayer and thanksgiving, focus on the positive aspects of community life, and imitate him.

4:10-20

Rejoicing in the Philippians' concern for him, Paul asserts that he has learned to be content in any circumstances. Acknowledging the gifts the Philippians have sent through Epaphroditus, as well as earlier contributions, he interprets these gifts as a contribution to his work and an act of worship.

4:21-22

With a traditional greeting and benediction, Paul concludes the letter.

Development of Christology in Philippians 2:6-11

Scholars generally acknowledge that at 2:6-11 Paul quotes an early Christian hymn to Christ, whether it was composed by Paul himself at an earlier time or by someone else. There is dispute, however, over the interpretation of the hymn. It seems almost self-evidently to contain a reference to the preexistence of Christ (vv. 6-7), and most scholars interpret it in that way. If they are correct, this means that Christians developed the view of Christ as a preexistent being at a very early date.

Some scholars interpret the hymn in a way that does not involve preexistence and claim that the notion of preexistence was a late development. Most, however, find such a reading strained. Not only does another Christ hymn, quoted in Colossians 1:15-20, seem to contain a notion of preexistence, but in several passages, Paul himself embraces such a Christology: 1 Corinthians 1:24; 8:6; and 10:1-5. The first two of these passages are of particular interest because they can be interpreted as applications of the motif of personified Wisdom to Christ.

Did Paul Have Opposition in Philippi?

What is behind Paul's outburst regarding circumcision in 3:2-11? We know that he contended with proponents of circumcision in Galatia, and some scholars have found similar groups at both Thessalonica and Philippi. On one theory, Christians who sought to bring Christianity into full conformity with Judaism dogged Paul in his missionary travels. Another view is that Paul was opposed, in these cities and in Corinth, by Jewish Christian gnostics who urged circumcision but also embraced a libertine lifestyle.

However, we have seen other possibilities for understanding the situation in Thessalonica, and the evidence for organized opposition within the church is slim with respect to Philippi. Paul could as easily be speaking in Philippians 3 of non-Christian Jews seeking to bring the Gentile converts into their own fold as he could of a group of Christians urging circumcision.

Galatians

The Story behind the Letter

Paul writes this letter in response to the news that missionaries have appeared in Galatia and convinced some of the people to accept a version of the gospel different from the one he preached when he was among them. According to their teaching, male Gentile converts must undergo circumcision, which would mean that all Christians are subject to the Jewish law. In response to this development, Paul writes to the churches in Galatia to win them back to the gospel he originally preached to them—the gospel without the law.

Paul addresses this letter to "the churches in Galatia," but it is unclear whether this means the old Galatian territory in the north-central region of Asia Minor or the larger Roman province of Galatia that included

territory to the south. Some think the "south Galatian" theory best accounts for the controversy over circumcision that dominates the letter, since we know that Jews were present in the south but have no indication of their presence in the north. However, the letter seems to presuppose a predominantly Gentile congregation, and those urging circumcision probably came from outside the congregation. Also, the term *Galatians* (3:1) was more commonly used as an ethnic designation, applicable to the north-central area, than of residents of the province. Thus, the majority of scholars today favor the "north Galatian" theory. Proponents of the south Galatian theory sometimes place the letter as early as 48 C.E., but those who favor the north Galatian theory usually favor a date in the mid-50s and look to Ephesus or Macedonia as the place of composition.

There has been much speculation about the nature of Paul's opponents in Galatia, but the most widely accepted opinion is that they were conservative Jewish Christians seeking to keep the Christian movement within the Jewish fold. Some scholars, noting that Paul's injunctions against licentiousness in 5:13-25 do not seem to fit such opponents, think Paul may have been fighting on two fronts. But this theory has not gained much support. Another theory is that of Walter Schmithals: Paul's opponents were members of a gnostic group embracing many Jewish elements but also advocating libertine behavior—a group that Schmithals believes also opposed Paul in Corinth, Philippi, and Thessalonica.[9] It is unclear that Christian Gnosticism even existed at this time, however, and this view has lost support in recent decades.

A Preliminary Note:
"Faith *in* Christ" or "Faithfulness *of* Christ"?

The concept of being justified, or pronounced righteous in God's sight, is a key element in Paul's thought in Galatians and Romans. But the Greek phrase he uses in this regard has been translated two different ways. One way indicates that people are justified by *their* faith in Christ, whereas the other way means that they participate in *Christ's* own faithfulness to God. Either way, human faith or faithfulness plays a role, and either way, justification is a gift of God, not a human accomplishment. Most translations take the first option, "faith in Christ," but many list the second as a possibility.

Points to Look For in Galatians

• Paul's sense of apostolic authority and his relationship to other apostles

• Paul's understanding of justification by faith/faithfulness and the role of the law

• Paul's appeal to experience and to scripture

• The role of the Spirit in Galatians

• Paul's emphasis on ethics/love

Notes on a Reading of Galatians

1:1—2:21

After a salutation in 1:1-5, Paul launches a biting criticism of his readers and defends the gospel he preached to them.

Paul's Arguments in 1:6—2:21

— **1:6-10.** Paul expresses astonishment that the Galatians have turned away from what he proclaimed to them in favor of "another gospel" and pronounces a curse on those who preach it.

— **1:11-24.** He recounts his own history to prove that he received his gospel directly from God, not human beings, playing down his association with the other apostles.

— **2:1-14.** He recounts his meeting with the other apostles in Jerusalem, claiming that they added nothing to his message but agreed that he should preach to the Gentiles and Peter to the Jews. He tells how he rebuked Peter at Antioch after Peter withdrew from eating with Gentiles when emissaries from James objected.

— **2:15-21.** He now makes a larger point: as a person in Christ, he is "dead" to the law, and Christ lives in him. And people are justified not by works of the law but by faith in Christ (or Christ's faithfulness).

3:1—5:1

Now Paul attacks the proponents of the "false gospel."

Paul's Arguments in 3:1—5:1

— *3:1-14.* Paul argues from the Galatians' experience. If they received the Spirit through a gospel without the law, the law is unnecessary. To accept circumcision is to turn from the Spirit to the flesh. Then he turns from experience to scripture: Abraham was justified because he believed (or trusted in) God before there was a law. The law brings a curse on those who seek justification through it, but Christ brings delivery from that curse.

— *3:15-18.* Paul uses an analogy: God's promise to Abraham is like a will that a person makes; once ratified, it cannot be annulled. The law cannot annul God's promise (of justification/righteousness), which was fulfilled in Christ.

— *3:19—4:7.* Now he has to explain why there was a law at all. It was a disciplinarian until Christ came but is now unnecessary. In 3:26, he makes use of "participation" language, signifying the believer's incorporation into Christ. In Christ, all human distinctions—Jew/Greek, slave/free, male/female—are obliterated; all are made one. To be under the law is to be like a minor or a slave, but Christ has redeemed those under the law and made them God's children who receive the Spirit.

— *4:8—5:1.* Paul again expresses distress and reminds the Galatians of the joy they experienced on first hearing the gospel. Then comes another argument from scripture, regarding the two sons of Abraham. The slave Hagar and her son (Ishmael) are prototypes of present Jews under the law. But the free woman (Sarah) and her son Isaac stand for Christians, free from the law.

5:2—6:10

Paul now turns to exhortation.

— *5:2-12.* Having been freed in Christ, the Galatians must not submit again to the "slavery" of circumcision. Contending that to do so is to sever oneself from Christ, Paul completes his line of logic with brutal humor (5:12): those demanding circumcision should go all the way and castrate themselves!

— *5:13-15.* He urges readers not to use their freedom in Christ for self-indulgence; they should abide by the command to love one's neighbor, which summarizes the entire law.

— *5:16-26.* He contrasts the works of the flesh with the fruits of the Spirit.

— *6:1-10.* He urges the readers to seek to restore transgressors, bear one another's burdens, and "work for the good of all, and especially for those of the family of faith."

6:11-17

Paul closes with further warnings against circumcision—contrasting circumcision and uncircumcision to the new creation in Christ—and a final blessing. By this point, the readers should feel shamed for departing from the gospel as they originally heard it. They should understand that justification by faith / Christ's faithfulness is incompatible with attempts to be justified by the law and that it was through the gospel without the law that they received the Spirit. They should also understand that life in the Spirit is not a life of self-indulgence but of love.

The Problem of the Stoicheia

Twice in Galatians Paul uses the Greek term *stoicheia*. The basic meaning of the word is "elements" or "fundamental principles," but precisely what it means and how it should be translated in any given passage is debated. Paul speaks in 4:3 of the "*stoicheia* of the world" and at 4:9 of "weak and beggarly *stoicheia*." When the ɴʀsᴠ renders the term "elemental *spirits*," it accepts the view that Paul refers to "demonic forces which constitute and control 'this evil aeon.'"[10] Walter Wink, however, argues that in

Galatians *stoicheia* refers "to those basic practices, beliefs, rituals, and celebrations which are fundamental to the religious existence of all peoples, Jew and Gentile alike."[11]

Concluding Comments

In Philemon, Philippians, and 1 Thessalonians, we observed Paul primarily as apostle and pastor. Galatians, too, is a pastoral letter, but it also exhibits Paul's theological thinking. His notions regarding righteousness / justification, law, and faith—stated only in the briefest form at Philippians 3:8-10—reach programmatic status in Galatians. Paul also develops the point that life in Christ is (as a "new creation") a radically new mode of existence, a life pervaded by the Spirit that stands in stark opposition to a life based upon "the flesh." Just what he means by "flesh" and "Spirit" will need some elaboration. And the same must be said of his use of "participation" language regarding Christians' relationship to Christ: "You . . . have clothed yourselves with Christ. . . . All of you are one in Christ Jesus" (3:27-28).

NOTES

1. ʀsᴠ. The ɴʀsᴠ obscures the point with the translation "*of* Jesus Christ."
2. Norman R. Petersen, *Rediscovering Paul: Philemon and the Sociology of Paul's Narrative World* (Philadelphia: Fortress Press, 1985).
3. Ibid., 169.

4. Ibid., 269; italics in original.

5. Abraham J. Malherbe, *Paul and the Thessalonians: The Philosophic Tradition of Pastoral Care* (Philadelphia: Fortress Press, 1987), 46–47.

6. Ibid., 2–3.

7. Robert Jewett, *The Thessalonian Correspondence: Pauline Rhetoric and Millenarian Piety* (Philadelphia: Fortress Press, 1986), 102.

8. Malherbe, *Paul and the Thessalonians*, 97.

9. Walter Schmithals, *Paul and the Gnostics*, trans. J. E. Steely (Nashville: Abingdon, 1972).

10. Hans Dieter Betz, *Galatians: A Commentary on Paul's Letter to the Churches in Galatia* (Philadelphia: Fortress Press, 1979), 204; see also 213–16.

11. Walter Wink, *Naming the Powers: The Language of Power in the New Testament* (Philadelphia: Fortress Press, 1984).

STUDY QUESTIONS

1. Reconstruct the "story" behind Philemon.

2. Explain the "socio-literary method" Petersen employs in studying Philemon. What does Petersen learn about the letter through this method?

3. Are Paul's ideas on slavery adequate for our own time in history?

4. Reconstruct the "story" behind 1 Thessalonians. What are the main theological themes Paul stresses in this letter?

5. Contrast the views of Malherbe and Jewett on the reason for Paul's writing 1 Thessalonians.

6. Reconstruct the "story" behind Philippians.

7. Why do some scholars think Philippians might be a composite of fragments?

8. Characterize Paul's relationship to the church at Philippi.

9. Reconstruct the "story" behind Galatians.

10. Characterize the understanding of Paul's relationship to the leadership of the Jerusalem church expressed in Galatians. From what source does Paul claim to have received the message he preached?

11. What issue was at stake in Paul's confrontation with Peter at Antioch?

12. Explain Paul's understanding of the Jewish law in Galatians.

13. What role does the Spirit play in Christian life, according to Galatians?

14. What are the competing views of the meaning of the term *stoicheia*?

15. What are the competing views of the identity of Paul's opponents in Galatia?

FOR FURTHER READING

Bassler, Jouette M., ed. *Pauline Theology*, vol. 1, *Thessalonians, Philippians, Galatians, Philemon*. Minneapolis: Fortress Press, 1991.

Betz, Hans Dieter. *Galatians: A Commentary on Paul's Letter to the Churches in Galatia*. Philadelphia: Fortress Press, 1979.

Cousar, Charles B. *Galatians*. Atlanta: John Knox, 1982.

Jewett, Robert. *The Thessalonian Correspondence: Pauline Rhetoric and Millenarian Piety*. Philadelphia: Fortress Press, 1986.

Malherbe, Abraham J. *Paul and the Thessalonians: The Philosophic Tradition of Pastoral Care*. Philadelphia: Fortress Press, 1987.

Osiek, Carolyn. *Philippians, Philemon*. Nashville: Abingdon, 2000.

Petersen, Norman R. *Rediscovering Paul: Philemon and the Sociology of Paul's Narrative World*. Philadelphia: Fortress Press, 1985.

1 and 2 Corinthians

10

Paul's Corinthian Correspondence

Our two canonical letters from Paul to the Corinthians mention two others that are now lost, one prior to 1 Corinthians (see 1 Cor 5:9) and another between 1 and 2 Corinthians (see 2 Cor 2:3-4). In addition, there is evidence that 2 Corinthians 10–13 was originally part of a different letter (but probably not to be identified with either of the lost letters already mentioned). Some scholars have thought that 1 Corinthians also is a composite of several letters, but not many accept this today. In any case, Paul wrote at least four letters to Corinth, and very likely five. As we will see, the letters that we have reveal a variety of problems that Paul dealt with in this congregation, and his responses reveal his views on several issues.

1 Corinthians

The Story behind the Letter

As is clear from 1 Corinthians 2–3, Paul founded the church in Corinth. According to Acts 18, he went there after leaving Athens and stayed with a couple from Rome, with whom he worked as a tent maker. In 1 Corinthians 16:19, he sends greetings from this couple, Prisca and Aquila, who are now with him in Ephesus. Romans 16:3 reveals that they were associates in his missionary activity.

He also mentions three others who preached in Corinth: Silvanus (Silas in Acts) and Timothy, both of whom worked concurrently with him (2 Cor 1:19); and Apollos, who came to Corinth after Paul had left (1 Cor 1:10-17). Acts 18:24-28 characterizes Apollos as an eloquent missionary and recounts how Priscilla (Prisca) and Aquila converted him from "the baptism of John" to Christianity in Ephesus.

After leaving Corinth, Paul received two communications from Corinth: a letter raising a number of questions, and a report from "Chloe's people" that painted a disturbing picture of the state of affairs in the church. Now in Ephesus (16:8), Paul writes to answer the Corinthians' questions and to speak to the problems revealed in the report. Scholars usually date the letter in the early to middle 50s C.E.

Points to Look For in 1 Corinthians

- Paul's emphasis on unity in Christ

- Paul's views on human wisdom

- Paul's views on eating meat offered to idols, marriage and divorce, and speaking in tongues

- The role of love and community in Paul's ethics

- Paul's views on eschatology

- Importance of the cross in Paul's thought

- Paul's use of irony

Notes on a Reading of 1 Corinthians

1:1—6:20

After a salutation in 1:1-3, in which Paul refers to his apostolic office, he offers a thanksgiving for the Corinthians that highlights their spiritual gifts (1:4-9). Then he addresses issues in the congregation.

— *1:10-18.* In response to a report from Chloe's people, Paul criticizes the divisions among them, which are based on loyalty to leaders, such as Peter and himself, and he appeals for unity.

— *1:19-31.* Employing irony and rhetorical questions, he contrasts human wisdom to God's wisdom—the message of the cross, which is foolishness to those outside of Christ. Not many of the readers are wise by human standards; no one should boast in anything but God. The implication is that some in Corinth claim to have wisdom.

— *2:1-16.* Paul's message was characterized not by wisdom but by a demonstration of the Spirit. But he refers to God's secret wisdom that the unspiritual, including "the rulers of this age," cannot grasp.

— *3:1-23.* Turning back to factionalism, Paul calls the readers "people of the flesh" and stresses that Christ alone is the foundation of the church, not he or Apollos, who are servants.

— *4:1-13.* Paul defends his ministry, implying that some have criticized him, and attacks those who act arrogantly. With powerful irony, he contrasts the vulnerability of the apostles to the attitudes of those who think they already know the fullness of the new age: "Already you have all you want!"

— *4:14-21.* In a more conciliatory tone, he interprets his admonitions as those of a father, but he returns to irony in a warning about an impending visit.

— *5:1-13.* Regarding other aspects of the report, Paul turns first to the case of a man having relations with his stepmother (prohibited by both Jewish and Roman law). This is a corrupting influence on the church. Paul details a punishment, presumably a ritual of excommunication.

— *6:1-11.* He condemns those who bring lawsuits against one another.

— *6:12-20.* Paul now launches a general condemnation of unrighteousness that leads to a confrontation with some views in the congregation. Quoting their slogans ("All things are lawful" and "Food is meant for the stomach") with apparent approval, he attacks their use of these premises. Freedom does not mean permission for immorality.

7:1—11:1

Paul now answers the questions the Corinthians raised in their letter.

— *7:1-16.* The first issues pertain to marriage, divorce, and sex. Paul expresses preference for celibacy. But he accepts marriage and counsels against celibacy within marriage, acknowledging the conjugal rights of both wife and husband (7:3). He prefers that the unmarried and widows remain single, but only if they can practice sexual self-control (7:8-9). Citing a command of Jesus, he counsels against divorce and states that those who do separate should remain unmarried (7:10-11). A believer married to an unbeliever should remain in the union if the unbelieving spouse consents; separation is permissible if the other party desires it.

— *7:17-24.* Paul now states the principle behind these views. It is better to stay in one's current state because of the near end of the age. Among his examples is slavery. Those who are in Christ belong to God and should not become slaves. But translators differ on whether 7:21 means that slaves who have the opportunity for freedom should remain in their present condition (NRSV) or should make use of the opportunity (RSV).

— *7:25-40.* Distinguishing his own opinion from a command of Jesus, Paul explains his preference that the unmarried and widows remain single: they should be free from the anxieties that come with marriage as they await the end of the age. But a wife is free to remarry if her husband dies.

— **8:1-13; 10:14—11:1.** Regarding food offered to idols, Paul on one level takes the side of those who accept this practice. He agrees that "no idol in the world really exists" and "there is no God but one" (8:4). And he grants the freedom to "eat whatever is sold in the meat market," even in the home of an unbeliever (10:25-26). But if eating food offered to idols confuses a "weaker" member—someone lacking full knowledge on this issue—then one should forgo the freedom and decline to eat (8:7-13; 10:28-29), for to cause another member to fall is a sin (8:12-13). The life of the community thus takes precedence over individual enjoyment. The actual worship of idols is forbidden, since those who participate in Christ's body cannot share the table of demons (10:14-22).

— **9:1—10:13.** Sandwiched between the two discussions of food offered to idols are Paul's thoughts on two other subjects. First, he defends his apostolic authority, which has apparently been challenged on the grounds that he has not exercised the apostolic right to financial support from the community. He has the right to such support and to a wife, but for the sake of the gospel, he chooses not to exercise these rights. This is part of a general strategy of entering into the situations of those to whom he preaches (9:19-22). Second, he recounts the story of the Israelites' disobedience in the wilderness as a warning against idolatry and sexual immorality.

— **11:2-16.** After his second treatment of food offered to idols, Paul commands women to keep their heads covered when praying or prophesying in worship, perhaps meaning that they should not let their hair flow loose. He supports this rule with an argument from nature that presupposes different hairstyles for men and women. But he asserts the mutuality between men and women. The statement falls short of true egalitarianism, since "neither was man created for the sake of woman, but woman for the sake of man" (11:9). But Paul clearly recognizes that "in the Lord woman is not independent of man or man independent of woman" (11:11).

— **11:17-33.** He criticizes the people's behavior at the Lord's Supper. In an allusion back to the problem of factionalism (11:19), he notes that some people are eating their meals and getting drunk before others arrive. He cites a tradition regarding Jesus' institution of the meal (11:23-26) as he accuses the Corinthians of desecrating the rite and violating their unity in Christ.

12:1—14:40

In 12:1, Paul turns to the topic of spiritual gifts (12:2-3), implying that one can actually be led astray by them. He does not oppose these gifts but implicitly criticizes those who might boast of having superior ones. The same Spirit distributes all of them (12:4-11), and all who are baptized into Christ "drink" of that Spirit (12:12-13). Since all members are parts of the body, none can claim superiority (12:1-31).

Paul nevertheless regards some gifts as "greater" than others—a point that leads into the "Love Chapter" (13). Subordinating all gifts to love, he presents it as a universal value. But it is clear that he speaks specifically of the self-giving love associated with Christ.

In chapter 14, he discusses speaking in tongues—the practice of ecstatic, unintelligible speech inspired by the Spirit—comparing this gift with that of prophecy. Speaking in tongues is valid, but it must be regulated to maintain orderly worship: only two or three persons should give utterances in worship, and only if an interpreter is present. The principle is that all aspects of worship should build up the community (14:26).

15:1-58

At 15:1, Paul turns to eschatology. Relating a traditional proclamation of Jesus' resurrection, he comes to the point in verse 12: some in the congregation deny the resurrection of the dead. Arguing that such denial undercuts Christ's own resurrection and their own deliverance from sin, he makes a declaration that ends in an account of the final events: Christ's resurrection; his return; the raising of

FIG. 10.1   **The Archaic Temple at Corinth and the Acrocorinth.** Photo by Marshall Johnson.

"those who belong to Christ"; the destruction of all competing authorities, including death; and finally, Christ's own subjection to God. In 15:29-34, Paul rounds out his argument, appealing both to the Corinthians' practice of receiving baptism in behalf of the dead and to his own empowerment to face difficulties.

Using the Stoic rhetorical device of diatribe, Paul raises a series of questions, only to declare how foolish they are (15:35-36). Then he explains the manner of the resurrection. Drawing on analogies from nature and the scriptural image of Adam, he describes resurrection as transformation of the person into a "spiritual body," rather than the resuscitation of "flesh and blood." The final resurrection will come before all now alive have died, and the living will be instantly transformed.

Paul closes his argument with a declaration of victory over death and a final exhortation to faithfulness. He has encircled the readers with logic, experience, scripture, and reference to experience. They should conclude that they cannot deny the resurrection without denying the heart and soul of their Christian faith.

16:1-24

Paul gives instructions regarding the collection for Jerusalem and his travel plans. After brief notes and further instructions, he adds greetings and closes with an expression of his love, but not before a final warning (16:22). The readers are left with the dual feelings of severe chastisement on the one hand and inclusion within the community on the other.

A Critical Note on 14:33b-36

Many scholars consider 14:33b-36 a later addition to the text by someone other than Paul. These verses interrupt the flow of thought and express a point (that women should keep silent in church) that seems to contradict Paul's presuppositions in 11:5. Another view is that here Paul again quotes a Corinthian slogan in order to refute it. Verse 36a should therefore read, "What? Did the word of God originate with you?" as in the RSV, and should be interpreted as a rejection of verses 33b-35.[1] On either suggestion, Paul did not forbid women to speak in church.

Knowledge, Wisdom, Status, and Gender: Paul's Opponents in 1 Corinthians

The Nature of the Problem in Corinth

Scholars have made many attempts to identify the group or groups Paul attacks in 1 Corinthians. Some have taken his reference to the slogans, such as "I belong to Paul" and "I belong to Apollos" in 1:10-17, as a sign that the church was split into several factions. And one view is that Paul is struggling against Jewish Christian gnostics. They claim a superior wisdom (1:18—2:14) and experience of the new age in its fullness (4:8-13), and they exercise radical freedom from the law (6:12-20; 8:1-13; 10:14—11:1). It has also been argued that the phrase "Let Jesus be cursed!" at 12:3 is among their slogans—a rejection of the physical person Jesus in favor of the spiritual Christ.[2]

However, the letter gives no hint of the complex mythological systems of developed

Gnosticism, and the phrase "Let Jesus be cursed!" may simply be a rhetorical device providing a contrast to the confession "Jesus is Lord."[3] Many scholars therefore characterize Paul's opponents simply as Hellenistic "enthusiasts"—persons so enamored of their sense of possession by the Spirit that they think they transcend the present age.

In any case, there were persons in Corinth who differed from Paul on some crucial issues, and their eschatology is a point of particular interest to scholars. Some think Paul was mistaken in assuming that their denial of resurrection (15:12) was a denial of eternal life. They may have rejected the Jewish notion of resurrection because they embraced the Greek idea of the immortality of the soul. Another view is that they pushed "realized eschatology" to the point of believing that the resurrection had already taken place.

Social Status of Those Paul Criticizes

Gerd Theissen argues that class conflict is in the background of 1 Corinthians.[4] It is clear from 1:26-31 that the Corinthian church was made up primarily of persons from the lower classes. Based on Paul's statements about specific persons in Corinth and some passages in Acts, however, Theissen determines that most of these were persons of considerable means. The phrase "Chloe's people," for example, suggests that this woman was mistress of a large household including slaves and/or servants; in other cases, the mention of houses or households is explicit. The community in Corinth apparently embraced a cross section of society.[5]

Theissen argues that the groups Paul identifies as "the weak" and (by implication) "the strong" fall out along class lines. "The strong" advocate freedom to eat meat offered to idols; only the affluent were frequently invited to banquets, and only they could have afforded meat as a regular part of their diet. "The weak" are scandalized by eating consecrated meat; the poor would have received meat most often through public distributions on ceremonial occasions and probably associated it with pagan worship. The affluent, moreover, would have been better educated and more interested in the speculative wisdom that characterized the Corinthian "enthusiasm."

Theissen also finds class conflict in the controversy over the Lord's Supper.[6] Of those who arrive early for the meal, Paul asks rhetorically (11:22), "Do you not have homes to eat and drink in?"—suggesting their affluence. It is difficult to know exactly what was going on: wealthy hosts might have provided better meals for their peers (a typical custom) or perhaps *only* the bread and wine for the poor. In any case, Paul brings a theological perspective to the conflict. He interprets the disruptions as part of the eschatological testing of the congregation (11:19), and he views the meal itself in an eschatological context: unworthy participation leads to condemnation at the judgment. The Corinthians' behavior is unworthy because it denies the unity the meal establishes (10:16-17).

Paul's criticism of some church members for taking others to court (6:1-11) may also reflect class conflict. Alan C. Mitchell thinks rich members are suing the poorer ones.

Ancient standards of honor and shame would discourage taking one's peers to court, and "people of higher statuses are more likely to litigate against people of statuses beneath them than vice versa."[7]

Status and Gender

Antoinette Clark Wire paints a rather different picture in her attempt to reconstruct the Corinthians' point of view through a study of the rhetoric of 1 Corinthians.[8] She believes that women prophets were among those attacked by Paul in this letter. And drawing on anthropological studies, she argues that the conflict was rooted in the different ways in which inclusion into the church affected the social standing of Paul on the one hand and these women on the other.

For Paul, an educated male, the decision to enter the Christian fellowship entailed a voluntary loss of status. For the uneducated segment in Corinth, however, that decision brought a gain in status. And that was particularly true for the women. They would have experienced greater freedom within the church than outside it and would have gained a new sense of empowerment.[9]

This difference in experience resulted in different perspectives. Paul stressed humility and emphasized that God inverts the values of the world. Having voluntarily accepted lower status, Paul expected those of low status to remain in that condition. But to the Corinthian women prophets, the new life in Christ meant a destruction of old boundaries. It brought them wisdom, power, and honor. Whereas Paul thought of them as arrogant persons

seeking social advantage, they must have thought of him as denying the social transformation God had brought about. And if Paul thought their claims to wisdom ignored the difference between this life and the next, they must have thought that he denied the power of the Spirit to work changes in human beings in this life.

Wire rejects the view of many scholars that 14:33b-36, which forbids women to speak in church, is a non-Pauline addition. And she argues that the conflict between Paul and the women is a central aspect of the letter. Comparing 1 Corinthians 12:13 to Galatians 3:27-28, she notes that although, in the latter context, Paul can proclaim that in Christ "there is no longer Jew or Greek . . . slave or free . . . male and female," in the present letter, he omits the reference to male and female. Although in other contexts he takes the more inclusive view, the conflict in Corinth leads him to reinforce a traditional social boundary.[10]

2 Corinthians

The Story and a Critical Problem

There is widespread agreement that 2 Corinthians is a composite of two or more letters of Paul. Chapters 1–9 presuppose that the Corinthian church has passed through a crisis that is now resolved. Paul extends forgiveness (2:10) and expresses his confidence in the church (7:16), but at 10:1 his tone changes abruptly. He becomes argumentative, speaking threateningly of a coming visit. In addition, 6:14—7:1 seems intrusive in its present context, and its severe attitude toward unbelievers is in tension with 1 Corinthians 5:10 and 7:12-16. Although some scholars treat it as a fragment of another Pauline letter, many believe it is a non-Pauline interpolation.

While scholars have proposed numerous explanations of the breaks in the thought flow, the following reconstruction of the story behind 2 Corinthians assumes that the canonical book combines two letters of Paul and a non-Pauline fragment (6:14—7:1). After writing 1 Corinthians, Paul pays a "painful" visit to Corinth (2 Cor 2:1). With the problems still unresolved, he sends an anguished letter, now lost, which he mentions in 2 Corinthians 2:3-4. Later, he sends Titus to Corinth, and Titus returns with basically good news. The letter has apparently accomplished its purpose, but some in Corinth are apparently hurt by Paul's harshness and his reneging on a promised visit (2 Cor 1:15—2:11). More seriously, a group claiming apostolic status has arrived in Corinth and is challenging his authority. From somewhere in Macedonia (2 Cor 9), Paul writes back (2 Cor 1–9) to express his joy over the healing that had taken place but also to lay the problems to rest.

Later, Paul learns that the rival apostles have gained adherents and pose a serious threat to his relationship to the Corinthian church. So he writes again (2 Cor 10–13) to defend his authority and discredit his opponents. All this correspondence presumably took place in the early to middle 50s.

Points to Look For in 2 Corinthians

- Paul's characterization of his own ministry, including his emphasis on his suffering and its redemptive effects

- Paul's contrasts between his ministry and that of the outside group and between the old and new covenants

- Paul's emphasis on reconciliation in chapters 1–9

- Paul's self-defense in chapters 10–13, including his use of irony

Notes on a Reading of 2 Corinthians 1–9

1:1—6:10

Following the salutation (1:1-2), Paul offers a blessing of God, who has sustained him and his companions in their suffering, which he interprets as having been for the sake of the recipients' consolation and salvation (1:3-11). Then comes the body of the letter.

— *1:12—2:11.* Paul reminds the readers of his conduct among them, which demonstrated his concern for them, and explains that his failure to visit was to spare them the pain of confrontation; instead, he wrote an anguished letter. He expresses forgiveness for a person who had caused trouble and urges the readers to forgive and console this person also. He adds a note about his anxiety when he missed contact with Titus.

— *2:12—3:18.* After a notation regarding his itinerary in 2:12-13, Paul turns to a discussion of his apostleship. He rejects personal credit but contrasts his ministry to that of those who came to Corinth with letters of recommendation. The success of his ministry in Corinth is his recommendation. Then he contrasts his ministry to that of the others as one of the Spirit and the new covenant rather than one based on the written law.

— *4:1—5:10.* Paul now contrasts his straightforward proclamation of the truth to others' underhanded ways and in 4:7 launches a poetic discourse on his sufferings. If "death" is at work in him, it is because he shares in Christ's sufferings and so that "life" might be at work in the readers (4:12).

— *5:11—7:16 (omitting 6:14—7:1).* Paul's discussion of his apostolic ministry has come full circle. Far from indulging in self-commendation, he has laid bare the nature of his work so that the readers can refute those who boast of externals. The entire argument culminates in the effect of Christ's death (5:16-21). The reader will understand that Paul's ministry needs no external validation; the word of reconciliation, grounded in the cross, is attested by his suffering on their behalf. He calls upon the Corinthians to be reconciled to God so that their original acceptance of grace might not be in vain (5:20—6:10). Reiterating his own sufferings on their behalf, he pleads for acceptance of his own ministry (6:11-12; 7:2-3), expresses his confidence in them (7:4), and rehearses the events leading to the harsh letter (7:5-16).

— *8:1—9:15.* Paul appeals to the Corinthians to complete the offering for the Jerusalem church, and concludes his points with an exclamation of thanks to God.

(*Critical note:* The original letter probably contained a closing that was deleted when it was joined with chapters 10–13, as was the opening of the attached letter. At 10:1, we find ourselves in the body of that letter.)

Perspective of 6:14—7:1

The passage 6:14—7:1, almost certainly a non-Pauline addition, deals with the relationship of community members to those outside, apparently forbidding marriage to unbelievers. "Beliar" is a name for Satan. Although the passage is Christian in orientation (v. 14), sharp dualism, the sense of separateness from the outside world, and the emphasis on purity are reminiscent of the Qumran literature.

Notes on a Reading of 2 Corinthians 10–13

10:1-18

Paul begins with an appeal to the Corinthians not to force him to make his upcoming visit unpleasant, warning that he is capable of disciplinary action, despite his opponents' charge that he is "humble when face to face" with them but bold toward them when away. In 10:7, he turns directly on his opponents with an argument touched with irony: apologizing for his own boasting, he exposes the opponents as the true boasters (10:13-17), and declining to compare himself to those who commend themselves (10:12), he exposes the absurdity of self-commendation (10:18).

11:1—12:10

The irony continues as Paul asks his readers (11:1) to indulge him in some "foolishness." Engaging in extended boasting and self-commendation, such as he has just criticized in his opponents, he defends himself against those he calls "super-apostles" in 11:5 and "false apostles" in 11:13. And he counters an apparent criticism of his practice of refusing financial support from the congregation by interpreting it as a sign of his love for the Corinthians (11:7-11)

Ironically playing the part of a fool from 11:16 to 12:10, Paul runs through a checklist of credentials, matching the opponents point by point and then turning to the one category in which they could not compete at all: his sufferings for Christ. In 12:1-4, the boasting reaches its climax as Paul speaks of a revelatory experience in which he was "caught up

into Paradise." But in 12:7-10, he mentions an unnamed physical infirmity that is a check against being too elated.

12:11—13:13

Paul explains that he has spoken as a fool because there is no avenue left open to him (12:11). His apparent point is that he has met arrogance with an ironical counter-arrogance! In 12:14, he returns to the theme of his coming visit, and starting at 13:1, he issues explicit warnings and exhortations. After a final appeal to the Corinthians to mend their ways (13:11), he closes the letter with brief greetings and a benediction.

Paul's strategy has been to dismantle his opponents' advantage by vacillating between straightforward speech and irony, constantly pushing the readers to look beyond appearances to their own human experience and to the character of the one who originally brought them to Christ.

Paul's Opponents in 2 Corinthians

Some scholars have assumed that in 2 Corinthians Paul is combating the same group he disputed in 1 Corinthians. The issues seem quite different in 2 Corinthians, however, and many recent commentators think they arrived on the scene after 1 Corinthians was written. While they were Jewish Christians of some sort (2 Cor 11:22-23), they apparently did not advocate circumcision, as did the group in Galatia. Nor is there any direct evidence of a gnostic orientation. In any case, they claimed charismatic gifts and apostolic status.

NOTES

1. David W. O'Dell-Scott, *A Post-Patriarchal Christology* (Atlanta: Scholars, 1991), 184–92.

2. Walter Schmithals, *Gnosticism in Corinth: An Investigation of the Letters to Corinth*, trans. John E. Steely (Nashville: Abingdon, 1971), 127.

3. Hans Conzelmann, *1 Corinthians: A Commentary on the First Epistle to the Corinthians*, trans. James W. Leitch (Philadelphia: Fortress Press, 1975), 204.

4. Gerd Theissen, *The Social Setting of Pauline Christianity: Essays on Corinth*, trans. John H. Schütz (Philadelphia: Fortress Press, 1982).

5. Ibid., 69–110.

6. Ibid., 145–68.

7. Alan C. Mitchell, "Rich and Poor in the Courts of Corinth: Litigiousness and Status in 1 Corinthians 6.1-11," *New Testament Studies* 39, no. 4 (1993): 576.

8. Antoinette Clark Wire, *The Corinthian Women Prophets: A Reconstruction through Paul's Rhetoric* (Minneapolis: Fortress Press, 1990).

9. Ibid., 58–71.

10. Ibid., 123–28.

STUDY QUESTIONS

1. Reconstruct the "story" behind 1 Corinthians.

2. What issues are at stake between Paul and his opponents in 1 Corinthians?

3. Summarize Paul's views, as expressed in 1 Corinthians, on sex, marriage and divorce, the eating of meat offered to idols, and participation in "pagan" worship.

4. Characterize Paul's understanding of the nature of Christian community as expressed in 1 Corinthians 12.

5. What is Paul's understanding of spiritual "gifts" in 1 Corinthians 13–14?

6. What does 1 Corinthians 15 reveal about Paul's eschatological views?

7. What use does Theissen make, in his sociological analysis of 1 Corinthians, of the categories of "the strong" and "the weak"?

8. Compare and contrast Wire's view on the controversy in 1 Corinthians with that of Theissen.

9. Why do many scholars think 2 Corinthians is composed of two or more separate letters?

10. What is problematic about 6:14—7:1, and what are the different views about its origin?

11. Reconstruct the "story" behind 2 Corinthians.

12. How does Paul meet the challenge regarding letters of recommendation in 2 Corinthians?

13. What, according to Paul, is the meaning of the sufferings he endures?

14. What strategy does Paul adopt in making his argument in chapters 10–13? Give your own evaluation of the advantages and disadvantages of such a strategy.

15. Why do many scholars think Paul is arguing against a different set of opponents in 2 Corinthians than he confronts in 1 Corinthians?

FOR FURTHER READING

Barrett, C. K. *A Commentary on the First Epistle to the Corinthians*. New York: Harper & Row, 1968.

———. *A Commentary on the Second Epistle to the Corinthians*. New York: Harper & Row, 1973.

Conzelmann, Hans. *1 Corinthians: A Commentary on the First Epistle of Paul to the Corinthians*. Translated by James W. Leitch. Philadelphia: Fortress Press, 1975.

Furnish, Victor Paul. *Second Corinthians*. Garden City, N.Y.: Doubleday, 1984.

Theissen, Gerd. *The Social Setting of Pauline Christianity*. Edited and translated by and with an introduction by John H. Schütz. Philadelphia: Fortress Press, 1982.

Wire, Antoinette Clark. *The Corinthian Women Prophets: A Reconstruction through Paul's Rhetoric*. Minneapolis: Fortress Press, 1990.

Romans

11

The Story behind the Letter

We can reconstruct the story behind the Letter to the Romans from 15:14-29. Convinced that he has completed his mission on the eastern end of the Mediterranean, Paul decides to extend his work to the west after delivering the collection for the Jerusalem church. He writes to the church in Rome to inform them that he will stop for a visit on his way from Jerusalem to Spain, likely in the hope of receiving their support for his work there (15:24). It is generally thought that he wrote during his three-month stay in Greece (Acts 20:1-3), probably Corinth, which would put the date of composition at 56–58 C.E.

Some interpreters think this letter is a summary of Paul's thought. According to one theory, he wrote to introduce himself to an important congregation that he did not found; others see it as a "round letter," sent to more than one church. Many scholars, however, maintain that Paul wrote to Rome to address issues between Jewish and Gentile Christians there.[1] Romans does bring together a number of themes that were central to Paul's thinking, but it is a genuine letter and not a theological treatise, and chapters 14–15 likely reflect a conflict that could have broken down partly along Jewish-Gentile lines. Given Paul's intention to visit Rome on the way to Spain, however, a letter of self-introduction would have been highly appropriate and would in fact have aided an attempt to mediate between Jews and Gentiles in the church. Jewish Christians, likely suspicious of Paul's attitude toward the law, might need an explanation of his views on justification/righteousness (Rom 1–8), and

Gentile Christians might have needed to be instructed on the role of Israel in God's plan of salvation (11:11-24).

Another issue concerns chapter 16, which contains greetings to people associated with the church in Ephesus. Not only does 15:33 sound like an ending, but in some manuscripts, the doxology in 16:25-27 comes at the end of chapter 15. On the "round letter" theory, chapter 16 could be an addendum to a copy sent to Ephesus, or it may have been a completely separate letter of recommendation on behalf of Paul's coworker Phoebe (16:1). However, chapter 16 makes sense as an ending to Romans if the persons mentioned there are Jewish Christians who left Rome during a period when Jews were persecuted but subsequently returned.

Whatever the case with chapter 16, the doxology in 16:25-27 is likely a non-Pauline addition. It occurs at various points in the manuscripts (after 14:23; 15:33; and 16:23) and is unlike any of Paul's other closings.

Points to Look For in Romans

- Arguments used by Paul to establish that all human beings, both Gentiles and Jews, are sinners

- The theme of "to the Jew first, and then to the Greek"

- Paul's understanding of justification/ righteousness by faith/faithfulness

- The parallel between Adam and Christ

- Paul's concept of dying and rising with Christ

- The role of the law

- The contrast between flesh and Spirit

- Paul's description of the new life in Christ

- Paul's statements on "the weak" and "the strong"

FIG. 11.1 **The Arch of Titus in Rome.** Photo © Scala /Art Resource, NY.

The Letter to the Romans: A Reading

1:1—3:20

Through an elaborate address and greeting, Paul introduces the readers to his understanding of the gospel and his ministry. As apostle to the Gentiles, he preaches the resurrection of God's Son in order to bring about "the obedience of faith." In the thanksgiving (1:8-15), he defines his coming visit in terms of mutual encouragement in the faith and states his intention to "preach the gospel" in the congregation. The net effect is to assert Paul's authority but also to allay fears that he might "lord it over" the congregation in Rome.

In 1:16-17, Paul gives a capsule definition of the gospel, which brings salvation for Jews first and then Greeks. It demonstrates God's faithfulness to the covenant promises and activity as a just judge.

Paul's first point is that God's wrath is revealed against all forms of ungodliness (1:18). When he argues that human beings are responsible for the wickedness they do, since certain aspects of God's being are evident in creation itself (1:19-32), it is clear that he is speaking of Gentiles, who do not have

FIG. 11.2 The Roman army taking the spoils from the Temple in Jerusalem. Detail from the Arch of Titus, Rome.
Photo © Vanni /Art Resource, NY.

the advantage of God's law. Identifying their sin as idolatry, he interprets the prevalence of same-sex intercourse as a sign that God has abandoned these idolaters to their own lusts.

Pointedly, Paul shifts his argument at 2:1. To any who feel comfortable in condemning others, he poses a series of rhetorical questions implying such persons' own guilt. Declaring these also subject to God's wrath, Paul then states that as those without the law are judged, so also are those with the law (2:12). And now he makes explicit what he had earlier implied: although Gentiles do not have the Torah, they do have a law "written on their hearts" (2:15) and are therefore accountable for their sin.

At 2:17, however, Paul turns his attention directly to the Jews. Having already stated in 2:12 that those who have sinned with the law will be judged along with those who sin without it, he now poses a series of rhetorical questions implicitly charging Jews with unfaithfulness. And then he contrasts physical circumcision to an inward disposition (2:25-29).

This indictment, however, raises a question. What about his earlier endorsement of the priority of Jews in God's plan of salvation? Resoundingly, he insists that this priority is real (3:2) and argues that human failure in no way nullifies God's faithfulness. What the readers should understand is that God, having made promises to Israel, cannot go back on them; nevertheless, if Israel itself rejects God, then God must exercise justice. Paradoxically, then, Israel's unfaithfulness becomes the occasion for the manifestation of God's justice. But this raises another question: Can God

hold Jews responsible for their sin, if that sin results in God's own glory? Paul insists that God's condemnation is just—deserved by those who receive it (3:8).

When in 3:9 Paul asks, "Are we any better off?" (that is, whether Jews are any better off than Gentiles), he returns to the question of Jewish "advantage" (3:1). His negative answer means that although the advantage is in one sense real, it does not affect salvation. The reason is that, as he demonstrates through scripture, all human beings—Jew and Gentile alike—are actually held under "the power of sin" (3:10-20).

The argument of chapters 1–3 thus concludes with a declaration of the universality of sin. The readers should understand that all humanity stands condemned and that no one is justified, or declared righteous, through the law.

3:21—8:39

With the phrase "but now," Paul signals a turning point in his argument. Having demonstrated the impossibility of a righteousness based on the law, he now announces the righteousness of God, based on faith, which is manifest in God's putting forth Jesus Christ "as a sacrifice of atonement" (3:21-26). This argument rests on two assumptions: first, that a just God cannot simply overlook sin; second, that God in the past has not passed judgment against sin but has shown "forbearance" toward it. The point is that now, through the death of Jesus Christ, God has acted justly by providing a way of judging the sinner—a way, however, that leads not to condemnation but to justification. That is to say, God's own righteous action in Christ results in the restoration of a right relationship between human beings and God.

Now the meaning of Paul's phrase "the righteousness of God," in 1:17, becomes clearer. In declaring that human beings stand justified before God through faith in Christ or the faithfulness of Christ, Paul is demonstrating that God has been faithful to the covenant made with Israel, but in a way that includes all humankind. God's righteousness is thus God's just judgment and faithfulness to the covenant (and all creation). It is perhaps also the human righteousness that God brings about through Christ. And, since Paul can speak of the gospel as "the power of God for salvation" (1:16), the righteousness of God revealed in that gospel is in some sense also the *power* through which God brings about human righteousness.

Paul's next point (3:27-31) is that if human beings are justified by faith/faithfulness, no one has grounds for boasting. Anticipating the reader's conclusion that the law is thus overturned, he insists that his teaching actually upholds the law. And for evidence, he turns to the Torah, arguing that Abraham himself was justified not by works of the law but by faith/faithfulness (4:1-25). God accounted him righteous because of his trust, even before his circumcision. Abraham therefore became the ancestor not of Israel alone (the circumcised) but of all humankind, since all would eventually be justified by faith/faithfulness. For, Paul argues, from the beginning God intended the promise to Abraham to reach beyond Israel. That is why justification/righteousness could not be based on the law.

"Therefore, since we are justified by faith"—Paul thus signals at 5:1 that he has made his point and can build upon it. Noting that justification creates peace between humanity and God, he piles up terms expressing the consequences of God's act in Christ: it provides access to *grace* and a basis for *hope* (5:2-5), and it demonstrates God's love, effecting reconciliation of humanity with God and signaling eventual salvation (5:6-11). Then, presenting Christ as the antitype of Adam, Paul contrasts the condemnation resulting from Adam's sin to the grace, righteousness, and eternal life issuing from Christ's obedience (5:12-19).

Declaring that when the law came in to increase sin, grace abounded all the more (5:19-21), Paul then pulls up short and raises the logical question: Should one then revel in sin to increase grace (6:1)? He answers by interpreting Christian baptism as an act of dying and rising with Christ, an incorporation into Christ that frees the believer from sin and opens up a new mode of existence. The "death" one dies in the rite is a death to sin. Then Paul restates his point with another set of metaphors (slavery to sin, slavery to God) and another term expressive of the new life—*sanctification*, being "set apart" by God for a holy purpose (6:15-23).

In 7:1, Paul's rhetorical question comes back to the law. Employing the metaphor of a woman's release from marriage through her husband's death, and reiterating the point in terms of dying and rising with Christ, he declares the Christian's freedom.

Because his argument links the law with sin and death, however, Paul must now anticipate the readers' questions: Is the law itself sinful, and does it bring death? Answering negatively in both cases, he gives a complex explanation. Sin uses the law to deceive human beings into thinking they can find salvation by obeying it. Because humanity itself is enslaved by the power of sin (7:14), the attempt to do good results in evil (7:21-23). Obedience to the law is thus a dead end. However, the law exposes sin for what it is (7:13) and thereby opens the way for an alternative solution to humanity's despair (7:21-25).

These last verses show that Christ provides what the law could not: deliverance from sin and death. But Paul states the point explicitly at 8:1 and elaborates on it in a passionate declaration of the nature of Christian existence. Life in Christ is lived "according to the Spirit," not "according to the flesh"; as such, it *is* "life and peace" (8:6)—that is, *authentic* human existence, the life of those who have become the children of God. The presupposition is that people must be "adopted" as God's children because the world apart from Christ is in bondage to sin. And for that reason, the process of adoption remains incomplete in the present. But Paul also proclaims a hope of deliverance that far outweighs the suffering that those in Christ must endure (8:18,

FIG. 11.3 **Saint Paul preaching to the Jews in the Synagogue at Damascus.** Byzantine mosaic, late twelfth century, Duomo, Italy.

31-39). The believer's "victory" over the world is a paradoxical one, since suffering remains. Yet it is the most profound victory imaginable, because Christians experience the one reality that makes real life possible: "the love of God in Christ Jesus our Lord" (8:39).

9:1—11:36

At 9:1, Paul introduces a new topic: the problem raised by most Jews' nonacceptance of Jesus. He expresses personal anguish over the fate of his fellow Israelites, but he is also concerned over whether Israel's failure means the failure of God's word. To demonstrate that God's word (that is, God's promise to Israel) has not failed, Paul uses biblical stories to distinguish between physical descent from Abraham and reception of the promise God gave Abraham. The point is that the rejection of Jesus by some Jews does not nullify the promise, since other Jews, along with Gentiles, receive that promise through Christ.

Because Paul believes that justification issues from God's mercy and is not a reward for human action (9:16-17), he can stress that those who receive the promise do so by God's *election* (9:11). But this raises the question of justice: If God elects those who will respond and those who will not, how can God pass judgment (9:14, 19)? On one level, Paul's answer is a simple assertion of the sovereignty of God; it is God's prerogative to choose the recipients of mercy and of wrath. If one focuses on the negative side of election, this answer may appear grossly inadequate. Paul's

emphasis, however, is on the positive side. God's seemingly negative acts—the rejection of Esau and the hardening of Pharaoh's heart—are not ends in themselves but serve to show God's mercy. Because Gentiles have found righteousness through faith (9:30), all God's actions play into the purpose of offering salvation as a free gift to everyone.

The focus, however, is not on Gentiles who found righteousness but on Jews who did not. Although desiring their salvation (10:1), Paul charges them with treating the law as a matter of works rather than faith (9:32) and contrasts their approach with the righteousness of God, which embraces both Jews and Gentiles (10:3-13). Then he quotes a series of biblical passages (10:18-21) to make his point: as God's word goes out to all the world, disobedient Israel becomes jealous.

With the question posed at 11:1—Has God rejected Israel?—the discussion of the Jewish people comes to a head. And Paul's answer is an emphatic "No!" To begin with, there is already a "remnant" (11:5), a small number of Jews who believe. Then, reasoning in rabbinic fashion from the lesser to the greater, he states that if Israel's trespass brings salvation to the Gentiles, the eventual *inclusion* of the whole Jewish people will have to mean something even greater!

At 11:13, Paul speaks specifically to Gentiles, undercutting any basis for gloating or pride with his metaphor of a wild shoot grafted onto a tree. Not only have Gentiles been incorporated into Israel's community, but they are subject to being "broken off," as were some Jews. The argument reaches a climax in the declaration that "all Israel will be saved" (11:26), and Paul summarizes the whole discussion in the statement that God has "imprisoned all in disobedience" only in order to "be merciful to all." The readers, sensing the depth of Paul's feeling, will grasp the appropriateness of the thanksgiving and doxology that conclude the argument (11:33-36). God has not only kept the promises to Israel but shown mercy to all humanity!

12:1—15:33

The phraseology of 12:1 ("I appeal to you therefore") combines with the "Amen" at 11:36 to mark the transition from the body of the letter to exhortations. It also coaches the readers to understand these exhortations as intimately related to what has gone before. The worship they should render is based on the "mercies of God" Paul has just recounted. And the call for a renewal of their minds in contrast to conformity to the world is based on the notion that, through Christ, God has set the world free from sin and death: the ethic Paul urges is that of the new age. In humility, all are to fulfill their functions within the body of Christ, as they are assigned by the Spirit, and their decisions should be grounded in a self-giving love that ministers to the enemy, seeks harmony within the community, and fully accepts the lowly.

Paul's injunctions on being subject to governing authorities (13:1-7) encourage a "quietistic," nonconfrontational relationship to the political order, and his statement on the near-ness of the end lends weight to all his exhortations (13:11-14). Coming on the wake of the broader exhortation not to conform to worldly standards, however, the assertion of rulers' authority presupposes the exercise of conscience (13:5), discernment of the good (13:3), and recognition of *God's* authority behind that of the ruler. Paul's statements in 13:8-10 put all the preceding injunctions in context: the one absolute requirement for Christians is the unqualified demand to love one's neighbor as oneself.

Beginning with 14:1, Paul addresses issues related to religious observances. He argues that observance of special days or dietary constraints cannot bring about salvation and cannot be made mandatory for Christians; to that extent, Paul sides against those he calls "the weak." Those who are "strong," however, must remember that love is the ultimate rule of the Christian life. They should make sacrifices to avoid causing others to stumble and should recognize that the practices of "the weak" are done out of devotion. But since the attitudes of the strong are rooted in similar devotion, the weak should honor their decisions also. As a broad rule, then, Paul proposes the exercise of individual conscience (14:5). The net result of the discussion is that Christians who make differing decisions on these matters are encouraged to live harmoniously with one another. And Paul concludes his argument by making just that point at 15:5-13.

The benedictory statement at 15:13 suggests to the readers that Paul has concluded his exhortations and is turning to other matters. That impression is borne out in 15:14

as he expresses general satisfaction with the Roman church and then explains his remarks in terms of his apostolic ministry (15:15-21). Should the readers retain suspicion regarding his teachings, they are implicitly asked to consider them in light of Paul's special calling.

Paul's delineation of his mission leads into an announcement of his ensuing visit, which he places in the context of his projected journeys to Jerusalem and Rome. His final appeal (15:30-33), therefore, serves to draw the readers into his ongoing ministry. The one who will visit them is one in whose ministry they share; they can therefore look forward to his visit as a time of mutual refreshment and joy.

16:1-23

By commending Phoebe to the congregation to whom he writes (16:1-2), Paul encourages the readers to accept her as a coworker in their mission. The greetings and commendations at 16:3-15 reaffirm his ties to the individuals mentioned and should strengthen the readers' resolve to continue in their work. These verses will also create a sense of solidarity, both between the congregation and Paul and within the Christian fellowship generally, which will make the exhortations in 16:17-20 seem appropriate. With final greetings, including a note from the scribe, Paul concludes the letter (16:21-23). (Some ancient manuscripts add a doxology as verse 24, but it is absent in the earliest manuscripts.)

16:25-27, a Benediction, Probably Added by Another Hand

In its setting at the end of chapter 16, the benediction provides a conclusion to the whole letter as it now stands.

NOTE

1. For articles outlining the various positions, see Karl P. Donfried, ed., *The Romans Debate*, rev. and expanded ed. (Peabody, Mass.: Hendrickson, 1991).

STUDY QUESTIONS

1. Reconstruct the "story" behind Romans. On what points do scholars disagree in the reconstruction of this story?

2. Why do many scholars think chapter 16, although written by Paul, might not have been part of his original letter to Rome?

3. How, according to Romans 1–8, are human beings enabled to stand justified before God? What are the steps in the author's argument on this matter? What role is played by his statement at 1:15 that the demands of the law are written on Gentiles' hearts?

4. What does Paul seem to mean by the phrase "righteousness of God"?

5. What does Christian baptism mean for Paul, and what role does his discussion of it in chapter 6 play in his argument?

6. How does Paul answer, in Romans 7, the hypothetical charge that because the law increases sin, it is itself sinful?

7. What, according to Romans 1–8, are the characteristics of the Christian life?

8. What role, according to Romans 9–11, does Israel play in God's plan for salvation? Explain why you do or do not find Paul's argument logical and/or meaningful at this point.

9. What is the specific meaning of Paul's metaphor of the body in Romans 12?

10. What advice does Paul give Christians in terms of their relationship to the Roman Empire?

FOR FURTHER READING

Cobb, John B., Jr., and David J. Lull. *Romans.* St. Louis: Chalice, 2005.

Donfried, Karl P., ed. *The Romans Debate*, rev. and expanded ed. (Peabody, Mass.: Hendrickson, 1991).

Johnson, Luke T. *Reading Romans: A Literary and Theological Commentary.* New York: Crossroad, 1977.

Perspectives on Paul

12

It is meaningful now to ask some questions about Paul's thought as a whole. In this chapter, I will first call attention to some key elements in Paul's theology and then, in the following two sections, examine his views from two hermeneutical perspectives. The final section will survey differing evaluations of the relevance of Paul's thought to moral issues in our contemporary world.

Cornerstones of Paul's Theology

Scholars are increasingly skeptical about approaches to Paul's writings that try to find in them a comprehensive, self-consistent system of beliefs. The letters were written for specific occasions, not as chapters in a systematic theology. Paul was, nevertheless, a theological thinker, and there are ideas that appear frequently in his letters. It thus seems legitimate to try to identify the central aspects of his thought that emerged over the course of his ministry.

Searching for a Center

"Juridical" Perspective
Ever since Martin Luther, whose reading of Paul's letters was a major factor in the Protestant Reformation, Protestant scholars have generally identified "justification by grace through faith" as the center of Paul's thought. From this perspective, the primary question for Paul was how human beings could stand "justified"

before God. And his answer was that justification came not through works of the law but through God's grace, which is appropriated by faith. Roman Catholic interpreters, however, have generally denied that justification is Paul's central concept, understanding it as "one of the many metaphors describing the new Christian existence." They have also insisted that Paul's understanding of God's grace does not rule out human cooperation with that grace in the process of salvation.[1]

Part of the difficulty in interpreting Paul is that the Greek term *dikaiosyne* can be translated either as "righteousness" or as "justification." It is thus unclear whether, when Paul speaks of "*dikaiosyne* by faith" (or faithfulness),[2] he means that the believer actually *becomes* "righteous" in the moral sense or is simply acquitted—that is, given a new standing before God. Catholic interpreters have tended toward the former view, and Protestants toward the latter,[3] which is often termed the "juridical" interpretation. According to the juridical reading, *dikaiosyne* is not a moral category but signifies a legal status: to be justified is to be acquitted before God on the basis of God's act in Christ, rather than one's own merit.

"Participationist" Perspective

Protestants and Catholics have recently come much closer in their readings of Paul. A major challenge to the dominant Protestant interpretation came early in the twentieth century from Albert Schweitzer, himself a Protestant,[4] who focused on what he called "mystical" passages: those expressing the believers' existence "in Christ" or in the "body of Christ" and the indwelling of Christ or the Spirit in believers. Schweitzer argued that these passages, rather than Paul's statements regarding justification, constitute the true center of his thought. The theme of justification comes into play only when Paul is addressing the controversy regarding the Jewish law, whereas the "mystical" theme appears in connection with other motifs such as the Spirit, resurrection, and ethics.

Pauline interpretation has always had a problem with the relationship between justification and ethics, or between faith and works. Many commentators have pointed out that for Paul, the "indicative" precedes and grounds the "imperative." That is, the proclamation that sinners are justified through Christ's sacrifice (the indicative) provides the basis for the ethical imperative: *because* sinners are already accepted by God, they can now be addressed with an ethical demand.

But just how does the ethical demand follow from justification? There is no connection, according to Schweitzer, between the two: Paul derives ethics not from justification but from incorporation into Christ. It is a fruit of the spirit, a natural result of one's new state of being. In other words, while mere acquittal carries with it no drive toward or empowerment for good works, the experience of a renewed life as a member of Christ's body does.

Catholic interpreters have had less trouble finding a connection between indicative and imperative. They have rejected the view that by *dikaoisyne* Paul means the mere fact of acquittal, devoid of moral content. From their perspective, the term refers to "the whole new being in Christ, the new relationship, the new creation, in which ethical uprightness is made possible and required."[5]

Many scholars have objected to Albert Schweitzer's use of the term *mysticism*, but some recent interpreters have defended modified versions of his thesis, generally preferring to speak of Paul's "participationist" language.[6] Although the precise relationship between Paul's notions of justification on the one hand and incorporation into Christ on the other remains a matter of debate, it seems clear that one cannot rightly understand Paul without taking both into account.

A Mediating Alternative: Sharing in the Faithfulness of Christ

The debate between the juridical and the participationist perspectives has proceeded largely on the basis of assumptions regarding the meaning of two Greek terms in Paul's thought. The first is the word *pistis*, which is usually translated as "faith." The second is the phrase *Iesou Christou*, which is usually rendered "*in* Jesus Christ." Translators and interpreters have generally thought that when these terms are used together, the reference is to *the faith that human beings place in Christ*, which justifies them before God. Some recent interpreters, however, argue that in Paul's usage, *pistis* should be translated as "faithfulness" and *Iesou Christou* should be translated as "*of* Jesus Christ." This would mean that it is *Christ's faithfulness to God*, in which human beings participate through their own faithful-

ness, that brings justification or righteousness.

Those who accept this view argue that it largely supersedes the debate as to whether justification merely changes human beings' status before God or actually changes their character. From this perspective, *pistis* is not merely "an interior attitude of belief or trust to be contrasted with outward behavior," but "an encompassing way of being in the world."[7] It *includes* moral behavior. Those who are truly "in Christ" not only have a new status before God but also are placed in a new *relationship* to God. They have entered a new sphere of influence, in which they are both called and empowered to do the good. They are granted a new life in the Spirit and are, in short, a "new creation" (2 Cor 5:17; Gal 6:15).

Community in Christ

Because Christian believers are "in" Christ, they are also in community with one another. "We have no evidence," J. Paul Sampley writes, "that Paul ever conceived of a solitary, isolated believer." Christians are "brought together by their shared death with Christ," not by virtue of common backgrounds or social standing.[8] Belonging to Christ, they have a responsibility to build up the community itself, to be productive members of the corporate whole. Each individual counts and is a recipient of special gifts from God, but the new life is a life lived in communion with other members of Christ's body.

Freedom in Christ

The new life in Christ is also a life in freedom. Those in Christ are free from the law, since there is no basis for salvation other than God's grace. To try to gain through obedience to the law what God has already given in Christ is an act of unfaithfulness, a failure to trust solely in God. The new life also means that those in Christ are free from the power of sin. Of course, they still live in the world and remain subject to temptation, death, and suffering. But they are no longer bound by the necessity of sin; by the power of the Spirit, they *can* do the good.

Flesh and Spirit

In their freedom, believers confront two possible modes of existence. They can live "according to the Spirit" or "according to the flesh." To live "according to the Spirit" is to make proper use of the power one has newly received; it is to follow the Spirit's promptings. Concretely, this means moral action, especially love. To live "according to the flesh," in contrast, is to turn away from the Spirit and live in another sphere of influence. In playing flesh and Spirit off against one another, however, Paul is not endorsing a dualism in which material reality is evil, as in Gnosticism. The flesh is, however, subject to domination by evil. To live "according to the flesh" is to live as if the material world were a self-sufficient reality, as if there were no Spirit; it is to live under an alien power in competition with that of Christ.[9]

This Age and the Age to Come

This alien power is that of Satan, who has, since the sin of Adam, held the world in bondage. This power, however, belongs to an age that is passing away. Through Christ's death and resurrection, God has inaugurated the eschatological age, a fact manifested in the Spirit's presence and in "spiritual gifts" such as prophecy and tongues. In living "according to the Spirit," believers participate already in the age to come.

However, the new age is not fully present, which is why believers cannot claim full knowledge. They live in an "in-between time," in which the competing powers are still in conflict, although the eventual outcome is apparent to them. As followers of a Messiah who died a shameful and humiliating death, Christians are not magically freed from the conditions of earthly existence. The cross of Christ must in some sense be their own, as it is also Paul's.

The Body

If for Paul *spirit* is a totally positive term and *flesh* usually negative, *body* is neutral. The body is the person as a whole, which is mortal but capable of redemption. Whereas "flesh and blood cannot inherit the kingdom of God" (1 Cor 15:50), life in the resurrection will be a life in a transformed body. Paul's use of the term *body* shows that he does not view matter itself as evil.

Human Hope and the Redemption of the Cosmos

Human beings are not all that will be transformed in the age to come. The "present evil age" is the result of a cosmic disruption brought about by sin. To say that Satan rules this age is to say that the universe itself—what we would call the natural world—is corrupted, exists under a curse. The fullness of the new age will bring not only human redemption but cosmic renewal. The life of the believer is therefore not only a life lived in faith/faithfulness, one that heeds the message of God's redemption of the world through Christ, but also a life lived in hope. To believe in Christ is to hope for final salvation and the restoration of the universe to its intended glory.

Above all, the life of the believer is a life of love, for faith/faithfulness becomes active in love. But Christians do not immediately and automatically become perfect, loving human beings. In the "in-between" time, they are continually in a process of growth. Paul is clear that believers are "at various stages in their faith journey toward maturity" and that "his life too is marked by a pressing on toward maturity or perfection."[10]

An Existentialist Interpretation of Paul

Paul's theology reflects the ancient world's thought patterns, which Bultmann termed "mythological." In Paul as well as the Gospel of John, however, Bultmann found evidence that the New Testament itself actually begins the process of "demythologizing," or existentialist interpretation.

An example of such interpretation is his treatment of Romans 6. In verse 5, he notes, Paul repeats an early Christian understanding of baptism as a guarantee of eventual resurrection to eternal life: "If we have been united with [Christ] in a death like his, we will certainly be united with him in a resurrection like his." In verse 4, however, he breaks the parallel between dying with Christ (in baptism) and eternal life: "so that, just as Christ was raised from the dead . . . so we too might walk in newness of life." In effect, Paul has reinterpreted the believer's resurrection as "an already present resurrection which realizes itself in ethical conduct."[11]

Because Bultmann finds that the New Testament itself begins the process of demythologizing, he argues for a contemporary mode of belief that rejects the "mythological" worldview it reflects. Salvation through the cross of Christ, for example, appears in the New Testament as a mythical event through which Christ atones for human sin through his blood and frees humanity by taking upon himself the consequences of sin. Existentialist interpretation reveals, however, that such views do not represent the deepest intention of the New Testament itself:

> Thus, to believe in the cross of Christ does not mean to look to some mythical process that has taken place

outside of us and our world or at an objectively visible event that God has somehow reckoned to our credit; rather, to believe in the cross of Christ means to accept the cross as one's own and to allow oneself to be crucified with Christ.[12]

In other words, when Paul says, "I have been crucified with Christ" (Gal 2:19), he shows that Christian faith does not at its base mean believing that Jesus' death created an objective change in God's relationship to the world. It does not mean that this death somehow actually accomplished the redemption of humanity, as if God could not accept human beings apart from it. What it does mean is that when human beings hear the proclamation of this event as redemptive and accept it as such, it in fact *becomes* so for them. The redemption takes place in human experience, not on a cosmic level.

A Freudian Interpretation of Paul

In a book entitled *Paul for a New Day*, Robin Scroggs uses Freudian theory to illuminate Paul's notion of justification. Scroggs notes that, according to Freud, the superego develops as a way of resolving a developmental crisis in childhood. Although Freud differentiated male and female development, in both cases the child at the oedipal stage represses desire,

internalizes the image of the feared parent, and directs aggression inward. The result is the emergence of the superego, the conscious part of which is the conscience. Accepting Freud's characterization of one's image of God as a projection of the father-image (which has nothing to do with the question of the actual *existence* of God), Scroggs finds a parallel between the child who is obedient in order to avoid punishment and Paul's understanding of humanity under the law:

> To be obedient to the Torah in an attempt to justify oneself by works covertly expresses that primal hostility and aggression against God the Father. Aggression is the reaction against the authoritative, awesome Father, who says "Thou shalt not ...," thus putting an end to freedom.[13]

Through his proclamation of justification by faith, Paul undermines this threatening image of God with the assertion that, through Christ, God has brought about reconciliation; the hostility is resolved. Reception of the new relationship, however, demands that human beings abandon their false (and unconsciously hostile) ways of seeking God's favor.

Paul as Ethicist

Paul is as controversial today as he was in the first century, particularly when his ethical views are under discussion. Social activists often find

Paul less than adequate when it comes to the issues of slavery and civil disobedience, yet some liberation theologians have enlisted him in their cause. Many conservative Christians cite Paul's letters in support of "traditionalist" views on same-sex relationships and the status and role of women, and for that reason, he is often condemned by feminists and advocates of lesbian/gay rights. In contrast, some interpreters find in him the inspiration for a "new morality" that revolutionizes traditional attitudes toward sex. It is thus important not only to pay attention to what Paul actually says on matters such as these, but also to note the presuppositions of those who have sought to evaluate his views.

It is also important to understand that Paul does not simply rattle off random pronouncements on ethical questions. He engages in a process of moral reasoning that is influenced by various cultural factors but is firmly grounded in his faith and theological understanding. And just as he himself engages in moral reasoning, he expects those to whom he writes to do the same. Although he can at a few points provide sayings of Jesus and lists of virtues and vices that serve as the boundaries of ethical reflection, he invites believers (Rom 12:2) to "discern" the will of God, that is, to puzzle out for themselves what is right and what is wrong.

This does not mean that they should do whatever feels comfortable to them, however, for Paul links the ability to carry out such reasoning to the renewed mind that one has in Christ. And he lays down specific criteria for discernment: "Projected deeds have to be evaluated in two ways: how they bear on the one who might do them and how they bear on others in the community of faith."[14] Thus, the final criterion for ethical action must be service to the community as a whole, the body of Christ.

Status and Role of Women

What roles should women play in the church? Should they be ordained as ministers? What is the role of a wife in relation to her husband? Conservative theologians cite the Pauline writings, more than any other part of the New Testament, in defense of the "traditional" answers to these questions: Women should be subservient to their husbands, and their roles in the church should differ from those of men. Most important, ordination should be reserved for males.

While support for all these answers can be found in letters attributed to Paul, the passages that make the sharpest distinction between female and male roles are found in those letters that many scholars believe Paul did not actually write. And within the undisputed letters, the clearest example of a distinction in roles is a passage (1 Cor 14:33b-36) that many scholars think is either a non-Pauline interpolation or actually the expression of a view that Paul is refuting.

In any case, there is strong evidence that Paul generally accepted women in prominent leadership roles.[15] He mentions Euodia and Syntyche (Phil 4:2-3), as well as Prisca and her husband (Rom 16:3-5), as fellow workers in spreading the gospel. Prisca's leadership role is underscored by the additional facts that she and Aquila hosted a church in their home and that Paul, against the custom, mentions her before her husband. And the reference to Chloe at 1 Corinthians 1:11 suggests that she exercised some type of authority in the church.

Paul's references to two other women illustrate how cultural bias can enter into interpreters' decisions about the meaning of a text. At Romans 16:1-2 he mentions Phoebe, to whom he applies the Greek term *diakonos*. The literal meaning of this word is "servant" or "helper," but it eventually came to designate a person ordained to a formal, ministerial office in the church. When used in this latter sense, it is usually translated "deacon." Paul generally employs the term in its nontechnical sense, but the phrase "of the church" in this passage suggests that he has an actual office in mind. Translators, however, assuming that a woman could not have held such a position, have traditionally avoided the term *deacon* at this point. Only a little short of two thousand years late, the NRSV has granted Phoebe the title of deacon and even suggested *minister* as an alternative rendering.

The second case is even more dramatic. At Romans 16:7, Paul sends greetings to two persons whom he apparently recognizes both as his predecessors in the faith and as apostles. As grammatical objects in the sentence, the names appear in the accusative case—that is, with a final *n*: Androniko*n* and Junia*n*. The first of these is the accusative form of the male name Andronic*us*, and the latter of the female name Juni*a*. Assuming that a woman could not have been an apostle, however, translators have posited a male equivalent, Juni*as*. But since we have no evidence of such a male form, it is probable that Juni*a* is original. This would mean that Paul recognized a woman as an apostle. Interestingly, some manuscripts read "Ju*l*ian" instead of "Ju*n*ian," which probably shows that bias was at work even among early manuscript copyists.

To say that Paul recognized women in leadership roles in the church does not mean he made no distinctions between men and women, however. In 1 Corinthians 11:2-16, he insists upon a restriction upon women during worship that does not apply to men.[16] And he also says, "The husband is the head of his wife," just as a man's head is Christ and Christ's head is God (11:3). We thus come upon a passage in which Paul seems not only to draw a distinction between male and female roles but even to place women at the bottom of a hierarchical power relationship: God, Christ, man, woman.

Nevertheless, in the course of his argument, Paul makes a remarkable point that does not serve his immediate interest at all: at 11:11-12, he injects a comment reasserting an egalitarian relationship between man and woman. Although Paul can resort to traditional thinking regarding women's status at some points, at others he can assert that "in Christ" all traditional distinctions among people are in some sense dissolved.

This latter point is explicit Galatians 3:28: "There is no longer Jew or Greek, there is no longer slave or free, there is no longer male and female; for all of you are one in Christ

Jesus." Scholars generally agree that here Paul quotes a baptismal formula current in the churches,[17] so we may assume that his egalitarian views are not innovative but reflect the radicalism of the earlier community. In fact, as Schüssler Fiorenza shows, Paul modified this radicalism in a more traditional direction.[18] But even though he was not always true to the principle at work in Galatians 3:28, it was an important influence on his thought and his action. And his counsel to some women to remain unmarried (1 Cor 7:8) is a challenge to the traditional, patriarchal family structure.[19]

In summary, from a feminist perspective, Paul's legacy is ambiguous. On the one hand, both his message and his practice involved a gospel in which traditional sex roles were transcended. On the other, he occasionally resorted to traditional distinctions and unwittingly laid the groundwork for the eventual resurgence of patriarchal structure in the church, a resurgence we will observe in chapter 13.

Same-Sex Relations

Are same-sex sexual relations acceptable for Christians? Should Christian churches accept persons involved in such relationships into the ordained ministry? Paul's writings stand at the very center of the controversy over these questions. In two passages in the undisputed letters (1 Cor 6:9-10 and Rom 1:24-27), he seems to condemn homoerotic sex. It is important, however, not only to note what Paul does and does not say on this subject, but also to ask the

more difficult question of why he says what he does.

It should be helpful, before addressing these passages, to make some observations about the attitudes toward homoerotic relations in the Greco-Roman world. First, one specific form of such relations was widely known and largely accepted in Paul's time: pederasty, the love of a man for a boy. In ancient Greece, the close relationship between mentor and student was an important aspect of the educational process, and when Plato praised such love, "his thought was not of a physical relationship but of a 'higher' form of love uniting two persons."[20] The physical dimension was probably present in many instances, however, and was widely accepted. By Paul's time, however, pederasty had come more and more to be associated not only with a physical relationship but with self-indulgent lust. In some cases, the boys were "call boys"—male prostitutes—or slaves, who were sometimes castrated.[21] We thus find some writers of the period who were critical of this practice. They tended to see it as a degenerate activity of the idle rich and generally directed their attention to the issue of exploitation of one person by another.[22]

Second, whereas there is much literature on male homoeroticism, there is very little on sexual relations between females. The sources we do have reveal the existence of woman-woman marriages, but they tend to condemn female homoeroticism in the severest terms. There is thus a striking discrepancy between attitudes toward male-male and female-female relations, which Bernadette Brooten attributes to a rigid definition of gender roles. The main problem with sex between women seems to have been that it placed them outside the realm of male protection and control.[23]

Third, although some literature from the period indicates an awareness of fixed sexual inclinations (what we would call "orientation"), most texts seem to treat homoerotic sex as freely chosen.

Paul's Views on the Issue

We turn now to the two passages in Paul's letters.

1 Corinthians 6:9-10. In 1 Corinthians 6:9-10, Paul lists several types of persons who will not inherit God's rule; on the list are two terms difficult to translate: *malakos* and *arsenokoites*. Both are associated with homoerotic sex. But what specifically does Paul mean by them, and why does he use them both? The root meaning of *malakos* is "soft," and Robin Scroggs argues that in a context suggesting pederasty, it would call to mind the "image of the effeminate call-boy."[24] The literal meaning of the second term, *arsenokoites*, is "a male who goes to bed," and many scholars think it refers to the (stereotypically) active partner in a homosexual relationship. Most likely, then, Paul uses both terms because he is thinking specifically of pederasty; his condemnation is of "call boys" and the adult males who use them.

Romans 1:24-27. In Romans 1:24-27, Paul cannot be thinking exclusively of pederasty, since he mentions female homoeroticism as well as male. It is also clear that he condemns such practices as "unnatural." However, it is equally clear that homoeroticism is incidental to Paul's main point. In Romans 1:1—3:20, he is arguing that all human beings are sinners, as a prelude to his declaration of universal grace in 3:21-26. The sin that he identifies in 1:18-23 is idolatry, not same-sex relations, and he does not even list the latter in his catalog of vices with which he concludes the illustration. He refers to homoeroticism as the *result* of sin: God abandons human beings to their lusts because of their idolatry. So Paul did not write Romans 1 in order to teach that homoeroticism is a perversion; rather, because he *assumed* it to be such, he used it as an illustration of humanity's overall corruption.

If we now ask why Paul made such an assumption, we may identify two sources of his attitude. Since pederasty was the most widely known and discussed form of same-sex relations, it is likely that his attitude toward homoeroticism in general was influenced greatly by it. This would mean that Paul thought of such relations as inherently lustful and exploitative.

The other source of Paul's attitude was Judaism: both the Jewish Scriptures and later Jewish texts condemned homoerotic practice, although the passages in which it is discussed are sparse. The scriptures give no rationale for the rejection, but it is interesting that only male homoeroticism is mentioned. This may indicate that a primary concern was that it diverted men from the task of procreation. Another reason may be that Jews associated same-sex relations with Gentiles and idolatry. The legal prohibition of such relations (Lev 18:22; 20:13) occurs in a law code (Lev 17–26) that distinguishes the Hebrew people from their neighbors who have "defiled" themselves through practicing various "abominations" (18:24-30; 20:23).[25]

Insights from anthropology regarding the notions of ritual purity and pollution are also helpful. As noted in chapter 2, ancient people had a deep-seated concern for what they perceived as the proper order of things. Leviticus 19:19—with its prohibitions against crossbreeding cattle, planting two kinds of seed in the same field, and wearing garments made of more than one kind of cloth—expresses this concern. Such forms of mixing presumably suggested the confusion of disparate elements and were thus rejected. Most important, animals that did not seem to fit the class to which they belonged were deemed unclean. For example, crustaceans, which live in the water but do not have scales and fins, are among the unclean creatures.

It seems likely that this sense of order is at work in the rejection of homoeroticism. Presupposed is a stereotypical view of active and passive roles in sex, defined along gender lines. Women who love women would be seen as not conforming "to the class of women, since they take on the active sexual roles that many authors of the period describe as unnatural for women."[26] And given the presupposition, male-male relations would involve one male playing the female role.

Paul's Views Today

What relevance do Paul's writings have to the contemporary Christian debate about same-sex relations? The issue is much more one of hermeneutics than of exegesis, and the answer depends largely upon how one understands the Bible as authoritative. On some models of biblical authority, Christians are obligated to accept Paul's views in a direct and literal way, even if they are expressed only in passing. On other models, the issue cannot be settled so easily. Some Christians might contend, for example, that since Paul knew nothing of sexual orientation in the modern sense, his statements cannot be applied without qualification to the contemporary question. Although some Greco-Roman texts show a consciousness of fixed sexual identities, Romans 1:25-27 suggests that Paul thought of same-sex relations as a simple matter of choice. His use of the verbs *exchanged* and *gave up* to describe a turn from what he considered "natural" to what he considered "unnatural" seems to imply "a conscious decision to act one way rather than another."[27] A similar argument is that we in the modern/postmodern world simply cannot share Paul's presuppositions regarding cosmic order that apparently undergirded both the purity laws in Leviticus and his views on same-sex relations. Finally, some interpreters would point out that Paul's emphasis on the guidance of the Spirit, the love commandment, and the process of *discerning* God's will (Rom 12:1-2) is more central to his thinking than are his specific views on same-sex relations.

Human Society and the Governing Authorities

Paul often gets low marks from social activists because he seems to have taught nonresistance to the injustices in the social and political orders of his day. He makes no explicit condemnation of slavery, and in Romans 13:1-7, he counsels his readers to "be subject to the governing authorities" and claims that these authorities "have been instituted by God." One must therefore ask whether there is any place in Paul's thought for efforts to change social structures or for civil disobedience for the sake of justice.

With respect to slavery, we have seen that in Philemon, Paul implies that it is wrong for a Christian to hold another Christian as a slave, and in Galatians 3:28, he states that in Christ "there is no longer slave or free." In 1 Corinthians 7:23, moreover, he speaks against selling oneself into slavery, and 7:21 may mean that slaves should opt for freedom if they have the chance. What we do not find, however, is encouragement to try to change the social system that endorses slavery. But in evaluating these facts, one should keep in mind the eschatological context of Paul's teaching: along with other early Christians, he looked for the imminent close of the age, when God's rule itself would restructure the social order.

Although Paul's eschatological views tended to discourage social activism in the modern sense, we do find Paul urging his readers to "seek to do good to all" (1 Thess 5:15), and when he gives instructions on living one's life in Philippians 1:27, he uses a verb that means "to live as a citizen," although translations generally obscure this.[28] So there is some basis for thinking that Paul had a sense of social responsibility beyond the church.

With respect to Romans 13:1-7, it is important to note that Paul does not command his readers to "obey" the authorities but to "be subject" to them. The difference is real: to be subject to a government is to recognize its right to exist, whereas to obey it means to comply with some specific law.[29] For example, Martin Luther King Jr. disobeyed laws he found unjust or unjustly applied while nevertheless recognizing governmental authority by accepting legal consequences of his actions. Because Paul shared the ancient Jewish and Hellenistic belief that governments were appointed by God, he could counsel loyalty to the state. But it is clear throughout Romans and Paul's letters in general that the Christian's ultimate sovereign is Christ. That he would have expected Christians to resist the Roman Empire when faith itself was at stake is unquestionable, as his own prison record makes amply clear.

In addition, there are subtle indications in Paul's letters of a critical attitude toward Roman power. His emphasis on the cross of Christ is itself an implicit challenge to the empire, since crucifixion was their trademark method of exterminating insurrectionists.[30] A similar challenge is implied in the Greek term he uses for Jesus' return at the end of the age (parousia). Since it was used in relation to the arrival of a king or emperor, to apply it to Christ suggests such a status for him. And when Paul mocks those who proclaim "peace and security" in 1 Thessalonians 5:3, he is probably criticizing language used by the empire in its claim to provide "peace to the provinces."[31]

Paul's Ethics Today: Competing Approaches

Anyone who wants to apply Paul's ethics to life in the modern world must face the question of *how* such an application is to be made. Some interpreters make such an application in a one-to-one fashion: to be faithful to Paul is to repeat in our situation the views he held in his. Others contend that such an approach is particularly problematic when dealing with Paul. For them, a rule morality—an ethical system consisting of specific rights and wrongs—runs into conflict with a key element in Paul's own thinking. If human beings are justified not by the law but by grace through faith/faithfulness, they argue, then Christian morality cannot consist of adherence to specific rules. While Paul certainly refers to such rules, the real heart of his morality is found in the process of discerning God's will (Rom 12:2), informed by the principle of faith working through love (Gal 5:6). Such interpreters do not find Paul's specific judgments irrelevant. But they argue that these judgments should be subordinated to an attempt to apply Paul's love ethic to the contemporary situation, taking into account the radical differences between the ancient world and our own.

These two approaches to Paul place him in an odd position in contemporary Christian thought. Quoted by the most conservative thinkers on specific issues, he is also hailed by the most liberal as the proponent of an open-ended mode of biblical interpretation. As Paul's letters themselves show, of course, this diversity in the interpretation of Paul goes all the way back to his own day. And as chapter 13 and the epilogue to part 3 will make clear, it was equally evident in the decades immediately following his ministry.

NOTES

1. Joseph Plevnik, *What Are They Saying about Paul?* (New York: Paulist, 1986), 57.
2. See the section "A Mediating Alternative: Sharing in the Faithfulness of Christ" on page 256.
3. Plevnik, *What Are They Saying?* 55–57.
4. Albert Schweitzer, *The Mysticism of Paul the Apostle*, trans. William Montgomery (New York: Macmillan, 1956; originally published in 1931).
5. Plevnik, *What Are They Saying?* 69.
6. See particularly E. P. Sanders, *Paul and Palestinian Judaism* (Philadelphia: Fortress Press, 1977), ch. 5.
7. John B. Cobb Jr. and David J. Lull, *Romans* (St. Louis: Chalice, 2005), 17.
8. J. Paul Sampley, *Walking between the Times: Paul's Moral Reasoning* (Philadelphia: Fortress Press, 1991), 37–38.
9. For a discussion of the terms *body*, *flesh*, and *spirit*, see Rudolf Bultmann, *Theology of the New Testament*, trans. Kendrick Grobel (New York: Charles Scribner's Sons, 1951), 1:192–210, 232–39.

10. Sampley, *Walking between the Times*, 47–48.

11. Bultmann, *Theology of the New Testament*, 1:140–41.

12. Rudolf Bultmann, *New Testament and Mythology and Other Basic Writings*, ed. and trans. Schubert M. Ogden (Philadelphia: Fortress Press, 1984), 34.

13. Robin Scroggs, *Paul for a New Day* (Philadelphia: Fortress Press, 1977), 13.

14. Sampley, *Walking between the Times*, 60.

15. Victor Paul Furnish, *The Moral Teaching of Paul: Selected Issues*, rev. ed. (Nashville: Abingdon, 1985), 101–12.

16. The Greek of verses 4-6 is somewhat ambiguous. Most interpreters have assumed that Paul wants Christian women to cover their heads with veils, according to Jewish custom, and this assumption has affected the English translations. Some recent interpreters, however, argue that he is insisting that the women keep their hair bound up rather than letting it down. If so, his real concern was to distinguish Christianity from ecstatic cults in which women danced with free-flowing hair.

17. Elisabeth Schüssler Fiorenza, *In Memory of Her: A Feminist Theological Reconstruction of Christian Origins* (New York: Crossroad, 1984), 229–30, 205–18.

18. Ibid., 219–36.

19. Ibid., 224–26.

20. Furnish, *Moral Teaching of Paul*, 59.

21. Robin Scroggs, *The New Testament and Homosexuality: Contextual Background for the Contemporary Debate* (Philadelphia: Fortress Press, 1983), 39.

22. Furnish, *Moral Teaching of Paul*, 59–63.

23. Bernadette Brooten, *Love between Women: Early Christian Responses to Female Homoeroticism* (Chicago: University of Chicago Press, 1996), 359.

24. Scroggs, *New Testament and Homosexuality*, 65.

25. See Norman H. Snaith, *Leviticus and Numbers* (London: Thomas Nelson & Sons, 1967), 126.

26. Brooten, *Love between Women*, 234.

27. Furnish, *Moral Teaching of Paul*, 73.

28. Victor P. Furnish, "Uncommon Love and the Common Good: Christians as Citizens in the Letters of Paul," in *In Search of the Common Good*, ed. Dennis P. McCann and Patrick D. Miller (New York and London: T&T Clark, 2005).

29. Furnish, *Moral Teaching of Paul*, 127.

30. Neil Elliott, *Liberating Paul: The Justice of God and the Politics of the Apostle* (Maryknoll, N.Y.: Orbis, 1994), 93.

31. Helmut Koester, "Imperial Ideology and Paul's Eschatology in 1 Thessalonians," in *Paul and Empire: Religion and Power in Roman Imperial Society*, ed. Richard A. Horsley (Harrisburg, Pa.: Trinity Press International, 1997).

STUDY QUESTIONS

1. Describe the roles played in Paul's thought by each of the following: Spirit, Spirit/flesh, body, faith/faithfulness, grace, *dikaiosyne*, freedom, love, present age/age to come, hope, resurrection, salvation, the death of Christ/the cross. Then discuss the relationship between Paul's "juridical" language and his "participationist" language.

2. Assess the potential of Bultmann's existentialist interpretation and Scroggs's Freudian interpretation for showing the relevance of Paul's thought today.

3. Give and defend your own views as to whether and how Paul's views on the status and role of women, same-sex relations, and the governing authorities have relevance for the contemporary discussion of these issues.

FOR FURTHER READING

Beker, J. Christiaan. *Paul the Apostle: The Triumph of God in Life and Thought.* Philadelphia: Fortress Press, 1980.

Elliott, Neil. *Liberating Paul: The Justice of God and the Politics of the Apostle.* Maryknoll, N.Y.: Orbis, 1994; Minneapolis: Fortress Press, 2006.

Furnish, Victor P. *The Moral Teachings of Paul: Selected Issues.* 2nd ed. Nashville: Abindgon, 1985.

———. *Theology and Ethics in Paul.* Nashville: Abingdon, 1968.

Keck, Leander E. *Paul and His Letters.* 2nd ed. Philadelphia: Fortress Press, 1989.

Sampley, J. Paul. *Walking between the Times: Paul's Moral Reasoning.* Minneapolis: Fortress Press, 1991.

Sanders, E. P. *Paul and Palestinian Judaism: A Comparison of Patterns of Religion.* Philadelphia: Fortress Press, 1977.

Schnelle, Udo. *Apostle Paul: His Life and Theology.* Translated by M. Eugene Boring. Grand Rapids: Baker, 2005.

Stendahl, Krister. *Paul among Jews and Gentiles.* Philadelphia: Fortress Press, 1976.

Theissen, Gerd. *The Social Setting of Pauline Christianity.* Edited and translated and with an introduction by John H. Schütz. Philadelphia: Fortress Press, 1982.

The
Disputed Letters

13

2 Thessalonians,
Colossians,
Ephesians,
1–2 Timothy,
Titus

Because the Pauline authorship of the letters treated in this chapter is in doubt, I will usually not try to place them in situations in Paul's life but will seek only to describe in broad fashion the circumstances to which they speak. The readers I posit in the reader-response analyses are therefore defined in a very general way. And I will refer not to Paul but only to "the author." When I do use the term *"Paul"* (in quotation marks), I indicate the role that the author has assumed in writing the letter.

2 Thessalonians

The Question of Authorship
and the Author's Purpose

One argument against the authenticity of 2 Thessalonians has to do with its relationship to 1 Thessalonians. The theme development, terminology, and wording of the two letters are so close as to suggest that the author of one had the other in hand while writing. Yet there are apparent discrepancies on specific points. In 1 Thessalonians 5:1-2, for example, "Paul" cautions readers that the day of the Lord will come without warning. In 2 Thessalonians 2:1-12, however, we find an apocalyptic scheme that seemingly undercuts the element of surprise and suggests to some interpreters a waning of the expectation of the imminent end of history. Another key point is the strange ending of 2 Thessalonians, in which the author makes such a point of claiming to be Paul as to recall Shakespeare's line about protesting too much.

Some scholars remain unconvinced on these points, however, and have attempted to explain why Paul would have written a follow-up to the earlier letter. Robert Jewett believes that eschatological fervor in Thessalonica led some members of the community to misunderstand 1 Thessalonians and claim that the "day of the Lord" had already arrived. So Paul wrote again to state his point more carefully.[1] If Paul did write the letter, we can assume that he did so shortly after writing 1 Thessalonians.

It is notable, though, that in none of the undisputed letters does Paul resort to an apocalyptic timetable to meet the challenge of eschatological enthusiasm.[2] And many scholars believe that the reference to a pseudo-Pauline letter (2:2), used by the author's opponents, reflects a time after that of Paul. The recent trend is thus to regard the letter as a pseudonymous work written after Paul's time, using the apostle's authority to combat an "erroneous" eschatological teaching. Some scholars think the writer's opponents taught a realized eschatology that denied apocalypticism altogether in the belief that the resurrection of the dead had already occurred. Others argue that they simply believed that the final events in the apocalyptic drama had already begun.

In any case, the letter is directed to readers who had suffered persecution (1:4-5) and whose minds were unsettled by the eschato-logical claims of some among them. The author's purpose is apparently "to demonstrate that the Day of the Lord is not present and simultaneously to give consolation and hope by pointing to Christ's inevitable, ultimate victory over all satanic forces."[3]

Notes on a Reading of 2 Thessalonians

1:1-12

The letter begins with a salutation and thanksgiving that stresses God's eschatological victory as an answer to the congregation's suffering.

2:1—3:5

"Paul" repudiates a letter purported to be from him, which claimed that the day of the Lord is already present. Specific events must take place before that happens: "the rebellion" and the revelation of "the lawless one." There is at present a force of some type (the *katechon*) restraining "the lawless one." Paul enjoins the readers to stand fast, keeping the traditions he taught them, and to pray for him.

3:6-18

"Paul" admonishes the idle and ends with greetings and an assurance that the letter is actually from him.

Problems of Interpretation

Several points in 2 Thessalonians remain obscure. The "rebellion" can hardly refer to the disobedience of humanity as a whole, since the Greek word (*apostasia*) indicates the falling away of someone who was formerly faithful. It could mean the eventual apostasy of some Christians or the continued Jewish rejection of the gospel.

No attempt to identify "the lawless one" has gained wide acceptance. Satan is among the suggestions, but at 2:9, this figure appears to be a subordinate in the hierarchy of evil. Other suggestions are the Roman Empire or emperor and a supernatural being of some sort. The lawless one, in any case, is related to a notion that was widespread toward the end of the first century: prior to Christ's return, an evil force would arise as an antitype of Christ.[4] The Johannine letters, for example, mention the expectation of an "antichrist" as current (1 John 2:18, 22; 4:3; 2 John 7).

The precise meaning of the term *katechon*, which is from a verb with a range of meanings from "hold back" to "oppress," is even more difficult to pin down. Whoever or whatever it is, the *katechon* precedes the revelation of "the lawless one" and restrains or presumes to restrain the latter's activity. Among the suggestions are the Roman Empire, Paul himself as a preacher of the gospel, Satan, and God. According to Gerhard Krodel, the *katechon*, "who fancies himself to be a restrainer" of evil, "represents the present power of oppression in the world"—oppression wrought by those who do not know God.[5]

Colossians

The Question of Authorship

Anyone who reads the letter to the Colossians in Greek after the undisputed letters is in for something of a shock. The sentences are longer and more cumbersome, and the text abounds with unfamiliar words.

Many interpreters also find subtle theological divergences. For one thing, the Christology of Colossians has a "cosmic" thrust not found in so developed a form in the undisputed letters. In Christ, "all the fullness of God was pleased to dwell" (1:19; see also 2:9), and through him "all things have been created" and "all things hold together" (1:16-17). He is the one who "disarmed the rulers and authorities" (2:15) and through whom "all things" were reconciled to God (1:20). While some of these phrases occur in a hymn the author quotes (1:15-20), others do not, so it is clear that the "cosmic" emphasis is the author's own.

Also, Colossians consistently presents salvation as already having taken place. At 2:12, for example, the writer declares that "you *were* also raised with him through faith." And although the theme of Christ's return appears at 3:4, there is no mention of the imminence of this event. Colossians also presents Christ as exercising sovereignty already in the present. In 1 Corinthians 15:28, Paul says that all things have not yet been subjected to Christ and that in the end, even Christ will be subjected to God, but at Colossians 3:11, we find that "Christ is all and in all."

While all commentators grant the differences between Colossians and the undisputed letters, many defend its authenticity. Some explain the differences by pointing to the specific nature of the "false teaching" that the letter opposes. Faced with what at least seemed to be a head-on challenge to the ultimacy of Christ, Paul had to struggle to make his point. Hence the new vocabulary and complex sentences; hence also the "cosmic" Christology and the emphasis on salvation and Christ's sovereignty as present.

As with 2 Thessalonians, however, the recent trend is to view Colossians as pseudonymous. An important factor is that it reflects more formalized views on the church, tradition, and Paul's apostleship than we find in the undisputed letters. The term *faith* now refers to a body of teaching, and Paul's apostolic office functions as its ensurer (1:5-8, 23, 25, 28; 2:6-7; 3:16). And while in the undisputed letters Paul speaks of Christians collectively as Christ's body, in Colossians Christ is the "head" of the body, which is designated by the term *church* (1:18; 2:19).

In addition, Colossians contains a clear statement of woman's subjection to man (3:18) and an injunction to slaves to obey their masters (3:23), neither of which has a clear parallel in the undisputed letters. These statements occur within a "household code" (a traditional compilation of social regulations) that the author has incorporated, whereas no such codes occur in the undisputed letters.

Among scholars who regard Colossians as pseudonymous, there is no consensus as to where to place the letter historically. Some

argue for the generation after Paul, while others think a follower of Paul might have written it while Paul was still alive. A compelling theory is that of Margaret Y. MacDonald, who makes use of a social-scientific model to understand this letter, along with Ephesians and 1 and 2 Timothy and Titus. The model identifies three stages in the development of an institution: community building, community stabilizing, and community protecting. MacDonald assigns Paul himself to the first stage, Colossians and Ephesians to the second, and the Pastorals to the third. The transition from the first to the second stages often comes following the death of a leader, and MacDonald believes that Colossians was written in response to a crisis created by Paul's death. In the new situation, it became important to stabilize the community's relationship to the social world beyond its border, and the household code, which in many ways mimicked the social system in that world, was introduced for that purpose.[6]

Points to Look For in Colossians

- Emphasis on the supremacy of Christ

- Emphasis on Paul's apostolic office

- Emphasis on the mystery of Christ's presence

- Refutation of alternative teachings and condemnation of unnecessary regulations

Notes on a Reading of Colossians

1:1—2:23

Following the prescript (1:1-2), which identifies Paul as the sender and the Colossian Christians as recipients, "Paul" offers a thanksgiving that reminds the readers of the gospel they have already heard (1:3-14). This leads into a hymn stressing Christ's supremacy over all things (1:15-20). These points follow:

— *1:21-23.* Christ's death has reconciling effects.

— *1:24-29.* "Paul" is commissioned to preach the mystery, which is "Christ in you."

— *2:1-5.* The readers should not be deceived by "plausible arguments."

— *2:6-15.* The readers should live on the basis of the true faith and avoid the "philosophy" of merely human origin. Christ is sovereign over all elements of the universe and all "rulers and authorities."

— *2:16-23.* "Paul" condemns the specifics of the "false" teaching—festivals, dietary regulations—as mere shadows of the true reality that have no effect, and to which the readers have already "died."

3:1—4:18

The implication of the preceding point is that Christ can accomplish what the "philosophy" cannot. Reasserting that the readers have been raised with Christ, "Paul" issues instructions on vices and virtues. The readers' new nature in Christ transcends all human distinctions (3:11), and they should bring it to realization by avoiding vices and embracing virtues. Then follows the household code (3:18—4:1), which defines the responsibilities of human relationships in hierarchical terms: husbands/wives; parents/children; masters/slaves.

The personal greetings at verses 4:7-17 strengthen the sense of a relationship between "Paul" and the readers, and references to two other communities (Laodicea and Hierapolis) suggest the letter's relevance to the church at large. A closing reference to Paul's imprisonment is a final reminder of his apostolic role in the progress of the gospel.

Nature of the Colossian "Heresy"

What was the "false teaching" or "heresy" that Colossians attacks? Suggestions range from a conservative Jewish Christianity such as Paul opposed in Galatia to an early Gnosticism. The emphasis on Sabbath observance and dietary regulations suggests Jewish influence, but there is no indication that circumcision was an issue. One can find an asceticism, characteristic of some gnostic sects, behind the slogans "Do not handle, Do not taste" (2:21) and in the claim to wisdom (2:23). And since the term *fullness* plays an important role in Gnosticism, the use of this word at 1:19 and 2:9 could undercut gnostic claims. However, there is no reference to the mythological systems characteristic of gnostic thought or any indication of "the radical dualism that marks the Gnostic spirit."[7] In sum, we cannot be very specific in describing the "heresy," except that it was syncretistic teaching combining Jewish elements with ideas that were at some point characteristic of Gnosticism.

On one final matter, the term *stoicheia* ("elements," "fundamental principles"), discussed earlier in relation to Galatians, occurs twice in Colossians (2:8, 20). Most commentators continue to treat the term as referring to cosmic beings. On Wink's interpretation, however, at 2:8 it means "the first elements or founding principles of the physical universe," for what the author attacks in this context is "philosophy" and "human tradition." In 2:20, however, the usage is parallel to that in Galatians; it means "the elements common to religion, pagan and Jewish alike."[8]

Ephesians

The Question of Authorship

Like Colossians, Ephesians has lengthy, complex sentences and an unusual number of words absent in the undisputed letters. And many of the unfamiliar words occur frequently in the later writings of the New Testament and Christian literature shortly after the New Testament period. Also, familiar Pauline terms are often displaced by alternatives: instead of "heaven," for example, one finds "heavenly places."

Ephesians also tends to present salvation as already present, making no mention of the imminence of Christ's return. It also speaks, as does Colossians, of Christ as the "head" of the body, which is the church. And whereas in the undisputed letters the word *church* frequently designates a local congregation, in Ephesians it is used only of the "worldwide" church.

Also significant is the view of the apostolic office. In 2:20, the author speaks of the church as "built upon the *foundation* of the apostles and prophets, with Christ Jesus himself as the cornerstone." And in 3:5, we read of the "*holy* apostles and prophets." Paul frequently defended his apostolic office, but in none of the undisputed letters does he speak of apostles and prophets as the church's foundation. Also, the specialized usage of "holy" seems at odds with his application of this term to the Christian community at large.

Another consideration is that there is so much overlap between Colossians and Ephesians that a literary relationship seems certain; the prevalent view is that the author of Ephesians used Colossians and expanded upon it. Interestingly, there is a shift in meaning in one of the most important instances of dependence. Whereas in Colossians the "mystery" of God's plan, revealed to Christians, is Christ's presence among them, in Ephesians the mystery is the unity of Jews and Gentiles in the church.

In Ephesians, we again find a household code with injunctions regarding women's subordination to their husbands and slaves' obedience to their masters. A final point is that many scholars regard Ephesians not as a "real" letter but as a treatise presented in letter form.

The best manuscripts do not contain a reference to Ephesus in the salutation, and the work is almost devoid of personal references. Nor does it address any specific problem, as do the other letters.

Some scholars defend the authenticity of Ephesians, but the arguments against it are strong. Margaret MacDonald assigns it to the community-stabilizing stage of institutionalization but sees it as belonging to a slightly later phase than Colossians.

Points to Look For in Ephesians

- The theme of unity: cosmic unity and the unity of Jews and Gentiles

- The theme of mystery

- Emphasis on the church as unified in Christ and the role of differing gifts within it

The Letter to the Ephesians: A Reading

1:1—3:21

Following the salutation, which establishes the letter as a writing of the apostle Paul, the author launches a lengthy doxology that introduces several key ideas. Christians are blessed "in the heavenly places," chosen "before the foundation of the world," and called to be "holy and blameless" before God. The readers will get a strong sense of their vocation as Christians and their place in an overarching mystery: God's plan to unite all things in Christ. The phrase "all things" stresses that God's plan is the reconciliation of all components of the universe. Assuring the readers at 1:11-14 of their eventual redemption, "Paul" encourages them to think confidently of the present in light of the eschatological future.

The intercessory prayer that follows (1:15-22) conveys a sense of the rich possibilities of Christian life in the present—wisdom, enlightenment, hope, power—that issue from Christ's exaltation.

In 2:1, "Paul" focuses on the readers' experience of salvation. Declaring that Christ has made Christians "alive" (2:5), he contrasts the new, resurrected state to the old life of sin. And presenting their salvation as issuing from God's grace (2:8), he places the present writing in the context of "his" other letters. Through the metaphor of a "walk" (obscured in the NRSV), he also issues a call for good works: although once walking in the ways of "this world," Christians are now enabled to live differently (2:1, 10).

Reminded in 2:11 that (as Gentiles) they once had no share in God's promises, the readers also hear that God has abolished the Jew/Gentile distinction. And the image of the new person resulting from the union of Jew and Gentile, together with the metaphor of "household of God" for the church, brings the cosmic unity of 1:10 into narrower focus. God's reconciliation of "all things" through Christ is manifest in the church's own inclusiveness.

The characterization of the church in 2:19-22 is a reminder of Christians' calling to be "holy and blameless" in 1:4. And now "Paul" introduces the metaphor of a temple: with Christ as cornerstone, apostles and prophets as foundation, it is a unified structure in which God's Spirit dwells.

The references to Paul's imprisonment in 3:1 and 3:13 place the intervening discourse on the "mystery" in the context of his own place in God's plan. The "mystery of Christ" has been revealed to the "apostles and prophets" and to Paul himself, who has received the insight that Gentiles are included in Christ's body. Also, Paul's commission to preach the gospel to Gentiles involves a declaration of the role of the church in God's purpose: it too is called to declare God's wisdom (which entails God's mystery/plan) "to the rulers and authorities in the heavenly places." The reference to Paul's sufferings in 3:13 thus becomes a word of encouragement to Christians who are themselves in mission.

FIG. 13.1 **The Temple of Emperor Hadrian in Ephesus, Turkey.** Photo © Erich Lessing /Art Resource, NY.

The doxology in 3:14-21 strengthens this word of encouragement and closes with a pronouncement of "glory in the church." The readers will finish this section with a feeling of empowerment as members of the church, graciously included by God's own mercy and called to a mission that is attested by the apostles, prophets, and Paul himself.

4:1—6:23

The words "I therefore" signal that "Paul" is about to draw out the implications of what has gone before. Beginning with general ethical exhortations, he places them in the context of an understanding of the church as united by Christ, a single faith, and baptism. Statements on Christ's ascension then ground a discourse on the various gifts given to church members. The readers are encouraged to understand that these gifts serve to "build up" the church and to provide a defense against false doctrine (4:14). And the notion of Christ's body, now removed from its cosmic context and made concrete, asks them to image the church as an organic unity. All individuals should think of their roles as essential to the whole and feel responsibility to maintain doctrinal purity and loving relationships with others.

In 4:17-24, "Paul" places general exhortations in the context of Christology. What the readers have learned in Christ contrasts with the way the "Gentiles" (which here means non-Christians) live. And by asking the readers to put away their old way of life, he implicitly presents their new ethical possibilities as the result of God's action in Christ.

"Paul" now turns to specifics, offering some initial instructions on behavior (4:25-32), which he sums up in the injunction to "be imitators of God" and "live [walk] in love" (5:1). Then comes a more detailed list of admonitions that closes with a call to constant thanksgiving (5:20). It is followed by a household code that includes instructions for wives, husbands, children, fathers, slaves, and masters (5:21—6:9). Here "Paul" presents both the subordination of the wife to the husband and the obligation of the husband to love the wife as analogous to Christ's relationship to the church. He presents marriage as holy but conceives it within the context of a hierarchical arrangement of power. And he links slaves' duty to obey their masters to their duty to obey Christ.

Duly admonished, the readers are once again encouraged, now with combat metaphors, to stand strong in the struggle against insidious powers (6:10-17). They will think back to the cosmic dimensions of Christ's body and of their mission as the church. And they will understand both ethical action and doctrinal fidelity as prime components in that mission. "Paul's" self-reference at 6:19-20, together with the closing comments and benediction, places all that has been said in the context of his apostolic authority.

The "Language of Power" in Ephesians 3:10: A Postmodern Rereading

In 3:10, the author declares that the church should make God's wisdom known "to the rulers and authorities in the heavenly places."

What are these "rulers and authorities," and how can the church preach in "heavenly" places? These questions play a crucial role in Wink's study of the "language of power" in the New Testament. As a way of understanding such language in our own context, Wink offers a "postmodern rereading" that draws on several hermeneutical perspectives, including liberation theology, existential interpretation, process thought, and Jungian psychology.

The New Testament uses several words and concepts for powers that enslave human beings: authorities, powers, rulers, thrones, evil spirits, angels, fallen angels, and angels of the nations—that is, "guardian" angels of specific peoples. While it might seem puzzling that apparently good powers, such as angels, are included in the list, Wink argues that "the powers" are both good and bad. They have their proper place in creation but can become evil through their ignorance of God's plan. And human beings can give them the absolute allegiance that belongs only to God: thus "even the good, made absolute, becomes evil."[9]

Interpreters have debated whether such terms as *rulers* and *authorities* refer to earthly institutions/persons or to supernatural beings. This issue comes to a head in Ephesians 3:10, where the church is commissioned to witness to these powers "in the heavenly places." This phrase clearly refers to the supernatural realm. At Ephesians 1:3, however, the author says that Christ has blessed *the church* in the heavenly places. Since the church is on earth, Wink concludes, "the heavenly places" must mean "that sphere where Christians, with one foot in each of two worlds, already experience the risen life in Christ."[10] "The heavenly places," in other words, refers not to a place spatially removed from earthly existence but to a transcendent dimension where "earth" and "heaven" intersect.

But how can the church witness "in the heavenly places"? In answering this question, Wink also proposes a solution to the problem of the "rulers and authorities." Acknowledging the difficulty that the mythological notion of heavenly powers poses for many people in our day, he suggests that we can best understand the "rulers and authorities" as "the inner and outer aspects of any given manifestation of power."[11] This statement will need elaboration.

As Wink's analysis shows, the New Testament writers refer to the powers in a way that embraces both the "earthly" and the "supernatural" senses—both human institutions/persons *and* supernatural beings. The reason is that they are projecting from their lived experience. Encountering an earthly government as oppressive, for example, they understand it as the manifestation of an evil supernatural force. While other interpreters have made similar points, Wink treats such projection as more than a fiction. Far from something "made up," it is a reflection of the impact of human institutions on the unconscious. Every such institution manifests some type of "inwardness" or "spirituality," whether positive or negative. It is pervaded with a sense of human dignity and worth, or it stifles creativity in an atmosphere of fear; it fosters cooperation and mutual respect, or it sets one group against another; it looks lovingly on the world at large, or it stands belligerently against anything outside itself. And when human beings *experience* the spirituality of an institution (whether positive or negative), they project that experience on the universe and create a myth—an observation Wink credits to Jung.[12]

In their "inward" manifestations, the powers are "the inner essence of outer organizations of power." In their "outward" manifestations, "they are political systems, appointed officials . . . laws—in short, all the tangible manifestations which power takes."[13] So what does it mean for the church to witness to them in "the heavenly places"? It means to seek to "convert" actual human institutions, to turn them away from their perversions to an understanding of their proper role in creation.

Restoration Eschatology, Cosmic Christology, and Ecological Theology

According to Ephesians 1:10, God will at the end time "gather up all things in [Christ]." This reference to the final "gathering up" of all things, paralleled by a similar phrase in Acts 3:21, clearly reflects the notion that the entire cosmos will be the object of God's ultimate redemption. It therefore stands alongside John 1 and Colossians 2 in exhibiting a decidedly cosmic dimension. Like these other passages, it has a strong appeal to theologians interested in ecological themes.

The Pastoral Letters: 1 and 2 Timothy and Titus

Designated the "Pastoral Letters" since the early eighteenth century, the three remaining disputed letters have much in common. All are concerned with ministerial functions but also speak to wider community concerns. They presuppose similar conditions in the church, speak to similar problems, and share distinctive characteristics of vocabulary and theological perspective. They are therefore probably the work of a single author. Margaret MacDonald places them in the third stage of institutionalization: community protecting. She sees them as concerned with internal stability, maintaining good relations with the outside world, and with evangelization. And she argues that they are in some respects responses to outsiders who have been critical of the community for promoting values contrary to those accepted in Greco-Roman society. As a result, they depart sharply from Paul's thinking on some issues, particularly the status and role of women.

The Question of Authorship

What the Pastorals have in common also sets them apart from the undisputed letters. The difference in word usage is striking. A number of shorter words appearing frequently in the other letters, such as the Greek terms for "now" and "therefore," do not occur in the Pastorals. And several key words in the Pastorals are found rarely or not at all in the other letters. For example, *eusebeia* ("godliness," "piety," or "religion") occurs ten times in the Pastorals but never in the undisputed letters. Such terminology closely parallels that of Christian writings from the second century.

Some linguistic differences have theological implications. In the undisputed letters, the word *pistis* ("faith" or "faithfulness") refers to a dynamic reality, the total act of self-giving. In the Pastorals, however, it generally designates a body of doctrine. And the Pastorals never use the term *Son* for Christ, never employ the formula "in Christ" in its "mystical" sense, and never mention the cross at all![14]

These letters also presuppose a situation quite different from that depicted in the undisputed letters. While the latter refer to various functions within the Christian community, authority seems to be primarily charismatic in nature. The term *episkopos* ("overseer" or "bishop") occurs once in the undisputed letters (Phil 1:1) but does not seem to be intended in the later, formalized sense. The bishops mentioned in the Pastorals probably did not possess the "monarchical" authority later associated with this term, but the discussions of the office of *episkopos*, along with those of deacon and elder, reveal a greater degree of formalization in church order than is evident in the undisputed letters. And the reference to an early form of ordination (1 Tim 4:14) suggests the beginnings of an institutionalized church. The emphasis on an ordained ministry dovetails with that upon formalized doctrine: a function of the officers of the community is to ensure sound doctrine.

Several scholars defend Pauline authorship because of the personal details in the letters, but others argue that such details might have been available through legend or projected from material in Acts and the other letters. And in some cases, the personal details speak against authenticity. While 2 Timothy 1:5 presents Timothy's faith as the product of Christian training in the home, Paul's reference to him as his own "child in the Lord" in 1 Corinthians 4:17 suggests that he was actually a convert.

Some scholars propose a compromise solution, arguing that the author expanded upon fragments of authentic letters. But such a view is difficult to substantiate and accomplishes little; one must still reckon with letters that are on the whole pseudonymous.

A final point is that the Pastorals draw extensively from Hellenistic sources—not only household codes, with their hierarchical views on women and slaves, but maxims from popular philosophy. Such borrowing, uncharacteristic of Paul, adds to the impression that these letters are pseudonymous works, written sometime between the last decade of the first century and the middle of the second.

Approaching the Pastoral Letters

The sequence in which these three letters were written is uncertain; the canonical arrangement is based on length. But because 1 Timothy and Titus share an emphasis on church regulations, it will be helpful to treat them in direct sequence. And because 2 Timothy focuses most clearly upon Paul himself, and thus provides a personal background for these regulations, it makes a good starting point.

Points to Look For
in the Pastoral Letters

- Emphases on proper behavior, sound teaching, and the opinion of outsiders

- Qualifications of specific officers and evidence of institutionalization

- Teachings on the status and role of women

- Opposition to gnostic teaching

Notes on a
Reading of 2 Timothy

1:1—3:9

With the salutation (1:1-2), the author establishes the letter as a communication from Paul to Timothy. "Paul" now refers to the tradition in which both he and Timothy stand and contrasts those who turned away from Paul with those who "refreshed" him (1:15-18). Then follow injunctions to Timothy: be strong, entrust Paul's teachings to the next generation, and accept his share of suffering (2:1-25). In 3:1-9, "Paul" prophesies that the "last days" will bring great distress and lists specific vices that will characterize the times. The ref-

erence to Jannes and Jambres, names given in Jewish tradition to Pharaoh's magicians who contended with Moses in Exodus 7, serves as a warning: those who oppose God come to a bad end (3:8-9).

3:10—4:22

The injunctions in 3:10-11, to look back over the apostle's career and place Paul himself at the center of attention, focus on Paul himself. But the following verses (3:12—4:5) use Paul's experience of suffering and deliverance as a basis for encouragement and exhortation:

— The godly will be persecuted, but God will be with them.

— Some persons will turn away from the truth to myths, but Timothy should continue in Paul's teaching, study the (Jewish) Scriptures, and pass on sound doctrine.

In 4:7, "Paul" notes that he has "fought the good fight," but the time for his "departure" (his death) has come. Then he focuses on his own situation in prison, noting that almost everyone has abandoned him. The readers are left with the image of Paul suffering in prison but rejoicing in an earlier deliverance that allowed him to continue his work and assured him of his place in God's heavenly rule. The final greetings and benediction bring the letter to a close, leaving the readers with the final impression that they have read a letter of Paul. They should be inspired by Paul's experience and encouraged to keep the faith as he did.

Notes on a Reading of 1 Timothy

1:1-20

The prescript identifies the letter as from Paul to Timothy, and 1:3-7 reveals its purpose: to warn against "false" teachings involving "myths," "genealogies," and the Jewish law. The readers will recognize a complex of ideas, current in their midst, that combines aspects of Judaism with gnostic speculation on the origin of the universe. Then "Paul" explains the proper function of the law: to instruct ungodly people (1:8-11). Following a thanksgiving and personal testimony, he then charges Timothy to "fight the good fight" (1:18-20).

2:1—6:21

A series of instructions on worship follows in 2:1-15: there should be prayers for all persons, including government officials; the men should pray, lifting up their hands without anger; women should dress modestly and "learn in silence with full submission"; no woman should teach or have authority over a man (2:12).

In 3:1-13, "Paul" lists qualifications for the offices of bishops and deacons. Bishops should be married only once, display moral qualities, be well thought of by those outside the community, and be able to manage their own households. (The male gender is assumed.) Deacons should display similar characteristics, but 3:11 mentions women, although it is unclear whether the reference is to women deacons or deacons' wives. (If there were women deacons, 2:11-12 shows that their duties were severely restricted.)

In 4:1, "Paul" refers to the "false" teachings of "later times," which the readers will identify with their own times. The heretics' prohibition of marriage and certain foods denies the goodness of God's creation. In 4:6-16, "Paul" warns against "myths and old wives' tales" and supports his injunctions with a reference to "the laying on of hands" (4:14).

In 5:1—6:2b, "Paul" gives instructions on the treatment of persons of varying status, including "widows," who seem to have constituted a formalized group. In 5:13-16, he lays down rules for younger widows, whom he characterizes as gossips and busybodies. After instruction to elders, an injunction to moderate wine drinking at 5:23 challenges the asceticism of the false teachers and affirms the goodness of creation. The injunction to slaves at 6:1-2 enhances the image of the church as an orderly household, moral by the standards of society at large.

The letter ends with more warnings against false teaching in 6:3-10, exhortations to Timothy in 6:11-16, an exhortation to the rich (6:17-19), a warning against "what is falsely called knowledge" (*gnosis*), and a brief benediction (6:20-21).

Notes on a Reading of Titus

1:1-16

The prescript in 1:1-4 establishes Paul as the writer and Titus, whom Paul has left in Crete, as the recipient and identifies the purpose of the letter as to strengthen "God's elect" (or chosen). "Paul's" reference to his commission to Titus in 1:5 to appoint elders reveals that the letter will explain how congregations should be organized. In 1:10-16, he discusses a problem with which bishops must deal: teachers who recommend circumcision and seek personal gain. The negative impression of these teachers is reinforced by the quotation of a line, attributed to the Cretan poet Epimenides,[15] that makes an ethnic slur against Cretans.

2:1-15

"Paul" exhorts Titus in 2:1 to the teaching of sound doctrine and includes a household code that encourages women and slaves to be sub-

missive. In 2:11-15, we find a summary statement on the ideal behavior of the community.

3:1-15

At 3:1-2, the author adds a list of admonitions, such as to submit to authorities and act courteously toward all people, which is given a Christian interpretation in verses 3-7. More injunctions follow, including specific references to the "false" teachings (3:9) and a word on dealing with factious people (3:10). Then "Paul" adds some personal notes and a final admonition (3:14) and closes with a greeting and benediction.

NOTES

1. Robert Jewett, *The Thessalonian Correspondence: Pauline Rhetoric and Millenarian Piety* (Philadelphia: Fortress Press, 1978), 191–92, 177–78.

2. Gerhard Krodel, "2 Letter to the Thessalonians," in *Ephesians, Colossians, 2 Thessalonians, the Pastoral Epistles*, J. Paul Sampley, Joseph Burgess, Gerhard Krodel, and Reginald H. Fuller (Philadelphia: Fortress Press, 1978), 75.

3. Ibid., 89.

4. Ernest Best, *The First and Second Epistles to the Thessalonians* (New York: Harper & Row, 1972), 283–86.

5. Krodel, "2 Letter to the Thessalonians," 94.

6. Margaret Y. MacDonald, *The Pauline Churches: A Socio-historical Study of the Institutionalization in the Pauline and Deutero-Pauline Writings* (Cambridge: Cambridge University Press, 1988), passim; and *Colossians and Ephesians* (Collegeville, Minn.: Liturgical Press, 2000), 8, 21.

7. Joseph Burgess, "The Letter to the Colossians," in Sampley et al., *Ephesians, Colossians*, 45.

8. Walter Wink, *Naming the Powers: The Language of Power in the New Testament* (Philadelphia: Fortress Press, 1984), 74–76.

9. Ibid., 49.

10. Ibid., 89.

11. Ibid., 5.

12. Ibid., 134.
13. Ibid., 5.
14. A. T. Hanson, *The Pastoral Epistles: Based on the Revised Standard Version* (Grand Rapids: Eerdmans, 1982), 3.
15. Walter Lock, *A Critical and Exegetical Commentary on the Pastoral Epistles* (New York: Charles Scribner's Sons, 1924), 134.

STUDY QUESTIONS

1. Summarize the arguments against Pauline authorship of each of the letters treated in this chapter.
2. What point does 2 Thessalonians make regarding eschatology?
3. What seems to be the specific nature of the Colossian "heresy," and how does the author argue against it?
4. What, according to Ephesians, is the role of the church in God's plan? How are the readers expected to express their loyalty to the church?
5. Explain how Wink intends his "postmodern" interpretation to enable contemporary readers to get hold of the "language of power."
6. How does the author of the Pastorals make use of the figure of Paul himself in 2 Timothy as a way of engaging the reader?
7. Characterize the "false teaching" combated in 1 Timothy.
8. In what ways does the author of the Pastorals present the church as an "orderly household"?
9. What attitude toward the world outside the church is expressed in the Pastorals? How do the "household codes" express this attitude?

FOR FURTHER READING

Dibelius, Martin, and Hans Conzelmann. *The Pastoral Epistles.* Hermeneia. Translated by Philip Buttolph and Adela Yarbro. Philadelphia: Fortress Press, 1972.

MacDonald, Margaret Y. *Colossians and Ephesians.* Collegeville, Minn.: Liturgical Press, 2000.

———. *The Pauline Churches: A Socio-Historical Study of Institutionalization in the Pauline and Deutero-Pauline Writings.* Cambridge: Cambridge University Press, 1988.

Sampley, J. Paul, Joseph Burgess, Gerhard Krodel, and Reginald H. Fuller. *Ephesians, Colossians, 2 Thessalonians, the Pastoral Epistles.* Proclamation. Philadelphia: Fortress Press, 1978.

Epilogue to Part Three

The writings of Paul's spiritual heirs in the late first and the second centuries express radically divergent understandings of what he was all about. In fact, we can see from 2 Peter 3:15-16 that the interpretation of Paul's letters had become problematic even before the New Testament period had ended. There should thus be little wonder that we find him claimed as an ally by persons with sharply opposing views today.

The passage in 2 Peter presupposes the existence of a collection of Paul's letters before the middle of the second century. We do not know which letters were in the earliest grouping, but by the end of the second century, the thirteen letters now in the canon were generally accepted as authoritative. Hebrews, which eventually made its way into the canon as a letter of Paul, was by this time accepted by many churches but did not as yet have a secure status.

Marcion's Interpretation of Paul

The earliest collection of Paul's letters whose contents we know was that of Marcion, who was excommunicated in 144 C.E. and later founded his own church. He also constructed a canon of scriptures that included only a shortened version of the Gospel of Luke and a collection of ten letters of Paul, from which the Pastorals were absent.

For Marcion, who was influenced by gnostic thought, Paul's contrast between law and grace necessitated a total denial of the authority of the Jewish Scriptures. He taught that the Jewish God was not the same as the Christian God, but an inferior, tyrannical deity who created the world out of evil matter. The Christian God, who appeared for the first time in Christ, was characterized by love and grace. Christ, who appeared on earth without being born and without a material body, came to rescue souls from this inherently corrupt world. Those who received him were required to abstain from all sexual intercourse and the eating of meat.[1]

Marcion edited the Pauline letters he used, excluding all positive references to the Jewish heritage. That is one way to deal with perceived contradictions, but it is not the only way. An alternative is to read some passages as symbolic rather than literal. This is the route taken by the teachers of the second-century Christian gnostic groups.

Gnostic Interpretation of Paul

A prominent Christian gnostic school was founded by Valentinus, who was born in Egypt and later taught in Rome. Although our knowledge of Valentinus himself is limited, anti-gnostic Christian writers of the period left detailed accounts of the teachings of his followers, each of whom offered a different version of a complex system of thought. And there are some Valentinian materials among the documents discovered at Nag Hammadi.

Gnostic mythologies are populated not with goddesses and gods but with "aeons," personified abstract notions that represent both spatial realms and "divine, semi-divine, or demonic beings."[2] These aeons make up the spiritual light-world known as "the Fullness." In the Valentinian system, the incomprehensible, perfect aeon named Fore-Father plants a seed in the womb of his female counterpart named Thought. The result is a lengthy chain of emanations of aeons in male-female pairs.

The inappropriate desire for knowledge on the part of one of the aeons disrupts the original harmony of the Fullness, and through a series of events, there appears the Demiurge, who thinks he is the true and only God and creates the material world. This world contains a spiritual element, but it must be awakened through knowledge (*gnosis*). Thus, the aeon Jesus, united with another aeon, Christos, sojourns in the world to impart this knowledge and bring salvation to human beings. But this salvation is not available to all. Some persons are simply "fleshly" and cannot be helped at all, while others are "spiritual" and predestined to return to the light. A third group, who are "psychic," can be saved only through the "spirituals."

In their reading of Paul,[3] the Valentinians made much of the distinction between the spirituals and the psychics. Paul's words *law* and *grace* provided a gold mine on this theme. According to the Valentinians, Paul taught that the spirituals are free from the law and exempt from sin and judgment. Lacking only the glory of the Father, they are justified by grace, which they receive through faith in the spiritual *Christos*. The psychics, however, who are under sin and subject to the law, are saved through faith in the psychical *Jesus*. It is they whom Paul has in mind when he says that "all have sinned" (Rom 3:23) and declares that the law is upheld (Rom 3:31).

The gnostics' negative view of material reality also played its part in Valentinian interpretation. They took Paul's phrase at Romans 8:3, "in the likeness of sinful flesh," to mean that the Son had only the appearance of a physical body. And assuming that Paul could not have referred to a bodily resurrection in Romans 6, they argued that he was speaking symbolically of the process of receiving *gnosis*. To be dead was to be ignorant of (the true) God, and to be resurrected meant to receive the knowledge they taught.[4]

Christian interpreters have generally assumed that the gnostics simply read their own systems of thought into Paul. Elaine Pagels, however, concludes that at many points, the Valentinians' theology was a genuine outgrowth of their reading of Paul, not a preconceived set of ideas imposed upon him. In this sense, the Valentinian teachers qualify as genuine interpreters.[5] It should also be said that their "realized eschatology," while clearly one-sided, did get hold of an important aspect of Paul's own teaching.

The Paul of Legend

The author of the Pastorals perpetuated Paul's legacy by enlisting his apostolic authority in the service of "sound teaching" and a church structure designed to maintain it. Marcion and the gnostics did so by interpreting Paul theologically. But there was yet another way Paul's memory was kept alive: early Christians told stories about him, some of which are collected in an apocryphal book called *The Acts of Paul*.

Dennis MacDonald has sought to determine the relationship between the Pastoral Letters and some of the stories in *The Acts of Paul*. In one of these, Paul plays the hero in a variant of the ancient tale on which George Bernard Shaw based his play "Androcles and the Lion." According to the original version, an escaped slave hiding in a cave befriends a lion by removing a splinter from its paw. The slave is eventually captured, condemned to death, and stands helpless in an arena as a lion is released upon him. When the lion, who turns out to be the slave's old friend, gently licks his feet, the spectators are moved to spare the man's life. The Pauline variation is wonderfully appropriate. Paul too is spared by a lion. But instead of removing a splinter in the earlier scene, he preaches to the lion, which immediately repents and is baptized![6]

Even more interesting is the story of Thecla, a young and beautiful woman who is converted by Paul's preaching on the eve of her wedding to the wealthy Thamyris and dedicates herself to a life of chastity. MacDonald summarizes:

> When Thamyris fails to woo her back from Paul, he and Thecla's mother, Theocleia, take her to the governor, who orders her brought to the theater naked to be burned at the stake. A hailstorm extinguishes the fire, and Thecla is saved. She finds Paul, tells him she will cut her hair short—i.e., like a man's—and follow him if he will baptize her. . . . Together they go to Antioch of Pisidia, where another frustrated would-be lover condemns Thecla before the governor. In spite of the protests of the women of the city . . . she is thrown naked to the beasts, baptizes herself in a pool of seals, is saved by a series of miracles, sews her mantle so that she will look like a man, and flees to Paul, who ordains her to teach.[7]

MacDonald believes that these stories were originally passed on by female storytellers. The dominant and sympathetic characters in every story are women, and men often appear in hostile roles. In the lion story, for example, Paul converts two women in prison, to the consternation of their husbands. The stories thus reflect a dissenting voice against the mores of a patriarchal society. The image of Thecla, a woman outside the traditional household and a teacher, legitimated women's independence and right to serve in leadership roles. It is significant that the stories seem to come from Asia Minor, where women were particularly prominent in church leadership.[8]

MacDonald thus argues that a primary motivation of the author of the Pastorals was to silence female storytellers who told such tales as later appeared in *The Acts of Paul*. In 2 Timothy 3:6-7, for example, "Paul" warns against "those who make their way into households and captivate silly women . . . who are always being instructed and can never arrive at a knowledge of the truth." And 1 Timothy 4:7 speaks explicitly against "old wives' tales."

The reason for silencing women was to protect the institution of the patriarchal household. It is thus understandable that the Pastorals not only object to stories that empower women but also reject the practice of celibacy (1 Tim 4:1-4), which encourages their independence. The statement that women are saved through childbearing (1 Tim 2:11-15) means quite literally that women should be kept in their place at home.[9]

The Paul of legend stands in marked contrast to the church officials who interpret the Pauline heritage in the Pastorals. "Nothing in the legends," MacDonald writes, "suggests that Paul or any other Christian could be characterized as moderate or dignified; rather, they are proudly presented as socially deviant, impudent, and incorrigible."[10]

Perspectives on the Issues

It is always tempting to caricature one's opponents. During the late first and early second centuries, the Pauline legacy developed in several different directions. While the options that appeared then cannot be equated with the ways in which twenty-first-century interpreters sort out the issues, it is meaningful to identify parallels. Modern opponents of women's ordination are in some sense heirs of the Pastoral Letters, and feminist theologians stand in some sense in the line of those ancient Christian women who told the story of Paul and Thecla. While it is important to recognize these connections, however, it is also important not to reduce the ancient issues to the modern ones but to see them in their original complexity.

It is easy, on the one hand, for interpreters who consider themselves "orthodox" to reject the noncanonical understanding of Paul out of hand. There can be little doubt that such readings distort Paul's thought. We may legitimately ask, however, whether such "distortions" are any greater than those found in the Pastoral Letters. Do the Pastorals rightly represent Paul's views on women? Does their emphasis upon "sound doctrine" do justice to Paul's understanding of faith?

It is also too easy, on the other hand, simply to condemn the Pastorals as representing a degeneration of an early, charismatic movement into a staid institution. In opposing Gnosticism, the Pastorals were preserving Christianity's Judaic heritage, with its emphasis upon the goodness of creation.

It is nevertheless true that the price the early church paid for preserving an affirmation of the material world was the adoption of a patriarchal structure. Whether that price was necessary is a matter of opinion, although it is important to reflect on the issue. It should be clear from the preceding investigation that theological speculation was indeed running wild and that loss of meaningful connections to the earliest level of the Jesus tradition and to the Judaic heritage was a real possibility. Whether the patriarchal structure was the only way to preserve those links is another matter.

Interpreters of the Pastorals have often concluded that the author recommends silencing women because they were particularly active in propagating gnostic teaching. MacDonald notes, however, that there are no discernible gnostic elements in the stories in *The Acts of Paul*.[11] Although we find gnostic teaching and women's stories lumped together in the Pastorals, this does not mean that such lumping was accurate. Alongside the anti-gnostic thrust of the Pastorals, we have also seen a general interest in settling down in the world. The author's attitude toward women seems motivated in part by a desire to accommodate to the dominant culture. Certainly, the church would acquire a "bad" reputation if its women became known as disrupters of households!

Because the developing institutional church adopted the patriarchal structure, many contemporary feminists look upon Gnosticism as more favorable to women's interests. As our description of Valentinianism showed, Gnosticism included feminine aspects in the deity, and there is evidence that women played active roles in gnostic circles. According to Elisabeth Schüssler Fiorenza, however, this does not mean that Gnosticism was pro-feminist:

Gnosticism . . . employed the categories of "male" and "female," not to designate real women and men, but to name cosmic-religious principles or archetypes. . . . In Gnosticism, the pneumatics [spirituals], men and women, represent the female principle, while the male principle stands for the heavenly realms, Christ, God, and the Spirit. The female principle is secondary, since it stands for the part of the divine that became involved in the created world and history. *Gnostic dualism shares in the patriarchal paradigm of Western culture. It makes the first principle male, and defines femaleness relative to maleness.*[12]

That both the early church and Gnosticism adopted aspects of the patriarchal ideology is hardly surprising; it was central to the dominant culture. The victory of patriarchy was not absolute, however. The church eventually made a place for celibate women and thus provided an escape from the household, although this status fell short of full equality.

Interpretation of Paul as a Hermeneutical Problem

The wide variation in the early readings of Paul provides a vivid illustration of hermeneutics in process, that is, the attempt of interpreters not simply to understand Paul in a technical, descriptive way but to make ultimate sense of his point of view. The discrepancies also illustrate, to be sure, the problematic character of hermeneutics: How does one decide between competing interpretations? But they can also be viewed as evidence that hermeneutical endeavor is a necessary corollary of the attempt to understand, that interpreters always bring some value-laden agenda to their work.

It should come as no surprise, then, that the hermeneutical issue arises in more recent attempts to understand Paul. Some of the variations in the attempt to characterize Paul's theology involve technical questions such as the meaning of certain terms and concepts, the motivation for a particular writing, and the nature of a conflict in which Paul was involved. At other points, however, interpreters understand Paul differently because they read him from different hermeneutical perspectives.

NOTES

1. Williston Walker et al., *A History of the Christian Church*, 4th ed. (New York: Charles Scribner's Sons, 1985), 67–68.
2. Hans Jonas, *The Gnostic Religion: The Message of the Alien God and the Beginnings of Christianity*, 2nd ed. (Boston: Beacon, 1963), 53–54.
3. See Elaine Pagels, *The Gnostic Paul* (New York: Random House, 1979).
4. Ibid., 28–33.
5. Ibid., 9.
6. Dennis R. MacDonald, *The Legend of the Apostle: The Battle for Paul in Story and Canon* (Philadelphia: Westminster, 1983), 21–23.

7. Ibid., 18–19.
8. Ibid., 26–53.
9. Ibid.
10. Ibid., 72.
11. Ibid., 63.
12. Elisabeth Schüssler Fiorenza, *In Memory of Her: A Feminist Theological Reconstruction of Christian Origins* (New York: Crossroad, 1983), 274; italics added.

STUDY QUESTIONS

1. Compare and contrast the "Paul of legend" with the gnostic Paul, the Paul of the Pastoral Letters, and the Paul who wrote the seven undisputed letters. State which aspects of these various "Pauls" you personally find acceptable or unacceptable, interesting or uninteresting, and explain why.
2. Give your own arguments as to whether the "mainstream" church was justified in rejecting gnostic teachings.
3. It has been argued that many gnostic teachings actually survived within the "mainstream" church. Give your own opinions regarding this claim.

FOR FURTHER READING

MacDonald, Dennis R. *The Legend and the Apostle: The Battle for Paul in Story and Canon*. Philadelphia: Westminster, 1983.

Pagels, Elaine. *The Gnostic Paul*. Philadelphia: Fortress Press, 1975.

THE GENERAL LETTERS
AND REVELATION

Prologue to Part Four

On the Margins: Inside

The nine canonical writings to be examined in part 4 form a diverse body of materials. One factor that binds them together, however, is that, with the exception of 1 John and 1 Peter, they were all subjected to some degree of dispute in their process toward final acceptance into the canon. In that sense, seven of them stand "on the margins" of the New Testament. Christians have valued some of these writings very highly through the centuries, however.

Tradition has assigned each of these works to an apostolic author, but in every case, modern scholars have raised serious doubts. As is the case with other New Testament writings, the titles are undoubtedly secondary, supplied not by the authors but by later Christians who preserved them. In chapter 14, I will examine the writings traditionally called the General Letters. This designation presumes (wrongly in at least some cases) that they were intended for the universal church as a whole, rather than for individual congregations. Hebrews, which was long considered Pauline, is sometimes included in this group, and I have followed that practice. I will treat the remaining writing, Revelation, in chapter 15. Of the canonical writings yet to be considered, I will give a full reading only of 1 John.

On the Margins: Outside

Other writings stand marginally outside the canon in the sense that they fulfill one or more of the following criteria: they appeared on one or more of the canonical lists in the early centuries, they were treated as scripture by some church leaders, and they were included in collections of New Testament texts. Unlike works such as the gnostic gospels that were branded heretical by the emerging majority church, they were often considered valuable resources for use in Christian worship. I have chosen to discuss five of these writings.

1 Clement

The letter that came to be known as *1 Clement* was sent from the church in Rome to the church in Corinth and is generally dated late in the final decade of the first century. An early and apparently reliable tradition attributes the actual composition to one Clement of Rome. A later tradition identifies this Clement as bishop of the Roman church, but many scholars discount it because the letter's terminology seems to indicate that the practice of investing exclusive authority in a single bishop in each church had not yet developed.[1]

The letter responds to an incident in the Corinthian church: a dissident group has deposed the established leadership. Clement (on behalf of the Roman church) defends the established leadership by referring to a chain of authority. As Christ is from God, so the apostles are from Christ. And it is the apostles who appointed the bishops and deacons. Many scholars see here the notion of apostolic succession, the belief that Jesus gave, through Peter and the other apostles, a formal authority to bishops. Helmut Koester argues, however, that because Clement does not connect specific apostles with specific churches, it is clear that he "is not interested in the doctrine of apostolic succession, but wants to speak generally about the continuance and stability of offices in the Christian churches."[2] It would seem, nevertheless, that we have here a clear step in the direction of such a doctrine, which in any case begins to take shape shortly after *1 Clement* and is found in explicit form by the end of the second century.

Clement speaks to the situation not only by condemning the removal of the leaders, but also by engaging in a long parenetic discourse, drawing on such sources as the Jewish Scriptures, sayings of Jesus, the letters of Paul, Christian traditions regarding Peter and Paul, and "pagan" materials as well. The bulk of the letter consists of an extended exhortation to maintain authentic Christian piety and ethical behavior.

Some scholars think there was a theological dispute behind the controversy between the rival leadership groups, and it is possible those who deposed the leadership were the spiritual heirs of Paul's opponents in 1 Corinthians. But there is no clear indication of this in the letter.

The writing is notable for its mention of the deaths of Peter and Paul and its use of the legend of the phoenix. According to this legend, when the bird dies, a worm is formed from its decaying flesh. Feeding off the carcass, it eventually grows into a new bird, which then repeats the cycle. Clement uses the story as an analogy to the Christian belief in the resurrection of the dead.

The *Didache*

The *Teaching of the Twelve Apostles*—or the *Didache* (Greek for "teaching"), as it is popularly known—is composed of two prior documents that an editor has brought together relatively intact. The first of these is a tractate on the "two ways," a kind of moral catechism that exists in slightly different forms as an independent document and as a part of the letter of *Barnabas*. The second is basically a manual of church order.

Many scholars think the first part is a slightly reworked Jewish document, but others dispute this. In its present form, in any case, it contains many points of contact with the Gospels. The two ways are the way of life and the way of death. The former is characterized by such virtuous activities as loving God, loving one's enemies, giving to the needy, and honoring church leaders. The way of death is that of those who are given over to such evils as murder, adultery, fornication, magic, and greed.

The church manual contains instructions for such practices as baptizing, fasting, and celebrating the sacred meal. The third practice is called the *eucharist* (Greek for "thanksgiving"), but some scholars doubt that this term is used here in the technical sense applied to the Lord's Supper and think it refers only to the love feast, or common meal, at a time after the Lord's Supper split off from it. It is possible, however, that the separation has not yet taken place. In any case, the instructions indicate an actual meal and exclude from it anyone who has not been baptized.

The manual also offers guidance on the treatment of apostles, teachers, and prophets and urges the election of worthy bishops and deacons. It also informs churches how to distinguish between true and false leaders among those who arrive as visitors, and it closes with an admonition about false prophets who will arrive in the last days.

The *Didache* claims to represent the teaching that Jesus gave to the "twelve apostles," but its final form clearly dates from the end of the first century or a little later. It has points of contact with several New Testament writings, most notably the Gospel of Matthew, which the final editor may have used.

Barnabas

The letter of *Barnabas* is really an anonymous treatise rather than a letter, and there is no reason to accept the early attribution of it to Barnabas, the companion of Paul. The greater part of the work is devoted to Christian allegorical interpretations of the Jewish Scriptures, and in this respect, it is similar to the canonical book of Hebrews. Unlike Hebrews, however, it is disparaging of the Jewish people, whom the author believes proved unworthy of the revelation given to them.

Addressing a wide range of topics in the scriptures, the author understands the dietary regulations as allegorical statements of moral commands. The prohibition against eating pork, for example, is really an injunction for human beings not to act like swine. What "Barnabas" considers the most important piece of wisdom in the treatise, however, concerns Genesis 14:14 and 17:23. As one commentator summarizes:

> When Genesis declared that Abraham circumcised 318 males of his household . . . , it meant to predict Jesus on the cross, for the Greek figures for 18 are iota eta (IH), the first two letters of Jesus' name, and the Greek figure for 300 is tau, or T, which could be taken as representing the cross. The allegorizing teacher who offered this interpretation was very proud of it. "No one has learned a truer lesson from me," he goes on, "but I know you are worthy of it." (*Barnabas* 9:8-9)

Allegorical interpretation appears bizarre to modern readers influenced by historical criticism. But it is in many ways typical of ancient Jewish interpretation in general and has clear points of contact within the New Testament—not only in Hebrews but, for example, in Paul's use of the story of Sarah and Hagar in Galatians 4:21-31.

The Shepherd of Hermas

The Shepherd of Hermas is an apocalyptic work that recounts three sets of visions of the author, Hermas, who identifies himself as a freed slave. Moralistic in tone, it extends a final call to repentance before a coming persecution and/or the end of the age. The presupposition is that those who refuse this opportunity to repent will be lost, as will any who do repent but later fall into sin. In offering a new opportunity for repentance, however, it gives a different answer than does Hebrews to the question of whether those who sin after baptism can subsequently be forgiven. Hebrews takes a harder line (6:4), proclaiming that there is in fact no forgiveness for those who fall from grace.

The book is devoted largely to moral instruction and the call to repentance. It contains very little explicit theology but is notable in several respects. An adoptionist Christology (the notion that Jesus became the Son of God during his life) is evident at some points, although at others, the preexistence of the Son is clear. And the writing seems to contain an early form of the notion of works of supererogation, good deeds above and beyond the commandments, which receive special merit from God.

Also, there is frequent reflection upon the question of poverty and riches. In an attempt to trace the social history of the writer's community, however,[3] Carolyn Osiek concludes that there were probably few upper-class persons to be found there. The "rich," on her account, were, like Hermas himself, former slaves who had become relatively successful in business and were abandoning their responsibilities to the church in favor of a quest for status in the wider society. Hermas's criticisms of wealth are thus an attempt to get such persons to exercise their duties to the rest of the community.

Apocalypse of Peter

The *Apocalypse of Peter*, which should not be confused with a gnostic work of the same name, purports to be the apostle Peter's account of revelations given to him by Jesus. Although some early church leaders considered it authentic, that judgment did not prevail; it is universally considered pseudonymous today.

Despite its eventual rejection, the work had some lasting influence on Christianity. It is the first example we have of a Christian writing that gives detailed descriptions of the rewards and punishments in heaven and hell, the kind of material later appearing in Dante's *Inferno*. Among those singled out for special punishment are blasphemers, people guilty of sexual sins, murderers, and slaves who do not obey their masters. The flavor is evident in the following excerpt:

> Then will men and women come to the place prepared for them. By their tongues with which they have blasphemed the way of righteousness will they be hung up. There is spread out for them unquenchable fire. . . . And the murderers and those who have made common cause with them are cast into the fire, in a place full of venomous beasts, and they are tormented without rest, as they feel their pains.[4]

The obvious point of comparison among the canonical writings is the book of Revelation. But as we will see, in Revelation the detailed descriptions of divine punishment are confined to the earthly sphere. And the *Apocalypse of Peter* is entirely lacking in the theme of vindication of the oppressed that is so strong in Revelation, whose author never would have listed disobedient slaves among the candidates for eternal torture.

NOTES

1. Cyril Richardson et al., trans. and eds. *Early Christian Fathers* (Philadelphia: Westminster, 1953), 36.
2. Helmut Koester, *Introduction to the New Testament*, vol. 2, *History and Literature of Early Christianity* (Philadelphia: Fortress Press, 1982), 290.

3. Carolyn Osiek, *Rich and Poor in the Shepherd of Hermas: An Exegetical-Social Investigation* (Washington, D.C.: Catholic Biblical Association of America, 1983).
4. Wilhelm Schneemelcher, ed., *New Testament Apocrypha*, vol. 2, *Writings Relating to the Apostles; Apocalypses and Related Subjects*, rev. ed., trans. R. M. Wilson (Philadelphia: Westminster John Knox, 1992), 628–29.

STUDY QUESTIONS

1. Based on the treatments of the noncanonical works in this prologue, try to formulate arguments both for their inclusion and for their exclusion. What aspects of each do you think you would value? What aspects might you not value? Why?
2. State why you agree or disagree with the author's statement that the approach to the Jewish Scriptures in the Letter of Barnabas is not that different from the approach employed in other New Testament writings.
3. Did the early Christians do the right thing in settling on a definite canon? Give arguments on both sides of the question.

FOR FURTHER READING

Grant, Robert M. *The Apostolic Fathers: A New Translation and Commentary.* 6 vols. Nashville: Thomas Nelson & Sons, 1964–69.

The General Letters

14

Hebrews,
James,
1–2 Peter,
Jude,
1–3 John

Hebrews

Searching for the Story

There is no consensus on the story behind the writing entitled "To the Hebrews." An old tradition in Alexandria assigned the work to Paul, although his name does not appear in it. On the basis of that tradition, the churches in the East had generally accepted it as canonical by the third century. Modern critical scholarship is virtually unanimous in rejecting Pauline authorship, however. Although Hebrews exhibits some similarities to Paul's letters, the author's style, vocabulary, and theology are quite different.

Some scholars have sought to find the author among the New Testament characters linked in one way or another with Paul: Barnabas, Apollos, Luke, Priscilla, Epaphras. None of these suggestions, however, has gained wide acceptance.

The original audience of the work is as difficult to identify as the author. The title reflects the early view that it was written to Jewish Christians on the verge of abandoning their Christian faith and reembracing Judaism. Some scholars accept this judgment because of its extensive quotations from the Jewish Scriptures and the detailed knowledge of Jewish institutions it presupposes. But Gentile as well as Jewish Christians accepted the authority of the Jewish Scriptures. And the author's dialogue is not with the living Judaism of the original readers' world but with the ancient sacrificial system described in Leviticus. However, attempts to prove that the audience was specifically Gentile do not fare much better.

Another problem is the writing's unusual form. Since it lacks the usual prescript or salutation found in letters, as well as the writer's self-identification, many scholars classify it as a sermon or theological treatise. However, it exhibits some characteristics of a letter. In chapter 13, the author offers specific exhortations and asks for the readers' prayers, and the conclusion in 13:22-25 (which contains a reference to Timothy) is a typical epistolary ending. Some scholars think that both verse 19 and this conclusion are later additions designed to present the work as a letter of Paul. But one may wonder why Paul's name was not added also. Some scholars thus accept the work as a real, although anonymous, letter.

As to the date of composition, all we can say is that it was probably written before the end of the first century, since it is apparently quoted in *1 Clement*. The place of composition is even more indefinite. Because the conclusion contains greetings from "those from Italy," some interpreters argue that the author wrote from Rome to Jewish Christians in Jerusalem. Others think the author, writing *to* Rome, is referring to Christians originally from Italy but residing in the place where the letter was composed.

Although we cannot be very specific in our reconstruction of a story behind Hebrews, the author regards the addressees as Christians in danger of falling away from their faith. At some point in their common history, they had probably experienced persecution and conducted themselves admirably in the midst of it. Now, however, some are neglecting communal worship and losing heart. The writer's broad intention is to rekindle the faith of the community and encourage perseverance. We thus find much of the work devoted to exhortation. Supporting this exhortation, however, is a complex theological statement rather different from anything else in the New Testament.

Points to Look For in Hebrews

- Contrast between the revelations in the old covenant and the new

- Emphasis on holding fast to the faith

- Emphasis on Jesus' unique status as high priest, who offered purification once for all

- Use of the figure Melchizedek in the author's argument

Notes on a Reading of Hebrews

1:1-4

The first four verses contain a refined theological statement identifying the subject of the discourse: a contrast between an earlier and partial revelation and a later and complete one. Although God spoke to the Christians' "ancestors" or predecessors "in many and various ways," God has now, in the "last days," spoken through the Son.

1:5—2:18

The Son's status is superior to that of angels (1:5-14). Assuming knowledge of the tradition that God gave the Torah through angels, the author issues a warning (2:1-4): if defection from God's earlier, incomplete revelation through angels merits punishment, how much more does defection from the full revelation through the Son. God subjected the world to human beings, but they do not now exercise the authority implied by this subjection. Jesus does, however; it is he who was "for a little while" made lower than the angels. He shared the fragile human condition, became the "pioneer" of salvation, and through his own death destroyed Satan's power and atoned for human sins.

3:1—5:10

Jesus is God's appointed apostle and high priest and was faithful to God, just as Moses was, but Jesus is superior to Moses as a son is to a servant (3:1-6). He is faithful over God's house, "and we are his house if we hold firm the confidence and the pride that belong to hope." This assertion leads to a warning in 3:7-19 not to turn away from God. The rebellious followers of Moses were denied entrance into God's "rest"—a term that refers both to the land of Canaan and to salvation (4:1-13). Because Christians have as their heavenly high priest Jesus, who is both Son of God and a person who can sympathize with human weakness, they should hold fast to their faith (4:14-16). High priests in general sympathize with human weakness and assume their offices only at God's call, but Jesus is high priest in

the line of Melchizedek by God's appointment (5:1-10).

5:11—10:25

This section provides an elaboration of the Melchizedek theme:

— *5:11-14.* The readers are spiritually immature and need basic instruction.

— *6:1-12.* They should press on to perfection, but those who were once enlightened but have fallen away cannot be restored to repentance.

— *6:13-20.* God's promise to Abraham is a basis of hope, which grants access to the inner part of the sanctuary (the Holy of Holies in the tent, the predecessor to the temple), where Jesus has entered as "a high priest forever, according to the order of Melchizedek."

— *7:1-10.* Abraham paid tithes to Melchizedek, priest of Salem (Gen 14:17-24), which indicates Melchizedek's superiority. Since Melchizedek had no ancestry (none is mentioned in Genesis), he remains a priest forever.

— *7:11-28.* Jesus is a high priest in the order of Melchizedek, not that of Aaron (Moses' brother, progenitor of the Israelite priesthood), which makes him superior. Other high priests must atone for their own sins and offer continual sacrifices; Jesus has no sins and offers atonement once for all.

— **8:1-13.** Other high priests offer sacrifices in an earthly sanctuary that is a shadow of the heavenly one; Jesus mediates a new covenant that is better than the old one, which is now obsolete.

— **9:1-22.** In the earthly sanctuary (the tent), only the high priest enters (thus access is limited); Jesus' priesthood is based on his own blood sacrifice and effects a true and lasting purification. He did so in the true (heavenly) sanctuary, not one made by human hands, and he will return to save those who await him.

— **10:1-25.** Neither the blood of animals nor continual sacrifices of other priests can take away sin, but Jesus' blood can. The readers should hold fast to their faith, be faithful in attending the community's gatherings, and encourage one another.

10:26—13:25

The definition of *faith* in 11:1-3 picks up on the quotation in 10:37-38 and serves as a prelude to examples of faithful action in Israelite history (11:4-40). In 11:13-16, the author notes that the exemplary folk of old kept the faith even in the face of unfulfillment, since they died before God's promises were realized. They lived as "strangers and foreigners on the earth," people "seeking a homeland." But God has prepared a "heavenly" country for them. The rehearsal continues, with emphasis on

FIG. 14.1 **The Western Wall in Jerusalem.** Photo by Gianfranco Moroldo © Alinari /Art Resource, NY.

the difficulties endured by the people of God, and concludes in 11:39-40. These heroes in the faith did not receive what God promised, "since God had provided something better so that they would not, apart from us, be made perfect."

The point of the whole argument thus becomes clear. The old covenant provided a promise, but not fulfillment; that has come only in Jesus. Those whom the author addresses thus experience that which the heroic figures of the past awaited in faith.

In chapter 12, the author exhorts the readers to remain faithful, looking to Jesus who persevered and was exalted to God's side. The admonition that they should accept tribulations as God's disciplining of them (12:7-11) leads to further exhortations and warnings (12:12—13:17). The letter ends with a request for prayer (13:18), a benediction (13:20-21), and an epistolary ending.

The call to join Jesus "outside the camp and bear the abuse he endured," coupled with the contrast between "no lasting city" and "the city that is to come" (13:13-14), makes a key point. The readers will equate the holy city of Jerusalem with "the realm of security and traditional holiness"[1] and conclude that, as his followers, they too are aliens in the present world. That is why they must bear abuse if they are to remain in solidarity with him. They will also understand that although Christians are privy to the "perfected" revelation in Christ, they are still, in some sense, like the heroic figures of the Jewish Scriptures, the "wandering people of God."[2]

A Critical Problem: Background of the Author's Thought

Much attention has been given to the background of the author's thought. There is a strong reliance upon the Jewish Scriptures, but the author seems dependent on the Septuagint and reflects many components of Hellenistic thought. Attempts to be more specific about influences have resulted in a variety of theories.

Ernst Käsemann found evidence of a gnostic background: the earthly/heavenly contrast, the notion of a heavenly redeemer, and the movement toward a heavenly homeland. This thesis, however, downplays the author's eschatological interests, and the emphasis on the world as God's creation (1:1) runs counter to gnostic thought.

Other scholars detect the influence of Philo, and there are numerous parallels. But there are also important differences, most notably the absence of allegorical interpretation. For many scholars, it is enough to note the general Hellenistic influence and possible affinities with Alexandrian thought, of which Philo may have been only one of many representatives.

Attempts have also been made to find direct links between Hebrews and the Dead Sea Scrolls. Here again, however, the more judicious judgment is that the author was familiar with broadly based Jewish notions also shared by the Essenes.

Regarding the Christian background, scholars have found similarities to both Paul and the Gospel of John. Most notable in the latter case are the author's use of the concept of "word" and the clear statement of Christ's preexistence. But it is not really possible to demonstrate direct dependence; what seems more likely is that the author drew from a fund of ideas spread widely within the early Christian community. As to Paul, some important theological differences should also be noted. Hebrews lacks the central Pauline contrasts of faith/works, flesh/Spirit, and Jew/Gentile, and it does not employ the notion of being "in Christ." Furthermore, Paul knows nothing of the notion of Jesus as high priest or of the impossibility of returning to the faith after willful defection.

In the end, we can say only that the author drew upon a wide range of ideas from early Christianity, the Jewish Scriptures, and Hellenistic thought.

The Old and the New in Hebrews

Graham Hughes, in his study of the interpretive method of the author of Hebrews, divides scholars into two groups. Those who think Hebrews was written to Jewish Christians turning back to Judaism generally read it as a polemic against Judaism. Those who think it was written to Gentile Christians see it as a more general call "for a more spiritualised conception of faith." From their point of view, "The Jewish motifs are employed simply as examples or symbols of an unworthily materialistic form of faith," and the author was more concerned to state doctrine than to exhort the readers to faithfulness.[3]

Hughes argues that neither of these views does justice to the author's main concern, which he identifies as the question of how God's word remains self-consistent despite being affected by historical developments. In other words, the argument in Hebrews focuses on the problem of the old and the new, how Christianity is related to the Hebrew faith that preceded it.

According to Hughes, the author solves the problem by reading the Jewish Scriptures from a Christian perspective, according to which incomplete and fragmentary revelations can be seen as part of a continuous process leading up to the final revelation in Jesus. When, however, the author asks how the Jewish Scriptures apply concretely to the life of a Christian congregation, the matter becomes more complex. Since in Christianity, Jesus is God's complete self-disclosure, Jewish institutions are understood as outmoded. One therefore finds a strain of realized eschatology in this work. This perspective changes, however, when the author addresses the community's awareness of its existence within the historical process—that is, its acknowledgment that the "city" it seeks is not yet present. At these points, one finds a futuristic eschatology and a sense of close continuity between the Christian community and the people of the Jewish Scriptures.

One must therefore reckon with both continuity and discontinuity in describing the relationship between old and new in Hebrews. Recognizing a kind of finality in the Christian revelation, it nevertheless presents the new community as continuing the pilgrimage of the people of old, responding to the word of the same God who has spoken in various ways throughout human history, although definitively in Jesus.

James

Searching for the Story

James begins with a salutation, but there are few other marks of a genuine letter. Consisting entirely of exhortations, the work lacks the references to specific people that characterize, for example, the letters of Paul. The author is self-identified as a teacher, and the document may be described as a parenetic treatise.

The author is also self-identified as James, and the work came into the canon on the supposition that it was written by James "the brother of the Lord," the longtime leader of the Jerusalem church. Most critical scholars, however, reject the traditional view of authorship because of the work's relatively polished Greek and its use of Hellenistic rhetorical devices and the Greek version of the Jewish Scriptures. In addition, its place in the Western canon was not fully secure until the end of the fourth century, and we have no sure evidence of its existence before the third century.[4] The author's self-identification as James is undoubtedly a reference to "the brother of the Lord," but the evidence just noted suggests that this is the device of a pseudonymous author.

The work seems to reflect more than one situation, which suggests that it has gone through several revisions. It is difficult to make judgments about the place or date of composition, but many scholars think the Hellenistic influence makes a date near the end of the first century likely. Pedrito U. Maynard-Reid argues that James must be read against the background of extreme social stratification and that it was written for a community of the poor.[5] While he accepts the traditional view of authorship and relates the work to an early period in Palestine, many of his observations hold good even on other presuppositions. The passages on wealth and poverty are probably rooted in the experience of the early Palestinian church, but they must have had relevance for the situation in which the work received its final form.

Many scholars find no real unity in the work, interpreting it as a string of largely unrelated exhortations. However, Peter H. Davids has offered an outline presupposing a unified structure, which I have followed here.[6]

Points to Look For in James

- The author's view on poverty and riches

- The author's view on faith and works

Notes on a Reading of James

1:1-27

Addressed as "the twelve tribes," the readers will understand that they as Christians consider themselves the "true Israel." The phrase "in the Dispersion" suggests that they are living outside Palestine.[7] The author offers wide-ranging advice:

- Accept life's trials as testing that leads to maturity.

- "Let the believer who is lowly boast in being raised up" (1:9).

- Do not say that temptation comes from God.

- Be slow to anger; be doers, not just hearers, of the word; and bridle one's tongue.

2:1-26

Two subjects dominate chapter 2: warnings against partiality toward the rich and the necessity of works as well as faith, with acts of mercy toward the poor illustrating "works." The rhetorical question in 2:5-7 assumes the poverty of the readers: "Is it not the rich who oppress you?" The reference to the "royal law" in 2:8-13 involves an appeal to both the Jewish Scriptures and Jesus' summation of the law. The statement on faith and works shows that mere belief in God's existence is of no value.

3:1—4:12

Injunctions on several topics follow in 3:1-18: the special responsibility of teachers, the use of judicious speech, and the necessity of acquiring the true, spiritual wisdom from above, rather than false, earthly wisdom. The author then enjoins readers to identify their "crav-

ings," which lead to conflicts, and contrasts God's way to the world's way with numerous imperatives, including prohibitions against slandering and judging one another.

4:13—5:6

The harsh indictment of the rich echoes prophetic literature in the Jewish Scriptures,[8] and the poor will hear it as a way of pointing up the sins of the merchant class in particular.

5:7-20

Beginning with a discourse commending patience in suffering while awaiting the final judgment, "James" now issues a series of injunctions, including a condemnation of oaths, a recommendation of prayers for the sick and confession of sin, and a final admonition to seek the restoration of those who fall away from the faith.

Theological Issues

James has often been disparaged among Protestants as theologically weak. Martin Luther, an avid proponent of a doctrine of "justification by grace through faith" based on Paul's writings, called it an "epistle of straw" because of its view of faith and works. And the relationship between this writing and Paul's thought has been the subject of much debate. Some interpreters try to press Paul and James into the same mold. But while Paul insisted that it is faith *and not works* that brings justification, the author of this writing believed that faith without works is ineffective. Thus, other scholars have argued that James was written in explicit opposition to Paul.

It is not clear, however, that the author is responding directly to Paul. The way in which the faith/works issue is cast suggests unfamiliarity with the subtleties of Paul's views. For this author understands faith as simply belief in the existence of one God (2:1), whereas for Paul, real faith does not exist in some privatized internal dimension of the self but involves one's whole being. There is therefore some truth in the claim that Paul and James do not really disagree, since they are to some extent talking about different matters.

Many scholars have noted that there is in fact little theology at all in the work. So little in James is distinctively Christian, in fact, that some scholars view it as a Jewish treatise only slightly reworked by a Christian redactor. The more recent judgment, however, is that it is dependent on the Jesus tradition, most particularly the kind of material underlying the Sermon on the Mount. And the charge of theological weakness is a matter of perspective. Liberation theologians criticize the neglect of this writing and find its attention to problems relating to social class and its emphasis on deeds of mercy an important corrective to the tendency to understand faith as a purely internal attitude. Thus, Cain Hope Felder, in a study carried out from a perspective defined by the interests of the black church, disputes the notion that James represents a "legalistic" point of view:

> There is a profound difference between "legalism" (rigid adherence to

religious regulations of the cultus to gain merit and guarantees) and moral obligations by which persons of faith are held accountable to God's law and purposes for humanity. . . . Christian faith, no less than God's moral law, for James, necessarily involves criteria for Christian social behavior.[9]

1 Peter

Searching for the Story

The prescript of 1 Peter presents this work as a letter from Peter to Christians in Asia Minor, but the excellent Greek and consistent use of the Septuagint suggest that it is not the work of a Galilean fisherman. Defenders of the traditional view point out that the author acknowledges use of a secretary (5:12), but there are also reasons to date the work after Peter's death (ca. 65–67). Many scholars have placed it near the end of the reign of the Roman emperor Domitian (81–96) on the supposition that it reflects a situation of official persecution of the church that fits this period. One may doubt this supposition, but one scholar who does so opts for a late date on other grounds. Arguing that most of the letter's intended recipients were in rural areas, John H. Elliott concludes that Christianity would not have had time to spread there before the last quarter of the first century.[10] Some scholars also argue that 1 Peter shows the influence of Pauline thought, which hardly sits well with the notion that it was written by Peter. Finally, the writing seems directed to churches that are predominantly Gentile, whereas Peter's mission was primarily to Jews (Gal 1:7).

One reading of the prescript supports the view that 1 Peter was written to bolster courage during a time of persecution. For some interpreters, the characterization of the readers as "the exiles of the Dispersion" means that, as Christians, they remain pilgrims on the earth with their true home in heaven. Elliott disputes this reading, however, arguing that the terminology of "homelessness" and "alienation" is used not metaphorically but sociologically. That is to say, the author addresses persons who are literally noncitizens and who have probably experienced economic deprivation as well. Their alienation is not from heaven but from society. Having joined the Christian movement in search of community, they soon found that their membership made them even more unacceptable to their neighbors.[11]

On this view, their suffering came not from the official persecution of the Roman Empire but from social ostracism from their neighbors, and the author's purpose was to counteract the disintegrating effects of this problem on the community. Thus, 1 Peter's use of household codes is less a sign of accommodation to the "bourgeois ethic" of the larger society, as many scholars have claimed, than an attempt to foster internal solidarity of the "household of God" (4:17).

The metaphorical use of "Babylon" in the conclusion (5:13) indicates that the letter was written from Rome. The references to Silvanus and Mark at this point are also interesting, since the reader will undoubtedly think of the companions of Paul, which raises a question as to why the author chose the name of Peter. As Helmut Koester comments, however, by the time the letter was probably written, both Peter and Paul were honored as martyrs, so that it mattered little which name was chosen.[12]

Points to Look For in 1 Peter

- The image of the church as a royal priesthood and holy nation, with a mission

- The sense of the church's apartness from the world, combined with advice to obey the authorities and live honorably in the sight of outsiders

- Advice given to women and slaves in the household code

- Emphasis on endurance of suffering

Notes on a Reading of 1 Peter

In the following notes, the divisions are based on John H. Elliott's *A Home for the Homeless*.[13]

1:1-2

The attribution to Peter lends the letter authority, and the address to "exiles of the Dispersion" encourages the readers to understand themselves as heirs of God's promises to

Israel and also of Israel's sufferings: they are God's people.

1:3—2:10

"Peter" begins with the declaration that the new birth in Christ brings hope for eschatological salvation, and this declaration becomes the basis for exhortation: the readers should maintain self-discipline, put away the desires that belong to the old life, nurture love rather than negative attitudes and deeds, and continue to feed upon the "spiritual milk" of Christian teaching. The poetic call in 2:4-10 addresses the readers as a spiritual house, of which Christ is the cornerstone, and as a royal priesthood commissioned to proclaim God's mighty acts.

2:11—4:11

Now addressing the recipients as "aliens," while designating outsiders to the community as "Gentiles," "Peter" increases their sense of apartness from the world. Even though acknowledging the hostility of outsiders, he counsels the readers to conduct themselves honorably so that "the Gentiles" (here meaning non-Christians) will learn to glorify God. Further injunctions are to obey the secular authorities, "honor everyone," "love the family of believers," and "fear God." Implying that Christians owe their ultimate allegiance to God, the author nevertheless assumes the possibility of living in relative harmony with the empire. Further commands are that slaves must obey their masters (2:18-25) and wives should obey their husbands and live simple and reverent lives (3:1-6). Husbands should honor "the weaker sex" (3:7), and the entire community should reject vengeance and pursue unity, humility, and love (3:8-12).

FIG. 14.2 Saint Peter, traditional founder of the church at Rome, holding the keys to paradise. Thirteenth-century Byzantine mosaic, Istanbul, Turkey. Photo © Werner Forman / Art Resource, NY.

Emphases in 3:13—4:11

— It is better to suffer for doing good, following the example of Christ, than for doing wrong. After his death, Christ preached "to the spirits in prison," those who died in the flood that Noah and his family escaped (3:19-20).

— Avoid licentious behavior, since the end is near, and all will have to give an accounting of their lives—which is why Christ preached to the dead: to give them a second chance.

— Maintain love for one another, and be good stewards of God's grace.

4:12-19

"Peter" now turns to the "ordeal" the readers face. Told that suffering as Christians is a sign

FIG. 14.3 *Christ Descending into Hell* by Canavesio, Giovanni and Giovanni Baleison. Fifteenth-century fresco in the Chapelle Notre Dame des Fontaines, La Brigue, Alpes Maritimes, France. Photo © François Guenet /Art Resource, NY.

that God's Spirit rests upon them, the readers will understand their present plight as a mark of their distinctive role in the world.

5:1-11

Applying the title "elder" to himself, "Peter" turns to the relationship between the elders of the communities and their "flocks." The fact that "Peter" has witnessed "the sufferings of Christ" shows that he has lived through ordeals similar to their own. Elders should exercise oversight and not seek personal gain; the people should obey them. All should be humble before God and resist the devil. A promise of eschatological deliverance (5:10) is followed by a brief doxology (5:11).

5:12-13

"Peter" concludes with greetings from a "sister church" and "Mark," as well as an additional word of encouragement.

The Sojourn among the Dead in 1 Peter 3:19 and 4:6

The notion of Christ's sojourn among the dead, which appears in a less developed form in Ephesians 4:8-10, has fascinated interpreters throughout history. Many scholars regard it as the application to Christianity of a theme of a descent into the underworld that was widespread in pre-Christian religions and Greek myths (Orpheus and Eurydice, Persephone). It found its way into the Apostles' Creed in the affirmation "He [Christ] descended into hell," a phrase deleted by many Protestant churches.

The related notion of "the spirits in prison" however, stands in a line of Jewish speculation regarding the generation destroyed in the flood of Genesis 6. In 1 Peter, the motifs are combined in order to deal with the question of the ultimate fate of persons who lived before Christ.

2 Peter and Jude

The story behind 2 Peter is entwined with that behind the Letter of Jude. The similarity in subject matter and wording makes literary dependence virtually certain; in fact, almost all of Jude is paralleled in 2 Peter. The consensus is that 2 Peter made use of Jude; the absence in the former of Jude's quotations from works eventually excluded from the Jewish Scriptures is best explained as the result of the intentional deletion of "suspect" material. And the fact that some passages in 2 Peter are obscure until read in light of their parallels in Jude suggests the author of 2 Peter unthinkingly deleted material that new readers would need in order to get the full meaning.

Jude

The Letter of Jude purports to be by Jude, "the brother of James," which would make him also the brother of Jesus mentioned in Mark 6:3 and Matthew 13:55. But along with its sophisticated Greek, two passages suggest a late date and pseudonymity. The reference to "the predictions of the apostles" in verse 17 presupposes a postapostolic age. And the phrase "the faith that was once for all entrusted to the saints" in verse 3 reflects the notion of a fixed body of doctrine, a concept that did not develop until late in the first century.

We have no way of identifying the original recipients of the letter. The characterization of the "heretics" the author attacks suggests a Gentile context, however, and the author was likely a Hellenistic Jewish Christian.

Many scholars think the references to the licentiousness of the "heretics" indicate that they were gnostics. Others find the evidence too scant to make such a judgment. In any case, they seem to have been itinerants who worked their way into the community to which the letter is sent (v. 4). And we know how the author viewed them: not only are they immoral, but they deny Christ (v. 4), reject authority, revile angels (v. 8), and seek personal gain (v. 11).

Notes on a Reading of Jude

The author reminds the readers of the apostolic faith and denounces the "heretics" by exposing their unworthiness. Verses 1-4 establish the writer's authority and explain the need for the letter. Verses 5-16 relate examples of God's judgment as a warning against false teachers and pronounce a woe upon them. Verses 17-19 summarize "Jude's" argument and lend apostolic authority with the claim that the apostles predicted the false teachers. The doxology in verses 24-25 reminds the readers of the writer's intention to keep them safe.

2 Peter

The dependence of 2 Peter upon Jude makes it unlikely that it was written by the apostle Peter, and there is much evidence to confirm this judgment. Not only do its language and rhetorical style show heavy Hellenistic influence, but there is strong indication that it comes from well after the apostolic age. It presupposes not only that the letters of Paul have been collected, but also that they have already attained the status of scripture (3:15-16). Furthermore, 2 Peter is mentioned by no Christian writer before the third century. Finally, although presented as a "testament" of Peter before his death, in which he predicts the appearance of false teachers in the later church, the author shifts from the future tense to the present when actually denouncing these teachers.

It is therefore clear that 2 Peter was not written before the last decade or so of the first century, and many scholars place it as late as 140 C.E. It was probably written after 1 Peter, since there is a rather clear allusion to it at 3:1-2. But scholars generally conclude that the two letters were written by different authors.

Like Jude, 2 Peter was written to combat teachings regarded by the author as heretical. Although some scholars regard the "heretics" as gnostics, a more recent judgment is that they were Christians who were accommodating their faith to popular Hellenistic ideas by deleting such traditional notions as apocalyptic eschatology and the divine inspiration of the Jewish Scriptures.

Notes on a Reading of 2 Peter

The author presents a "testament" left by the apostle Peter, warning the church of such teachings as those the readers are now encountering. "Peter" reminds these readers of the fundamentals of the faith and warns them regarding the fate of those who fall away from the truth.

FIG. 14.4   Saint Peter preaching and Saint Peter's crucifixion. Ivory panels, fourteenth century c.e., Paris. Photo by Gérard Blot
© Réunion des Musées Nationaux /Art Resource, NY.

The salutation in 1:1-2 establishes the letter as authoritative, and in 1:3-15, "Peter" reminds the readers of their faith and enjoins them to fulfill that faith with specific virtues. The reference to Peter's imminent death lends weight to the appeal. In 1:16—3:13, the author contrasts the message regarding Jesus' "power and coming" to "cleverly devised myths." An apparent reference to the transfiguration scene in the Gospels (Mark 9:2-13) reinforces the impression that it is Peter who is writing and also suggests the majesty that will accompany Jesus' eschatological return. A major component of the argument is the claim that the church's teaching is based on prophecy, and true prophecy is contrasted with false. "Peter" also claims that the rise of the false teachers was predicted, and he explains the delay in Christ's return as a way of granting extra time for repentance. In 3:14-18, he cites Paul's letters as scripture and concludes with further exhortations and a doxology.

Theology, Doctrine, and the Hermeneutical Question

Although Jude and 2 Peter are deeply concerned about doctrinal purity, they contain virtually no theology at all. To this extent, they are similar to the Pastoral Letters. In none of these writings do the authors try to refute their opponents with argumentation; they simply condemn them. Jude and 2 Peter go much further in this direction and take on a harsher polemical tone. But in the Pastorals no less than in Jude and 2 Peter, we can hear the echoes of a time in which the dynamic, open-ended kind of theological reflection characteristic of Paul is giving way to sheer doctrinal pronouncement.

Many scholars and theologians for this reason portray all these writings as degeneration from the creative early years of Christian thought. Others, however, see the movement toward doctrinal stability as necessary and inevitable in light of tendencies toward fragmentation. I will not try to settle the debate here but will only point out that it involves a question that is at base hermeneutical. To what extent is theological endeavor a perpetual process of formulation and reformulation, and to what extent must it involve the strict definition of boundaries?

The Letters of John

Searching for the Stories

None of the letters of John actually claims to have been written by a person of that name. The first of these, which bears hardly any traits of a letter, does not name an author at all. The two shorter writings, which follow the form of a Hellenistic letter rather closely, indicate simply that they are sent by "the elder." The similarity in language and theology between the Gospel of John and these three books, however, convinced the early church that all were written by the same person.

That person was presumed to be John the son of Zebedee, one of "the Twelve," who was also identified with the "beloved disciple" of the Gospel. Although many modern scholars reject all aspects of this traditional view, we may still ask whether the letters were written by the person who wrote the Gospel and whether the three letters themselves had a common authorship.

Opinion is divided on both questions, but there is reason to answer the first negatively. Despite similarities in thought between the Gospel and the letters, there are significant differences in emphasis. While the Gospel stresses Jesus' divine nature, both 1 and 2 John are more concerned to assert that the Son of God came "in the flesh," and 1 John contains a stronger emphasis on futuristic eschatology than does the Gospel. Also, the phrase "the beginning," which seems at first glance to bind 1 John (1:1) so closely to the Gospel, might actually count in the other direction. In the Gospel, it refers to the creation of the world, but in 1 John, it indicates the initial stage of the Christian tradition. Many scholars also claim that 1 John reveals a later historical situation, since the opponents it attacks are not those outside the community but false teachers within it.

Not all critics are convinced by such evidence, since it could be replied that the author changed tactics to meet a new situation. And the question is complicated by the possibility that the Gospel has gone through one or more revisions. Some scholars believe that the person who wrote 1 John, while not the author of the original version of the Gospel, was responsible for its final state.

The question of whether the author of 1 John also wrote 2 and 3 John is even more difficult, because the latter two works are so brief as to yield little evidence. But there is little reason to doubt that 2 and 3 John were written by one person, "the elder."

Given the difficulty of all these questions, any attempt to tell the story behind the letters of John will be speculative. But there is one point on which all scholars agree. Whether written by one, two, or more authors, the four Johannine writings came from the same Christian community, which was marked by a distinctive theological outlook.

In chapter 8, we noted Raymond E. Brown's view that the Johannine community was made up originally of Jewish Christians who developed a high Christology involving belief in the preexistence of the Son of God, were expelled from the synagogue, and began to receive Gentile converts.

According to Brown, the letters of John date from a stage in the community's life somewhat later than that in which the author of the Gospel wrote.[14] After this community separated from those Jewish Christians who would not accept its high Christology, it went through a period of internal conflict. Some members began to emphasize Jesus' divine nature to the point of compromising his full humanity. Brown refers to this group as the secessionists, because they apparently separated from the rest of the community.

In the opinion of many scholars, the letters of John oppose a fully gnostic point of view characterized by "docetism" (from the Greek verb *dokeo* meaning to "think" or "seem"), the view that Jesus only "seemed" to be human and had no real human body at all. But Brown thinks the secessionists had not moved that far, since they too were Johannine Christians and it would be difficult to justify a truly docetic Christology on the basis of the Gospel of John. What they denied, according to Brown, was not that Jesus was human, but only that the human Jesus had significance for salvation. They understood salvation as the result of the knowledge of God that Jesus brought, not of any action that took place in the world, such as his death on a cross.

The letters of John associate the secessionists with a number of specific views. We may assume from 1 John 1:8, 10 that they claimed to have reached a state of sinlessness. This view is consistent with their strong sense of union with God and their rejection of futurist eschatology. The emphasis on commandments in 1 John is also evidence that the secessionists thought ethical behavior was unnecessary for salvation.

On some other matters, we must be more careful about accepting the author's characterization of the opponents. Many scholars take the charge that the secessionists lack love (1 John 1:9) at face value, assuming that those who deemphasized the humanity of Jesus and the importance of commandments would feel no sense of obligation to the human neighbor. Brown thinks it more likely, however, that each camp was characterized by internal solidarity on the one hand and animosity toward the opposition on the other. The author of 1 John may well have appeared as unloving to those called "antichrists" and "liars" (1:18, 22) as they did to that author! And they undoubtedly understood the author's group, not theirs, as the one that had fallen away from the truth.

On Brown's view, 1 John was written for the author's immediate community, the home base of Johannine Christianity, in order to combat the teachings of the splinter group. Because the potential readers were close at hand, there was no reason to use the format of a letter. In 2 John, however, "the elder" writes to a Johannine house church some distance away to warn about the secessionists and to urge rejection of any missionaries whose views do not conform to "the teaching of Christ" (as the author defines it).

The story behind the Third Letter is the most difficult to reconstruct. In it, "the elder" writes to one Gaius, praising him for "faithfulness to the truth" and criticizing someone named Diotrephes. The elder charges the latter with usurping authority and refusing to welcome some group, presumably emissaries from the home base community. We do not, however, know the specifics of the controversy—why, for example, Diotrephes turned the travelers away. The elder does not speak directly about the secessionists of 1 and 2 John. But was Diotrephes a secessionist? Or did he think the emissaries were? We do not even know whether Diotrephes and Gaius were in the same local community, or what specific office (if any) each held.

Brown thinks Diotrephes was an early example of a local leader invested with great authority, such as the bishops of the Pastoral Letters. He agreed with "the elder" in rejecting the secessionists but disagreed about authority in the church. Whereas "the elder" retained a community-based version of authority, charac-teristic of the earlier stages of Johannine Christianity, Diotrephes thought that controversies were best dealt with through concentrated power. He therefore assumed the authority to expel members from the community (v. 10) and probably dealt with the problem of false teaching by rejecting all missionaries. When he refused to accept the emissaries from the home community, "the elder" wrote to Gaius, who may have received the missionaries after their rejection by Diotrephes (vv. 3, 5-8), to shore up support for a confrontation on this issue.

We do not know who won the immediate dispute. But if Brown's view is correct, we do know which point of view ultimately prevailed: the church finally invested authority in the office of bishop. So it is likely that the letters of "the elder" represent a model of community-based authority within Johannine Christianity that disappeared as the Johannine churches were absorbed into the church at large. The apparent acceptance of Peter's authority in (the Gospel of) John 21 is a sign that only a modified version of this type of Christianity was ultimately acceptable to the wider body. For it was a revised, "ecclesiastical" version of the Gospel of John that achieved canonical status.

Points to Look For in 1 John

- Emphasis on love within the community

- Dualisms of life and death, light and darkness

- The author's view of the secessionists

- Emphasis on Jesus as the Christ

The First Letter of John: A Reading

1:1-4

The author, using the first person plural, discloses an intention to declare "what was from the beginning." Three terms in the introduction are reminiscent of the prologue to the Gospel of John: "the beginning," "life," and "word" (*logos*). But the emphasis is not on the preexistent *logos*, as in the Gospel, but on the extension of that word through the tradition of the community. The readers are thus addressed by the Johannine community itself. And the author's description of the community's experience of the Word lends concreteness to the community's witness: they have "seen" it with their eyes, "touched" it with their hands. The eternal Word, having become manifest in an actual human being, continues to be manifest in a tangible way in their midst.

1:5—3:10

In 1:5, the author specifies the content of the tradition, the "message" that has brought life, fellowship with God, and joy: God is pure light, containing no darkness at all. And here the qualified dualism of the Gospel of John reappears. To say that God is light is to say that God is the source of the illumination that engenders authentic human existence. But to mention darkness is to recognize an antithetical force in the world, a power that opposes all that is good. Against the background of this dualism, the author implies in 1:6 that some who claim fellowship with God actually walk in darkness, and goes on to assert that it is

those who walk in the light who alone have such fellowship.

The readers will know who is meant by the persons the author condemns for claiming sinlessness (1:8). Hearing that those who are in the light are cleansed and forgiven through "the blood of Jesus," they will conclude that all human beings stand in need of such forgiveness. The reference to atonement in 2:1-2 combines with the appeal to the readers as "little children" to clarify the author's view of sin: those in the light should not sin, but if they do, they are forgiven through Christ's sacrifice.

Lifting up the necessity of obeying Jesus' commandments, the author focuses on the specific command, defined in the Gospel of John as both old and new: to love one's fellow believers (2:3-11). The declaration that "the darkness is passing away" interprets the Johannine dualism in terms of a futuristic eschatology. Although passing away, the darkness is still present in the world. But to say that "the light is already shining" is to acknowledge the Johannine tradition of fulfillment in the present.

At 2:12-14, the author offers assurances to the readers: their sins are forgiven; they do have knowledge of God. Then an admonition, once again reflective of Johannine dualism, follows in verses 15-17: the readers must not love the world, which stands in opposition to the Father and is passing away.

The proclamation at 2:18 that "it is the last hour" makes explicit the eschatological point subtly indicated earlier. And the references to "antichrist," again presuming knowledge of the subject on the readers' part, identify the object of the author's scorn. Now the identity of the group the author opposes is clear: it is those who "went out from us," the secessionists. They are the "antichrists," and their presence is a sign of the nearness of the end.

In 2:22-25, the author plays those who deny that "Jesus is the Christ" against those who confess the Son and thereby know the Father also. Although the specific point of contention is not mentioned, the readers will recognize in the conjunction of "Jesus" with "Christ" something that the secessionists deny, rendering their Christology inadequate. And the reference to what the readers "heard from the beginning" will remind them that this confession of Jesus stands at the center of their tradition. That tradition once again appears as the source of authority, and verses 26-27 invite contrast with the teachings of the secessionists. In proclaiming that the community members have no need of teachers, since they are anointed (presumably by the Spirit), the author binds the Spirit and the tradition together. This move undercuts the secessionists' position, since they too undoubtedly appealed to the Spirit as justification for their views: Did not the Gospel of John (16:13) promise that the Spirit would guide the community "into all the truth"? The statement on anointing in 2:26-27 suggests that the tradition is open-ended yet not simply free-floating, since what was heard in the beginning remains the point of departure.

The injunction in 2:28 to "abide in him" shows that abiding in Christ and remaining true to the tradition are equivalents, and the reference to Jesus' coming stresses the eschato-logical significance of remaining in the truth. The author also promises (v. 29) confidence to those who so "abide" and presents right action as the sign of one's relation to Christ. This thought leads in 3:1-3 to a brief discourse on what it means to be "children" of God. In this discourse, use of "the world" in its negative sense and additional eschatological references reinforce the distinction between the readers and the secessionists.

The reference to those who commit sin at 3:4 again points to the secessionists, and the declaration that those who abide in Christ do not sin points up two incompatible modes of existence. If the statement that those in Christ do not sin sounds very much like the secessionists' view, the readers will nevertheless remember that the author has condemned the claim to sinlessness, has written of atonement and confession of sin, and in the present context continues to press the obligation to "do what is right" and love one's fellow community members.

3:11—5:12

In 3:11, the author both builds on the immediate context and signals a new beginning. The reference to "the message you have heard from the beginning" points back to 1:5 and indicates an expansion upon that message. But it is in fact love, mentioned in 3:10, that constitutes the new summation of the message. In verses 12-17, the story from Genesis 3 of Cain's murder of his brother contrasts the two ways of existing in the world. Those who hate their fellows are murderers like Cain, abiding "in death." But those who abide in life, rather than death, will be hated by "the world" and are called to imitate Christ in laying down their lives for others. The rhetorical question in verse 17 then brings the point home in terms of economics: that the haves cannot claim to manifest God's love if they ignore the needs of the have-nots.

After an injunction to actual deeds (as opposed to mere words) of love at 3:18, the author offers assurance in verses 19-24. Those who worry about whether they are in fact "from the truth" need only ask themselves whether they obey the commandments, specifically the commandment to love, which the author links to the confession of Jesus Christ as God's Son.

Verse 24 also states that the readers may be certain of Christ's presence in them by the testimony of the Spirit. The author acknowledges in 4:1 that there are many spirits in the world, noting the presence of false prophets, and provides a way to test the spirits manifest in the various teachings: any true spirit will confess "that Jesus Christ has come in the flesh." Then the statement in 4:4-6 assures the readers that they are from God, contrasting true believers with "the world."

In 4:7, the author breaks out into a poetic sequence, bracketing an exposition on the relationship between God and love with injunctions to realize love in the community. Love is the necessary sign of the knowledge of God and is descriptive of the essence of God's own being, and God's love is revealed in the sending of the Son as a sacrifice for sin. Although human beings cannot see God, those who love one another in Christ can experience God's presence (4:12).

Reemphasizing several points in 4:13-21, the author also presents love as the basis for confidence in the day of judgment and contrasts it with fear. "Perfect love," in fact, "casts out fear." Verse 20 uses a logical argument to reveal the absurdity of the separation of love of God from love of neighbor, and the term "liar" underscores the point.

In 5:1-4, the author extends the love theme through an analogy: as love of a parent entails love of the child, so love of God entails love of God's children. Since God's children are those who confess Jesus (the human being) as the Christ, it is clear that the author's own faction within the community is meant. The secessionists are thus excluded as unloving, whereas the readers can prove themselves to be God's children by loving one another. But the faith of those who accept Jesus as the Son of God conquers the world.

A reiteration in 5:5 of the theme of conquering leads into a discourse on the Son of God in verses 6-12. The reference in 5:6 to the view that relates Jesus' coming to "water only" presumably points to some aspect of the secessionists' teaching, which probably had something to do with the statement of John the Baptist in the Gospel (John 1:26)—"I baptize with water"—and the more inclusive formula "the water and the blood" presumably refers to the death scene in John 19:34, where blood and water pour out of Jesus' wounded side. It would be consistent with the author's earlier statements to see here an insistence that Jesus' atoning death on the cross is an essential aspect of Christian faith.

In 5:9, the author contrasts God's own testimony to mere human testimony, which again reflects the secessionists' views, very likely their appeal to John the Baptist. The statement in 5:11 that this testimony is God's gift of eternal life in the Son indicates that it is believers' own possession of eternal life that constitutes God's testimony. Since eternal life is the sign that one is truly related to God through the Son, the author can then (5:12) give assurance that a true confession of Jesus brings life, whereas a defective confession leads to death.

5:13-21

Restating the purpose in writing at 5:13, the author reminds the readers of the earlier statement of purpose in 1:4 and so brackets all the intervening material as the main body of the writing. At this point, the author wants to secure the readers' knowledge that they do have eternal life. After presenting that knowledge as the ground of confidence in prayer, the author turns in 5:16-17 to the issue of praying for those who sin. The community should pray for those who commit sins that do not lead to eternal death, but not for those who commit sins that do. The probable implication is that since the secessionists' position makes them guilty of mortal sin, prayer for them is ineffective.

With the emphatic, threefold use of the phrase "we know," the author now offers a final set of assurances regarding the readers' knowledge of God. Having earlier denied the secessionists' claims to sinlessness, the author can now (5:18) address the readers with the more positive, empowering statement that "those who are born of God do not sin." Including in the assurances the affirmation that

the God known in Christ is the true God, the author closes with a warning against idolatry.

Notes on a Reading of 2 John

In the salutation, "the elder" establishes a link with tradition and a bond with the recipients. He then enjoins the love commandment as central to the community's tradition, identifies as "the deceiver" and "antichrist" anyone who denies "that Jesus Christ has come in the flesh," and warns against receiving any who "go beyond" traditional teaching. With the essential point made, the elder indicates in closing (v. 12) that he will say more when he visits in person. The final greeting from the elder's own church community brings the letter to a close on a note of confessional solidarity.

Notes on a Reading of 3 John

Following the salutation, the elder commends Gaius for his hospitality and then addresses the issue of Diotrephes, who has refused the emissaries he has sent, rejected his authority, and spread false rumors. In verse 11, the injunction to do good implies that to follow the elder's advice is to do God's will. The elder's testimony on behalf of Demetrius, possibly one of the emissaries, will commend the latter to Gaius. The closing reference to a visit suggests that the elder has more to say on the issue, and the final greeting plays up the close relationship between the elder and the members of Gaius's community. Gaius will finish the letter with a strong sense that to refuse the emissaries is to deny the tradition through which he has learned "the truth."

Note on "Antichrist"

Students of literature know that a hero needs an opponent. The creator deities of ancient Middle Eastern mythology battled primordial monsters representing chaos and thus shaped an organized and habitable world. Even Judaism, for all its insistence on the oneness and sovereignty of God, made a place for Satan when it embraced apocalyptic thought. It is thus hardly surprising that as messianic thought developed in Judaism, various "anti-messiahs" were introduced to play a role in apocalyptic dramas, or that the New Testament picked up on this theme.

Just as there were no self-consistent, unified concepts of either a Messiah or an anti-Messiah in pre-Christian Judaism, so in the New Testament there is no unified concept of an "antichrist." In the New Testament, in fact, the term appears only in the Johannine letters. But there are several images of an eschatological opponent of Christ. The Synoptic Gospels, for example, mention "false christs" (Matt 24:24) who will arise to lead people astray. We have already seen that 2 Thessalonians 2:9 mentions "the lawless one," who appears as an eschatological antitype of Christ, and in chapter 15, we will see that the broad notion appears in more than one form in the Revelation to John.

Post–New Testament Christian writings continued the tradition. And later interpreters tended to put together all the diverse images, including those in the Jewish Scriptures, to create self-consistent *concepts* of an antichrist, which, century after century, they identified with one after another historical figure.

What is interesting about the use of the term *antichrist* in the Johannine letters is that they apply it to the secessionist movement. And this identification shows that the eschatology of the letters is related to that of the Gospel on the one hand, and the church at large on the other, in a complex way. At one stage, the Gospel of John reshaped traditional, futurist eschatology of the wider church, giving it a strong realized component. The letters, which for the most part move back toward futurist thought, nevertheless introduced a new kind of realized eschatology. Their claim that the antichrist has already appeared means that the present moment (the time in which the letters are written) is in their view the "last hour," the actual beginning of the eschatological drama.

NOTES

1. Harold W. Attridge, *The Epistle to the Hebrews: A Commentary on the Epistle to the Hebrews* (Philadelphia: Fortress Press, 1989), 399.
2. Ernst Käsemann, *The Wandering People of God: An Investigation of the Letter to the Hebrews*, trans. Roy A. Harrisville and Irving L. Sandberg (Minneapolis: Augsburg, 1984).

3. Graham Hughes, *Hebrews and Hermeneutics: The Epistle to the Hebrews as a New Testament Example of Biblical Interpretation* (Cambridge: Cambridge University Press, 1979), 2–3.

4. Some scholars find allusions to James in late first-century materials, but these are vague parallels that might simply be drawn from a common tradition.

5. Pedrito U. Maynard-Reid, *Poverty and Wealth in James* (Maryknoll, N.Y.: Orbis, 1987).

6. Peter H. Davids, *The Epistle of James: A Commentary on the Greek Text* (Grand Rapids: Eerdmans, 1982), 27–28.

7. Some commentators think this phrase reflects a "pilgrim" theology such as that in Hebrews and indicates that Christians in this world are away from their true home in heaven. There is little in the writing to suggest such an interpretation. See John H. Elliott, *A Home for the Homeless: A Sociological Exegesis of 1 Peter, Its Situation and Strategy* (Philadelphia: Fortress Press, 1981), 38, 45.

8. Isa 3:10; Prov 1:11; Wis 2:10, 12, 19.

9. Cain Hope Felder, *Troubling Biblical Waters: Race, Class, and Family* (Maryknoll, N.Y.: Orbis, 1989), 130–31.

10. Elliott, *Home for the Homeless*, 87.

11. Ibid., ch. 1.

12. Helmut Koester, *Introduction to the New Testament*, vol. 2, *History and Literature of Early Christianity* (Philadelphia: Fortress Press, 1982), 293.

13. Elliott, *Home for the Homeless*, 234–36.

14. Raymond E. Brown, *The Community of the Beloved Disciple: The Life, Loves, and Hates of an Individual Church in New Testament Times* (New York: Paulist, 1979); and *The Epistles of John* (Garden City, N.Y.: Doubleday, 1982).

STUDY QUESTIONS

1. What is it possible to say about the authorship and original audience of Hebrews?
2. What problem does the author of Hebrews seem to be addressing?
3. What is distinctive about the way Jesus is presented in Hebrews?
4. What is the role of the list of heroic figures in Hebrews 11?
5. Explain the role of each of the following concepts in the argument of Hebrews: Melchizedek, shadow (or copy) versus reality, Jesus' faithfulness to God.
6. What is it possible to say about the authorship and original audience of James?
7. Martin Luther thought James was theologically weak, but contemporary liberation theologians think highly of it. Explain why, in each case.
8. Summarize the teaching of the Letter of James on poverty and riches.
9. What is it possible to say about the authorship and original audience of 1 Peter?

10. How does the author of 1 Peter expect Christians to relate to the outside world?

11. Why do scholars think 2 Peter is dependent upon Jude? What can be said about the authorship of these two works?

12. To what specific problems are 2 Peter and Jude directed, and what are the authors' strategies for dealing with them?

13. What is it possible to say about the authorship of the Johannine letters?

14. At what stage of the Johannine community's development was each of these letters written, according to Raymond Brown's theory?

15. What, on Brown's view, was the teaching of the "secessionists"?

16. What is central in Christian teaching, according to 1 and 2 John?

17. Give your own arguments as to why each of the works studied in this chapter should or should not have been accepted into the canon.

FOR FURTHER READING

Hebrews

Jewett, Robert. *Letter to Pilgrims: A Commentary on the Epistle to the Hebrews.* New York: Pilgrim, 1981.

Johnson, William G. *Hebrews.* Atlanta: John Knox, 1980.

James

Laws, Sophie. *A Commentary on the Epistle of James.* San Francisco: Harper & Row, 1980.

Maynard-Reid, Pedrito U. *Poverty and Wealth in James.* Maryknoll, N.Y.: Orbis, 1987.

Tamez, Elsa. *The Scandalous Message of James: Faith without Works Is Dead.* New York: Crossroad, 1990.

1–2 Peter, Jude

Boring, M. Eugene. *1 Peter.* Nashville: Abingdon, 1999.

Elliott, John H. *A Home for the Homeless: A Sociological Exegesis of 1 Peter, Its Situation and Strategy.* Philadelphia: Fortress Press, 1981.

Watson, Duane Frederick. *Invention, Arrangement, and Style: Rhetorical Criticism of Jude and 2 Peter.* Atlanta: Scholars, 1988.

1–3 John

Brown, Raymond E. *The Community of the Beloved Disciple: The Life, Loves, and Hates of an Individual Church in New Testament Times.* New York: Paulist, 1979.

Perkins, Pheme. *The Johannine Epistles.* Wilmington, Del.: Michael Glazier, 1979.

Smith, D. Moody. *First, Second, and Third John.* Louisville, Ky.: Westminster John Knox, 1990.

The Revelation to John

15

Searching for the Story

Many people who know nothing else of the Bible are aware of claims that Revelation contains prophecies regarding the "end of the world" that are being fulfilled in our time. And yet many who have some familiarity with the Bible will name Revelation as the most puzzling of all the biblical books, and quite a few find it either frightening or morally repugnant. It is therefore important to pay careful attention to the story behind this writing.

Who Was the Author?

The author identifies himself as John. By the middle of the second century, many Christians assumed he was one of the Twelve, the son of Zebedee, who had supposedly written the Gospel and letters of John also. And by the end of that century, the churches of the West had accepted the work as apostolic and canonical. In the East, however, many leaders denied apostolic authorship, and the canonical status of Revelation was not secure until the end of the fourth century.

Linguistic differences between Revelation and the Gospel and letters of John have been noted since the third century, and many scholars argue that the author of the Gospel of John cannot have written the other works. For one thing, Revelation is permeated with futuristic eschatology, whereas the Gospel has a strong strain of realized eschatology. Nor is there any reason to identify this John with the son of Zebedee.

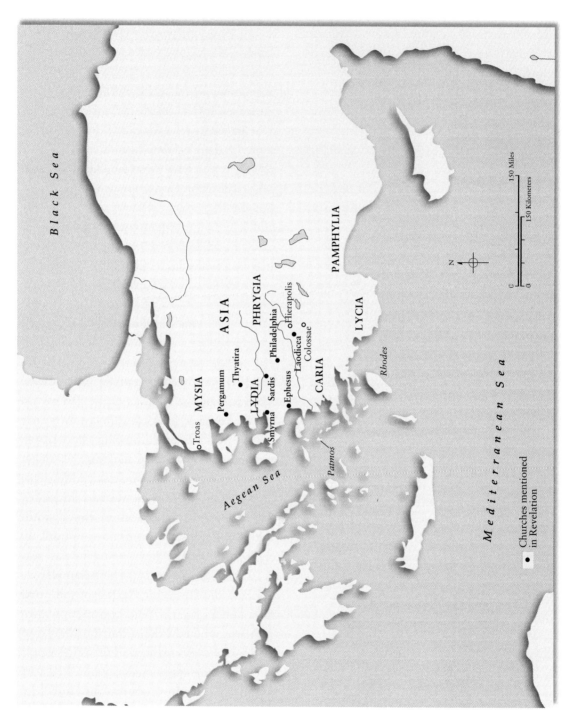

FIG. 15.1   Map of the churches in Revelation.

Nevertheless, some scholars find enough similarity between Revelation and the other works to think its author was associated with the Johannine community. At Revelation 19:13, for example, Jesus is called "the Word [*logos*] of God." Others, however, find the similarities superficial.

The author's knowledge of Jewish apocalyptic literature is evident. In fact, the entire genre gets its name from this writing, which came to be known as "the Revelation (*apokalypsis*) to John" on the basis of the author's designation at 1:1, "The revelation of Jesus Christ." It is also clear from 1:3 that the author understands the work as prophecy. And we may presume that he lived in Asia Minor, since the work is an extended letter to seven churches in that region and the scene of his vision is on the isle of Patmos, just off its western coast.

In What Sense Is Revelation "Prophecy"?

In popular thinking, prophecy is virtually synonymous with prediction. Those who understand Revelation on this model believe that John predicted events centuries removed from his own time. According to one version of this approach, Revelation gives a preview of human history from the first century to the "end of the world." Another version, which appeared in the late nineteenth century, is represented in many popular writings and is often endorsed by media evangelists. On this view, John's predictions concern only the end

of history, not its entire sweep, and are being fulfilled in our own time.

Critical scholars understand Revelation differently, partly because they understand prophecy differently. The Hebrew prophets saw God at work in the sociopolitical events of their times. They often declared God's displeasure with the actions of the Israelite people and their monarchs and thus spoke of a coming judgment. But they expected this judgment in the immediate future. On other occasions, they spoke of the promise of God's eventual restoration of Israel and/or Judah. In some instances, they envisioned this restoration in the near future, and in others, they spoke more vaguely, in the vein of "someday." But they did not give an outline of events centuries ahead. They sometimes declared what was to happen in the future, getting it right in some instances and wrong in others, but "prediction" is an inadequate understanding of their primary intentions.

In contrast, apocalyptic works such as the book of Daniel do contain detailed "predictions" of events to come. But these works were written pseudonymously, in the name of heroes of earlier ages. By writing in the name of persons in the distant past, the apocalyptic authors made their reviews of events that were actually in the past look like predictions of the future. Typically, when an apocalyptic writer deals with the actual future, the "predictions" become extremely vague.

For critical scholars, John was a prophet who used the apocalyptic medium to speak to readers in his own time about the events of that time. Revelation is not a book about the distant future, which would have remained meaningless to persons in the first century. It does speak of the eschatological future, of the end of the age, but John clearly believed the eschatological events to be very near (1:3; 2:16; 3:11; 6:11; 10:6; 12:12; 22:6, 7, 12, 20).

John wrote Revelation because he believed that his readers were about to face persecution (2:10; 7:14) and knew that some of them had already suffered in some degree (2:3, 9, 19). His statement in 1:9 probably means he was banished to Patmos by Roman authorities because of his faith. Early Christians believed that Jesus' resurrection had inaugurated the eschatological age. Given that belief, and given an apocalyptic tradition that often included a period of "woes" just preceding the end of the age, it was natural for John to conclude that the end was near. So he wrote to the churches of Asia Minor to bring hope in the midst of tribulation, interpreting their present distress as a prelude to God's final victory.

Whom Did the Author Oppose, and When Did He Write?

John also wanted to admonish his readers to avoid certain teachings and practices. In 2:6, 15, he rails out against a group he calls the Nicolaitans, and at 2:20-25, he disparages a prophet by dubbing her "Jezebel," an infamous idolater in the Jewish Scriptures. He also condemns both "Jezebel" and another group to which he applies names from the Jewish Scriptures (2:14) for approving the practice of eating meat offered to idols. But

we saw in part 3 that Paul had no objection to that practice as long as it did not unsettle other Christians. So what was it about these groups that offended John?

According to a Christian writer in the late second century, Revelation was written near the end of the reign of the Roman emperor Domitian, which lasted from 81 to 96 C.E. Although some modern scholars place the work earlier or later, the majority think this is the most likely time of composition. Revelation seems to presuppose the demand for emperor worship, and Domitian demanded homage before statues of himself. This does not mean that Christians were being put to death in great numbers, as they were half a century later. The government was apparently not at this point seeking out Christians in a systematic way. But documents from a few years later show that when persons were accused of being Christians, the authorities would execute them if they refused to sacrifice before the emperor's image and/or curse Christ. A similar practice was probably in effect during Domitian's reign.

Some interpreters think Revelation was written under the emperor Nero in the 50s C.E. or under Galba in the 60s. However, the author employs a metaphorical identification of Rome with Babylon, the nation that destroyed the temple earlier in Israelite history, and we can document this usage among Jews only after the destruction of the second temple in 70.

In any case, John wrote in a situation in which Christians faced the possibility of death for refusing to perform a sacrifice to the emperor. And in such a situation, the eating of meat offered to idols took on a different meaning than it did for Paul. In John's eyes, it was outright idolatry. It seems likely, in fact, that all the groups he opposed advocated an accommodation to the ways of the Roman Empire, full participation in business and social activities. But for John, the empire was an agent of Satan. So when he wrote to encourage Christians to "keep the faith," he meant that his readers should not compromise with the demands of the empire just to keep themselves alive. They should be prepared, if necessary, to go to their deaths.

Who Were the Readers?

If John seems uncompromising, it is important to note another aspect of the story behind Revelation. The fact that Christians were singled out for persecution reveals their marginalized status in the empire. Eugene Boring writes:

> They were considered to be adherents of a sect that primarily appealed to the lower classes, a sect that had no long history or glorious institutions. . . . Christians were thus considered to be unpatriotic and irreligious, sometimes being called "atheists" because they had no "gods." Thus, they were likely candidates to become scapegoats for disasters, such as the fire which destroyed much of Rome in 64.[1]

From the perspective of such a community, anyone who advocates accommodation to the larger society threatens the identity of the smaller community. To do so in a time of overt persecution is to compound the injury.

Christians and Jews in Revelation

It is important to remember both the background of persecution and the sense of vulnerability that John and other Christians felt when one comes upon a passage such as 2:9: "I know the slander on the part of those who say that they are Jews and are not, but are a synagogue of Satan." By the time of Christianity, Judaism was a well-established religion in the Roman Empire. And although Jews were considered strange by the general populace and often harassed in various ways, the empire had learned to tolerate them and accord them a measure of respect. They were exempt from military service and any obligation to participate in the emperor cult.

When Christianity became a separate religion, it lost the special status accorded Jews. And, given the precarious position of any group that could not participate fully in the emperor cult, it was almost inevitable that the bitterness between Christians and Jews would increase during a time of persecution. Because Christians threatened the very structure of Judaism by including uncircumcised Gentiles in a faith that claimed Jewish roots, Jews would be inclined to distance themselves from Christians, perhaps even to the point of denouncing them to the authorities.

Against such a background, John made harsh statements against non-Christian Jews. In so doing, he reflected a tragic instance of the frequent situation in which rival marginalized groups, powerless in the face of the dominant power structure, turn their anger on one another.

The Author's Use of Symbolic Language

An important aspect of the author's language is its symbolic nature. Most interpreters recognize that John did not intend for images such as the great beast rising out of the sea (13:1) and the locusts with tails like scorpions that torture human beings (9:1-11) to be interpreted literally. But there are different ways in which symbolic language functions.

Some interpreters assume that every symbol in the book has an exact meaning, corresponding in a one-to-one fashion to something outside the text. For these interpreters, just as Rome stands for Babylon, each of the "woes" visited upon the earth by angels in chapters 8–9 points to some definite set of events the author expected to take place. Interpreters at the other extreme deny that any of the symbols have exact meaning or point to specific realities in the actual world. Even Babylon, from this perspective, does not stand in simplistic fashion for the Roman Empire but functions more generally as a symbol of oppressive, God-denying power in any time or place.

There is increasing recognition that John's use of such language falls somewhere between the two extremes. Some of the symbols seem

to have a definite reference, most notably Babylon. But to try to interpret Revelation as a whole by simply "decoding" it is to miss an important aspect of the author's intention. It would be absurd, for example, to try to assign a referent in the actual world to the "event" John envisions at 20:14, the casting of Death and Hades into the lake of fire. As Schüssler Fiorenza notes:

> The symbolization and narrative movement of Revelation elicits emotions, feelings, and convictions that cannot, and should not, be fully conceptualized. . . . The mythopoetic language of Revelation is akin to poetry and drama. Therefore, any adequate exploration and comprehension of Revelation has to experience the evocative power and "musicality" of the book's language since it was written to be read aloud as a liturgical poem and to be heard in the worship gatherings of the Asian communities.[2]

In the following treatment, I will keep in mind that the book's symbolic language is the powerful, emotionally charged language of the open-ended symbol, which grows out of the impact of deeply lived experience on human persons and communities. And since John probably wrote the work to be read aloud in Christian worship, I will try to recapture something of the impact this work would have had in that context. It will therefore be more appropriate to speak of "hearers" than of "readers."

The Symbolic Number 666

No biblical passage has fascinated people more than Revelation 13:18, which invites the reader to interpret the symbolic number of the great beast, 666. On one level, the symbolism seems broad. Because 7 symbolizes perfection, 6 stands for imperfection, so 666 may indicate the highest degree of imperfection, or ultimate evil. On another level, however, 666 seems to have a definite reference, since John says, "It is the number of a person." That reference is probably to the emperor Nero, making use of the practice of *gematria*, which assigns numerical values to the letters of the alphabet. Following an alternative way of spelling Nero Caesar in Hebrew (documented in the Dead Sea Scrolls), its numerical value is 666. And in some manuscripts, the number is 616, the numerical value of Nero Caesar according to the usual spelling in Greek.

This does not mean that John wrote during Nero's time, however. There was a current belief that Nero had not really died but was in hiding and about to return, and the reference in 13:3 to a "mortal wound [that] had been healed" on one of the beast's heads is probably an allusion to that belief. Nor should we think that John meant the identification literally. As Boring comments, "His picture-language warns, 'Beware, it is Nero all over again,' just as one might say of a new dictatorial anti-Semitism that many might see as innocuous, 'It's Hitler all over again.'"[3] The point is that the current situation in Rome was as dangerous to Christians as was the time of Nero, who engaged in active persecution.

Notes on a Reading of Revelation

For these notes, the text divisions are based on Elisabeth Schüssler Fiorenza's *Invitation to the Book of Revelation*.[4]

1:1-8

The opening words command the hearers' attention and create positive expectations with the declaration that "the time [of the end] is near" and indications of the sovereignty of God/Christ.

1:9—3:22

In 1:9-20, John's self-identification as a brother who has shared in the persecution creates solidarity with the recipients, and the vision of Christ ("one like the Son of Man") creates a sense of awe. John is awestruck, but the figure's compassionate response is a reminder that Christ's resurrection brings deliverance from death. The scene sets the stage for a reception of the prophetic message to the seven churches.

This message, stretching from 2:1 to 3:22 and presented as the words of Christ, includes compliments, encouragement, and chastisement. John praises such qualities as endurance, faith, service, and love and condemns backsliding (2:4) and lack of enthusiasm (3:15-18). More specifically, his condemnation or praise relates to the congregations' attitudes toward groups and teachings he rejects. Eating food offered to idols and fornication (presumably a metaphor for idolatry) are singled out (2:14). Central to the letters is a call to "conquer," that is, to be "faithful unto death" (2:10), and a promise of reward for those who obey that call.

The reference to Satan's throne in the message to Pergamum (2:13), a major center of the emperor cult, contrasts with the reference to God's throne at 1:4. The political content of the message is clear: to side with the empire is to side with Satan.

4:1—9:21

The vision of heavenly worship in 4:1-22 rekindles a sense of wonder, as the promise to disclose "what must take place after this" directs attention to the future. In 5:1-5, the search for one worthy to open the seals creates a moment of suspense, which is broken by the appearance of "the Lion of the tribe of Judah," whom the hearers will recognize as Jesus. In a dramatic clash of images, however, what John actually sees is a little lamb, "standing as if it had been slaughtered." The paradox is stunning: the crucified Christ represents the ultimate power in the universe.

In 6:1, the Lamb starts to open the seals. The first four of these release horses and riders that bring war, famine, and death upon the world. The image of the first rider evokes associations with the Parthians, who were a constant threat to Roman power, and links the end of the age to the dissolution of Roman power. The fifth seal reveals an image of the martyrs who were killed "for the word of God" underneath the heavenly altar, and the sixth unleashes an earthquake that terrifies everyone, from kings to slaves, and then a triumphant vision. First, John sees 144,000 people from the tribes of Israel, symbolic of the "completed" church, and then a multitude of persons from all nations surrounding God's throne and giving praise.

The silence at the opening of the seventh seal in 8:1 creates a sense of anticipation. Then seven angels with trumpets appear, and the trumpets of the first six release a series of woes upon the earth, recalling the plagues visited on the Egyptians in the story of the exodus (Exod 7–10). Human beings are subjected to various tortures, and a third of all people die in the plagues. But associations with the exodus story are reminders that the goal of that story was liberation, and in 9:20-21, the reason for all these woes is identified as encouragement to repentance, although repentance does not come.

10:1—15:4

An interlude follows before the seventh trumpet sounds. Another angel appears and opens a scroll, which unleashes the sound of the seven thunders, but John is forbidden to write what the thunders say. His eating of the scroll in 10:9 recalls a similar scene in Ezekiel 3:1-3, and its bitter/sweet taste suggests the dual quality of prophecy, which brings both God's judgment and ultimate redemption.

John's measuring of the temple at 11:1-2

recalls Zechariah 2:1-5, where a similar action signifies God's protection in the face of coming destruction. But the death of the two prophetic witnesses shows that God's protection does not mean exemption from suffering.

The seventh trumpet in 11:15 brings another vision of heaven, which ends in a glimpse of the ark of the covenant. This vision, following the proclamation that God destroys "those who destroy the earth" (11:18), dramatizes the superiority of God's power over oppressive forces.

In chapter 12, an initial vision of a goddess-like woman leads into accounts of a dragon's pursuit of her and the male child to whom she gives birth and a war in heaven between the forces of the dragon and those of Michael the archangel. Michael's victory leads to a sequence on earth in which the dragon pursues the woman's other children.

In 12:9, John identifies the dragon as Satan, and the child and the woman's other children clearly stand for Jesus and those who follow him. The either/or choice between the church and the empire is heightened by the regal appearance of the woman in 12:1, which casts her as an antitype of Roma, the goddess of Rome.

FIG. 15.2   The four horsemen of the Apocalypse, from a thirteenth-century book on the Apocalypse. British Library, London.
Photo © HIP /Art Resource, NY.

The seven-headed beast that rises from the sea in 13:1 and worships the dragon is easily associated with Rome, and the hearers will understand its "mark" as participation in Roman society. They will also decode its symbolic number (666) as a reference to Nero but will likely, in light of the reference to a mortal wound on one of the heads that had been healed (13:3), identify the current emperor as the returned Nero.

Despite the description of the beast's power, the vision of the Lamb and 144,000 in 14:1-4 is a reminder of God's power. Furthermore, the remainder of chapter 14 gives assurance of God's final victory, reinforced by 15:1-4, when a song of praise to God is preceded by assurance that the next series of seven plagues will bring God's wrath to an end.

15:5—19:10

The seven angels of 15:1 receive bowls full of God's wrath and proceed to pour them out on the earth in scenes that once again recall the plagues in Exodus. The seventh bowl brings the sequence to a climax as a voice announces the completion of the drama of judgment, and Babylon/Rome, together with the cities, islands, and mountains of the world, disintegrates (16:12-21).

The judgment of "the great whore who is seated on many waters" (17:1) views the

FIG. 15.3 *The Fall of Babylon* (1831) by John Martin. British Museum, London. Photo © British Museum /Art Resource, NY.

destruction of Rome from a different angle. The identity of the whore as the empire is made plain by her identification with Babylon (17:5), the allusion to the blood of Christian martyrs she has drunk (17:6), the seven mountains (= seven hills of Rome) on which she sits (17:9), and the description of her as "the great city" (17:18).

The mood shifts in chapter 18. The earth is illumined with the splendor of an angel, who pronounces a dirge over the fallen city. The injunction in 18:4 to "come out" of Babylon is a warning to resist the allure of Roman civilization and power.

The kings and merchants of the world mourn the whore, and there are painful ironies in the description of her destruction. Once wallowing in luxury, she has seen her wealth "laid waste" (18:17). Associating her wealth with "fornication" (18:9), John concludes the long list of her cargo items with "slaves—and human lives" (18:13). The indictment is clear: her wealth was based on exploitation.

The irony is heightened at 18:20 as those who had once traded with the whore turn from mourning to a joyous proclamation of God's justice. In 18:21-23, the description of all that the city once was is not mere gloating but expresses a genuine sense of tragedy. Still, 18:24 gathers up all that has been said about the evil at the heart of the magnificent empire. As dazzling as she was, she was a murderer.

At 19:1, the scene shifts once again to heaven, where there is rejoicing and praise of God.

19:11—22:9

The final events are related: Christ appears, imaged as a rider on a white horse, leading the armies of heaven to victory over the beast and its armies (19:11-21). Christ reigns for a thousand years, while Satan is imprisoned (20:1-6). Satan is released, fights a final battle, is defeated, and is thrown into the lake of fire (20:7-10). Then the dead are judged, and Death and Hades are thrown into the lake of fire (20:11-15).

Dramatically, John now (21:1-2) recounts his vision of the new heaven and earth and the new Jerusalem. In the new order, heaven and earth are united, and God dwells among human beings. When the voice from the throne says, "See, I am making all things new," it is clear that the eschatological order is not totally new, created out of nothing, but a renewal of what already is.

A description of the new Jerusalem (21:9—22:7) culminates in a vision of the heart of the city, where John sees the river of life and the tree of life, which will recall the Garden of Eden. It is a vision of ultimate peace and reconciliation.

22:10-21

John receives a command not to seal up the prophecy, and Christ announces that he will come soon and exercise judgment. That announcement becomes the occasion for exhortation in 22:14-16, but the poetic invitation in 22:17 stresses grace by presenting the water of life as a gift.

In 22:18, John directs the hearers' attention to the writing itself, reasserting its prophetic character and warning against altering its words. The audience will be reminded of the claim that the content of this writing was given in a revelatory experience, and they will be comforted by the promise and blessing in verses 20-21. They have been assured of ultimate vindication and justice in the near future, reminded that the God they worship is the ultimate power in the universe, and inspired by the visions of eschatological peace.

Reflections on the Sources and Structure of Revelation

No careful reader of Revelation will miss the complexity of the progression of eschatological "events" throughout the several visions. Efforts to plot out a continuous chronology of these events have been so unsuccessful that many scholars think that the series of visions describe roughly the same events over again from alternative angles. Evidence for this view is found in the fact that partial visions of eschatological glory occur throughout the book.

The complex structure of Revelation, then, is partly explained by the author's purpose, which was not to outline a chronology of coming events but to inspire hope and confidence in his readers. By using multiple symbols, he immersed the audience in imaginative portrayals of both God's judgment and the blessedness of God's eschatological rule. His appeal was not to the intellectual urge to calculate but to the deep-seated emotional needs of his readers.

There is, however, another reason for the work's complexity. John's visions are, at least for the most part, literary creations, not scenes that he actually saw in a dream or trance. For they reflect not only the canonical Jewish Scriptures but other apocalyptic texts. To some extent, that is, John's account was shaped by the extensive literary sources he employed. The notions of a thousand-year messianic reign and of the eschatological woes were only two of the many items he drew from the standard apocalyptic repertoire.

Differing Evaluations of Revelation

For some Christians obsessed with apocalyptic themes, Revelation is the most important book in the New Testament. For others, and for many persons outside the church, it is a highly problematic book. Martin Luther found it theologically inadequate, and many scholars and theologians see in it a subchristian desire for revenge. The writer D. H. Lawrence, who called it the "Judas" in the New Testament, thought it reflected an envy of the strong and a hatred of civilization.[5]

From liberation perspectives, Revelation has received mixed reviews. Feminist evaluations are often negative. Tina Pippin finds strong misogynist tendencies in the work, particularly the depiction of God's vengeance brought upon the whore, symbol of Rome, in chapters 17-19 and in the punishment of the woman called Jezebel in 2:22-23.[6] Schüssler Fiorenza likewise notes that Revelation encourages readers "to perceive women in terms of good or evil, pure or impure, wife or whore."[7] However, she finds great value in the work from a liberation perspective when it is approached with a carefully defined hermeneutical lens. And her defense of Revelation against Lawrence's criticism reflects the views of many liberation theologians:

> Revelation's theology is not so much interested in describing the "reversal of fate," because of an unchristian resentment of civilization or of the city, as it is in spelling out hope and encouragement for those who struggle for economic survival and freedom from persecution and murder.[8]

Adela Yarbro Collins finds both positive and negative traits in Revelation from a social-psychological perspective.[9] She interprets it as a way of dealing with the discrepancy between "what is" and "what ought to be" that involves two strategies. First, it induces a kind of catharsis, or cleansing of emotions, akin to that which Aristotle attributed to Greek tragedies. It enables readers to identify, express, and ultimately manage their fear of Roman power and resentment of Roman wealth. Second, it seeks to convince the audience "that what ought to be *is*."[10] By announcing an already-determined

future in which the forces of oppression are overcome, John enabled the audience to participate imaginatively in eschatological peace in the present.

Yarbro Collins also argues that Revelation offers two ways of "containing aggressive feelings."[11] The first is transference. John never depicts the Christian believers as engaged in combat with Rome or Satan, but he does present Christ and God as defeating and judging these forces. The second is internalization. John enjoins his readers to accept martyrdom and to embrace rigorous lifestyles in relation to wealth, sexuality (see 14:4), and participation in the general culture. Psychologically, this means turning aggressiveness inward on oneself.

In terms of evaluation, Yarbro Collins criticizes Revelation for achieving human dignity through "the degradation of others." But she also recognizes that it "serves the value of humanization insofar as it insists that the marginal, the relatively poor and powerless, must assert themselves to achieve their full humanity and dignity."[12]

Another problem that some interpreters have found with Revelation is the deterministic view of history—the notion that God is in total control of the course of human events and that this course has been mapped out in advance. Making use of process thought, however, Ronald Farmer reads Revelation in a different light, focusing on the vision at Revelation 4–5, in which the Lamb receives a scroll. In 5:2, the angel asks, "Who is worthy to open the scroll and break its seals?" Since the scroll apparently contains God's redemptive plan, the implication is that God's intention to redeem the world depends on human action. And this means that God is not in total control of events.

Also, the statement at 5:3 that no one was found worthy dramatizes the announcement in verse 5 that "the Lion of the tribe of Judah, the Root of David, has conquered, so that he can open the scroll and its seven seals." The messianic image here clearly suggests militaristic, coercive power. This image, however, is balanced by that of the "Lamb standing as if it had been slaughtered" in 5:6. Not only are lambs associated with gentleness, but the fact that this one bears the marks of a violent death calls to mind the notion of Jesus as the innocent one whose death is a sacrifice for sin.

The presence of contradictory images, Farmer argues, forces the audience to interpret each in light of the other. The image of Jesus as conquering lion interprets his death: it is victory, not defeat. And that of Jesus as lamb interprets his role as conqueror: God, through Jesus, conquers precisely through "suffering, redemptive love." As in process thought, the lamb imagery suggests that God achieves the divine purposes not through coercion but through the persuasive power of what appears as weakness.

On the literal level, the strain of imagery in Revelation that presents God's power as persuasive is incompatible with the deterministic strain that presents divine power as coercive. Farmer argues, however, that it is possible to hold the two perspectives together if one interprets the deterministic strain nonliterally, that is, as an imaginative expression of the view that "suffering, redemptive love will eventually triumph, that it is the most powerful force in the universe."[13]

Yet another problematic aspect of Revelation is its seemingly negative attitude toward nature. As in apocalyptic literature generally, the coming of the new age involves the dissolution of the existing universe. One passage in particular has seemed to many interpreters to involve God's condemnation of the earth: 12:12, where a voice from heaven proclaims, "But woe to the earth and the sea." Barbara Rossing argues, however, that the word usually translated as "woe" should be rendered as "alas," as it is in other places in the New Testament. The passage would thus indicate not God's condemnation of the earth, but God's lament over it. And this is consistent with Revelation's indictment of Rome and its allies as "those who destroy the earth" (11:18).[14]

From Rossing's perspective, we might venture a positive evaluation of Revelation from a postcolonial perspective with respect to ecological concerns as well as on the issue of economic exploitation: God stands in solidarity with both the earth and human victims of colonization against an oppressive and destructive empire. But we would still have to ask whether its apocalyptic way of stating that solidarity risks compromising its own vision of ultimate peace and reconciliation. Therefore, the judgment of many interpreters is that Revelation can convey an important message of justice, but only if read through a hermeneutical lens that ensures that the cry for justice does not degenerate into a thirst for revenge.

NOTES

1. M. Eugene Boring, *Revelation* (Louisville, Ky.: John Knox, 1989), 11.
2. Elisabeth Schüssler Fiorenza, *Invitation to the Book of Revelation: A Commentary on the Apocalypse with Complete Text from the Jerusalem Bible* (Garden City, N.Y.: Doubleday, 1981), 18–19.
3. Boring, *Revelation*, 164.
4. Schüssler Fiorenza, *Invitation*.
5. D. H. Lawrence, *Apocalypse* (New York: Viking, 1932), 14–15.
6. Tina Pippin, *Death and Desire: The Rhetoric of Gender in the Apocalypse of John* (Louisville, Ky.: Westminster John Knox, 1992), 76.
7. Elisabeth Schüssler Fiorenza, *The Book of Revelation: Justice and Judgment* (Philadelphia: Fortress Press, 1985), 199.
8. Schüssler Fiorenza, *Invitation*, 173.
9. Adela Yarbro Collins, *Crisis and Catharsis: The Power of the Apocalypse* (Philadelphia: Westminster, 1984).
10. Ibid., 154.
11. Ibid., 156.
12. Ibid., 171–72.
13. Ronald L. Farmer, *Beyond the Impasse: The Promise of a Process Hermeneutic* (Macon, Ga.: Mercer University Press), 98.
14. Barbara R. Rossing, "Alas for Earth! Lament and Resistance in Revelation 12," in *The Earth Story in the New Testament*, ed. Norman C. Habel and Vicky Balabanski (Sheffield: Sheffield Academic Press, 2002).

STUDY QUESTIONS

1. What can be said about the authorship of Revelation?
2. Describe the situation of the original audience, and explain why the author uses such dramatic language to address this situation.
3. What are the competing views regarding how the "events" mentioned in Revelation are related to actual human history? How do the interpretations of critical scholars differ from those of many popular interpreters?
4. What is the function of the letters to the seven churches in Revelation 1–3?
5. What emotions might chapters 4–9 elicit from those who hear it read? What is the intended function of the "eschatological woes" described in these chapters?

6. With what or whom would a first-century reader have identified the symbols of the beast, Babylon, and the whore?

7. What effect might it have had on a first-century congregation to hear chapters 17–22 read aloud during worship?

8. Evaluate the claim that Revelation predicts events in the twenty-first century.

9. Does the book of Revelation have any relevance, *when not interpreted literally*, for people living in our place and time? Compare and contrast the views of Yarbro Collins and Schüssler Fiorenza on this issue, and then give reasons for your own judgment.

10. Explain the role of the distinction between coercive and persuasive power in Farmer's interpretation. Then give your own evaluation of his reading.

11. In what specific ways does Revelation suggest the necessity of hermeneutics in interpreting the New Testament?

12. How does Barbara Rossing's reading speak to ecological and postcolonial concerns?

FOR FURTHER READING

Boring, M. Eugene. *Revelation*. Louisville, Ky.: John Knox, 1989.

Yarbro Collins, Adela. *Crisis and Catharsis: The Power of the Apocalypse*. Philadelphia: Westminster, 1984.

Minear, Paul. *I Saw a New Heaven and a New Earth: An Introduction to the Vision of the Apocalypse*. Washington, D.C.: Corpus, 1968.

Pilch, John J. *What Are They Saying about the Book of Revelation?* New York: Paulist, 1978.

Schüssler Fiorenza, Elisabeth. *The Book of Revelation: Justice and Judgment*. Philadelphia: Fortress Press, 1985.

———. *Invitation to the Book of Revelation: A Commentary on the Apocalypse with a Complete Text from the Jerusalem Bible*. Garden City, N.Y.: Doubleday, 1981.

Epilogue

After the New Testament

The New Testament leaves the historian of Christianity in midstream, for much that is characteristic of the church in later centuries is absent: the explicitly stated doctrines, the hierarchical ecclesiastical structure, the institutionalized ministry.

We do, of course, find the foundations of later developments in doctrine and church organization. The major writings share a general understanding of Jesus as Messiah and Son of God as well as other beliefs such as a final judgment and the resurrection of the dead. And some of the later books manifest an explicit concern for the purity of a body of beliefs. The Pastoral Letters, in particular, reflect a movement toward institutionalized authority. And finally, the New Testament in general gives us clear evidence of the practice of baptism and the observance of the Lord's Supper.

With all of this, however, we are still a long way from the highly institutionalized church, with a formally stated body of doctrine, that entered the Middle Ages. But the transition was not long in coming. By the end of the second century, the writings of Irenaeus, the bishop of Lyons, reflected a situation in which each church was under the authority of a single bishop and this authority was understood in terms of apostolic succession. That is to say, the belief was securely in place that Jesus appointed specific apostles over specific churches and that they in turn appointed bishops, who passed on the apostolic authority in an unbroken chain. Irenaeus could therefore speak of a worldwide church sharing one apostolic faith. In time, a formalized understanding of the ordained ministry was worked into the notion of apostolic succession.

Irenaeus specifically associated the church in Rome with Peter and Paul and provided a list of bishops that succeeded them, down to his own time. Gradually, because of the unique status of Rome in the empire, the bishop of that city began to assert authority over other churches. Eventually the bishop of Rome was accorded formal authority over the church in general: he was the pope (or "papa") of the church universal, standing in a line of succession beginning with Peter.

The church that thus emerged from the New Testament period understood itself as catholic, or universal, and apostolic, the authentic continuation of the faith delivered by Jesus to the apostles. But in naming itself universal, it was in fact distinguishing itself from other bodies that claimed a common heritage. From the beginning, there were groups that dissented from what became the majority view. We have seen that some scholars believe there were early groups that followed Jesus but did not attach saving significance to his death. And in any case, there were conservative Jewish Christian groups that never accepted the way in which others dispensed with the Jewish law; continuing for a time as small sects, they eventually died out. In the second century, the gnostics and Marcionites were excluded. So also was a group known as the Montanists, who stressed the renewal of prophecy and eschatological fervor and demanded a more rigorous Christian lifestyle than was prevalent in the late second-century churches.

Further splits came in the ensuing centuries as a result of the effort to settle the issues surrounding the doctrine of the two natures of Christ. The eventual formulations excluded three major groups along the way: the Arians, who denied that the Son was coeternal with the Father; the Nestorians, who argued that the two natures of Christ remained separate; and the Monophysites, who argued that the two natures merged completely into one, and whose doctrine survives in the Coptic Church in Egypt today.

The church that defined itself early on as catholic and apostolic is the ancestor of most of the Christians of the world. But it has not remained whole. A split between its eastern and western regions resulted in a distinction between the Roman Catholic Church on the one hand and a group of national churches under the umbrella of Eastern Orthodoxy on the other. The western church was rent asunder yet again in the Protestant and English reformations, and these divisions were followed by innumerable divisions down to the present time.

Recent years have brought a strong movement toward reunification, however, and all bodies that issue from the "apostolic and universal" church that emerged in the early centuries can look to a common heritage. But one must never forget, in reflecting on the nature of Christianity and the meaning of its writings, that there have been and are other groups who have shared at least part of that heritage.

Evaluating the New Testament: The Necessity of Hermeneutics

At a corner of Central Park, a man waves a Bible and cites John 3:7, urging his hearers to be born again. Meanwhile, a woman in Nicaragua speaks of Jesus, who challenged the power structure through his action in the temple, as liberator of the oppressed. As you have worked through the present text, it has taken you a long way since the little panorama in chapter 1 that posed the problem of multiple interpretations of the New Testament. No serious reader can have failed to sense the reality of that problem as we approached the materials from numerous perspectives.

The problem of varying interpretations, however, is only one dimension of a much deeper question. We have also encountered differing viewpoints among the various New Testament writings. For example, if the formula Paul quotes in Galatians 3:28 proclaims that, in Christ, female and male are no longer divided, the Pastoral Letters are equally clear in asserting male authority. We have even observed tensions within the individual writings themselves. The unavoidable question is whether and how readers can understand and evaluate the New Testament in its totality.

If we broaden our concern beyond the canonical writings to the early Christianity that produced them, yet another aspect of the problem appears. The books of the New Testament are selections from a wider range of materials that the early communities produced. When we survey all the types of early Christianity that died out after a time, and then imagine all the ways in which the movement might have developed but did not, some crucial questions arise. To what extent is the kind of Christianity that survived as the "mainstream" movement the inevitable result of Jesus' words and deeds, and to what extent is it the result of contingent factors and of decisions that might have been made differently? Does the New Testament as a finished product ultimately express, or does it perhaps in some ways betray, the deepest insights of the Jesus movement? The path from Jesus' open-ended parables to the tight doctrinalism of Jude, 2 Peter, and the Pastorals is, one must admit, a rather long trek. And one can easily question whether the route is a straight one.

Although it might seem otherwise, my intention here is not to drive readers into despair. It is, rather, to raise for a final time the question of hermeneutics. Hermeneutics, as noted in chapter 1, has two dimensions. On the theoretical level, it explores the question of how understanding takes place. But on the more concrete level, a given hermeneutical perspective will entail a specific strategy for finding meaning in a text. My point is that now, after having given close attention to the writings in the New Testament, and having approached those writings from several different angles, you should be prepared to reflect more deeply on the question of how to read these writings, the question of strategies for understanding and evaluating them in a more than superficial way.

For many interpreters, the tasks of understanding and evaluating the New Testament are relatively simple. One takes the writings at face value, perhaps making use of historical criticism to determine their original meanings. And then one decides for or against them—that is, decides whether to accept or reject their various claims to truth, assertions of value, and moral injunctions.

For those who take this approach, whether they are Christian believers, adherents of other faiths, or secular interpreters, the encounter with the ancient text is essentially a one-way conversation. That is to say, the meaning of the text is fixed, unchanging. It makes a clear and definite claim, and the interpreter's first task is to understand that claim in an objective way that is untarnished by her or his own prejudices, preconceptions, and desires. The second task, which is often understood as entirely separate, is to evaluate the witness of the text, to make positive or negative judgments about it. These two tasks, taken together, constitute one rather widespread hermeneutical strategy.

There are, however, more complex hermeneutical approaches that are more like dialogues than one-way conversations. From these perspectives, the tasks of understanding and evaluation, while generally regarded as relatively distinct, cannot be separated so easily. Interpreters who employ such approaches therefore allow their own world pictures, interests, and concerns a much greater role in the discovery, and perhaps creation, of meaning. And because they recognize something problematic about understanding the biblical writings, they adopt strategies that seek to look beneath the face value, or surface meaning, of the texts.

Although I suppose it is evident that my own hermeneutical stance fits within the second broad category, I would also hope that I have not prejudiced the case against those who approach the New Testament in a more "straightforward" way. My intention has not been to force a particular interpretive strategy upon readers but to confront you with the hermeneutical problem—a problem that is, I maintain, ultimately unavoidable. However we choose to read the New Testament, our way of reading is in fact a choice, and that is no less true of the first broad hermeneutical division than of the second. Those who desire an informed and thoughtful evaluation of the New Testament writings must give attention to the question of reading strategy.

I do not mean, however, to insulate hermeneutics from criticism. A number of theorists have charged that it is simply a sophisticated way of saving the text at all costs—that is to say, a way of making a text that is unacceptable appear acceptable. I would grant that hermeneutics can, in fact, degenerate into such a practice. It is up to you to decide in any given instance whether a hermeneutical move is just such an act of desperation. My conviction, however, is that, at its best, hermeneutics does not deny the interpreter the right to reject a text. What it does is to help ensure, by exposing a broad potential for meaning in a text, that the decision to accept or reject is not made on a superficial basis. In the end, it should be said that even the decision to reject a text involves a hermeneutical decision as to how it is to be read.

So here, finally, are the two points for which I do want to argue, and which I hope this text has helped to demonstrate. If we wish to read the New Testament with genuine understanding, we must pay close attention to what it actually says. We must, in other words, nurture an appropriate objectivity. But if our reading and understanding are to be more than superficial, we will also have to nurture an appropriate subjectivity by opening ourselves to an encounter with the New Testament writings on the deepest level. And if we are to do that, then we cannot escape the question raised in the second half of Jesus' query of Luke 10:26 (Today's English Version): "What do the Scriptures say? *How do you interpret them?*"

Glossary

Agrippa II (28 c.e.–ca. 100 c.e.). Son of Agrippa I (Herod Agrippa), great-grandson of Herod the Great, and the last reigning member of the Herodian Dynasty. He ruled a mostly Gentile kingdom, under Roman appointment, that eventually included Galilee and parts of Judea. In Acts 25–26, Paul, under arrest, defends himself before Agrippa II just before his departure to Rome to pursue his appeal to Caesar.

Allegory. A type of story whose various elements point symbolically to realities, with which the readers/hearers would be familiar, outside the story world. Although an allegory may be considered a type of parable, most scholars think Jesus did not tell allegories. In some cases, however, the parables of Jesus have been made into allegories by the Gospel writers or earlier handlers of tradition, while other allegories in the Gospels may have been created after Jesus' death.

Apocalyptic literature. A type of writing in exilic and postexilic Judaism involving a revelation given to a human subject by a heavenly messenger. The revelation can consist of secrets of the heavenly realm and/or a divinely ordained plan for history. Apocalypses of the historical type generally focus on a dramatic end to history followed by the resurrection of the righteous to eternal life.

Apocrypha. A term, used largely in Protestantism, to refer to a collection of ancient Jewish writings, most of which were included in the Septuagint but did not become a part of the final canon of the Jewish Scriptures. They are considered "deuterocanonical" (belonging to a second level of canonicity) by the Roman Catholic Church, and several of these books appear in the Greek and Slavonic Bibles, but not in the Catholic, or in the appendixes to one or more of these canons. The literal meaning of the term is "hidden," and it has sometimes been used to designate materials considered heretical; in the present context, however, it indicates only a secondary status. In Catholicism, the term *Apocrypha* is used for the writings Protestants call the Pseudepigrapha. See **Pseudepigrapha.**

Apocrypha, New Testament. A term applied to a wide range of early Christian writings not included in the canon. These vary widely in theological perspective, from what came to be known as orthodox to what was considered severely heretical. Many of them are the products of sectarian groups of Christians that eventually died out. The term is somewhat misleading, since the books considered New Testament Apocrypha are not really parallel to the Apocrypha (see **Apocrypha**) of the Jewish Scriptures. The latter have a kind of secondary canonical status among Christians (although not among Jews), whereas the former have no official standing at all in relation to the canon.

Apostle. Literally "one who is sent"—an emissary, agent, or ambassador. The Christian usage seems related to a Hebrew term with similar meaning. In the early church, an apostle was understood as someone belonging to the first generation of Christians with a special divine commission for mission and leadership. The circle of apostles included, but was not limited to, "the Twelve"—those believed to have been called into leadership by Jesus himself. Paul considered himself an apostle and was apparently widely accepted as such, and he recognized a few others beyond the Twelve as having this status also.

Archetype. Literally an original pattern from which all copies derive. In Jungian psychology, the archetypes are specific patterns of thinking that all human beings share by virtue of their common evolutionary history, and the notion of "the self" is the controlling archetype, which guides human beings toward their ultimate fulfillment.

Babylonian Empire. More technically designated Neo-Babylonian, an empire that flourished from 625 to 529 B.C.E. Centered in the city of Babylon in Mesopotamia, it extended eastward and included Palestine. In 587, following an attempt of Judah to gain independence, the Babylonians sent the ruling class into exile in Babylon. The period from that point until 538, when the conquering Persian king decreed that the Judahites could return home, is known as the Babylonian exile.

B.C.E./C.E. Abbreviations for Before the Common Era and Common Era—nonreligious alternatives, respectively, to B.C. and A.D.

Canon. A Greek word designating a reed and, by extension, anything straight (as reeds are straight). This term also took on the metaphorical meaning of rule, measure, or standard, so in the early church, it was applied to religious law and doctrine and to a list of writings understood to provide an authoritative standard of faith. The various books of the Bible thus constitute a canon, and those included are termed "canonical."

C.E. See **B.C.E./C.E.**

Cosmic empathy. A term used by the author of this book to describe the perception, common in prehistorical society, that all components of reality are organically related and that all aspects of the universe, including those that moderns consider inanimate, are pervaded with vitality and feeling.

Covenant. In Hebrew thought, a relationship between God (Yahweh) and the people of Israel, including two components: God's promise to be with the people (evidenced by God's prior actions on their behalf) and the people's obligation to serve and obey God.

Demystification. The process of explaining some phenomenon, which previously appeared to be mysterious and/or supernatural, in such a way as to render it intelligible in nonmysterious terms. Whereas ancient people tended to view nature as mysterious, modern science has tended to demystify it, often explaining it in mechanistic fashion.

Demythologizing. See **Existentialist interpretation.**

Deuterocanonical. See **Apocrypha.**

Devil, the. From a Greek term (*diabolos*) meaning "slanderer," used in the Septuagint to translate "Satan." In the New Testament, the devil and Satan are basically interchangeable designations for the archfiend, author of evil and cosmic opponent of God.

Diaspora. A Greek word meaning "dispersion." In biblical studies, it refers to the Jewish people living outside the homeland, beginning in the period of the Babylonian exile.

Diatribe. A type of argumentation, probably used in philosophical schools, in which the speaker (or writer) uses vivid images and rhetorical questions to take up and refute arguments of imaginary opponents.

Dispersion. See **Diaspora.**

Docetism. From a Greek word meaning "to think" or "to seem," the doctrine, considered heretical by what emerged as "mainstream" Christianity, that Jesus, as a divine being, only seemed to have a physical body. Many forms of Gnosticism embraced a docetic Christology.

Eschatology. Teaching regarding the "last things," the end of history or of the present age.

Essenes. A Jewish faction in the Hellenistic period, characterized by sectarian teachings and strict community discipline. They do not appear in the New Testament but are mentioned in other ancient sources. The majority of scholars identify the community at Qumran, who produced the Dead Sea Scrolls, as Essenes.

Exegesis. From a Greek term whose root meaning has to do with leading out, a statement, a narrative, or an interpretation. In biblical studies, exegesis is systematic interpretation of the meaning of a text. See also **Hermeneutics.**

Exile, Babylonian. See **Babylonian Empire.**

Existentialist interpretation. An approach to biblical interpretation first proposed by the German scholar and theologian Rudolf Bultmann. Bultmann's method involved looking for an "existential" meaning—a meaning not dependent upon supernatural categories, but referring to human existence as all persons experience it—beneath the mythological language of biblical texts.

Exodus, the. The event recounted in the Jewish Scriptures (Exod 14) wherein God, acting through Moses, led the Hebrews out of slavery in Egypt, parting the waters of the sea for them as they went.

Feminist criticism. An approach to the interpretation of texts from the explicit standpoint of a commitment to full equality for women. Feminist critics engage in such operations as critiquing the patriarchal nature of texts, recovering the lost history of women by reconstructing history through the critical use of texts, and challenging traditional interpretations of texts on the basis of explicit attention to questions of particular interest to women.

Galilee. A region in northern Palestine where Jesus grew up (in the town of Nazareth) and carried out most of his ministry.

Gentiles. A term derived from a Latin term used to translate Greek and Hebrew words that literally mean "the nations," employed only when those words are taken to have the specific connotation of non-Jews as opposed to Jews. *Gentile* thus means "non-Jew."

Gnosticism. A modern term, based upon the Greek word for knowledge, that refers to a wide range of religious teachings dating from the second century C.E. (and perhaps earlier). Gnostics typically claimed to possess a secret knowledge that ensured their immortality, and they tended to see the physical universe as completely under the sway of evil, so that the goal of religious enlightenment was the eventual escape of a divine spark within the individual from this world into the realm of light. Many gnostics considered themselves Christians, although the church eventually defined its beliefs to exclude them. See also **Docetism.**

Gospel(s). From an Anglo-Saxon (and Middle English) term meaning "good news," a translation of the Greek *euangelion*, which has the same meaning. In New Testament Christianity, the gospel is first of all the message, or proclamation, about Jesus Christ. By extension, it is also applied to the four narratives of Jesus' life in the New Testament.

Hasidim. A Hebrew term with the literal meaning of "those who practice *hesedh.*" *Hesedh* connotes a rich range of meaning including such notions as loyalty, mercy, and loving-kindness. In the broad sense, then, persons who are particularly faithful and loyal to God are termed hasidim. In the period of the Maccabean Revolt, those who refused to comply with orders from the Seleucid king to violate the Jewish law became known as the Hasidim.

Hasmonean Dynasty. The Jewish dynasty that ruled following the Maccabean Revolt, 142–63 B.C.E.

Hellenism. A term referring to Greek culture. It is most frequently applied to the culture of the Hellenistic Age (see **Hellenistic Age**).

Hellenistic Age. Most narrowly, the period from the death of Alexander the Great (323 B.C.E.) to the ascendancy of Octavian (later to become Caesar Augustus) in 31 C.E. But Hellenistic culture permeated the Roman imperial period also.

Hermeneutics. A technical term relating to the process of interpretation. Once used to simply indicate the rules of interpretation, it has taken on two broader connotations. One is philosophical reflection on the conditions under which the understanding of the text takes place. The other is methodology for extracting meaning from the text, most especially methodology designed to overcome a specific problem, such as discrepancy between the worldview of the text and that of the interpreter.

Herod. A native of Idumea who was appointed "king of the Jews" by the Roman emperor and came to be called Herod the Great. He reigned as a vassal of the Romans from 37 to 4 B.C.E. He appears in the Gospel of Matthew as a jealous king seeking the life of the child Jesus.

Herod Antipas. A son of Herod the Great, who ruled Galilee and Perea after his father's death. He appears in the New Testament as the Herod who questions Jesus in Jerusalem prior to his trial.

Hierarchical. A descriptive term from a Greek word referring to someone who is a steward or keeper of sacred things. A hierarchical power structure is a system of authority in which persons are arranged according to rank.

Historical criticism. An approach to the study of materials from the past that attempts to place them in their original historical contexts; often called the historical-critical method. Interpreters employing this method seek objectivity by trying to take up a disinterested attitude toward the results of investigation, distancing themselves from their own beliefs and commitments. They try to bridge the gap between their own worldview and that of the materials in view by immersing themselves in the historical world of the latter.

Holy Spirit. In the Jewish Scriptures, the power and/or presence of God, operative in such divine activities as empowering heroes, inspiring rulers and prophets, creating the world, and sustaining life. The Spirit was also associated with the eschatological expectation, and in the New Testament, it is understood as descending upon Jesus and as empowering both individual Christians and the church collectively. In post–New Testament times, Christian theology defined the Holy Spirit as the third person of the Trinity, alongside the Father and the Son.

Irony. A mode of expression in which the speaker or writer intends a meaning that is the exact opposite of that which the words would normally carry; also, a situation in which the result of events is the opposite of what one would normally expect. Sarcasm is a form of irony.

Isis. An Egyptian female deity, originally envisioned as the consort of the god Osiris. In Hellenistic times, Isis worship underwent extensive syncretism in which various other deities were identified with her. Among some worshippers, she came to be understood as the one universal deity.

Israel. The Hebrew/Jewish people; their homeland as a totality; or the northern monarchy that split off from the south (Judah) following the death of King Solomon.

Jamnia. See **Yabneh.**

Jewish Palestine. See **Palestine.**

Josephus, Flavius. A Jewish historian living in the first century C.E. A commander of Jewish forces during the war against Rome in 66–70, he gained favor with the Romans following his surrender. Residing in Rome and living on an imperial pension, he spent his remaining years writing. Although his works must be used critically, they are an important source for the period.

Jubilee, Year of. A year of emancipation and restoration. Leviticus 25:11 provides that the "fiftieth year shall be a jubilee." Although some scholars interpret the passage to refer to a one-time occurrence, it has generally been taken to mean that every fiftieth year should be such, as the culmination of a cycle of seven sabbatical years. In any case, the Jubilee Year entailed the emancipation of any Israelite who had become enslaved to another Israelite and also the return of property that had been sold during the period to the original owner or family. Scholars debate whether it was ever put into practice.

Judah. The name of one of the twelve tribes of Israel, and of one of the twelve sons of Jacob, whom tradition named as the ancestors of these tribes. Upon the division of ancient Israel into northern and southern monarchies after the death of Solomon, the southern region took the old tribal name Judah as its designation. In the period after the Babylonian exile, this region became known as Judea.

Judea. See **Judah.**

Kingdom of God. See **Rule of God.**

Koine. A Greek word meaning "common." The language of the Hellenistic world, a simplified form of Greek, is called the *koine.*

Liberation theology. A type of theological thinking that stresses God's identification with and action on behalf of the poor and oppressed and values engagement with the world rather than abstract speculation. The term in its narrowest sense refers to a particular strain of Latin American thought originating in the 1960s, but it is increasingly used in a broad sense that includes other perspectives with related interests, such as certain types of Black, feminist, and Asian theological thought.

Logos. A Greek term with a wide range of meanings, including "word," "speech," "subject," "reckoning," and "reason." The Stoics used it to indicate both the divine principle in which all reality coheres and a spark of divine within each human being. The Gospel of John uses it to indicate God's eternal Word that became incarnate in Jesus.

LXX. Abbreviation for the Septuagint.

Maccabean War. The insurgency of the Jewish people, led by one Judas, nicknamed Maccabeus ("The Hammer"), against the Seleucids (one of the Hellenistic monarchies) in 168–167 B.C.E. It eventually resulted in victory and the founding of the Hasmonean Dynasty.

Manuscript(s), biblical. Copies of the biblical writings dating back to the ancient world. None that we possess, however, are the original or autograph copies. Thus, textual critics must seek to reconstruct approximations of the originals from the various manuscripts.

Mediterranean world. The area surrounding the Mediterranean Sea, including Italy, Greece, Asia Minor, Syria, Israel/Palestine, and the northern coast of Africa. Anthropologists identify certain cultural traits that bound this broad area together in ancient times.

Messiah. Literally "anointed," in Judaism, the kingly figure expected to serve as God's agent in bringing in an age of peace and justice in the future. Rooted in the ideology surrounding the reign of David, the concept developed over a great expanse of time and probably did not take its final form until after the time of Jesus.

Midrash. A type of Jewish commentary on the scriptures intended to explain their meaning and apply them to the situations in which the interpreters lived.

Mishnah. In the broad sense, Jewish laws passed on orally rather than in written form; eventually applied to a written compilation of such materials, arranged topically, in the second century C.E.

Monotheism. The belief that there is only one god.

Mysteries. A term applied to a broad range of religious phenomena in the Hellenistic world, characterized by initiation through secret rites, that generally promised a renewed life in the present and immortality after death.

Myth. From a Greek term meaning "story" or "legend," in the field of religion, a traditional story passed on in a community in order to provide a sense of the nature of reality and the people's place in it. In Bultmann's usage, the term carries further implications. See **Mythological.**

Mythological. Having the character of myth. In Bultmann's demythologizing project, it refers to a view of reality involving belief in the supernatural in which ultimate or otherworldly reality is presented in terms that properly apply only to this world. Thus, for example, God is envisioned as "above" the earth. See **Myth.**

Narrator. In literary criticism, the voice in a narrative—whether anonymous or that of a character—that tells the story. The narrator is not to be confused with the author, an actual person.

New Testament Apocrypha. See **Apocrypha, New Testament.**

Orthodox. From Greek roots for "straight" and "thinking," correct, as opposed to wrong or heretical, religious doctrine. This term is also used in relation to one branch of Judaism and in the formal names of one family of Christian churches—Greek Orthodox, Russian Orthodox, etc.—that is parallel to Roman Catholicism and Protestantism.

Palestine. As used in relation to the ancient world, the preferred term to refer to the total area in which the ancient Israelites, the twelve tribes, had their homeland. *Israel* is ambiguous, since it can also designate the Hebrew people or only the northern monarchy in the period following the death of King Solomon. The term *Palestine* is derived from the name of one of the tribes of the "sea people," the Philistines, who entered the land in the early twelfth century B.C.E. and struggled with the Israelites for domination. Some recent scholars use the term "Jewish Palestine," indicating that in the period in question, the region was home to Jewish society and religion.

Pantheism. The belief that the universe as an entirety is divine, and that nature is the only god there is.

Parable. A story suggesting metaphorical meaning but demanding creative interpretation on the part of the audience. The authentic parables of Jesus must be distinguished from allegories, which have a more definite and limited range of meaning. See also **Allegory.**

Patriarch. From Greek roots meaning "father" and "to rule," a founder, forefather, or ruler of a family or tribe. The patriarchs in the Jewish Scriptures—among whom Abraham, Isaac, and Jacob are primary—were the forefathers of Israel.

Patriarchal. Pertaining to a patriarch or father. A patriarchal system is a male-dominated, hierarchical, and multigenerational social arrangement in which primary power is invested in the oldest living male in the extended family. Feminist hermeneutics is particularly interested in critiquing the patriarchal presuppositions of biblical texts.

Pharisees. A Jewish faction in the Hellenistic period, apparently drawn from the retainer class. Rivals of the Sadducees, they advocated strict obedience to the details of the law and held certain beliefs, such as the resurrection of the dead, not contained in the Torah. They appear in the Gospels, where they receive extremely negative characterizations, as opponents of Jesus.

Pilate, Pontius. The Roman procurator of Judea, 26–36 C.E., who presided at the trial of Jesus in the Gospels.

Postcolonialism. As used in literary studies, a sensitivity (generated by the collapse of colonial arrangements) to the ways in which literature tends to reflect the values and attitudes of conquering nations with respect to colonized peoples. Originally used in relation to Western colonialism, it has been appropriated by biblical studies in recent years. In this context, it is a way of evaluating biblical texts with respect to their possible complicity in conquering nations' attempts to control subjugated peoples by convincing them to adopt the imperial ideology. In New Testament studies, for example, postcolonial criticism might ask whether a text reflects pro-Roman or anti-Roman sentiments.

Postmodernism. An intellectual movement that appeared in the late twentieth century and moves away from the confidence, characteristic of the modern Western world, that human reason is able to comprehend the nature of reality. Postmodernists stress that all such attempts are carried out from some perspective limited by culture, bias, experience, and so on. One variety of postmodernism tends to be agnostic on the question of God and extremely skeptical of human claims to knowledge; another, known as constructive postmodernism, which is rooted in process thought, thinks provisional understandings of reality are possible and that it is meaningful to construct new models of God in light of recent scientific theory.

Process thought (also *process theology; process philosophy*). A philosophy that appeared in the twentieth century and that stresses the dynamic quality of reality, viewing the most basic realities as events rather than things, and sees all components of the universe as interrelated. Process thought envisions God not as a being separate from the universe but as the mind of the universe. Emphasizing freedom, it understands God's power as relational or persuasive rather than absolute or coercive.

Prophet. In Israelite religion, a person commissioned by God to bring a message to the people in a particular set of circumstances. Because prophets announced God's intentions, they were also understood in a secondary way as predicting the future, but only through God's power. In early Christianity, prophets spoke to Christian communities in the name of the risen Jesus.

Pseudepigrapha. A largely Protestant designation for a group of ancient Jewish writings, outside both the Jewish canon and the apocryphal/deuterocanonical books. Roman Catholics generally use the term *Apocrypha* for the books Protestants call the Pseudepigrapha. The term *Pseudepigrapha*, which indicates pseudonymous authorship, derives from the fact that some of these works, such as the *Psalms of Solomon* and *2 Enoch*, claim authorship by biblical characters.

Q. A hypothetical document purported to have been used by the authors of Matthew and Luke, defined primarily by the material these two have in common with each other but not appearing in Mark.

Qumran. An ancient settlement near the Dead Sea, uncovered in twentieth-century excavations; the site of the discovery of the Dead Sea Scrolls. The majority of scholars believe that Qumran was inhabited by Essenes.

Rabbi. At first, a title accorded to revered teachers. In the period following the establishment of the academy at Yabneh (see **Yabneh**), there was a succession of such rabbis, and the type of Judaism they helped fashion became known as Rabbinic Judaism. In time, the rabbinate became a formalized status marked by ordination.

Rabbinic Judaism. See **Rabbi.**

Retainer class. According to modern sociological analysis, a class of persons in agrarian societies who were directly responsible to the governing class. Among them were government officials, educators, and soldiers. The scribes and Pharisees in the New Testament probably belonged to the retainer class.

Rhetorical criticism. A study of texts in light of the standardized forms of expression (rhetoric) employed in the ancient world.

Rule of God. Most basically, God's action in the manner of a monarch, reigning over human society, and also the sphere of such action. The notion underwent many changes over the course of time. In the prophetic and apocalyptic traditions, it came to refer to a time in the future, but in the wisdom tradition, it meant something always present. There is much scholarly debate as to its precise meaning in the teaching of Jesus. Traditionally, the Greek term (*basileia tou theou*) has been translated as "kingdom of God."

Sadducees. A Jewish faction in the Hellenistic period, drawn from the upper echelons of the priesthood and thus belonging to the ruling class. Rivals of the Pharisees, they were concerned primarily with the temple cult and rejected all beliefs (such as resurrection of the dead) not found in the Torah. They appear in the Gospels as opponents of Jesus, although not as frequently as the scribes and Pharisees.

Samaria. The region in Palestine to the north of Judah and the south of Galilee and named for the capital city of the old northern monarchy (Israel). In the postexilic period, the Samaritans were bitter enemies of the Jews. The two peoples shared roots in the ancient Hebrew faith, but the Samaritans were at this point a separate society with their own version of the Torah, which constituted their sole canon, and for a time, they had their own temple.

Satan. In the New Testament, the supernatural archfiend who opposes God on a cosmic level. This usage, however, developed late in Jewish history, appearing in the apocryphal/deuterocanonical writings and the Pseudepigrapha but not in the canonical Jewish Scriptures. Derived from a root with the meaning "obstruct," it appears in the latter not as a proper name for the archfiend but as the designation for a prosecutor or accuser in the heavenly court or a spirit. Alongside Satan, other names, such as Belial, were applied to the archfiend.

Scribes. Persons skilled in such tasks as copying documents and keeping records. The temple employed scribes, who were responsible for copying the Torah and were considered experts in its interpretation. In the New Testament, "the scribes" are usually portrayed in a negative light and associated with the Pharisees as opponents of Jesus. They probably belonged to the retainer class.

Septuagint. The ancient Greek translation of the Jewish Scriptures; abbreviated LXX.

Social-scientific criticism. In biblical studies, a broad term indicating any approach to a text that employs methods drawn from the social sciences, such as sociology and anthropology.

Syncretism. The process of combining formerly distinct traditions. The Hellenistic Age was characterized by extreme religious syncretism.

Synoptic Gospels. The Gospels of Matthew, Mark, and Luke. These three Gospels are designated the "Synoptics" (meaning "seeing together") because, as opposed to the Gospel of John, they share a great deal of wording and sequence.

Synoptic problem. The question of the literary relationships among the Synoptic Gospels (Matthew, Mark, and Luke), raised by the complicated pattern of similarities and differences among them.

Torah. The Hebrew term for the first five books of the Jewish Scriptures, understood to be the most important part and attributed to Moses. The root meaning of the word has to do with pointing the way, and it is sometimes translated as "instruction." The Torah contains both law and narrative, but it was translated in the Septuagint as *nomos*, the Greek word for "law."

Two-document hypothesis. The predominant solution to the Synoptic problem; the view that Mark was the first of the Synoptic Gospels written and that the authors of Matthew and Luke drew upon both Mark and another document, which scholars term Q. See **Q; Synoptic Problem.**

Wisdom. A type of literature found in the Jewish Scriptures that involves reflection on life as ordinarily experienced, apart from specific reference to distinctively Hebraic notions such as covenant. In a philosophical strain of this tradition, there eventually emerged the personified figure of Wisdom—imaged as a female, because of the feminine gender of the noun—who was present with God at creation and whose presence permeates the universe. There is evidence that the notion of personified Wisdom played a part in the development of Christology.

Yabneh (also *Jamnia; Jabneel*). A town near the coast of the Mediterranean in northern Judah. At the time of the Jewish revolt against the Romans in 66–70, the Pharisee Yohanan ben Zakkai secured Roman permission to establish a Jewish academy there. It became an important center for the preservation of Jewish tradition, and its establishment signaled the beginning of what became known as Rabbinic Judaism. See **Rabbi.**

Yahweh. The distinctive Hebrew/Jewish name for God. According to ancient tradition, this sacred name should not be pronounced, except once a year by the high priest in the Holy of Holies, the innermost sanctuary of the temple.

Zealots. A coalition of freedom fighters probably formed in a late phase of the Jewish rebellion against Rome in 66–70 C.E. At one time, scholars believed the Zealots were a longstanding revolutionary party that would have been active during the time of Jesus, but the recent trend is away from this view.

Index